FLAT WORLD, BIG GAPS

FLAT WORLD, BIG GAPS

Economic Liberalization, Globalization,
Poverty and Inequality

edited by
JOMO K.S.
with
JACQUES BAUDOT

Orient Longman

Zed Books
London and New York

TWN
Third World Network

Published in association with the United Nations

Flat World, Big Gaps was first published in 2007.

Published in association with the United Nations

Published in the Indian Subcontinent, South East Asia (except Malaysia and Singapore), West Asia, China and Africa by
ORIENT LONGMAN PRIVATE LIMITED
Registered office: 3-6-752 Himayatnagar, Hyderabad 500 029 (A.P.), India
Email: info@orientlongman.com *Website:* www.orientlongman.com
Other offices: Bangalore / Bhopal / Bhubaneshwar / Chennai Ernakulam / Guwahati / Hyderabad / Jaipur / Kolkata / Lucknow / Mumbai / New Delhi / Patna

Published in the UK, Europe, USA, Canada and Australia by
ZED BOOKS LTD
7 Cynthia Street, London N1 9JF, UK and
Room 400, 175 Fifth Avenue, New York, NY 10010, USA
www.zedbooks.co.uk
Distributed in the USA on behalf of Zed Books by
Palgrave Macmillan, a division of St Martin's Press, LLC
175 Fifth Avenue, New York, NY 10010, USA

Published in Malaysia and Singapore by
THIRD WORLD NETWORK
131 Jalan Macalister, 10400 Penang, Malaysia.
www.twnside.org.sg

Published worldwide by the United Nations and distributed worldwide via the UN specialized network of agents.
United Nations Publications
2 United Nations Plaza, Room DC2-853, New York, NY 10017, USA.
http:/unp.un.org *Email:* publications@un.org

United Nations' sales number: E.06.IV.5
ISBN: 978-81-250-3067-6 Pb (Orient Longman)
ISBN: 978 1 84277 833 3 Hb (Zed Books)
ISBN: 978 1 84277 834 0 Pb (Zed Books)

A catalogue record for this book is available from the British Library
US CIP data is available from the Library of Congress

Cover designed by Andrew Corbett, Cambridge, UK
Typeset at Tulika Print Communication Services, New Delhi, India
Printed in India by Orion Printers Private Limited, Hyderabad 500 004

Contents

List of Tables

List of Figures

Preface

Perhaps more than other recent United Nations convened summits and conferences, the 1995 Social Summit at Copenhagen is often credited with having focused international attention on the social and distributional dimensions of recent economic development trends. During 2005, three major publications focused on issues of economic inequality and equity. In mid-year, the Secretariat issued its *2005 Report on the World Social Situation* on *The Inequality Predicament*, to critical acclaim. Not long thereafter, the United Nations Development Programme (UNDP) also considered such issues in its annual *2005 Human Development Report* just before the September Summit to consider progress towards achieving the Millennium Development Goals (MDGs). In quick succession, the World Bank issued its *2006 World Development Report* (WDR) on *Equity and Development*, praised by some as its best ever *World Development Report* and attributed to the leadership of its Chief Economist and Senior Vice President, Francois Bourguignon.

While it is generally agreed that international income inequality increased from the early 19th century until the mid-20th century, it is also believed to have declined in the first three decades after World War Two (Maddison, 2001; Bourguignon and Morrison, 2001). However, there is now a lively debate over whether it has continued to fall since the 1980s, i.e. the period associated with recent globalization.

While some insist that there is considerable and increasing evidence of growing global inequality (e.g. UNDP, 1999), much depends on what is being measured and how. There is no unambiguously strong evidence that inequality has sharply and consistently increased—or declined—since the last two decades of the 20th century. Milanovic's (2002a) finding of a sharp increase in global inequality between 1988 and 1993 seems to contradict the findings of others for the 1980s and 1990s, who use different methodologies as well as data, for different, time periods. Meanwhile, Sutcliffe's chapter three suggests that inequality has been growing at the extremes for both rich and poor, as intermediate income groups in the world's population move closer together (see Palma's chapter 5; Melchior, 2001). But actual trends here are moot—others suggest that the world's 'middle class' has remained relatively stable (Maddison, 2001), shrunk (Milanovic, 2000b) or grown (Sala-i-Martin, 2002a, 2002b).

Maddison's later (2001) historical income estimates do not point to considerable decline in inequality since the 1980s, as suggested by his earlier estimates (Maddison, 1995). It also seems likely that while inequality has grown rapidly in China and has probably also worsened in India, the rapid growth of these populous economies in recent decades has served to reduce world inequality, as most global inequality measures are mainly influenced by inter-national disparities. The overall impression—that inter-country inequality in the last two decades of the 20th century either fell or levelled off (Firebaugh, 1999) or 'was roughly stable' (Bourguignon and Morrison, 2001)—thus actually obscures the otherwise varied and even contradictory trends underlying the data, measures and methodologies (Sutcliffe chapter).

Milanovic (2002a, 2005, chapter 1 in this volume) has since suggested that the sharp increase in world inequality during 1988–1993 was slightly reversed in the next half-decade (1993–1998) and then slightly reversed yet again during 1998–2003. Although there is little evidence of stability in world income distri-bution, there is no consensus on what has changed. Milanovic (2002b) as well as Bourguignon and Morrisson (2001) emphasize that there is little evidence of income convergence on a global scale, while others (e.g. Quah, 1996; Milano-vic, 2003) suggest a bipolar distribution (i.e. convergence around 'twin peaks'), contradicting those claiming convergence (e.g. Sala-i-Martin, 2002a, 2002b).

Nonetheless, despite weak evidence for their case, advocates of economic globalization continue to claim that it has helped to promote economic growth throughout the world, and to bring about global convergence in terms of econo-mic development, incomes and human welfare. On the contrary, there has been a significant slowing of growth since the 1980s, a period normally associa-ted with contemporary globalization. In this volume, Weisbrot, Baker and Ros-nick (updating Weisbrot, Naiman and Kim, 2000) show that economic growth has slowed dramatically in the last two and a half decades (1980–2005) in most developing countries, as compared with the previous two decades (1960–1980).

During 1960–1980, output per person grew by an average, among countries, of 83 per cent, while average growth was 33 per cent during 1980-2000. Eighty-nine countries—77 per cent, or more than three-quarters—saw their per capita growth rates fall by at least five percentage points from the 1960–1980 period to the 1980–2000 period. Only 14 countries—13 per cent—saw their per capita growth rate rise by as much between the two periods.

There has been a sharp slowdown in per capita income growth for the vast majority of low- and middle-income countries with a few notable exceptions, mainly in East Asia, notably China, as well as India, which together account for almost forty per cent of the world's population. Hence, while most countries have been worse off in the last quarter century compared to the previous two decades, rapid growth in Asia has improved the welfare of much of the world's population despite the increased inequality in most countries over the same period.

However, the contribution of economic growth to employment and hence income and welfare, has also changed. For every percentage point of additional GDP growth, global employment grew by only 0.30 per cent between 1999 and 2003, compared to 0.38 per cent during 1995–1999 (ILO, 2005). Economic growth was more employment-intensive in the Sub-Saharan African as well as the Middle East and North Africa (MENA) regions. Much of this growth in employment has involved self-employment, especially in the informal sector and agriculture, where 'decent work' conditions are far from assured. Wage inequality seems to be increasing globally (see Palma in this volume), as highly skilled workers improved their wages between 1990 and 2000 (ILO, 2005).

Most other recent work suggests some increases in inequality at a time of economic globalization (for an exception, see Sala-i-Martin, 2002a, 2002b), but the trends are not clear cut, as many other things are happening at the same time, and correlation does not mean causation. Milanovic (1999) found inequality in the distribution of individual incomes and spending to be very high, and more unequal in 1993[1], compared to 1988. Milanovic (2005) showed a slight reversal of this trend in 1993–1998, while his chapter here suggests another slight increase in inequality during 1998–2003. Milanovic has found world household Gini coefficients to be higher than for any single country when adjusted for purchasing power parity (PPP), and even higher when using current US\$ incomes.

As this volume will show, there is considerable evidence to suggest that while income distribution at the world level may not be unambiguously increasing, income inequality has worsened in most countries in the world in recent decades. Rapid growth and welfare improvements in East Asia, India and a few other places as well as more modest growth elsewhere has resulted in significant poverty reduction in most of the world with the clear exception of Sub-Saharan Africa where economic stagnation over three decades has exacerbated poverty there. Despite a significant reduction in poverty rates in South Asia, the number of poor has continued to increase, especially outside India, where growth in the sub-continent has been highest. The number earning less than \$2 daily (1.38 billion) has not declined, though the proportion has declined from 57 per cent in 1994 to just below half in 2004 (ILO, 2005).

The last two to three decades have also seen changing government roles, with more regressive impacts, e.g. with tax systems becoming less progressive, or even more regressive. In many countries, income tax rates have become less progressive, causing direct taxes and the overall tax structure to become less progressive, if not more regressive, in impact. Meanwhile, the share of direct taxes has declined compared to the generally more regressive indirect taxes. This has been accompanied by various efforts to reduce overall tax rates, in line with supply-side economic philosophy, which became especially influential during the 1980s, despite being dismissed as 'voodoo economics' by (later) President George H.W. Bush.

Lower tax revenues and increasing insistence on balanced budgets or fiscal surpluses have constrained government spending, especially what is deemed social expenditure, with some deflationary consequences. Privatization has sometimes succeeded in temporarily obscuring or postponing likely fiscal crises or contractionary budgetary policies. Privatization in many countries temporarily increased government revenues, enabling governments to balance budgets in the short term or even achieve surpluses on the basis of one-off sales incomes. In the transition economies of Eastern Europe and the Commonwealth of Independent States (or the former Soviet Union), privatization has rapidly led to unprecedented concentrations of wealth, power and income.

Some (e.g. Stiglitz, 2002) argue that IMF policy prescriptions have reduced cumulative economic growth and the economic welfare of hundreds of millions of people. IMF policies in the economies of the former Soviet Union contributed to one of the worst economic disasters in the history of the world in the nineties, with Russia losing more than half its national income. According to a senior World Bank researcher, the poor did not gain as much from economic growth in countries to which the IMF lent money as they did in places with no programs: "The poor in developing countries are often better off when their governments ignore the policy advice of the International Monetary Fund and World Bank" (Easterly, 2000).

Nonetheless, IMF and World Bank policymakers claim that their reforms often require necessary short-term pain for the sake of long-term gain, though there is little evidence to that effect. If globalization and other economic liberalization policies have not led to increased growth, it becomes extremely difficult to defend these policies. The 'costs' of these changes—the destruction of industries, unemployment, the harsh 'austerity' medicine often demanded by these institutions and by international financial markets—have become burdens to society without any clear compensating benefits.

Meanwhile, China, India and other countries that have not scrupulously pursued IMF and World Bank economic programs have seen more of their people lifted out of poverty by economic growth than nations taking advice from the Washington-based Bretton Woods international financial institutions. Understandably, globalization proponents are reluctant to claim credit for China, which maintains a non-convertible currency, state control over its banking system, and other major violations of IMF/Bank prescriptions, or even for India, which remains far less open than most other developing or transitional economies after two decades of pro-business—rather than liberal market—reforms. No region has accelerated its growth rate by adopting policies imposed as conditionalities on borrowing countries.

In chapter one, Branko Milanovic distinguishes three concepts of international inequality—first, among countries' mean incomes, second, among countries' mean incomes weighted by their populations, and third, among individuals in the world, which he favours. Conceptual and methodological matters greatly influence the measurement of inequality and trends over time. He shows that global inequality exceeds inequality in the most unequal of countries, and that most global inequality is explained by inter-national, rather than intra-national disparities. He cautions against easy attribution of recent trends to globalization and also considers the debate over whether inequality matters.

Chapter two by Mark Weisbrot, Dean Baker and David Rosnick compares the 1980–2005 period with the previous two decades (1960–1980). The last quarter century has seen much slower growth and reduced social progress for most low- and middle-income countries. However, it is difficult to conclusively show a clear relationship between any particular policy change (e.g. globalization, trade or financial liberalization, structural adjustment or stabilization) and socio-economic outcomes, especially across countries, as many changes are taking place at the same time, and causality is difficult to attribute. Nonetheless, with some important exceptions—notably China and India - the recent period has been characterized by slower growth for most countries, which has been exacerbated by generally weaker social policy commitments.

In the third chapter of this volume, Bob Sutcliffe critically reviews the literature to ascertain whether there has been a recent trend towards growing or diminishing income inequality. He also discusses some methodological and data problems in the measurement of world income inequality, focusing on some recent attempts to do so before offering his own estimates. He suggests that there is no simple straightforward answer to the question of whether or not the world has become more or less unequal, as the variety of methods used to measure income inequality are often legitimate on their own terms. By comparing these methods, Sutcliffe offers a complex picture, showing that inequality is declining in some ways while increasing in other ways. He insists that there has undoubtedly been an enormous, recent increase in the gap between the very rich and the very poor, i.e. between the two poles of the income distribution, however measured.

Next, Albert Berry and John Serieux review trends in economic growth and income distribution internationally, focussing on the last decades of the twentieth century, in chapter four. Their survey of international economic growth and income inequalities presents estimates of world economic growth for the last three decades, and changes in inter-country and inter-personal world income distribution between 1980 and 2000. They suggest that while growth slowed in the 1980–2000 period with some important exceptions, average within-country inequality worsened, but the world distribution of income among individuals improved slightly, mainly due to the exceptional economic performances of China and India. Otherwise, the slowdown in economic growth was even more dramatic; world income distribution unequivocally worsened, and poverty rates remained largely unchanged.

Gabriel Palma then argues in the fifth chapter that recent trends in national income inequalities in this era of globalization have seen a trend towards globalizing inequality. He argues that two opposing forces have been at work. At the two extremes of the distribution, there has been an increasing disparity in the income shares appropriated by the top and bottom four deciles across countries. Meanwhile, there has been a remarkable consistency of the income share going to the middle deciles (5 to 9). He suggests that the forces of globalization have resulted in a new situation where virtually all inter-country diversity in income distributions is due to differences in what the rich and the poor get in each country.

In chapter six, David Woodward and Andrew Simms make the case for re-distribution to address poverty in light of inequality by arguing that only a small share of world economic growth actually contributes to reducing poverty, however defined. Current understanding of 'pro-poor growth'—as growth which trickles down to the poor or that proportionately favours the poor relatively more—can only modestly enhance the lot of the poor. The consequences have been exacerbated by economic growth and greater intra-national inequalities, including smaller total income shares for the poor, in most economies in the last quarter century.

The remaining chapters in this volume look at recent income distribution trends in the major regions or groups of countries in the world. John Weeks reviews inequality trends in some developed OECD countries in chapter seven. He argues that income inequality has increased in several, but not all, developed countries over the last two decades of the twentieth century. Increased income inequality in some countries suggests that the deregulation of markets has resulted in further concentration of economic power, which is the fundamental cause as well as the consequence of both wealth and income inequalities.

Next, Heather Boushey and Christian Weller review recent trends in inequality and household economic distress in the United States of America (USA) in chapter eight. There is considerable evidence that income inequality in the USA has increased over the past few decades. While employee compensation as a share of national income has declined, wage inequalities have risen as the profit share of national income has increased. However, increased and less costly access to credit may have softened the implications of greater income inequality. According to the authors, there is no empirical support for the claim that greater inequality is due to or has encouraged faster productivity growth, but there is some evidence that rising inequality is correlated to slower demand growth.

Mihaly Simai then reviews recent poverty and inequality trends in the Eastern European and Commonwealth of Independent States (CIS) transition economies. His chapter nine considers the causes and consequences of inequality and poverty east of the new frontiers of the European Union, mainly in the CIS countries. Poverty and inequality were previously partly mitigated by the former socialist states' social policies. However, the transition processes have significantly redistributed wealth and income, often resulting in new, more extreme sources of poverty and inequalities. Despite some economic improvements, most CIS countries experienced massive economic contractions during their transitions, and while poverty has grown in most CIS countries, some governments have tried to mitigate its harsher consequences.

Next, in chapter ten, Pedro Sainz reviews recent trends in Latin American equity, dealing mainly with the social welfare consequences of the stagnation of Latin American GDP per capita since the 1980s. According to the author, the transformations experienced during this period following major structural reforms after the 1980s' debt crises have increased foreign economic and political influence in Latin America, with negative consequences for income equity and poverty. The only important counter-tendency to these trends has been increased public social expenditure since the nineties, which has partially offset, but not eliminated, the increased inequality associated with the economic reforms.

Maria Cristina Paciello's eleventh chapter examines the determinants of income distribution in the Middle East and North Africa (MENA) since the 1960s. Drawing on available data for Algeria, Egypt, Jordan, Morocco, Tunisia, and Turkey, she argues that the MENA region has been characterized by two main income distribution trends. Contrary to the common view that the region has experienced significant improvements in income distribution over time, she shows that its relatively high inequality has changed little. However, the increasing inequality experienced by most developing countries since the 1980s, following stabilization, structural adjustment and other economic reform policies, do not seem to have occurred in MENA.

Next, in chapter twelve, Alemayehu Geda and Abebe Shimeles consider the consequences of economic openness, particularly trade liberalization, for inequality and poverty in Africa. Their chapter examines whether greater global economic integration has influenced poverty and inequality in Africa. The patterns of trade and finance in Africa are explored as these are presumed to be the main ways by which African economies are linked to the rest of the world. They conclude that trade liberalization has been strongly associated with poverty and inequality in the continent.

In chapter thirteen, Parthapratim Pal and Jayati Ghosh survey the trends and causes of inequality and poverty in India during the recent period of economic liberalization. Their survey of the evidence suggests both regional and 'vertical' increasing inequality as well as persistent poverty since the early 1990s. They identify some macroeconomic policies likely to have been responsible for this, including: fiscal discipline, regressive tax reforms and spending cuts; financial sector reform which has reduced institutional credit flows to small producers, including farmers; liberalization of foreign and domestic investment regulations, leading to more skewed investment patterns, exacerbating regional inequalities; and trade liberalization, which has adversely affected employment generation and livelihoods.

Jomo K. S. then critically reviews the widespread claim of growth with equity in East Asia in chapter fourteen. East Asian economies have undoubtedly reduced poverty very dramatically, but this has been mainly due to growth and structural change, rather than more egalitarian growth or progressive redistribution. Income inequality has been low in the Republic of (South) Korea and Taiwan province, due to initial conditions following land reforms in the early 1950s, but has risen in recent years with economic liberalization. Trends in Thailand, Malaysia and Indonesia have been less clear, with poverty going down, but inequality apparently not decreasing significantly and possibly increasing in recent years. The evidence suggests that the common claim of egalitarian growth in East Asia may be exaggerated, if not erroneous.

Finally, in chapter fifteen, Ranja Sengupta and Jayati Ghosh survey recent inequality trends in China. With rapid growth and strengthened (private) property rights, China has experienced rapidly increasing inequality and unemployment despite sustained rapid growth and considerable poverty reduction. The chapter attempts to document and analyse the inequalities that exist in China, not only in income and consumption, but also with reference to other indicators such as employment, wages, access to education and health. The authors consider rural-urban, regional and gender dimensions of these inequalities over time. The effects of economic policies, including patterns of public expenditure, as well as the nature and pattern of foreign direct investment, have shaped China's increasing inequality. They conclude that reversing increasing inequality in China will require broad based and multidimensional policy initiatives directly addressing various sources of inequality.

NOTES

[1] Milanovic (1999) highlighted the following aspects of global inequality:
- The bottom 5 per cent grew poorer while the richest quintile gained 12 per cent in real terms, i.e. more than twice as much as mean world income (5.7 per cent).
- The richest one per cent of people in the world received as much as the bottom 57 per cent, i.e. less than 50 million, received as much as the poorest 2.7 billion, or more than 54 times as many people.
- An American with the average income of the poorest US decile is better off than two-thirds of the world's population.
- The top decile of the US population had the aggregate income of the poorest 43 per cent of the world's people, i.e. the total income of 25 million Americans was equal to that of almost two billion people, or almost 40 times as many people.
- The ratio of the average income of the world's top 5 per cent to the bottom 5 per cent rose from 78 in 1988 to 114 in 1993.
- 75 per cent of the world population received 25 per cent of the world's PPP-adjusted income, and vice versa.
- 84 per cent of the world population received 16 per cent of the world's unadjusted US$ income, and vice versa.

REFERENCES

Amin, Samir (1976). *Unequal Development: An essay on the social formations of peripheral capitalism.* Translated by Brian Pearce. Monthly Review Press, New York.
Arrighi, Giovanni (1994). *The Long Twentieth Century. Power and the Origins of Our Times.* Verso, London.
Bagchi, Amiya (2006). 'The Developmental State Under Imperialism'. In Jomo K. S. [ed.]. *Globalization Under Hegemony: The Changing World Economy During The Long Twentieth Century.* Oxford University Press, New Delhi.
Balibar, Etienne (1970). "From Periodization to the Modes of Production". Louis Althusser and Etienne Balibar. *Reading Capital.* Pt 2. New Left Books, London: 209–24.
Barber, Benjamin R. (2003). *Fear's Empire: War, Terrorism, and Democracy.* Norton, New York.
Bourguignon, François, and Christian Morrisson. (2002). "Inequality among world citizens: 1820–1992". *The American Economic Review* 92 (4), September: 727–44.
Dapice, David. (2003). "Does the 'Hyper-Power' Have Feet of Clay?" *YaleGlobal* 3 March.
Easterly, William. (2000). "The Lost Decades: Developing Countries Stagnation in Spite of Policy Reform, 1980–1998". Processed, December, Development Research Group, World Bank, Washington DC.

Ferguson, Niall. (2002). *Empire: How Britain Made the Modern World*. Penguin, London. Published in the US as *Empire: The Rise and Demise of the British World Order and the Lessons for Global Power*. Basic Books, New York (2003).

Ferguson, Niall. (2004). *Colossus: The Rise and Fall of the American Empire*. Penguin Press, London. Published in the US as *Colossus: The Price of America's Empire*. Penguin, New York.

Firebaugh, Glenn (1999). 'Empirics of World Income Inequality'. *American Journal of Sociology* 104 (May): 1597–1630.

Go, Julian. (2004). "Waves of American Empire, 1787–2003: US Hegemony and Imperialist Activity from the Shores of Tripoli to Iraq". Processed, Sociology Department, Boston University, Boston.

Hardt, Michael, and Antonio Negri. (2000). *Empire*. Harvard University Press, Cambridge, MA.

Ikenberry, G.J. (2001). "American Power and the Empire of Capitalist Democracy". *Review of International Studies* 27: 191–212.

Ikenberry, G. J. (2004). "Illusions of Empire: Defining the New American Order". *Foreign Affairs* 83 (2), March/ April: 144–54.

ILO (2005). *Key Indications of the Labour Market*. Fourth edition, International Labour Office, Geneva.

Johnson, Chalmers. (2004). *The Sorrows of Empire: Militarism, Secrecy, and the End of the Republic*. Metropolitan Books, New York.

Jomo K.S. (1986). *A Question Of Class: Capital, the State, and Uneven Development in Malaya*. Oxford University Press, Singapore.

Lindert, Peter, and Jeffrey G. Williamson. (2001). "Does Globalization Make The World More Unequal?". NBER Working Paper 8228, National Bureau of Economic Research, Cambridge, MA.

Louis, William Roger, and Ronald Robinson. (1994). "The Imperialism of Decolonization". *Journal of Imperial and Commonwealth History* 22 (3): 462–511.

Maddison, Angus. (1995). *Monitoring the World Economy, 1820–1992*. Organisation for Economic Cooperation and Development (OECD), Paris.

Maddison, Angus. (2001). *The World Economy: A Millennial Perspective*. Organisation for Economic Cooperation and Development (OECD), Paris.

Mann, Michael. (2003). *Incoherent Empire*. Verso, London.

Melchior, Arne. (2001). "Global income inequality: beliefs, facts and unresolved issues". *World Economics* 2 (3), July–September.

Milanovic, Branko (1999). "True World Income Distribution, 1988 and 1993: First Calculation Based on Household Surveys Alone". Policy Research Working Paper 2244, Poverty and Human Resources, Development Economics Research Group, World Bank, Washington, D.C.

Milanovic, Branko. (2002a). "True World Income Distribution, 1988 and 1993: First Calculation Based on Household Surveys Alone". *Economic Journal* 112 (476), January: 51–92.

Milanovic, Branko. (2002b). "Worlds Apart: Inter-National and World Inequality, 1950-2000". Processed, Research Department, World Bank, Washington, DC.

Milanovic, Branko. (2003). "Income Convergence during the Disintegration of the World Economy, 1919–39". Processed, World Bank, Washington DC.

Moreno-Brid, J.C., E.P. Caldentey and P. R. Napoles. (2004). "The Washington Consensus: A Latin American Perspective Fifteen Years After". *Journal of Post-Keynesian Economics*. 27 (2) Winter 2004–05: 345–63.

O'Rourke, Kevin. (2001). "Globalization and Inequality: Historical Trends". NBER Working Paper Series No. 8339, National Bureau of Economic Research, Cambridge, MA. (http://www.nber.org/papers/w8339)

Quah, Danny. (1996). "Twin Peaks: Growth and convergence in models of distribution dynamics". *Economic Journal* 106 (437), July: 1045–55.

Said, Edward (1979). *Orientalism*. Vintage Books, New York.

Said, Edward (1993). *Culture and Imperialism*. Knopf, New York.

Sala-i-Martin, Xavier. (2002a). "The Disturbing 'Rise' of Global Income Inequality". NBER Working Paper 8904, National Bureau of Economic Research, Cambridge, MA. (http://www.nber.org/papers/w8904)

Sala-i-Martin, Xavier. (2002b). "The World Distribution of Income (estimated from individual country distributions)". NBER Working Paper 8933, National Bureau of Economic Research, Cambridge, MA. (http://www.nber.org/papers/w8933)

Sharpe, Andrew (2003). "Angus Maddison Rewrites Economic History Again". *Challenge* 45 (4), July/August: 20–40.

Spiro, P.J. (2000). "The New Sovereigntists: American Exceptionalism and Its False Prophets". *Foreign Affairs*, November/December.

Stiglitz, J.E. (2002). *Globalization and its discontents*. Norton, New York.

Sutcliffe, Bob. (2003). "A more or less equal world? World income distribution in the twentieth century". PERI Working Paper No. 54, Political Economy Research Institute, University of Massachusetts, Amherst. Also *Indicators, a journal of social health*, 2 (3), Summer.

Todd, Emmanuel (2003). *After the Empire: The Breakdown of the American Order*. Columbia University Press, New York.

Toye, John (1986). *Dilemmas of Development*. Blackwell, Oxford.

Weisbrot, Mark. (2004). "The Unbearable Costs of Empire". Processed, Center for Economic Policy Research, Washington DC.

Weisbrot, Mark, Robert Naiman, and Joyce Kim (2000). "The Emperor Has No Growth: Declining Economic Growth Rates in the Era of Globalization". Processed, Center for Economic and Policy Research, Washington DC.

Williams, William Appleman [ed.](1973). *The Contours of American History*. New Viewpoints, New York.

Williamson, Jeffrey G. (1997). "Globalization and Inequality: Past and Present". *World Bank Research Observer* 12 (2), August: 117–35.

Acknowledgements

At the beginning of 2004, the United Nations Secretariat commissioned a number of regional studies to provide support to the preparation of the International Forum for Social Development on 'Equity, Inequalities And Interdependence' held at the United Nations in New York on 5–6 October 2004. This was the last meeting of a forum created in 2001 by the Department of Economic and Social Affairs (DESA), and financed by voluntary contributions, to promote debate on the implementation of the commitments made in Copenhagen in March 1995 at the World Summit for Social Development and confirmed in Geneva in June 2000 by a special session of the General Assembly. The overarching theme of this International Forum was "Open Societies, Open Economies: Challenges and Opportunities". Other issues it considered during its four year programme—which were closely related to questions of equity and inequality at national and global levels—included the financing of social development, and international migrants and development. The summaries of these meetings are available on the Forum's website: http://www.un.org/esa/socdev/IFSD/index.html

All but one of the regional studies undertaken for the October 2004 meeting of the Forum were revised for publication as DESA Working Papers, with many considerably abridged for publication in this volume. Besides a new paper on the Middle East and North Africa, other additional papers were solicited to address more general thematic issues, broaden the scope of the inquiry and advance the contemporary debate on recent global inequality trends.

This book would not have seen the light of day but for the untiring efforts of Diane Loughran, who worked hard on some of the most difficult chapters and DESA Working Papers on which they are based. Lauren E. Anderson, Tanima Bossart, June Chesney, Saroja Douglass, Julie Pewitt and Patience Stephens worked conscientiously to copy-edit these chapters for publication while Valerian Monteiro was creative and innovative in preparing the Working Papers for publication. Judith Brister and Dominika Halka assisted in myriad ways. Johan Scholvinck, Director of the Division for Social Policy and Development in DESA, provided unstinting support for the preparation and completion of this book. We are grateful to all of them for their respective contributions.

10 April 2006   JOMO K. S.

1
Global Income Inequality:
What it Is and Why it Matters

BRANKO MILANOVIC[1]

Global inequality is a relatively recent research topic. The first calculations of inequality across world citizens were done in the early 1980s (Berry, Bourguignon and Morrisson, 1983; Grosh and Nafziger, 1986). This is because in order to calculate global inequality, one needs to have data on (within-country) national income distributions for most of the countries in the world, or at least for most of the populous and rich countries. But it is only from the early to mid-1980s that such data became available for China,[2] Soviet Union and its constituent republics and large parts of Africa.

Before we move to an analysis of global inequality, however, it is useful to set the stage by delineating what topics we shall be concerned with and what not. This is necessary, precisely because of the relative underdevelopment of the topic, reflected in the fact that the same or similar terms are often used in the literature to mean different things. We need to distinguish between inequality among countries' mean incomes (inter-country inequality, or Concept 1 inequality, as dubbed by Milanovic, 2005), inequality among countries' mean incomes weighted by the countries' populations (Concept 2 inequality), and inequality between the world's individuals (global, or Concept 3 inequality).

Concept 1 inequality deals with convergence and divergence among countries, and although this line of work was at first couched in inequality terms (see Baumol, 1986), most of the later work used cross-country regressions and ß convergence.[3] In such regressions, each country/year is one observation. This line of research, which has generated a huge literature, is interesting for a number of reasons, but it has very little to tell us about income inequality among world citizens. This is basically because countries are of unequal population size. Thus, a fast increase in the income of a poor small country will not have the same effect on global inequality as the same per capita increase in a poor and populous country.

Concept 2 inequality tries to take this into account by weighing each country by its population. It is a low-cost approach since it requires knowledge of only two variables: mean income, which is approximated by gross domestic income

(GDI) per capita, and population size. The first such calculations were done by Kuznets in 1954 (see Kuznets, 1965: 162ff).[4] Some thirteen years later, as part of their first study of purchasing power parity (PPP), Kravis, Heston and Summers (1978) calculated Concept 2 inequality for the non-socialist world.

There are two reasons for the enduring popularity of this approach (for recent examples, see Schultz, 1988; Boltho and Toniolo, 1999; Firebaugh, 2003). First, Concept 2 inequality is the largest component of global inequality. Global inequality is, by definition, composed of population-weighted international inequality (Concept 2 or between-inequality), and inequality due to income differences within countries. The relationship is shown in equations (1) and (2) for Gini and Theil coefficients respectively, where y_i = per capita income of i-th country, p_i = population share of i-th country in total world population, π_i = share of i-th country in total global income, n = number of countries, G_i = Gini coefficient of national income distribution, T_i = Theil coefficients of national income distribution, and L = the so-called overlapping component.[5] Since the 'between' component is by far the larger, accounting for between $\frac{2}{3}$ and $\frac{3}{4}$ of global inequality (depending on what inequality measure one chooses), Concept 2 inequality can be used as a lower-bound proxy to global inequality. Moreover, its movements can be presumed to track changes in global inequality. Second, the data requirements for the calculation of Concept 2 inequality are modest.

$$Concept\_3\_Gini = \sum_{i=1}^{n} G_i\, p_i\pi_i + \frac{1}{\mu}\sum_{i}^{n} \sum_{j>i}^{n}(y_j - y_i)\,p_i p_j + L \qquad (1)$$

Concept 2 Gini

$$Concept\_3\_Theil = \sum_{i=1}^{n} p_i T_i + \sum_{i=1}^{n}\left(p_i\, \frac{y_i}{\mu}\right)\ln \frac{y_i}{\mu} \qquad (2)$$

Concept 2 Theil

Of course, what Concept 2 inequality does not take into account are within-country inequalities. In calculating Concept 2 inequality, we implicitly assume that each individual within a country has the same per capita income (and thus $G_i = T_i = L = 0$). This last assumption needs to be abandoned if we want to calculate 'true' global inequality across individuals. But in order to abandon it, one must have access to national income distributions which are available only from household surveys. It is this 'jump' that makes such a big difference in data requirements between Concept 2 and Concept 3. From being 'modest', the data requirements now become huge, since, ideally, we should have access to national income distributions from all the countries in the world.

This leads to a very important, albeit not sufficiently appreciated, difference between Concepts 2 and 3. This is not a conceptual difference, but rather the difference in what is a commonly used metric of welfare. To be sure, Concept 2 inequality can be calculated using either GDIs per capita or mean disposable incomes retrieved from countries' household surveys (HS). It is however almost never calculated using the latter because HS means are much more difficult to obtain than from national accounts (NA) data. In contrast, Concept 3 inequality *must* be based on household surveys because the only sources of distributional data are, as said before, household surveys. Because there is no world-wide household survey, this means that the best one can do is to combine individual countries' surveys, and use disposable per capita income or personal per capita consumption as welfare indicators.

Now, the first problem is that there is a definitional difference between GDI which comes from national accounts, and disposable income which comes from surveys. Second, there has been a recent tendency for these two measures not to move in unison in several important countries (see Deaton, 2005). Thus, even if everything else were fully comparable, a commonly calculated Concept 2 measure that uses national accounts data will differ from an equivalent Concept 2 measure calculated using household surveys because welfare indicators are different and because they have recently diverged for reasons that are not yet quite clear.[6]

This review will deal only with studies of global or Concept 3 income inequality.[7] The way to estimate global inequality is to calculate Concept 2 inequality using nation accounts data, and to combine it with the empirical observation that within-country income distributions tend to follow a log-normal pattern. Then, the only additional piece of information needed is a Gini coefficient, or some other summary inequality statistic describing national income distributions. They are published in various compendia of Gini coefficients such as the WIDER and Deininger-Squire databases, etc.

Under the assumption of a log normal distribution of income, the inequality statistics allow us to derive an estimate of the variance of each national distribution. Once we know the variance and the mean, and given the assumption of log-normality, we can estimate the entire distribution, that is, each fractile's income. It is then a relatively simple task to combine these national distributions into a single world-wide income distribution, particularly so if one uses an exactly decomposable measure of inequality like the Theil coefficient or the variance of logs. This was precisely the approach followed by many early and some recent studies of global inequality (Berry, Bourguignon and Morrison, 1983; Grosh and Nafziger, 1986; Quah, 1999; Shultze, 1998; Chotikapanich, Valenzuela and Rao, 1997). At times, this approach can be refined by using a bit more information than what is contained in a Gini or Theil index. Sala-i-

Martin and Bhalla have used quintiles of income distribution to get a better handle of national distributions and thus a more precise estimate of global distribution. All these methods can be considered *tatonnements*, groping for the global distribution.

These methods are quite ingenious, given their rather minimal information requirements. But they are also very 'costly', because it is often the numerous assumptions, rather than the data, that drive the results. A lot of assumptions are made simultaneously (e.g. that each country's distribution is log normal; that GDP per capita gives the correct mean income, and that its under or over-estimation, compared to household surveys, is constant across poor and rich alike), and it is nearly impossible to tell the impact of each separate assumption on the results. Further, since even the minimal data requirements (national Ginis) are not satisfied annually, authors are led to make additional assumptions (for example, that national inequality does not change or changes in an assumed fashion), so that in the end, the part of the results driven by various assumptions may vastly outstrip the part based on actual data. The best recent examples of such approaches, which are often thinly disguised Concept 2 inequality calculations, are Bhalla (2002) and Sala-i-Martin (2002a; 2002b). In Bhalla's (2002) calculations of global inequality, only one out of his 24 distributions is based on actual data, while 23 are 'derived' through assumptions; in Sala-i-Martin's (2002a) paper, the ratio is one actual to four 'derived' distributions.[8]

Compared to this method, the quantum leap is to directly use household surveys from as many countries as possible (ideally, all). This was done by Milanovic (2002; 2005) and by the World Bank (2005). Here, in principle, global inequality is calculated the same way one calculates within-country inequality, using not national accounts data, but survey data. Another quantum leap in this line of research will occur when these, so far disparate, national surveys are standardized, or a single world-wide household survey is conducted. We shall come back to this in the third section. Now, we have to briefly cover some methodological issues that are very important in this type of research although they seldom receive the attention they deserve.

SOME METHODOLOGICAL ISSUES

We start with the simplest question of all: what is 'income' in calculations of global inequality? As we have seen, most of the early work used national accounts data, that is GDI per capita expressed in the same currency (international or PPP dollars). This is because household survey data for many countries were simply unavailable (and even when they existed, researchers could not get them because the statistical agencies refused to release them).[9] There are currently three main sources of world wide data on GDI per capita across time and across countries. They are World Bank data, available in World Bank World Development Indicators (WDI), the Penn World Tables, and Angus Maddison's data. The advantage of using GDI per capita as 'income' is that these numbers are relatively uncontroversial, even if the three sources do not always agree among themselves. We know what is meant by GDI per capita and we know that these values do give some generally accepted mean incomes of all nations.[10]

The main drawback of this approach is that GDI per capita is not 'income' in any recognizable sense to any individual or household. Gross domestic income includes components such as corporate investment from retained profits, build-up of stocks, government spending on defence, etc., which are not part of even broadly defined household disposable income. In addition, publicly financed health and education are part of GDI per capita, but not included in household per capita disposable income unless one is able to impute—which is quasi impossible in a multi-country context—these values back to individual house-holds based on survey data on school attendance and use of medical services.

Another drawback is that the combination of GDI per capita with some distributional statistics (to reflect national income distribution) mixes two aggregates, calculated from different sources, and this 'mixing' is not distri-bution-neutral. On the one hand, we are using country GDI per capita, and on the other, we are applying to this mean, distributional parameters obtained from surveys of household disposable income.[11] It was already explained that the two instruments are different by definition. But in addition, such an adjust-ment is not distribution-neutral. We know that surveys tend to under-represent capital income or under-survey rich people (see Mistiaen and Ravallion, 2003).[12] Thus, a simple scaling-up of all survey incomes by a given parameter will reduce poverty below what it really is and underestimate inequality.[13] When a different mean (GDI per capita) is applied to a survey-based distribution, we implicitly allocate the difference between GDI per capita and disposable house-hold per capita income across all households (more exactly, in proportion to reported household income). Poor people's incomes are increased in the same proportion as rich people's incomes. But if most of the difference between the two concepts is due to the unreported income of the rich, then this approach wrongly inflates the incomes of the poor.

Now, the income of the rich, which accounts for the bulk of the difference between GDI and disposable income, is of two types: first, the definitionally different part, which consists of publicly-financed health and education, corporate profits, etc., that are consumed by the rich, but also by the middle-classes and some poor in *rich* countries;[14] second, the income of rich people in each individual country that is missed out by surveys (e.g. property incomes). All actual recipients of these incomes are globally-rich because the middle-class and even the poor from the rich world are in the top quintile of the global income distribution, but the difference between the two aggregates is spread much more widely: some of it is imputed to the poor in the poor countries which, we know, receive none of it.

Consider the following example. Let the poverty line $PPP1 per capita per day. Let the average per capita disposable income from surveys of several groups of the poor in India be $0.75, $0.8, $0.85. Now, suppose (very realistically) that India's GDI is some 35 per cent higher than disposable income. We know that most of this 35 per cent is received by the rich, either because they benefit more from publicly-funded public services, or because they fail to report their property incomes. What the authors (in particular, Sala-i-Martin, 2002a; Bhalla, 2002) then do is to multiply the incomes of the poor by the factor of 1.35. Then, suddenly, none of them is poor any longer: they have all crossed the poverty threshold. Pure magic![15]

But if we decide that 'income' in global studies should be the same concept as in national studies of inequality—that is per capita disposable household income—the problem is not solved yet. This is because national definitions of survey income are very different, and the more countries we include, the more different they become. A huge effort, conducted by the Luxembourg Income Study, has gone into standardization of national definitions. A similar project is underway at the World Bank using Living Standards Measurement Surveys (LSMS). Yet, the standardization covers only a small portion of all countries and surveys.

The main differences arise in the treatment of self-employed income (what are business expenditures for the self-employed?), valuation of home-consumption, including owner-occupied housing,[16] treatment of publicly-provided health and education benefits, and the use of top-coding of high incomes (where all incomes above a certain ceiling are coded as equal to that ceiling).[17] For different countries and at different levels of development, differences in the treatment of these categories are not equally important. For poor countries, it is the problems of valuation of own consumption and self-employed income that are the most difficult and that can make individual incomes often move up by a factor of 2 or more; for the rich countries, it is the treatment of publicly-provided health and education benefits that is of most concern. Swedish disposable income with them or without them is quite different. For countries with extravagantly rich individuals, it is the underestimation of capital incomes which is of concern.

But there is no agreement that 'income' in global inequality studies should be income at all. Many people think that rather than income, one should look at consumption or expenditures as the true indicator of the standard of living. This debate mirrors the debates in individual countries since obviously inequality can be measured using either income or consumption. What lends this debate an added importance in the case of global inequality is that in many countries, household surveys ask questions about income only, while in other countries, they ask for both, or for expenditure only. Then, a global study of inequality has to do what all national studies try to avoid, that is to mix household survey data that use two different concepts of 'income': disposable income and consumption. This introduces an error whose direction and magnitude cannot be estimated.

Although in the last few years, there has been a trend toward the use of consumption measures (not the least through the efforts of the World Bank and the influence it has exerted on the choice of survey instruments in the former communist countries and in Africa), we are still far from unanimity on this issue. In the study of global inequality based on 1998 benchmark data, Milanovic (2005: 104) used 63 consumption instruments and 59 income instruments. This represents a significant increase in the number of consumption instruments compared with ten years before (80 income-based and 22 consumption-based distributions), but for some of the most important countries (like China), one still depends on income data alone. If a guess had to be ventured, it could be said that there is likely to be a tendency toward greater use of household per capita consumption as the main welfare indicator. While quite defensible from a strictly methodological perspective, this will open up a number of issues of comparability since most historical income distribution statistics (e.g. in the United States, UK, France, Germany) are income-based. One thus needs to weigh methodological and quality improvements in snapshots of recent income distribution against the breaks in historically existing series.

Considering the problems of the appropriate welfare indicator, other methodological issues are easier to deal with. Whatever 'income' is, that 'income' should be expressed in per capita terms, and should be equal for the members of a household. This means that the two issues often debated in national inequality studies are 'solved' here: the issue of equivalence scales, and intra-household inequality. They are 'solved' because at the current level of statistical development, there is simply no way to account for economies of scale and size across different countries.

The main reason for this is that economies of scale and size depend on the relative prices of public and private goods (if housing is very cheap, economies of size will be small) and they systematically differ between poor and rich countries (see Lanjouw and others, 2004). Until we have a better handle of the relative prices of public and private goods,[18] we cannot adjust internationally for equivalent units. The use of a given equivalence scale for all countries in the world would be much more arbitrary than the use of per capita calculations. Similarly, we lack information about within-household inequalities.[19]

Another issue on which there is agreement is that whatever 'income' is, it needs to be adjusted using a country's relative price level. In other words, we need to use PPP exchange rates to translate domestic currencies into international dollars. Ideally, of course, one would like to move toward a better adjustment where, at least for some large countries with less than fully integrated markets, PPP exchange rates would differ between different parts of the country (e.g. the price level in the richest Chinese province is estimated to be 76 per cent higher than in the poorest; see Brandt and Holz, 2006).

Another concern is that the relative prices faced by different parts of the income distribution are not the same. According to Pogge and Reddy (2002), relative food prices faced by the poor in poor countries are higher than implied by the use of a single all-consumption PPP.[20] Food prices are what really matters for the poor, and the use of a lower overall price index will artificially boost poor people's incomes in India and elsewhere in poor countries.[21] Pogge and Reddy advocate a cross-country project akin to the one currently conducted by World Bank's International Comparison Project which would generate PPPs relevant for the very modest, principally food, basket consumed by the poor across the world. But so long as within-country (e.g. provincial) PPPs and PPPs differentiated by income class are not available, we are obliged to use a single PPP exchange rate per country.

How about the use of market (rather than PPP) exchange rates in global inequality calculations? This is a useful complement because it gives us a different insight into inequalities. If one is interested in global purchasing power or ability to affect the world economy, then conversion of local incomes into actual US dollars makes sense. But there are relatively few instances where we are interested in this, and most of our interest in global inequality is really based on the desire to compare living standards of different people. For that purpose, PPP exchange rates are, of course, better.

How Great is Global Inequality?

There is general agreement about the size of global inequality, and there is general disagreement about the recent direction of change of global inequality. Table 1.1 shows the results for global inequality obtained by a number of authors using quite different techniques: most of them mix national accounts

TABLE 1.1
Global inequality (in Gini points) in the 1990s, according to various authors

Author	Year	Gini value	National mean incomes from:	National income distributions from:
Milanovic (2005)	1993	66	Household surveys	Household surveys
Milanovic (2005)	1998	65	Household surveys	Household surveys
Bourguignon and Morrison (2002)	1990s	66	GDI (Maddison)	Household survey estimates
Sala-i-Martin (2002a)	1998	61	GDI (Penn World Tables)	Ginis and quintiles from HS
Bhalla (2002)	2000	65	GDI (Penn World Tables and WDI)	Ginis and quintiles from HS
Dikhanov and Ward (2001)	1999	68	National consumption (WDI)	Ginis and quintiles from HS
Dowrick and Akmal (2001)	1993	71	GDI	Ginis and quintiles from HS
Sutcliffe (2003)	2000	63	GDI (Maddison)	Ginis and quintiles from HS
Chotikapanich, Valenzuela and Rao (1997)	1990	65	GDI (Penn World Tables)	Ginis for HS

Key: HS: household survey; GDI: Gross Domestic Income; WDI: World Development Indicators (World Bank).

information (using GDI per capita as mean income) and household survey information, and only a few use household surveys directly. In all the studies however, the recipients are individuals (inequality is expressed on a per capita basis), and national incomes are converted into international (PPP) dollars although the PPP exchange rates may be drawn from different sources. All Gini values for the 1990s, with the exception of the two extremes (61 and 71), lie within a relatively narrow range between 63 and 66. The similarity in the results is even more remarkable when one realizes that the standard errors of these estimates are between 2 and 3 Gini points,[22] and that most of the estimates are consequently within one standard error of each other.

As for the direction of change—comparison between 1990s and 1980s—there is no unanimity. Sala-i-Martin and Bhalla, using very similar methodologies, argue that global inequality has declined by between 3 and 4 Gini points. Dikhanov and Ward as well as Bourguignon and Morrison find an increase of about 1 Gini point. Sutcliffe concludes that there was no change, and Milanovic finds an increase of 3 Gini points between 1988 and 1993, followed by a decline of 1 Gini point in the next five years.[23] His most recent (and unpublished) calculations for 2002 show another small increase of about

1 Gini point. Thus, according to Milanovic, there are zigzags. They are explained by the slow growth of rural incomes in India and China as well as the economic collapse of Eastern Europe in the early 1990s, both of which contributed to global inequality. When both developments were reversed in the next five-year period, global inequality decreased. But these are zigzags caused by specific economic events in large countries, not a trend.

This lack of unanimity on changes, and disagreements on whether there is any trend at all, stem not only from the differences in methodology, but paradoxically, also from the very similar results that all authors obtain regarding the overall *level* of inequality. The reason is as follows. Different methodologies yield similar inequality levels, but they do so with quite a lot of noise caused by measurement problems. Mean incomes, whether obtained from surveys or national accounts, are not consistently calculated, and key data sources disagree among themselves. The computation of Concept 2 inequality using GDI per capita—a metric on which there is apparently least dispute—from World Bank or Maddison's data series will differ by several Gini points. This is because, as pointed out by Sutcliffe (2003), Maddison's data include estimates for a number of worn-torn or otherwise 'excluded' countries like Sudan, Afghanistan, Somalia, the Congo, Cuba, North Korea, etc., that are almost invariably poor and not included in the World Bank database. In addition, Maddison's growth rates for China are less than the official rates and those used by the World Bank. It is then not surprising that when one superimposes estimates of national distributions on one or another set of GDIs per capita to generate global inequality, the choice of the GDI database will clearly influence the end result.[24]

Income distribution data, particularly when extrapolated from quintiles or from Gini coefficients, are even noisier. Furthermore, due to the absence of income distribution data for many countries, some authors (e.g. Bhalla and Sala-i-Martin) resort to very dubious assumptions, e.g. that income distributions do not change over time or change in a certain (linear) fashion or everyone in a country has the same income. In most cases, this myriad of assumptions and measurement errors tend not to bias the results in one direction only, but probably to offset each other, producing relatively similar levels of inequality. But when one re-estimates global inequality for another year, while the level hardly changes, the result is (on account of the measurement error, if nothing else) likely to be slightly different. It is that slight difference that is then interpreted as the evidence of a change, or in some cases, even of a trend.

How big is a Gini of around 65? It is larger than the inequality found in any single country including South Africa and Brazil, two of the most unequal countries in the world, whose Ginis are in the upper fifties or low sixties. The Gini coefficient however does not give an intuitive feel for how large global inequalities are. A better way to look at it is to consider how the overall pie is distributed among different fractiles of the distribution. Thus, for example, the top 5 per cent of individuals in the world receive about 1/3 of total world (PPP-valued) income, and the top 10 per cent get one-half. If we take the bottom 5 and 10 per cent, they receive 0.2 and 0.7 per cent of total world income respectively. This means that the ratio between the average income received by the richest 5 per cent and the poorest 5 per cent of people in the world is 165 to 1 (Milanovic, 2005). The richest people earn in about 48 hours as much as the poorest people earn in a year.

Another important question is to ask how much of global inequality is due to differences in the mean incomes of countries and how much is due to income differences within countries. Some 70 per cent of global inequality is 'explained' by differences in countries' mean incomes. This is a sharp reversal from a situation which existed around the time of the Industrial Revolution when more than half of the (admittedly very rough) estimate of global inequality was due to income differences within nations (see Bourguignon and Morrisson, 2002).[25] Then, in contrast to today, the differences between countries' mean incomes were relatively small. For example, in 1870, the average (un-weighted) GDI per capita of the ten richest countries was 6 times greater than the average (un-weighted) GDI per capita of the ten poorest countries. In 2002, the ratio was 42 to 1.[26]

While income inequality between countries is the largest component of global inequality, overlaps between countries' distributions (that is, some people from a poor country being better off than some people from a rich country) are not negligible either.[27] We illustrate this in Figure 1.1, which plots the position of each 5 per cent (ventile) of different countries' distributions in the global distribution. Consider the line for France. We calculate the mean income (in international dollars) of each French ventile from the lowest (first) to the highest—arrayed on the horizontal axis—and then find their positions in the global income distribution. As can be seen, the poorest 5 per cent of Frenchmen have a mean income which places them in the 72nd percentile of the world income distribution; the richest 5 per cent have incomes which place them in the top percentile of the world. Hence, French income distributions span the range between the 72nd and 100th percentiles in the world. Consider now rural Indonesia at the bottom of the figure. Here, the range is from the 4th percentile to the 56th percentile in the world. The two distributions (France and rural Indonesia) do not overlap at all.[28] But this is not the case if we compare Brazil and France: more than a third of all Brazilians are richer than the poorest 5 per cent of the French.[29]

The figure illustrates not only that inequality due to within-country

FIGURE 1.1

The position of different countries' ventiles in global income distribution

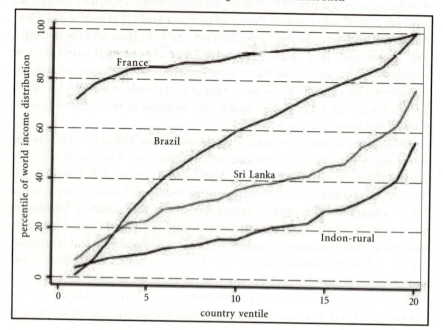

distributions is still significant, and that countries are not homogeneous entities composed of either rich and poor people only, but will have practical implications when we discuss global transfers (see the fifth section). In short, if transfers were to flow from mean-income rich to mean-income poor countries, and we do not a priori know who their beneficiaries are, a glance at Figure 1.1 immediately convinces us of the need to take recipient countries' income distributions seriously. This is because of the probability that money raised from a French citizen will end up in the pockets of somebody who is richer than he, is higher if money is transferred from France to Brazil than if it is transferred from France to rural Indonesia. But we shall return to this topic below.

IS THERE A LINK BETWEEN GLOBALIZATION AND GLOBAL INEQUALITY?

It is often implicitly assumed that the changes in global inequality can be interpreted as telling us whether globalization leads to widening or shrinking income differences among individuals in the world.[30] However, the causal link between globalization and global inequality is very difficult to make. To see this, consider several ways in which globalization affects inequality among individuals in the world. The first channel goes through globalization's effects on within-country distributions. As we would expect from economic theory, the effect varies between rich and poor countries. In the simplest Hecksher-Ohlin world, globalization would increase demand for, and the wages of, low-skilled labour in poor countries and the wages of high-skilled workers in the rich world. Consequently, we would expect income distribution in poor countries to become 'better' and income distribution in rich countries to get 'worse'.

This is not, however, consistent with what has been observed over the last twenty years when distributions in poor, middle-income and rich countries have tended to grow more unequal (Cornia and Kiiski, 2001). This is an issue which has recently been studied a lot and is still the subject of intense debate: Is openness to blame for increasing wage and income differences in the US? Is openness associated with rising income inequality in poor countries? For example, Milanovic (2005) and Ravallion (2001) find that openness is associated with increased inequality in poor countries, and lower inequality in rich countries, while Dollar and Kraay (2002) argue that there is no systematic effect of openness on inequality.[31]

Then, and this is the second channel, globalization may differently affect mean incomes in poor and rich countries: in other words, it might lead to divergence or convergence in country incomes. There is no unanimity on this point either. Most authors agree that openness is positively associated with mean income growth, but some of them (Sachs and Warner, 1997; World Bank, 2002) find the effect stronger for poor countries, while others (DeLong and Dowrick, 2003; Dowrick and Golley, 2004) argue that the openness premium has been larger for rich than for poor countries during the last twenty years.[32] The first group of authors would expect openness to lead to shrinking differences in national mean incomes. Therefore, they have to explain away the observed divergence in mean country incomes by the lack of openness among the laggards. According to the second group of authors, the divergence is an indication that the effects of openness might change over time, and that openness, even if positive for all on balance, may exacerbate inter-country inequality.

Third, the effects of globalization may vary between populous and small countries. This area has not been much explored except in the context of the rather limited (in scope and number) studies of small island economies. Yet, one can imagine that globalization may play out differently in populous countries with large domestic markets, or in small niche economies like Hong Kong, Singapore or Luxembourg, than in middle-size countries.

And finally, and possibly, most importantly, the effect of globalization on global inequality will depend on history, that is on whether populous countries happen to be poor or rich at a given point in time. To see this, assume for a moment that globalization has a positive impact on the growth rates of populous and poor countries, and has no effect on within-country income distributions. This will, in the current constellation of world incomes (see Figure 1.2), mean that India and China would be expected to catch up with the rich world, while their national distributions will not change, and global inequality will tend to decrease.[33] There would be both mean-income convergence and reduction of global inequality. But let us decouple the poor and populous countries. Suppose that India and China are rich (and still populous) and let most poor countries be relatively small. Now, mean income convergence will continue, but the effect on global inequality will be ambiguous. China and India will benefit from the pro-big bias of globalization, but since they would be rich, globalization will be less beneficial to them than to poor countries. These two effects will pull in opposite directions, and global inequality may go down or up. Moreover, if populous countries are generally poor, the convergence effect is nil, globalization on average favours small countries and leads to the widening of national income distributions, then the overall effect must be to increase global inequality.

Figure 1.2

Distribution of people according to GDI per capita of the country where they live, 2000

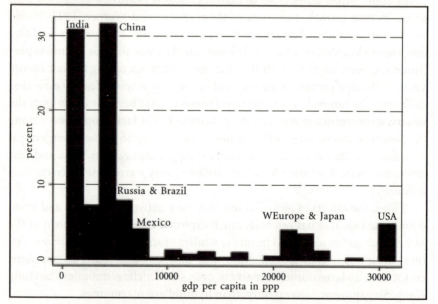

This illustrates a key point: even if the effects of globalization on within-country inequality, mean income convergence, and populous vs. small countries, are unambiguous and do not change over time, globalization's impact on global inequality will vary depending on where along the international income distribution, countries with different attributes happen to lie at a given point in time. The implication is, of course, that all statements about the relationship between globalization and global inequality are highly time-specific, contingent on past income history, and not general.

Does Global Inequality Matter?

There are two views on this matter (as on pretty much everything else discussed here). One group of people believe that global inequality is irrelevant. There are two reasons why it may be so. According to Bhagwati (2004), even calculation of global inequality is 'lunacy' as it is a mere number. There is no 'addressee' to whom this mere number matters because there is no global government and there is no global civil society. According to this view, national inequalities matter because they become the stuff of political discourse; they are used to form political parties or platforms, and to organize interest groups. But at the global level, none of that exists because there is no global polity.

Another reason adduced for the irrelevance of global (or for that matter, all) inequality is that only changes in absolute income matters to the poor and the rich alike (Krueger, 2002; Feldstein, 1999). In the words of Anne Krueger (2002), "Poor people are desperate to improve their material conditions…rather than to march up the income distribution [ladder]". Thus, even if the absolute income gap between an average American and an average African increases, these authors are unconcerned. After all, they argue, the average African would be a bit less poor. This, of course, assumes that our income relative to the incomes of others does not matter. Yet, this conclusion is at odds with psychological studies that invariably show that people do not care only about their absolute income, but also about where they stand in the social pyramid, and also whether they think this position to be fair (Graham and Felton, 2005; Frank, 2005).

Or—differently—global inequality may matter. On this side of the issue, there are also different approaches. For Pogge and Reddy (2002) and Singer (2002), global poverty and global inequality are ethical issues. Hence, the rich world cannot disown all interest in global poverty and inequality: to some extent, the fate of every individual in the world affects us. Distributional justice within a nation, and in the world as a whole, is—from an ethical perspective—the same thing (see Singer, 2002: Chapter 5).

There are also more pragmatic reasons why global inequality may matter. Kuznets (1965 [first published in 1954]: 173–74) formulated the following half a century ago: "Since it is only through contact that recognition and tension are created, one could argue that the reduction of physical misery associated with low income and consumption levels…permit[s] an increase rather than a diminution of political tensions [because] the political misery of the poor, the tension created by the observation of the much greater wealth of other communities…may have only increased."

When people observe each other and interact, it is no longer simply a national yardstick that they have in mind when they compare their incomes with the incomes of others, but an international or global one. What globalization does is to increase awareness of other people's incomes, and therefore, the perception (knowledge) of inequalities among both the poor and the rich. If it does so among the poor, then their aspirations change: they may no longer be satisfied with small increases in their own real income, if they know that other people are gaining much more. Therefore, the process of globalization by itself changes the perception of one's position, and even if globalization may raise everybody's real income, it could exacerbate, rather than moderate, feelings of despondency and deprivation among the poor.

Globalization, in that sense, is no different from the process which led to the creation of modern nation states out of isolated, and often mutually estranged, hamlets. National income distribution was similarly an abstraction for the people who did not interact with each other, and almost ignored each others' existence and way of life. However, once nation-states came into existence, national inequality became an issue—simply because people were able to compare their own standards of living and to make judgments as to whether these income differences were deserved or not. If one believes that the process of globalization would slowly lead to the formation of a global polity, then global inequality will indeed become a relevant issue. For it is difficult to envisage that a fully free exchange of goods, technology and information, transfer of capital, and some freedom in the movement of people can go on for a long time without creating a global polity of sorts and requiring decision-making processes at the global level.

If so, then we need to develop some rules for global redistribution. The first rule, which may be called Progressivity 1 rule (a companion to Concept 1 inequality), is that funds should flow from a (mean-income) rich to a (mean-income) poor country. This requirement is easily satisfied. Even today, bilateral aid is given by rich to poor countries (not the other way round). But in a globalized world, this is not enough. Redistribution needs to be globally progressive—that is, to satisfy the same criteria that we require from

FIGURE 1.3
Globally progressive transfer

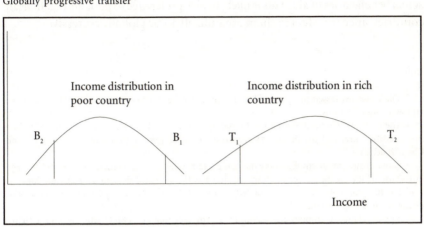

Income distribution in
poor country

Income distribution in rich
country

B$_2$ B$_1$ T$_1$ T$_2$

Income

Note: T: tax payer. B: beneficiary.

redistribution within a nation-state. This means that the tax-payer ought to be richer than the beneficiary of the transfer. But both Progressivity 1 and global Progressivity may be satisfied (as shown in Figure 1.3 by points B$_1$ and T$_1$) while the beneficiary is a relatively rich individual in a poor country and the tax payer a relatively poor individual in a rich country. And it is precisely the perception that many transfers end up in the pockets of the rich elite in poor countries which is fuelling the current discontent with multilateral and bilateral aid. Thus, the third requirement ought to be that transfers be such that inequality decreases in both donor and recipient countries. This will happen only if the tax payer is relatively rich, even within his/her own country, and the beneficiary is relatively poor in his/her country. This situation is illustrated by points such as T$_2$ and B$_2$.

Now, these three requirements regarding global transfers will be more easily satisfied when the income distributions of rich and poor nations do not overlap. This is, for example, the case of France and rural Indonesia (illustrated in Figure 1.1). Even if the distribution of aid money among Indonesian beneficiaries is random, global progressivity will be satisfied since there are practically no people in rural Indonesia who are better off than even the poorest Frenchmen. But this is not the case if we look at a transfer between France and Brazil. There, assuming that the tax payer belongs to the French middle class (say, around the median of French income distribution), a purely random allocation of aid to Brazil will still yield a non-negligible probability of 10 per cent for a globally regressive transfer.[34] This means that in the design of global transfers, one needs to take into account national income distributions to determine the actual beneficiaries of aid. This is likely to give preference to poor and egalitarian countries since transfers to them are unlikely to be globally regressive.

Notes

[1] The views expressed are personal and should not be attributed to the World Bank or its affiliated organizations.

[2] The first post-Cultural Revolution household survey in China was conducted in 1978. The first available rural and urban surveys are from 1980 and 1981 respectively (see Ravallion and Chen, 2006: 3).

[3] Some of the initial emphasis on inequality, rather than on â coefficients, can still be seen in the use of the sigma convergence where sigma is the standard deviation of income logs.

[4] For the year 1949, Kuznets calculated a Concept 2 inequality that covered around a third of the world's population.

[5] The overlapping component accounts for the fact that somebody who lives in a richer country may have an income lower than somebody from a poorer country (and the converse). L is calculated as a residual, and this is why the Gini index is, unlike the Theil index, not exactly decomposable.

[6] This area—understanding why national accounts and household survey averages move differently—represents one of the most important areas for further research. Bhalla (2002) must be credited through his, at times single-minded, insistence on using national accounts data for highlighting this issue.

[7] And with global inequality conventionally defined as inequality in relative, not absolute, incomes, and using conventional measures of inequality like the Lorenz curve, Gini coefficient or Theil index. The focus on absolute inequality, however, has its own uses (see Atkinson and Brandolini, 2004; Svedberg, 2003; Ravallion, 2004). Similarly, relative income inequality, with the use of different inequality aversion parameters (reflecting, in principle, different welfare judgments), will produce ambiguous results, even where conventional statistics yield a clear outcome (see Capeau and Decoster, 2004: Table 5).

[8] For a critique, see Milanovic (2005: 119–27).

[9] This is still the case with many countries that refuse to release micro data to any institution or individual. Such countries are quite diverse, ranging from Japan to Algeria. There is thus a paradoxical situation that a number of expensive instruments like household surveys exist in the world; yet, they cannot be used because of misplaced policies of some countries' statistical offices. The issue of confidentiality, with which they sometimes defend their practice, is clearly bogus since no researcher can ever identify the participating households. Are we to believe that a researcher in 2006 is going to identify the Japanese households that took part in a survey conducted in 1973?

[10] It has not always been like that. Consider the problems of converting Communist countries' national accounts methodology to the national accounts statistics (NAS) system, and of course, the issue of the deliberate falsification of national accounts.

[11] The difference in coverage and definition between national accounts and surveys means that, even if everything were perfectly measured, it would be incorrect to apply inequality or distributional measures—which are derived from surveys—which measure one thing, to means—which are derived from national accounts—which measure another (Deaton, 2003: 35).

[12] Income from property is notoriously underestimated in household surveys (even leaving aside the fact that most surveys do not include capital gains at all). Concialdi (1997: 261) claims

that the best available French household surveys underestimate capital incomes by about 40 per cent. Wagner and Grabka (1999) estimate German property income to be underestimated by almost one-half compared to national accounts data. In Japan, according to Ishizaki (1985), only 12 per cent of property income is 'captured' by household surveys (quoted in Bauer and Mason, 1992: 407).

[13] We speak of scaling-up, rather than scaling-down, because GDI per capita is normally greater than household per capita disposable income.

[14] Disposable household income, retrieved from surveys in West European nations, amounts to about 60 per cent of GDI. A bulk of that difference is explained by health and education consumption. Publicly-financed health and education as a share of GDI is much less in poor countries.

[15] On the additional pitfalls caused by the use of averages from national accounts and distributions from household surveys, see Ravallion (2000), Deaton and Dreze (2002), and Deaton (2003).

[16] For example, in 1990, the Chinese statistical office changed the valuation of grain output produced by rural households from state-mandated to market prices. This generated a large change in calculated poverty rates and a break in the rural mean income series (see Ravallion and Chen, 2005).

[17] For example, the US Current Population Survey 'top-codes' all very high wage and capital incomes. Similarly, the maximum capital gain that can be recorded in the survey is $149,999 per household annually.

[18] And also relative prices of child vs. adult goods if we are to adjust for household composition, and not only for household size.

[19] Schultz (1998) however tries to account for intra-household inequality by using gender gaps in schooling (for each country) to estimate gender gaps in income at the household level.

[20] This means that the ratio of food prices consumed by the poor in (say) India compared to the food prices of the same goods in the US is higher than the ratio between the overall price level in India and that in the US.

[21] The reason behind such income overestimation is as follows. The weights in the 'world' consumption basket of goods and services are decisively influenced by the prices and structure of consumption in rich countries since they are obviously the largest consumers. Then, a relatively high consumption of services in poor countries—which are cheap there, but are assessed at much higher 'world' prices—tends to show poor countries' (and poor people's) incomes to be higher than they 'really' are. One possible way to adjust for this is to move from the commonly used Geary-Khamis index, which has this property, to more 'neutral' price indices (Afriat or EKS) where the weight of rich countries is less (see Dowrick and Akmal, 2001).

[22] One has to be careful in the interpretation of the standard error. The standard errors are obtained using simple 'bootstrapping' techniques, so they basically show how sensitive the estimated Gini coefficient is to any single observation (Milanovic, 2002). These results do not include any information about the reliability of the underlying national income distributions (viz, how correctly incomes are measured).

[23] The World Bank's *World Development Report, 2006* uses mean log deviation as the measure of global inequality. It finds that it has decreased between 1994 and 2000 from 0.87 to 0.82 (see World Bank, 2005: 64).

[24] For example, Concept 2 inequality calculated using World Bank GDI per capita data from 138 countries shows a decrease of some 3 Gini points between 1985 and 2000. The same concept calculated using Maddison's data over the same period for about 160 countries shows a decline of only 1 Gini point (author's unpublished calculations).

[25] This is an estimate based on the Theil decomposition between inequality due to the differences in incomes between six country groups, namely 'Africa', 'Asia', 'Japan, Korea and Taiwan', 'Latin America', 'Eastern Europe', and 'Western Europe and its offshoots', and

inequality within country groups. Since there are no data on income distributions for most countries in the world prior to 1950, Bourguignon and Morrison use estimates for a few select countries to 'impart' the same distributions to other countries in the group. Their between-component accounts for some 30 per cent of global inequality. Obviously, if they had data on all countries' distributions, the between-component would have been larger. However, it is unlikely to have exceeded one-half of global inequality.

[26] Both calculated from Maddison (2004) data.

[27] Note that in a world of large between-country income differences, and very small within-country inequalities, there would be no overlap at all, and 100 per cent of global inequality would have been 'caused' by between-country differences.

[28] This is, of course, true at the level of ventiles. It is quite possible, even likely, that there are some individuals in rural Indonesia who are richer than some individuals in France. If we conducted the analysis in terms of national percentiles, rather than ventiles, there would be some overlap. But it would be clearly minimal.

[29] Even if at each given ventile, the income of the French is higher than the income of the Brazilians. This means that French income distribution is first-order dominant over the Brazilian distribution (as is, for example, the Sri Lankan over the rural Indonesian), even though the French and Brazilian distributions do overlap (unlike the French and the rural Indonesian).

[30] We define globalization in terms of an outcome variable: increased share of trade and direct foreign investments in GDI. This is quite acceptable when we have income inequality as the left-hand side variable since inequality moves in response to outcomes (higher or lower trade). But one could also define globalization in terms of policies (e.g. lower trade barriers).

[31] For a review of the literature, see Winters, McCulloch and McKay (2004). The role of trade in increasing wage differentials in rich countries is the subject of a voluminous controversy (for some examples, see Freeman, 1995; Slaughter, 1999).

[32] According to them, the openness premium was larger for poor countries in the 1960–1980 period, but then changed in the last two decades. For some speculation on what might have triggered that change, see Dowrick and Golley (2004: 53).

[33] We are concerned with effects at one point in time only. Independent changes in population may, by affecting the weights in the inequality statistics, influence changes in global inequality on their own. For example, China's impact on global inequality can be decomposed between income per capita growth effects and population growth effects. Jiang (2006) finds that one-third of China's contribution to reducing global inequality is due to its population growth.

[34] Differently put, 10 per cent of Brazilians have higher income than the median Frenchman.

REFERENCES

Atkinson, Anthony B., and Andrea Brandolini (2004). Global world inequality: Absolute, relative or intermediate. Paper prepared for the 28th Conference of the International Association for Research in Income and Wealth, Cork, Ireland, 22–28 August.

Bauer, John, and Andrew Mason (1992). The distribution of income and wealth in Japan. *Review of Income and Wealth* 38 (4): 403–28.

Baumol, William (1986). Productivity growth, convergence, and welfare: What the long-run data show. *American Economic Review* 76, December: 1072–116.

Berry, Albert, Francois Bourguignon and Christian Morrisson (1983). Changes in the world distribution of income between 1950 and 1977. *Economic Journal* 93, June: 331–50.

Bhagwati, Jagdish (2004). *In Defense of Globalization.* Oxford University Press, New York.

Bhalla, Surjit (2002). *Imagine There is No Country.* Institute for International Economics, Washington, DC.

Boltho, Andrea, and Gianni Toniolo (1999). The assessment: the twentieth century-achievements, failures, lessons. *Oxford Review of Economic Policy* 15 (4), Winter: 1–17.

Bourguignon, Francois, and Christian Morrisson (2002). The size distribution of income among world citizens, 1820-1990. *American Economic Review* September: 727–44.

Brandt, Loren, and Carsten Holz (2006). Spatial price differences in China: Estimates and implications. *Economic Development and Cultural Change*, forthcoming. http://ihome.ust.hk/~socholz/SpatialDeflators.html.

Capeau, Bart, and Andre Decoster (2004). The rise or fall of world inequality: A spurious controversy. WIDER Discussion Paper No. 2004/02, UNU-WIDER, Helsinki. http://www.wider.unu.edu/publications/publications.htm.

Chotikapanich, D., R. Valenzuela and D.S.P. Rao (1997). Global and regional inequality in the distribution of income: Estimation with limited and incomplete data. *Empirical Economics* 22: 533–46.

Concialdi, Pierre (1997). Income distribution in France: The mid-1980s turning point. In Peter Gottschalk, Bjorn Gustafson and Edward Palmer (eds). *Changing Patterns in the Distribution of Economic Welfare: An International Perspective*. Cambridge University Press, Cambridge: 239–64.

Cornia, Giovanni Andrea, and Sampsa Kiiski (2001). Trends in income distribution in the post WWII period: Evidence and interpretation. WIDER Discussion Paper No. 2001/89, UNU-WIDER, Helsinki.: http://www.wider.unu.edu/research/1998-1999-3.1.publications.htm. Revised version published in Giovanni Andrea Cornia (ed.). *Inequality, Growth and Poverty in an Era of Liberalization and Globalization*. Oxford University Press, Oxford, for UNU-WIDER, Helsinki, 2004: 26–55.

Deaton, Angus (2003). Measuring poverty in a growing world (or measuring growth in a poor world). NBER Working Paper No. 9822, June, National Bureau of Economic Research, Cambridge, MA. http://www.wws.princeton.edu/~deaton/working.htm. Revised version published in *Review of Economics and Statistics* 87, February 2005: 1–19.

Deaton, Angus, and Jean Drèze (2002). Poverty and inequality in India: A re-examination. *Economic and Political Weekly* September 7: 3729–748.

DeLong, Bradford, and Steve Dowrick (2003). Globalization and convergence. In M. Bordo, A.M. Taylor and J. Williamson (eds). *Globalization in Historical Perspective*. Chicago University Press, Chicago.

Dikhanov, Yuri, and Michael Ward (2001). Evolution of the global distribution of income, 1970–99. Processed, August, World Bank, Washington, DC.

Dollar, David, and Aart Kraay (2002). Growth is good for the poor. *Journal of Economic Growth* 7: 195–225.

Dowrick, Steve, and Jane Golley (2004). Trade openness and growth: Who benefits. *Oxford Review of Economic Policy* 20 (1): 38–56.

Dowrick, Steve, and Muhammed Akmal (2001). Contradictory trends in global income inequality: A tale of two biases. Processed, 29 March, Australian National University, Canberra. http://ecocomm.anu.edu.au/economics/staff/dowrick/dowrick.html, published in *Review of Income and Wealth* 51 (2), June 2005: 201–30.

Feldstein, Martin (1999). Reducing poverty not inequality. *Public Interest* Fall: 33–43.

Firebaugh, Glenn (2003). *The New Geography of Global Income Inequality*. Harvard University Press, Cambridge, MA.

Frank, Robert H. (2005). Positional externalities cause large and preventable welfare losses. *American Economic Review* 95 (2): 137–51.

Freeman, Richard B. (1995). Are your wages set in Beijing? *Journal of Economic Perspectives* 9 (3), Summer: 15–32.

Graham, Carol, and A. Felton (2005). Does inequality matter to individual welfare? An exploration based on household surveys in Latin America. Center on Economic and Social Dynamics Working Paper No. 38, Brookings Institution, Washington, DC.

Grosh, Margaret E., and E. Wayne Nafziger (1986). The computation of world income distribution. *Economic Development and Cultural Change* 34: 347–59.

Ishizaki Tadao (1985). Is Japan's income distribution equal? An international comparison. *Japanese Economic Studies* 14 (2): 30–55.

Jiang Zhiyong (2006). China component in international income inequality. *Population Research and Policy Review,* forthcoming.

Kravis, Irving, Alan Heston and Robert Summers (1978). Real GNP per capita for more than one hundred countries. *Economic Journal* 88: 215–42.

Krueger, Anne O. (2002). Supporting globalization. Remarks at the 2002 Eisenhower National Security Conference on 'National Security for the 21st Century: Anticipating Challenges, Seizing Opportunities, Building Capabilities', 26 September. http://www.imf.org/external/np/speeches/2002/092602a.htm.

Kuznets, Simon (1965). *Economic Growth and Structure: Selected Essays.* Oxford University Press, New Delhi.

Lanjouw, Jean, Peter Lanjouw, Branko Milanovic and Stefano Paternostro (2004). Relative price shifts, economies of scale and poverty during economic transition. *Economics of Transition* 12, September: 509–36.

Maddison, Angus (2004). World population, GDP and GDP per capita, 1-2000 AD. Data set, Organization for Economic Cooperation and Development, Paris. http://www.eco.rug.nl/~Maddison/.

Milanovic, Branko (2002). True world income distribution, 1988 and 1993: First calculations based on household surveys alone. *Economic Journal* 112 (476), January: 51–92.

Milanovic, Branko (2005). *Worlds Apart: Global and International Inequality, 1950–2000.* Princeton University Press, Princeton, NJ.

Mistiaen, Johan, and Martin Ravallion (2003). Survey compliance and the distribution of income. Working Paper No. 2956, January, World Bank, Washington, DC.

Pogge, Thomas W., and Sanjay Reddy (2002). Unknown: The extent, distribution, and trend of global income poverty. Processed, July 26, Columbia University, New York. http://www.columbia.edu/~sr793/povpop.pdf.

Quah, Danny (1999). 6 x 10^9: Some dynamics of global inequality and growth. Processed, December, London School of Economics, London. http://econ.lse.ac.uk/staff/dquah/p/9912sbn.pdf

Ravallion, Martin (2000). Should poverty measures be anchored to the national accounts? *Economic and Political Weekly* 34, August 26: 3245–252.

Ravallion, Martin (2001). Growth, inequality and poverty: Looking beyond averages, *World Development,* 29 (11), November: 1803–815

Ravallion, Martin (2004). Competing concepts in inequality debate. *Brookings Trade Forum, 2004.* Brookings Institution, Washington, DC: 1–23.

Ravallion, Martin, and Shaohua Chen (2006). China's (uneven) progress against poverty. *Journal of Development Economics,* forthcoming.

Sachs, Jeffrey, and David Warner (1997). Fundamental sources of long-run growth. *American Economic Review* 87 (2): 184–88.

Sala-i-Martin, Xavier (2002a). The disturbing 'rise' of world income inequality. NBER Working Paper No. 8904, April, National Bureau of Economic Research, Cambridge, MA. www.nber.org.

Sala-i-Martin, Xavier (2002b). The world distribution of income. NBER Working Paper No. 8905, May, National Bureau of Economic Research, Cambridge, MA. www.nber.org.

Schultz, T.P. (1998). Inequality in the distribution of personal income in the world: How it is changing and why. *Journal of Population Economics* 11 (3): 307–44.

Singer, Peter (2002). *One World: The Ethics of Globalization.* Yale University Press, New Haven.

Slaughter, Matthew (1999). Globalization and wages: A tale of two perspectives. *World Economy* 22 (5), July: 609–29.

Sutcliffe, Bob (2003). A more or less unequal world? World income distribution in the 20th century. Working Paper No. 54, Political Economy Research Institute, University of

Massachusetts, Amherst. Published as: World inequality and globalization. *Oxford Review of Economic Policy* 20 (1): 15–37.

Svedberg, Peter (2003). World income distribution: which way. Institute for International Economic Studies, Stockholm. Published in: *Journal of Development Studies* 40 (5), June 2005: 1–32.

Wagner, Gert, and Markus Grabka (1999). Robustness assessment report (RAR) Socio-Economic Panel, 1984–1998. Processed, German Socio-economic panel, Berlin. http://www.lisproject.org/techdoc/ge/ge94survey.doc.

Winters, Alan, Neil McCulloch and Andrew McKay (2004). Trade liberalization and poverty: Evidence so far. *Journal of Economic Literature* 42, March: 72–115.

World Bank (2002). *Globalization, Growth and Poverty: Building an Inclusive World Economy*. Policy Research Report, World Bank, Washington, DC.

World Bank (2005). *World Development Report, 2006: Equity and Development*. Oxford University Press, New York, for World Bank, Washington, DC.

2
The Scorecard on Development:
25 Years of Diminished Progress[1]

MARK WEISBROT, DEAN BAKER and DAVID ROSNICK

Over the past 25 years, a number of economic reforms have taken place in low and middle-income countries. These reforms, as a group, have been given various labels: 'liberalization', 'globalization' or 'free-market'[2] are among the most common descriptions. Among the reforms widely implemented have been the reduction of restrictions on international trade and capital flows, large-scale privatizations of state-owned enterprises, tighter fiscal and monetary policies (higher interest rates), labour market reforms, and increasing accumulation of foreign reserve holdings. Many of these reforms have been implemented with the active support of multilateral lending institutions such as the International Monetary Fund (IMF) and the World Bank, as well as the G-7 governments, and have often been required in order for countries to have access to credit from these and other sources. But regardless of origin, labels or political perspectives, there is a general consensus that the majority of developing countries have benefited economically from the reforms, even if they have sometimes been accompanied by increasing inequality or other unintended consequences (De Rato, 2005).

This chapter looks at the available data on economic growth and various social indicators—including health outcomes and education—and finds that, contrary to popular belief, the past 25 years have seen sharply slower rates of economic growth and reduced progress on social indicators for the vast majority of low and middle-income countries. Of course, it is still possible that some or even all of the policy reforms of the past 25 years have had net positive effects, or that they will have such an impact at some point in the future. But the fact that these effects have not yet shown up in the data, for developing countries as a group—and that, in fact, the data show a marked decline in progress over the last quarter-century—is very significant. If the data and trends presented below were well known, it would very likely have an impact on policy discussions and research. Most importantly, there would be a much greater interest in finding out what has gone wrong over the last 25 years.

In order to evaluate the progress of the last 25 years, it is necessary to have a benchmark for comparison. In other words, for the world as a whole, there is almost always economic growth, technological progress, and therefore, social progress over time. The relevant question is not whether there has been income growth and social progress, but the rate of such progress as compared with what has been feasible in the past.

For this chapter, we have chosen to compare the past 25 years (1980–2005)[3] with the previous 20 years (1960–1980). This is a fair comparison. While the 1960s were a period of exceptional economic performance, the 1970s suffered from two major oil shocks that led to worldwide recessions: in 1974–1975, and again at the end of the decade. The seventies were also a period of high inflation in both developing and developed countries. So this twenty-year period is not a particularly high benchmark for comparison with the most recent 25 years. If the 1950s were included, it would have made the benchmark for comparison higher, since the 1950s were generally a period of good growth for the developing world. But there is not much good data for the 1950s; and many of the developing countries did not become independent until the late 1950s or 1960s.

STANDARDS OF COMPARISON

One way to compare the performance of the two periods (1980–2005 and 1960–1980) would be to simply compare how each group of countries did in the first period, with the same group of countries' performances for the second period. The problem with such a comparison is that it may be more difficult to make the same amount of progress from a higher level than when starting from a lower level. For example, this is certainly true for some levels of life expectancy: it would be more difficult to raise life expectancy from 70 to 75 years than to raise it from 50 to 55. A comparison of the same countries for the two periods would therefore tend to find a diminished rate of progress simply because of this inherent difficulty that comes from progress during the first period. This is not what we want to measure.

To get around this problem, we divide the countries into five groups, depending on their starting point at the beginning of each of the two periods. For example, if we look at Figure 2.1, there are five groups of countries sorted by per capita income. The middle quintile includes countries with an income per person between $2,364 and $4,031 (in constant 2000 dollars). These are countries that started out either in 1960 or 1980 with a gross domestic product (GDP) per person in this range. The other quintiles range from the poorest ($355–$1,225) to the richest ($9,012–$43,713).

FIGURE 2.1

Average annual growth by income quintile and period

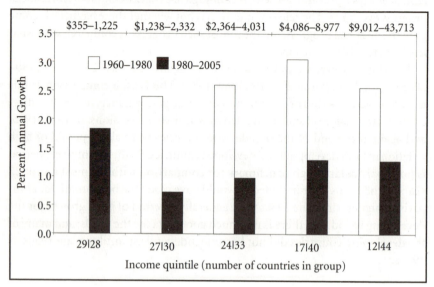

Source: Penn World Tables 6.1, April 2005 IMF World Economic Outlook, author's calculations

Looking at the middle quintile, at the bottom of the graph, we can see that there were 24 countries that started the 1960s in this range of per capita GDP ($2,364 to $4,031), but 33 countries started the 1980s in this range. This is to be expected, as some of the countries from the bottom two quintiles moved into the middle quintile as a result of their growth during the first period.[4] On this basis, we can make a fair comparison—not of the same countries over time, which would suffer from the problems described above—but between all the countries that started the first period at a certain level of income, and all the countries that started the second period at that same level. We can do the same for the social indicators as well.

In fact, this methodology should bias the data towards finding better results for the second period. There should generally be possibilities for countries to gain by borrowing from the technology and practices of other countries that are richer or have achieved higher levels of the various social indicators. As a result of the progress made in the first period, there were far more possibilities for faster improvement in the second period. For example, in the case of life expectancy (Figure 2.2), there were only 16 countries at the start of the first period (1960) with life expectancy of more than 69 years. This meant that countries in the next lowest grouping, with life expectancies from 63 to 69

FIGURE 2.2
Life expectancy at birth, total

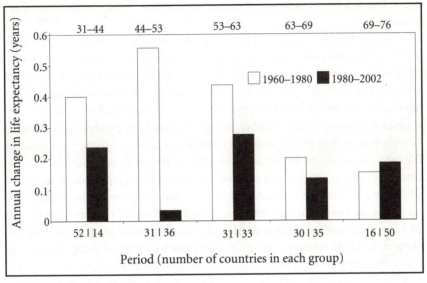

Source: World Bank (2005)

years, would have a relatively limited number of countries from which to adopt better public health measures, medicines or medical practices. However, at the start of the second period (1980), there were 50 countries with life expectancies of more than 69 years. This should have provided a far larger set of practices that the countries in the second grouping (with life expectancies from 63 to 69 years) could adopt to improve health care in their own country in the second period. The same would also be true for all the countries further down the ladder in life expectancy. In other words, it is reasonable to expect that countries starting at any particular level (e.g. of income or life expectancy) will perform better in the second period (1980 to 2005), simply because the advance of technology and knowledge over 20 years has created more and better practices that are available to be adopted.

THE SLOWDOWN IN ECONOMIC GROWTH

The growth of income (or GDP) per person is the most basic measure of economic progress that economists use. Of course, this ignores the distribution of income, as well as environmental and health outcomes. And there are things that raise GDP that do not increase human welfare: e.g., more people buying cigarettes and alcohol, and then having to be treated for resulting health impairment. But as a broad measure of economic progress, it is by far the most important.

When we look at GDP per person, we are deliberately factoring out population growth, since any growth in the economy that is only due to population growth does not improve living standards. Ignoring for the moment any change in labour force participation, we are really looking at productivity growth. For developing countries especially, it is the increase in productivity over time that enables a country to have higher living standards. As productivity grows, a smaller proportion of the country's resources is allocated to the necessities of life, and more can be dedicated to education, health care, and investment in future growth. In general, and especially over long enough periods of time, productivity growth will improve the lives of the majority of the population, including the poor.[5] To the extent that any of the reduced progress over the last 25 years measured by social indicators, as noted in subsequent sections of this chapter, is due to economic changes—and much of it is—it is almost certainly due to declining growth rates, rather than changes in the distribution of income.[6]

Figure 2.1 shows the annual rate of growth of GDP (or income) per capita for the two periods (1960–1980 and 1980–2005). The 175 countries are divided into quintiles according to their per capita income at the start of each period, as explained above. There is a pronounced slowdown in growth for each quintile, except for the bottom quintile. Taking the three middle quintiles first, which are all low and middle-income countries, the difference between the two periods is striking. In the fourth quintile, marked by incomes between $1,238 and $2,332, growth falls from 2.4 per cent annually in the first period to 0.7 per cent in the second period. To get an idea how much difference this makes over time, at 2.4 per cent growth the country's income per person will double in about 29 years. At 0.7 per cent growth, it would take 99 years.

The declines in the next two quintiles are also severe. The middle quintile, with GDP per capita between $2,364 and $4,031, drops from a 2.6 per cent growth rate in the first period to 1 per cent in the second. The second quintile ($4,086–$8,977) falls even further: from 3.1 per cent in the first period to 1.3 per cent in the second period. Even the top quintile, which at $9,012 to $43,713 contains a mixture of middle-income and high-income countries, shows a sizeable fall-off in growth, from 2.6 per cent in the first period to only 1.3 per cent in the second period. It is worth noting that in the top quintile, the result is mainly driven by the middle-income countries.

As noted above, the comparison in each of these quintiles is not for the same countries over the two periods, but for the countries that start each period at the level of income defined by the per capita income boundaries of the quintile. Some countries will move up to higher levels, as we would expect on the basis of progress between 1960 and 1980. So, for example, the Gambia, Indonesia, Lesotho and Sri Lanka, all started out in the bottom quintile in 1960, but began the second period (1980) in the next quintile up. Botswana, Morocco and Thailand moved two quintiles, from the bottom to the third (middle) quintile. At the bottom of the table, the number of countries in each quintile, for 1960 and 1980 is listed.

The only group which does not show a slowdown in growth is the bottom quintile, with per capita income between $355 and $1,225 annually, where growth increases slightly, from 1.7 to 1.8 per cent. However, this is still a bad average performance for the poorest developing countries. It is worth noting that this result is reversed without China and India, despite the fact that that China and India are counted in the averages here with no more weight than small countries such as Burundi or Mali. That is, the averages are not weighted by either GDP or population. (Since China and India together account for approximately half the population of the developing world, their experiences are discussed separately in the last section.) So it is only the large jump in their growth rates in the second period that drives the improvement for the bottom quintile. It is also worth noting that the improvement for the bottom quintile is also dependent on the countries that were not in the data set for 1960–1980, but are included for 1980–2005.

In any case, there is no ambiguity about the overall result, which does not depend on how the countries are divided into groups or whether the new countries are included. There is a sharp slowdown in the rate of growth of per capita income for the vast majority of low and middle-income countries. This is probably the most important economic change that has taken place in the world during the last quarter century. It is much more difficult to reduce poverty or inequality in the face of such a growth slowdown. When a country's economy is growing, it is at least possible for the poor to share equally or even disproportionately in the gains from productivity growth. When there is very little growth in income per person, such improvements are much harder to achieve, and may be politically impossible to the extent that poverty alleviation depends on actually reducing the current incomes of the middle and upper classes.

One region that has been particularly affected by this growth slowdown has been Latin America. Income per capita for the region grew by more than 80 per cent from 1960–1979, but only by about 11 per cent during 1980–2000 and 3 per cent for 2000–2005. This has been a drastic change. If Brazil, for example, had continued to grow at its pre-1980 rate, the country would have European living standards today. Mexico would not be far behind. Instead, the region has suffered its worst 25-year economic performance in modern Latin American history, even including the years of the Great Depression.

Latin America is a region that adopted many of the policy reforms that have characterized the last 25 years. The average tariff on imported goods was cut by about half from 1970 to 2000 (World Bank, 2005). Controls on the inflow and outflow of investment were either removed or drastically reduced in most countries. Privatization of state-owned enterprises was undertaken on a massive scale: it amounted to 178 billion dollars in the 1990s, more than 20 times the value of privatization in Russia after the collapse of the Soviet Union (World Bank, 2001: 186). Latin American countries also adopted more than 80 IMF programs during the last 25 years. These programs generally required higher real interest rates as well as budget cuts, which led to reductions in social spending as well as other forms of liberalization.

As a result of this long-term economic failure, many Latin Americans have blamed the reforms, which are often labelled 'neoliberalism' there. In the last seven years there have been a number of elections—in Argentina, Brazil, Ecuador, Uruguay and Venezuela—where the winning candidates campaigned against neoliberalism. In many other countries in the region, these reforms led to political unrest Still, the long-term growth slowdown, whether in Latin America or in the developing world generally, has attracted little attention or debate in policy circles in the United States.

REDUCED PROGRESS IN HEALTH OUTCOMES

As would be expected in a period of sharply reduced economic growth, the last 25 years also show slower progress on health outcomes. Figure 2.2 shows the result for life expectancy, with countries divided into quintiles according to their life expectancy at the beginning of each period. As can be seen in the graph, there is a noticeable slowdown in all groups except the highest quintile, which contains countries where life expectancy is between 69 and 76 years.

The biggest drop was in the fourth quintile, with life expectancy between 44 and 53. These countries saw an average annual increase of 0.56 years for 1960–1980, but almost no progress, 0.03 per cent, for the second period. Over 20 or 25 years, this makes a large difference. For the first period, countries in this quintile increased their life expectancy by about 11 years. If this rate of improvement had continued, the countries in this quintile in the second period would have raised life expectancy by 12 years; instead they saw an increase of only 0.7 years.

The middle and bottom quintiles also show reduced progress. The bottom quintile, with life expectancies between 31 and 44 years, falls from 0.4 years to 0.24 years annual improvement. Over the 22 years of the second period, this means that life expectancy would have increased by 4 years more than it actually did, if not for this fall-off in the rate of progress. For the middle quintile, with life expectancies between 53 and 63 years, there is a decline from 0.44 to 0.28 years of annual improvement. The second quintile shows a smaller reduction, from 0.20 to 0.14 years. It is worth noting that even this difference is not insignificant, adding up to a difference of about one year of life expectancy over the 22 years.

A significant part of this story is Sub-Saharan Africa, which dominates the bottom two quintiles for the 1980–2005 period, and has some impact on the middle quintile. However, even if all the Sub-Saharan African countries are removed from the data, there is still a decline in progress for the bottom three quintiles, with no change for the second. So the decline in progress on life expectancy occurs across a broad range of low and middle-income countries, and is not confined to any particular region. Furthermore, the reduced life expectancies from HIV/AIDS and even the armed conflicts in Africa are not necessarily completely exogenous. Per capita income in Sub-Saharan Africa grew by a modest, but still significant 36 per cent from 1960 to 1980. From 1980 to 2000, income per capita actually declined—a rare event in modern economic history over a 20-year period—by about 15 per cent. It is possible that some countries may have been able to deal with the HIV/AIDS and other public health crises at least somewhat more effectively if not for the economic collapse of the second period. Also, the spread of AIDS is itself partly a result of the increased trade and travel, including migrant and transport labour, associated with international economic integration. For all the benefits that countries can gain as a result of increased commerce, a potential drawback is the more rapid spread of diseases. Finally, it is possible that the continent would have seen less armed conflict over the second period if not for the economic collapse that took place.

Figures 2.3 and 2.4 show the life expectancies of males and females respectively. The boundaries for the five quintiles are different from each other and from the overall boundaries in Figure 2, because of the higher overall life expectancy for females. But the quintiles are roughly comparable. The results are similar to the overall result in Figure 2 for the bottom four quintiles, with somewhat more of a decline in the second quintile for females. The top quintile is different, with males actually showing an improvement in the growth of life expectancy in the second period, while females do not. The increase in progress for male life expectancy in the top quintile is driven by high-income countries.[7]

Figures 2.5 and 2.6 show the mortality rates for male and female adults

FIGURE 2.3
Life expectancy at birth, male

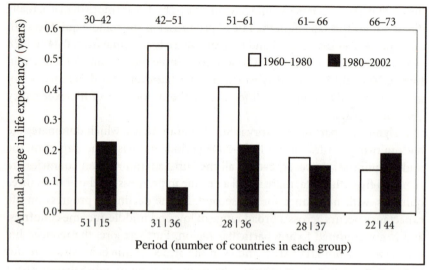

Source: World Bank (2005)

FIGURE 2.4
Life expectancy at birth, female

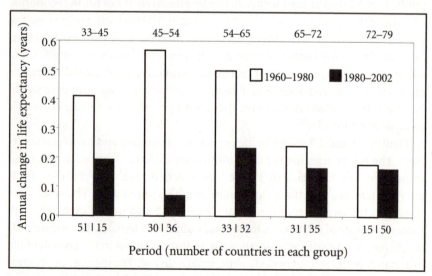

Source: World Bank (2005)

FIGURE 2.5
Adult mortality rate, male

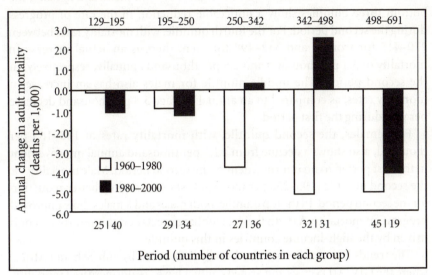

Source: World Bank (2005)
Note: These mortality rates measure the probability of a 15-year old dying before age 60 (in deaths per 1,000.)

FIGURE 2.6
Adult mortality rate, female

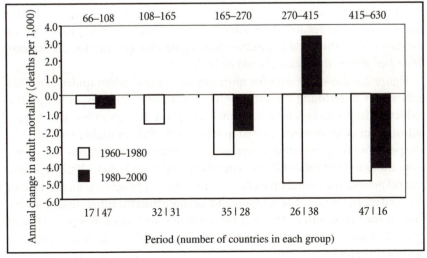

Source: World Bank (2005)
Note: These mortality rates measure the probability of a 15-year old dying before age 60 (in deaths per 1,000.)

respectively.[8] These are arranged in the opposite direction from the previous charts, with the worst quintiles on the right. For both males and females, the bottom three quintiles show a noticeable reduction in the rate of progress during the second period. For the fourth quintile, with mortality rates between 270–415 for women and 342–498 for men, there is an actual increase in mortality of 3.4 per thousand and 2.6 per thousand annually, respectively, in the second period. The middle quintile for males also has an increase in mortality rates, as compared to an annual average 3.8 per thousand decrease per year during the first period.

For females, the second quintile, with mortality rates of 108–165 per thousand, also shows a decline from a 1.7 per thousand annual improvement in the first period to no improvement in the second period. Male mortality for the second quintile (195–250 per thousand) shows a slightly better reduction for the second period. In the top quintile, both males and females show improved progress on mortality. As with the data for life expectancy, this improvement is driven by the high-income countries in this quintile.

The trends in mortality are also heavily influenced by Sub-Saharan Africa, where the HIV/AIDS crisis and armed conflict have greatly increased mortality. According to the UNDP, the conflict in the eastern part of the Democratic Republic of the Congo has resulted in an estimated 3.8 million "excess deaths" from just 1998–2004, as compared with what would have occurred in the absence of war. But a decline in the rate of improvement of adult mortality for low and middle-income countries is not determined by Sub-Saharan Africa. If the Sub-Saharan African countries are eliminated from the data set for Figure 2.4, the bottom two quintiles still show huge declines in the rate of improvement of mortality, with the middle quintile showing no change. And for the reasons described above, the region should be included.

Figure 2.7 shows the data for mortality rates for children under five. This data shows a declining rate of progress for all five quintiles, although the reduction in progress is relatively small in the top two quintiles. The biggest fall-off is for countries in the worst quintile, with child mortality rates of 227–390 per thousand. The rate of progress—average annual reduction—falls from 5 per thousand for 1960–1980 to 3 per thousand from 1980 to 2002.[9] For this second period, the cumulative effect of this reduced progress is an increase in the child mortality rate of 44 per thousand, or more than the entire child mortality rate for the best quintile. The next two quintiles, with child mortality rates of 154–227 and 80–154 per thousand also show a significant decline in progress in reducing child mortality.

Figure 2.8 shows the decline in infant mortality rates for the two periods, arranged by quintiles. Once again, the reduction in progress is across the board.

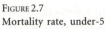
Figure 2.7
Mortality rate, under-5

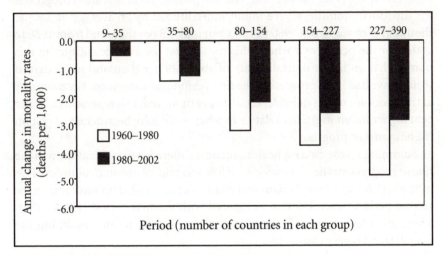

Source: World Bank (2005)

Figure 2.8
Mortality rate, infant

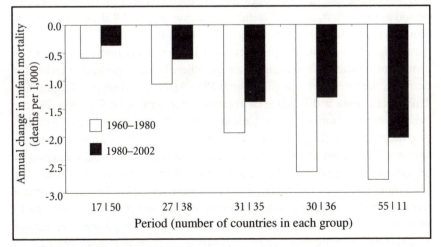

Source: World Bank (2005)

Even the top two quintiles, not influenced by Sub-Saharan Africa, show declining progress for the 1980–2002 period. The sharpest fall-off in the rate of progress is for the fourth quintile, where infant mortality fell by an average of 2.6 per thousand each year from 1960 to 1980, but only 1.3 per thousand from 1980 to 2002. For the period as a whole, this means that the average country in this quintile has an infant mortality rate of about 29 per thousand more than it would have had if the progress of the first period had continued. For a country at the midpoint of this quintile, e.g., 122 per thousand, this represents a 31 per cent higher infant mortality relative to what could have been achieved just on the basis of past progress.

Summing up the data on health outcomes, there is a significant drop in the rate of progress for the vast majority of low and middle-income countries. This is true for life expectancy, infant and child mortality and adult mortality in the second period (since 1980) as compared with the first period (1960–1980). There are a few groups of countries that run counter to this result, but the overall trend is very clear.

REDUCED PROGRESS IN EDUCATION

Given the sharp slowdown in economic growth, it would not be surprising to find that public spending on education did not increase as much in the second period as in the first, and that is indeed the case. Figure 2.9 shows the average annual change in public spending on education for the two periods, as a percentage of gross national product (GNP). There is a reduction in the rate of growth of education spending in all quintiles. For the middle quintile, for example, the rate of growth falls from 0.10 to 0.04 percentage points annually. This would make a difference of about 1.3 per cent of GDP over a 20 year period—for illustration, for the United States today this would be $150 billion of education spending per year. The top quintile, with countries spending between 5 and 8 per cent of GDP on education, shows an actual reduction of education spending during the second period. Some of this is undoubtedly due to demographics, as the higher income countries especially experienced a reduction in the number of school age children. However, this would be less of an explanation in countries that were not already spending a large percentage of their GDP on education. The slower rate of increase in public spending on education for the middle three groups is unlikely to just be a result of demographic changes.

Given the slowing growth in expenditures on public education, we would expect reduced progress in educational outcomes, unless there were large and

FIGURE 2.9
Public spending on education, total

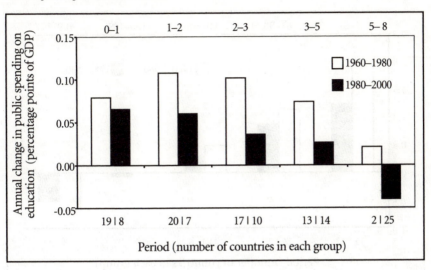

Source: World Bank (2005)

FIGURE 2.10
Primary school enrolment, total

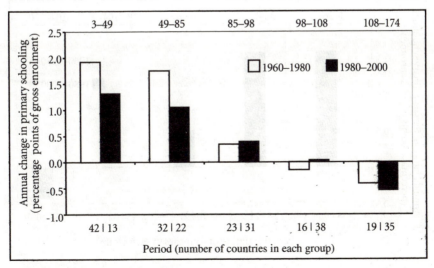

Source: World Bank (2005)

FIGURE 2.11
Primary school enrolment, male

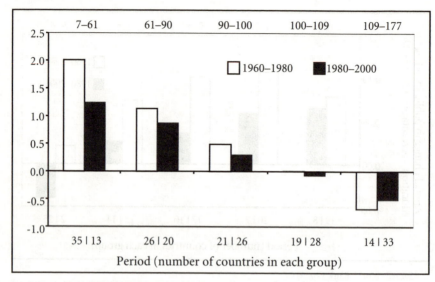

Source: World Bank (2005)

FIGURE 2.12
Primary school enrolment, female

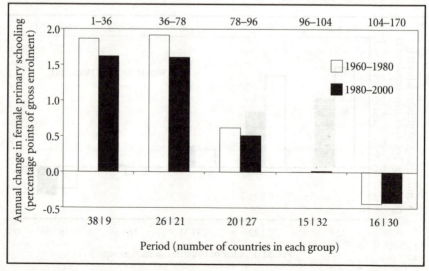

Source: World Bank (2005)

FIGURE 2.13
Secondary school enrolment, total

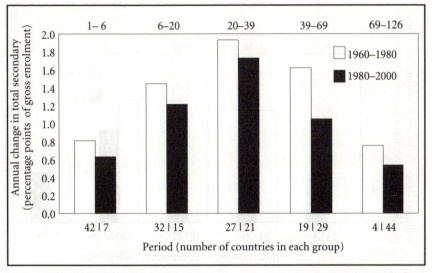

Source: World Bank (2005)

FIGURE 2.14
Secondary school enrolment, male

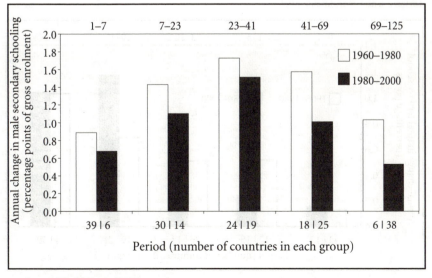

Source: World Bank (2005)

FIGURE 2.15
Secondary school enrolment, female

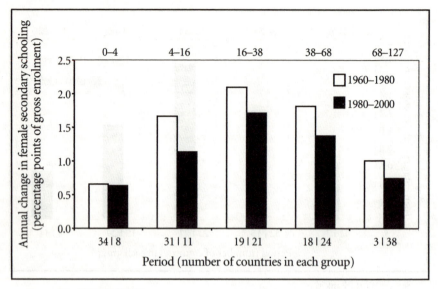

Source: World Bank (2005)

FIGURE 2.16
Tertiary school enrolment, total

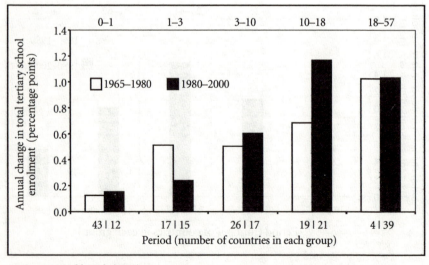

Source: World Bank (2005)

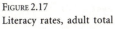

FIGURE 2.17
Literacy rates, adult total

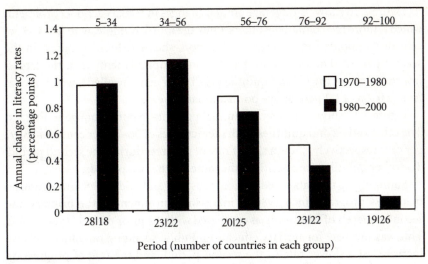

Source: World Bank (2005)

widespread improvements in the efficiency of education. Figure 2.10 shows the average annual change in the percentage of students enrolled in primary school. It measures the number of students enrolled as a percentage of their age groups. It is possible for the number to exceed 100 per cent, as in the top two quintiles, due to adults taking remedial or literacy classes. The bottom two quintiles show a noticeable decline in the rate of growth of primary school enrolment from the first to the second period. The middle quintile is nearly flat, and the second quintile (with enrolment between 98 and 108 per cent) shows some improvement. The top quintile shows a faster rate of decline in the second period as compared with the first, but that is not necessarily harmful; for the higher income countries, it could represent a reduction in the number of adults that need remedial primary education classes. Figures 2.11 and 2.12 look at the same changes in primary school enrolment broken down by gender, for male and female primary school students and school-age children. The overall changes are similar, although the levels of enrolment for females are lower than for males, reflecting a widespread gender bias in education that prevails in many developing countries.

Figures 2.13, 2.14 and 2.15 show changes in secondary school enrolment overall, and for males and females respectively. There is a decline in the rate of growth of secondary school enrolment—again, as a percentage of the population in this age group—across all quintiles, from the first period to the second. The only exception is the bottom quintile for females, with an average enrolment of 0–4 per cent, which is flat.

Figure 2.16 shows the average annual changes in tertiary school enrolment, which is more mixed than the others. Only the fourth quintile, with just 1–3 per cent of its population in tertiary education, shows reduced progress in the second period. The others are flat or show improvement, with the largest improvement in the second quintile (10–18 per cent enrolled), which moves from a 0.7 to a 1.2 percentage point annual increase.

Figure 2.17 shows the average annual percentage point change in literacy. The third and second quintiles, with literacy rates of 56–76 per cent and 76–92 per cent respectively, show a slower rate of progress during the second period. The other quintiles are essentially the same for the two periods.

Summing up the data on education, most low and middle-income countries made less progress since 1980 in increasing enrolment at the primary and secondary levels of education, as compared with the prior period (1960–1980). This was not true for tertiary education. Public spending on education also increased at a slower rate in the second period, and the rate of progress on literacy also slowed. This, together with the slowdown in economic growth, could explain the reduced progress for low and middle-income countries on the educational front. The changes in measures of educational progress are not as pronounced as indicators of health outcomes, or of economic growth, but they are overwhelmingly in the same direction, showing reduced progress since 1980.

EXCEPTIONS: CHINA AND INDIA

There are a few countries that have actually grown much faster since 1980 than in prior decades. Among them are China and India, the world's two most populous countries—China now has 1.3 billion people and India about a billion. Since these countries have adopted some 'globalizing' or 'liberalizing' reforms over the last 25 years, it is sometimes argued, on the basis of these countries' experiences, that the overall set of reforms implemented by low and middle-income countries worldwide have been a success.

There are two arguments here. First, since these two countries contain close to half of the entire population of the developing world, if we look at people, rather than countries, the policy changes of the last quarter century have succeeded. The problem with this argument is that if we are looking at policy changes, we need to look at countries. Individuals do not control the investment, trade, interest rate, budget and other economic policies that affect their ability to make a living. It is their governments that make these choices. But if a set of policy reforms is implemented over a long period of time in 80 or 90 countries, and only a few show higher growth rates—and the vast majority show slower, and often drastically slower growth—this provides at least a prima facie case that the reforms have failed. This is true even if those few success stories happen to be countries with a lot of people.

The other argument is that a few success stories demonstrate that the reforms can work, if only they are correctly implemented. It is possible that all the other countries did not implement them fully enough, or in the right way. One of the World Bank's answers to sceptics has been to group countries into 'globalizers' and 'non-globalizers', and to show that the globalizers have grown faster over the last decade or so. The globalizers were the countries that showed the most rapid increase in trade as a percentage of their economies (see Dollar and Kraay, 2001).

But even if it were true that some set of globalizing countries—i.e., the ones that correctly implemented a set of liberalizing reforms—could be found to do better than the rest during the last 25 years, it would still not explain the long-term drop in the average rate of growth for the period. In Latin America, for example, Chile is the only country that has grown at a faster rate over the last 25 years than it did previously.[10] Whatever Chile did that was successful, it would not explain why the last 25 years have been such a disaster for Latin America. It is simply not plausible to argue that Chile is the only country in the region that carried through the recommended reforms far enough to achieve benefits. If the nature of the reforms is such that anything less than full implementation leads to sacrifice without gain, and the political obstacles are so great that few countries can attain this level of reform, then most countries would probably be making the right decision by not attempting to follow the reform path. A handful of success stories cannot explain the sharp slowdown in economic growth in the vast majority of low and middle-income countries.

China has been most often cited as a globalization or liberalization success story, including trade and investment liberalization. And indeed, since 1980, it has had one of the fastest growing economies in world history: GDP per person grew by an incredible average of 7.15 per cent, increasing six-fold in 25 years to become the second largest economy in the world. But it did so under a set of economic policies strikingly different than the reforms implemented in the vast majority of low and middle-income countries.

First, China did not liberalize its trade in most goods until it could compete in those areas in world markets. As late as 1992, its average tariff was still over 40 per cent, about four times the level that Latin America had in 1974, before liberalization there. To the extent that trade liberalization contributed to China's growth, it may be because it was done carefully, so as not to disrupt existing production—unlike the indiscriminate opening up to imports that was adopted in many other countries.

In fact, China's transition to a mixed economy, with increasing use of markets, was carried out gradually and carefully. There were pilot projects, Special Economic Zones (in the 1980s) to experiment with foreign capital and technology, and gradual liberalization of prices. All this was deliberately designed so as to be able to correct mistakes and expand upon successes, a logical thing to do when policy makers are entering uncharted territory. As late as 1996, state owned and collective enterprises accounted for 75 per cent of urban employment; even today, 25 years into China's economic transition, they still account for more than one-third of urban jobs (Prasad [ed.], 2004). This stands in sharp contrast to the 'shock therapy', massive and rapid privatization, and rapid decontrol of prices that led to an economic collapse and the loss of nearly half of Russia's GDP in five years. That China has been able to manage its transition without any such setbacks—and by contrast, with record-breaking economic growth over a 25-year period—is a compelling example of how important economic policy decisions can be.

Even today, China's banking system is dominated by four state-owned banks, which have more than 60 per cent of the nation's deposits, assets, and credit. Foreign influence in the financial system is minimal. And even after the recent revaluation of the Chinese renminbi, which included some changes to allow more flexibility in its peg to the dollar, foreign currency flows remain strictly controlled.

Foreign direct investment (FDI) in China has soared from $19 billion in 1990 to more than $53 billion annually today (World Bank, 2005), and it has certainly contributed to China's growth. But even here, the government has had a very big role in shaping and directing this investment, and approving investments that would fit in with the country's development goals. These include such priorities as producing for export markets, a high level of technology (with the goal of transferring technology from foreign enterprises to the domestic economy), hiring local residents for managerial and technical jobs, and not competing with certain domestic industries. China's policy toward foreign investment has therefore been directly opposed to the major worldwide reforms of recent decades, including the rules of the World Trade Organization (WTO); the same is also true in the important area of intellectual property.

In short, China's economic success over the last quarter-century cannot simply be summed up—as it so often is—as an example of the success of the overall package of reforms that most developing countries have adopted over the last 25 years. The same is true for India, which is a less spectacular, but still important exception to the general slowdown of growth after 1980. The Indian economy has grown by an average of 3.8 per cent annually, per capita, from 1980 to 2005, more than double the 1.6 per cent annual rate from 1960 to 1980.

But it is difficult to attribute this transformation to globalizing reforms. As in China, the big increase in economic growth in India took place more than a decade before liberalization began. India's growth took off in 1980, more than a decade before the liberalizing reforms of 1991. Tariff revenue, measured as a share of imports or GDP, actually increased significantly during the 1980s, as did other measures of trade protection. Similarly, trade increased several times faster in India in the 1990s than it did in the 1980s. Beginning in 1991, the government embarked upon a rapid reduction of trade barriers, privatization, some deregulation of financial markets, measures to encourage foreign direct investment and other reforms. But growth did not increase over its 1980s' rate.

So while there is plenty of room for debate over what caused India to increase its growth rate at a time when most developing countries were moving in the opposite direction, the 1990s' reforms do not look like the main answer (Rodrik and Subramanian, 2004). India's success story also included such non-orthodox policies as strict currency controls. Even after the liberalization of the 1990s, India retained a higher level of protection for its domestic markets than most other developing countries.

Conclusion: What Went Wrong?

The past quarter century has seen a sharp decline in the rate of growth for the vast majority of low and middle-income countries. Accompanying this decline has been reduced progress for almost all the social indicators that are available to measure health and educational outcomes.[11] The methodology of this chapter precludes the possibility that this reduced economic and social progress was a result of "diminishing returns", i.e., the increased difficulty of progressing at the same rate from a higher level. It is therefore likely that at least some of the policy changes that have been widely implemented over the last 25 years have contributed to this long-term growth and development failure. In some of the financial and economic crises that took place in the late 1990s, for example, in Argentina, East Asia and Russia, it seems clear that policy mistakes contributed to severe economic losses (Radelet and Sachs, 1998; Cibils, Weisbrot and Kar, 2002).

But it is generally difficult to show a clear relationship between any particular policy change and economic outcomes, especially across countries. There are many changes that take place at the same time, and causality is difficult to establish. It is certainly possible that the decline in economic and social progress that has taken place over the last 25 years would have been even worse in the absence of the policy changes that were adopted. But that remains to be demonstrated. In the meantime, a long-term failure of the type documented here should at the very least shift the burden of proof to those who maintain that the major policy changes of the last 25 years have raised living standards in the majority of developing countries, and encourage scepticism with regard to economists or institutions who believe they have found a formula for economic growth and development. Indeed, some economists have recently concluded that more "policy autonomy"—the ability of countries to make their own decisions about economic policy—is needed for developing countries.[12] Most importantly, the outcome of the last 25 years should have economists and policy-makers thinking about what has gone wrong.

NOTES

[1] Acknowledgements: Egor Kraev, Luis Sandoval, Dan Beeton, Ji Hee Kim, Jamie Strawbridge, and Nihar Bhatt provided research assistance for this paper.

[2] The latter term, as well as 'free trade', is inaccurate as a matter of economics, since the reforms have included very costly forms of protectionism—e.g. increased patent and copyright protection—as well as such policies as fixed exchange rates, which are the opposite of 'free-market' policies.

[3] For some indicators, the most recent data does not extend to 2005, e.g., life expectancy goes only to 2002.

[4] In this data set there are also 65 countries (out of 175) for which there are only data for the 1980–2005 period, and not for 1960–1980. The number of countries in each group also changes as countries move up from one quintile to the next on the basis of progress in the first period.

[5] See e.g., Dollar, David and Aart Kraay (2000). A remarkable exception to such long-term trends has been the United States over the last 30 years, where the median wage has increased only about 9 per cent, while productivity increased by more than 80 per cent.

[6] This is not to say that redistribution—whether from existing income or wealth, or new income created through growth—is unimportant or undesirable. Indeed, as the UNDP points out, it can potentially make a large difference in poverty reduction (see UNDP, 2005: 64–71).

[7] This includes Australia, Belgium, Canada, France, Germany, Kuwait, Luxembourg, and New Zealand.

[8] These mortality rates measure the probability of a 15-year-old dying before age 60 (in deaths per 1,000)

[9] For *World Development Indicators*, February 2005, the last available year for such data is 2002.

[10] This is mostly since 1990; the Chilean economy grew by more than 60 per cent per capita in the 1990s.

[11] It is worth noting the limited basis of the comparisons used in this analysis. In particular, it would have been desirable to measure national performances on a variety of environmental measures. Unfortunately, there are no widely available sets of data for most countries on these measures; if such data could be assembled, this would be an important part of a more complete evaluation of the progress of the last quarter-century.

[12] This is the conclusion of Birdsall, Rodrik and Subramanian (2005: 136–52) With regard to China, the authors ask rhetorically, "Would China have been better off implementing a garden-variety World Bank structural adjustment program in 1978 instead of its own brand of heterodox gradualism?"

REFERENCES

Birdsall, Nancy, Dani Rodrik and Arvind Subramanian (2005). How to Help Poor Countries. *Foreign Affairs* 84 (4): 136–52.
Cibils, A., Mark Weisbrot and Debayani Kar (2002). Argentina Since the Default: The IMF and the Depression. Processed, Center for Economic and Policy Research, Washington, DC.
De Rato, Rodrigo (2005). The world's lender must redefine its role to stay relevant. *Financial Times*, 14 September: 15. Available from http://www.lexisnexis.com/ (accessed 15 December 2005).
Dollar, David, and Aart Kraay (2000). Growth Is Good for the Poor. Processed, Development Research Group, World Bank, Washington, DC.
Dollar, David, and Aart Kraay (2001). Trade, Growth, and Poverty. Processed, World Bank, Washington, DC.
IMF (2005). *World Economic Outlook: Globalization and external imbalances.* World Economic and Financial Surveys, International Monetary Fund, Washington, DC.
Prasad, Eswar [ed.] (2004). *China's Growth and Integration into the World Economy: Prospects and Challenges.* IMF Occasional Paper No. 232, International Monetary Fund, Washington, DC.
Radelet, Steve, and Jeffrey Sachs (1998). The East Asian Financial Crisis: Diagnosis, Remedies, Prospects. *Brookings Papers on Economic Activity.* Brookings Institution, Washington, DC.
Rodrik, Dani, and Arvind Subramanian (2004). From Hindu Growth to Productivity Surge: the Mystery of the Indian Growth Transition. NBER Working Paper No. 10376, National Bureau of Economic Research, Washington, DC.
UNDP (2005). *Human Development Report 2005: International cooperation at a crossroads: Aid, trade and security in an unequal world.* United Nations Development Programme, New York.
World Bank (2001). *Global Development Finance, 2001.* World Bank, Washington, DC.
World Bank (2004). *World Development Indicators, 2004.* World Bank, Washington, DC.
World Bank (2005). *World Development Indicators, 2005.* World Bank, Washington, DC.

3
A Converging or Diverging World?[1]

BOB SUTCLIFFE

The richest human beings in history—from Croesus to Henry Ford—were not as rich (in terms of the absolute real value of what they owned or received as income) as the richest people alive today. At the beginning of 2005, the world had seven and a half million people with non-property wealth of more than $1 million (Merrill Lynch and Capgemini, 2005), of whom 691 were dollar billionaires (*Forbes Magazine,* 2005); some sports and rock music stars had incomes of more than $30 million a year, and the annual pay of the highest paid corporate chief executive officer (the head of Yahoo!) was greater than $100 million (AFL-CIO, Executive PayWatch, 2005).

This latter figure was, according to World Bank estimates, the same as the combined income of at least 300,000 of the world's poorest people. Unlike the rich, the poorest people alive today are as poor as the poorest people in history. Millions of people throughout the world often see on television harrowing pictures of masses of people literally dying for lack of food or other basic needs. While economists can and, of course, do argue about how we can measure such things, the common observer would surely, if asked, say that economic inequality among the human race is not only high, but higher than it has ever been, and is probably rapidly diverging further.

Anyone desirous of a more systematic answer would find that professional economists are much divided about how economically unequal the human population is, and if it is becoming more or less so. The reason for the discrepancies is that, when it comes to advancing beyond an impressionistic view of this question to the use of rigorous measures, a large number of methodological questions are encountered, to which different writers give different answers. The main ones can be summarized as:

1) Inequality of what? (income, wealth, or some other measure related to welfare, such as longevity);
2) Inequality among/between whom? (the countries of the world, men and women, capitalists and workers, different ethnic groups, rural and urban

dwellers, the healthy and the sick, the old and the young, or all human individuals);

3) How to compare incomes in different currencies?
4) Using data from where?
5) Using what measure? (integral statistical measures of inequality or, more simply, the ratio of the rich and the poor).

In this chapter, I shall first try to review some of the answers given to these five methodological questions and explain some of my own choices. Then, I will outline a series of calculations about inequality, its level and evolution, using a variety of methodologies and data sources. Finally, I will sum up the answer to the question posed in the title as I see it, and comment on the state of debate on the question.

FIVE METHODOLOGICAL QUESTIONS

What Variable?

In modern times, income has been the most commonly used indicator of economic welfare and economic development. It may be the average income of a country or of households, or the personal incomes of individuals. The overwhelming majority of recent writings about inequality, therefore, concentrate on measuring this variable. This is partly because, of all the possible candidates, income is the variable about which the greatest amount of data is available. There are fewer studies of the distribution of wealth, for example, than of the distribution of income, partly because of limitations in the availability of data; but also, the central role of people's income in determining their material situation in life seems instinctively important. In spite of this, the measurement of income is problematic, and there have been endless debates about how to do it, or about what other variables might be more significant.

In the results of recent calculations and discussions, a trend can be discerned: comparing incomes tends to suggest that the world is more unequal than proposed alternatives, notably, the frequently proposed alternative, life expectancy; also, using life expectancy, rather than income, as the crucial variable has a greater tendency to suggest that, over time, there is convergence, rather than divergence. Since writers and commentators tend to choose their variables to produce conclusions they feel ideologically and politically comfortable with, we can see a tendency, at present, to escape from the disturbing conclusions produced by studies of income towards the more comforting ones resulting from adding another convergent indicator, such as life expectancy.

The United Nations Development Programme (UNDP) launched its Human Development Index (HDI) in 1990, not as a measure of inequality as such, but as a means of dethroning income per head from its traditional place as the privileged indicator of development. However, as UNDP emphasized at the time, human development was distributed in a much more equal way than income per head. The index is made up of three indicators: the logarithm of income per head, life expectancy at birth, and education (a combination of adult literacy and combined enrolment ratios). Plausible maximum and minimum values are assigned to each indicator, and the value of each indicator for each country is assigned a value between 0 and 1 according to its position between the extremes. The HDI is the arithmetical average of these three values, and can therefore itself vary between 0 and 1; but nearly all the developed countries are necessarily close to 1. This is because they are close to an upper limit for life expectancy which seems to be approaching a biological maximum; they have close to 100 per cent levels of literacy and educational enrolment and so are approaching a logical maximum (100 per cent) for the combined education indicator. Only income has no logical upper bound, but the difference between poor and rich countries is strongly attenuated in the HDI by taking the log, instead of the actual value; this has the effect of reducing the ratio between the countries with the highest and lowest gross domestic products (GDPs) per head from 63 to 1 to 3.7 to 1. All this means that the very structure of the index prevents countries with a high level from raising it more than marginally. Countries with a lower level have some way to go and can attain significant percentage increases in the index. The result is that all progress in less developed countries translates into international convergence.

With many variables other than income whose distribution we could measure, one of several problems tends to arise. Sometimes, the variables are too specific; their distribution in a population measures particular outcomes which are not necessarily universally accepted as indicators of welfare. This is why the inventors of the Human Development Index looked for indicators of potential or capacity, rather than particular outcomes, such as the possession of particular goods or services. Other variables, which sound as if they should measure welfare, such as happiness or life-satisfaction, have aroused much interest among economists recently; but no satisfactory way has yet been found to make such variables sufficiently objective.

Ever greater amounts of data about social and economic variables and their distribution are produced, either by public authorities or by social science research, and they are increasingly used to give a more detailed picture of the many kinds of inequality in human societies; but they have not yet displaced income as the most commonly compared criterion in the systematic measurement of inequality. So, for the most part, the rest of this chapter restricts itself to looking at the distribution of income as the measure of convergence or divergence.

It is a pity, in a way, that the growing discussion of distribution involves over-using the variable that more recent contributions to development thinking have tried to demote from its earlier position of primacy. However, we may draw some comfort from the fact that one of the chief criticisms levelled against the use of income per head is precisely that it did not take distribution into account.

Inequality among/between Whom?

Inequality is ubiquitous in human society; and much of the social sciences can be seen as a response to some kind of inequality. If humans were all equal, there would be less need for social science. That means that there are many inequalities which could be examined. Much of the discussion of development has implied a primary interest in distribution between large groups of countries, labelled rich and poor, developed and underdeveloped, North and South, and so on. The interest here is the gap between two or sometimes more groups of countries which are considered qualitatively different. This gap is a crude, but often revealing, measure of world inequality; but it would not pass many of the tests which statisticians demand of a measure of inequality. In particular, it measures a gap, but, as a measure, does not take into account the size of the population on either side of the gap.

An adequate measure of world inequality has, at least, to weight the observed levels of income by population. Many calculations have been done of indexes of world inequality by comparing the income per head of countries and weighting them by the size of their population. These I will call measures of intercountry distribution. All the well-known measures of inequality can be calculated in this way. The problem with it is that it involves, in effect, assuming that all the population of a country have the same income (the income per head). There seems something very suspect about ignoring inequalities within countries and only comparing those between them. There could, however, be two justifications for doing it. First, there is an enormously greater quantity of data on the relative national income per head of different countries than on the internal distribution of that income. So, granted this limitation, we can obtain much more information, albeit inadequate, by looking at country averages. Second, as we shall see later, nearly everyone who has studied the subject agrees that intercountry differences are responsible for much more of world inequality than intracountry differences. So, if we observe both a level and trend in inter-country distribution, they are likely to tell us quite a lot about what is happening to world distribution in general.

Ideally, however, it would be more enlightening to combine intercountry and intracountry inequality figures to produce a more accurate estimate of what I will call global inequality, to distinguish it from intercountry inequality. To calculate global inequality, we need to have good surveys of income distribution within countries. The number of these is growing, but their quality leaves a lot to be desired. Also, since they involve expensive and time-consuming surveys of thousands of people, they are not done very often. Very few countries have annual estimates of inequality, but virtually all of them have annual estimates of the national income.

Comparing Incomes—How?

One question about data on incomes has caused huge confusion, and it is necessary to be clear about it. When looking at the distribution of income in the world, we have to reduce incomes of different countries to one standard. Traditionally, it has been done by using exchange rates and converting the income of each country to the currency of a single country (usually to the US dollar). As a result, the international component of inequality appears to change when exchange rates change, which is highly misleading.

Until recently, that was the only way things could be done; but now we have data based on 'purchasing power parity' or PPP (the comparative buying power, or real equivalence, of currencies). Many problems remain with PPP values, but they are the only way to make coherent comparisons of incomes between countries. They produce estimates, however, which are astonishingly different from exchange rate-based calculations. For instance, the US income per head is 34 times the Chinese income per head, converting with exchange rates, but only 8 times as great using PPP (and incidentally, on PPP estimates, the total size of the US economy is now only 1.7 times that of China, and on present trends, will be overtaken by 2011). So when we make this apparently technical choice between two methods of converting one currency to another, we come up with not only different figures on income distribution, but also with two totally different world economic (and thus political) pictures.

One way of looking at this is to say that PPP is the equivalent of correcting economic figures for inflation. So PPP eliminates price differences among places similarly to how inflation-adjustment eliminates the distorting effects of price differences over time. As a result of the work of a few economists, historical estimates have now been produced of the level of income per head of different countries which are comparable over time and over space. While, in practice, there remain many defects in the PPP figures we have, this is nonetheless a massive breakthrough for economists and economic historians. The greatest enthusiasts for it describe it as the economic equivalent of decoding the human genome.

Data from Where?

The recent great upsurge of interest in calculating world inequality and its trends has gone hand in hand with the improvement of comparative national income or product figures between countries. There are now three easily available series of historical national income figures in PPP, or international prices as they are sometimes referred to; thirty years ago, there were none. The first is produced by the group at the Organization for Economic Cooperation and Development (OECD) led by Angus Maddison (2001; 2003). I have used his figures in the long-term comparisons below, since they begin at an earlier date (some as early as 1820) than the second set of estimates by a team centred at the University of Pennsylvania and related to the United Nations International Comparisons project. This team produces the Penn World Tables (current version 6.1) (Heston, Summers and Aten, 2002), which calculate many more macroeconomic variables in PPP terms than Maddison, starting for most countries in 1960. I have used these in one of the comparative calculations below. The third series is produced by the World Bank, begun in 1975 (World Bank, 2005a). I have used these in nearly all the calculations for recent dates, mainly because they are kept more up to date than the other data sets, and are very easy to use in combination with distribution estimates.

For intracountry distribution of income, there are a number of sources of data, principally the World Income Inequality Database (http://www.wider.unu.edu/wiid/wiid.htm)—which started life as an extension of a much used database, which I have used in my historical calculations, compiled by Deininger and Squire (1996) of the World Bank—and the Luxembourg Income Study (www.lisproject.org). Serious students of inequality need to consult these. In the calculations below of recent trends in world inequality, I have used almost entirely the growing set of data on income distribution published in the annual *World Development Indicators* (*WDI*) by the World Bank (2005a). This consists of information based on household surveys during the last ten years or so for a growing number of countries (122 in the 2005 issue of *WDI*). These data are easy to obtain and use, but it cannot be said that they are adequate. Some of them are old, there is no guarantee that they are obtained using consistent methods, and any detailed study of what has happened to inequality in any given country will need to acquire much more detailed data from other sources. They will be referred to below because of their convenience.

In principle at least, these data allow inter and intracountry data to be combined to produce an idea of global inequality; but the intracountry dimension of inequality which is being added is that between households. There are other kinds of intracountry inequality which these data do not touch, for instance, gender or ethnic-based inequalities. Some of the most serious dimensions of gender inequalities take place within households, and so household surveys cannot usually provide information about that.

What Statistical Measure?

I have used a variety of simple statistical measures in the calculations below. First is the simple calculation of the gap between incomes per head of broad groups of countries. The main integral statistical measure of inequality which I use is the Gini coefficient. This is a measure of the degree of inequality among a population which aims to take all its members into account. The resulting measure, varying between 0 for complete equality and 1 for maximum inequality, can be affected by changes in distribution at any point in the distribution. The smaller the groups into which the population is divided, the more accurate is the measure of inequality.

In addition to the Gini coefficient, there are a number of other measures which many statisticians and researchers believe offer more useful results than the Gini coefficient. These include the Theil index and the mean logarithmic deviation, both of which are increasingly popular. I have not used them, partly because, like many other people, I have spent a lifetime with the Gini coefficient and have a greater instinctive understanding of it than of the others; but also, the conclusions about recent changes in intercountry and global inequality outlined below are not changed when another statistical coefficient is used. In all the recent studies of which I am aware, different measures produce very similar results.

In terms of results, there is a more basic choice of statistical measures. This is between an integral measure, such as the Gini, and a ratio of the extremes of a distribution. This is a very important choice, since it is possible for integral measures, such as the Gini, to move in one direction, while the ratio of extremes moves in another.

Is an integral measure better than a ratio of extremes? The ratio of extremes has the advantage that it can be understood much more intuitively, while integral measures, such as the Gini coefficient, are more abstract and require more explanation. However, the ratio of extremes only compares two parts of the available data, and so, at best, can give a limited view of the distribution. On the one hand, measures of the ratio of extremes can, in some cases, use all the available data (for instance, by measuring the ratio of the top to the bottom half of the population); but even here, they present no more than a relation of two summary figures. On the other hand, the ratio of extremes may be a better indicator of social justice than integral measures.

Ratios of extremes can be used to look at ratios between the incomes of defined groups, usually percentages, of the population with specified relative income levels: for instance, the ratio of the income of the highest 20 per cent to that of the lowest 20 per cent. Any similar ratio can be used, from the 'Robin Hood ratio' (top 50 per cent to bottom 50 per cent) to the ratio between the top and bottom 1 per cent, or even less, of the population. In these measures of inequality, the intervening figures do not enter into the conclusion (except in the special case of the 50/50 formula which, of course, includes all values).

CALCULATING INEQUALITY

Convergence and Divergence between North and South

We can start a review of measurements of inequality with one which is both simple and revealing. It is simply the gap between the average income of the rich countries of the North and that of the rest of the world (the South as a whole and various geographical components of it). It is clear in Figure 3.1 that—in spite of decolonization, thousands of economic development plans, billions of dollars in aid, the operations of dozens of multilateral development agencies, thousands of non-governmental organizations (NGOs) and billions of words— the gap between the North and the South widened continuously from 1950 to 1990. For Africa and Latin America, the gap has continued to grow until the present; but since 1980, Asia, and China in particular, has been closing it. After 1990, the faster growth of Asia has outweighed the relative decline of Africa and Latin America, and so, the relative position of the South as a whole has very marginally improved. The contrast between these two opposed tendencies is a central feature of world distribution during the last two or three decades, and will be referred to again.

The Recent Course of Intercountry Inequality

The gap tells us quite a lot about inequality, but does not provide a single summary indicator of it. We can, however, process exactly the same data in a more sophisticated way by taking our knowledge of the population and national

FIGURE 3.1

Ratios of different groupings of countries of the South to the average income of the North

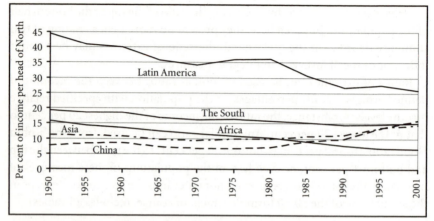

Source: Author's calculations based on data in Maddison (2003).

Note: The North =Australia, Canada, Japan, New Zealand, USA and Western Europe; The South = the rest of the world except for Eastern Europe and ex-USSR; Asia includes China, but not Japan.

FIGURE 3.2

Three PPP estimates of the intercountry Gini coefficient, 1960–2000

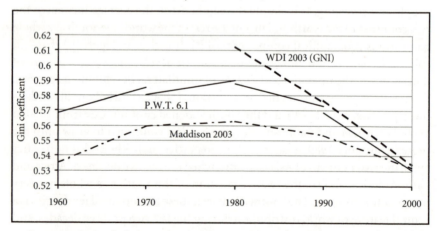

Sources: Author's calculations using data from Maddison 2003; Heston, Summers and Aten 2003; World Bank 2003.

Note: The PWT and WDI series have steps, because for each decade, the maximum number of countries with figures for both ends of the decade has been chosen. That means some discontinuity since, in each decade compared, there is a different (growing) number of countries. The Maddison figures show only one small discontinuity in 1990, due to the change to independent estimates for the component countries of the USSR, Czechoslovakia and Yugoslavia in that year; otherwise, there are no blank spaces in his data.

income of virtually every country of the world and calculating from them an overall coefficient of inequality in different years. The Gini coefficient, which I have used, basically measures the cumulative total of the differences between a country's income and the world average, weighting each country's difference by its population.

Since not all the available estimates of income are the same, I have calculated the coefficient using the three different sources of PPP income data mentioned above. Up to 1960, Maddison's data are the only ones available. They show a long-term and very substantial increase in world intercountry inequality from 1820 to 1980. After 1960, Maddison's figures can be compared for the period from 1960 with the data from the Penn World Tables (version 6.1); and from 1980, a three-way comparison is possible, including the World Bank's *WDI* figures. Decadal comparisons are shown in Figure 3.2.

As far as their direction of movement is concerned, all three PPP data sets are consistent with an inverted 'U' which rises up to 1980 and falls in the two subsequent decades. Since 1980, according to this measure, intercountry distribution of income has been growing less unequal; but the degrees of change between the three sets are mysteriously different. The *WDI* figures show the largest fall and Maddison the smallest. By 2000, they were giving more or less the same reading.

Since Maddison has estimated his data for more years and more countries than the other sources, it pays to look at the intercountry Gini coefficients

FIGURE 3.3
Intercountry Gini coefficients, including and excluding China

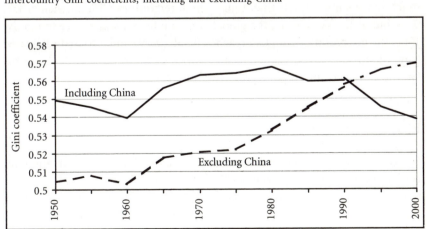

Source: Author's calculations using data in Maddison (2003).

which his data generate in a little more detail, with a view to understanding more of what has happened. Figure 3.3 shows the five-yearly Gini coefficient for the whole world since 1950. It falls (greater equality) from 1950 to 1960, probably due to the post-war recovery of Europe and Japan in relation to the USA. It then rises strongly until 1980 (more inequality) due to many factors, but mostly the rapid growth of the developed countries and the disappointing growth of the South, which we already observed in another way in Figure 3.1. It then falls again up to 2000. This again has many causes, but probably the most important one is hinted at by removing China from the figures. Inequality then rises continuously and quickly from 1960 to 2000. The interpretation that all of the apparent drop in inequality after 1980 is due to China is too simplistic, since China and other parts of the world interact. So, while it is instructive to omit the figures for China, the influences of China, both for and against equality, remain. What the removal of China does do, is to emphasize the enormous importance of developments in this one huge country to the interpretation of the world, though not only in respect of income distribution.

In the Long Term

Bourguignon and Morrison's (2002) study is the only one to attempt to trace the long-term history of global distribution. They base their calculations on Maddison's GDP figures from 1820 (Maddison, 1995), using a wide range of sources as well as some estimation to adjust them for distribution. They conclude that global, like intercountry, inequality increases more or less continuously from 1820 onwards, but that the intercountry component increases faster than the intracountry component. At the start of the period, when countries were at much more similar levels than today, the intercountry Gini coefficient was 0.16, but at the same time, the global Gini coefficient was nearer to 0.5. By 1960, the intercountry Gini had reached 0.535 (very similar to that calculated from Maddison's most recent data and shown in Figure 3.3), while the global Gini was 0.635 (Bourguignon and Morrison, 2002).

RECENT DECADES

Continuing with the story as Bourguignon and Morrison tell it, the Gini coefficient went on rising from 0.635 in 1960 to 0.657 in 1980, and remained stable until 1992 (where they end the story, as Maddison did in his earlier 1995 book). So the trend is rising inequality from 1820 to 1980, and then,

TABLE 3.1
Global Gini coefficients, 1960–2000

Year	1960	1970	1980	1990	2000
Bourguignon & Morrisson 2002 (Maddison 1995)	0.635	0.650	0.657	*0.657	
Sutcliffe 2003 (Maddison 2001)			0.667	0.650	0.627
Sala-i-Martin 2002a (PWT 6.0)		0.657	0.662	0.654	0.633

Sources: Bourguignon and Morrisson (2002); Sutcliffe (2003); Sala-i-Martin (2002a).

Notes: Sources of income data are in parentheses. Sources of distribution data are explained in the source articles. * = 1992

stabilization; and during this period, the contribution of intracountry inequality falls, and that of intercountry distribution rises.

For recent decades, a number of studies attempt, as Bourguignon and Morrisson have done, to combine national income figures with internal distribution figures to estimate the movement of global distribution. The results of three of these are given in Table 3.1. There are differences among these three studies regarding the sources of income data (shown in parentheses in the table) and in the way they introduce distribution. Bourguignon and Morrisson as well as Sutcliffe estimate for benchmark years only. The former use various sources of distribution data; the latter uses the Deininger–Squire dataset and the *WDI*. Sala-i-Martin (2002a) makes annual estimates of distribution using Deininger–Squire and fitting trend lines. Despite these differences, the methods produce global Gini values which are very close for years for which they all have figures; and they show either a stabilization or a reversal of the earlier rising trend from 1980 onwards.

Other recent estimates, using some combination of the same sources of data and measures of inequality other than the Gini coefficient (e.g., Firebaugh, 2003), also arrive at broadly similar conclusions. It has to be concluded that all approaches which use PPP income data and then weight them in some way by available internal distribution figures show, as all PPP estimates of intercountry distribution, a decline in inequality since 1980 as measured by one integral measure, be it the Gini or some other coefficient. This has now been demonstrated a sufficient number of times; and the conclusion seems to be rooted in the data.

This, of course, does not mean that it is the correct conclusion; other methodologies and data may give different answers. For one thing, these global distribution estimates retain one of the main sources of error of the intercountry estimates, namely, the fact that not all of national income reaches households which can use them to finance welfare-related benefits. The only way to reach a different conclusion is to question the validity of the data, to use a different methodology, to measure with a different statistical measure or to use a different variable or combination of variables to measure income or welfare.

'True Distribution' through Direct Use of Household Surveys

Branko Milanovic's (2002) 'true distribution' uses a different methodology and produces results apparently inconsistent with other recent studies, although it remains a variant of global distribution, and its comparisons are made using PPP conversions. However, since it uses household surveys as raw material, it does not need to go through the stage of imputing the incomes of groups by weighting the national income estimates by the groups' shares. The previously described global distribution method of income imputing implicitly allocates the difference between total household income and total GDP pro rata, that is, investment and state spending are assumed to be distributed in the same way as household consumption. Milanovic's method completely eliminates this problem. However, it then leaves another one: relative welfare is clearly not restricted to household consumption, since it also, at a minimum, includes the amounts of social spending on free services which contribute to welfare received by each group but which do not figure directly in household expenditure (education, health and a share of infrastructure). Milanovic discusses this problem, but does not solve it.

If we are interested in the global distribution of welfare, then, in principle, Milanovic's method is surely the most accurate. Its problem is that it rests on the comparability of the household studies which he uses. The problem of data and the infrequency of PPP benchmark studies means that he produces estimates of inequality for two years, 1988 and 1993. First, as he mentions, it is striking that his estimates of the global Gini coefficient for these years are 0.63 and 0.66, respectively. This is extremely close to those produced by the other methods examined above. His principal conclusion is, quite rightly, that this shows the world has a level of inequality scarcely encountered in national economies.

His second conclusion, however, differs from that of other studies. Between two dates, lying within the period in which other studies find a falling level of inequality, Milanovic's Gini estimate rises. It remains to be seen if, over a longer period, this method will reproduce this difference. In any case, the existing difference needs to be explained. It would appear, from Milanovic's discussion of this, that the reason is not the fact that he does not use GDP per capita figures (since a similar result appears when he does so, as a control), but that his distribution data permit a more detailed breakdown of internal inequality than the mixture of quintile data used by other global inequality studies, in particular for China and India.

Rising inequality between urban and rural incomes in these two giant countries accounts for much of the difference between his results and those of other studies. The difference seems to be largely due to the fact that his method catches the sharp growth in urban–rural inequality in China and India, while those which use overall national figures do not. It is strongly to be hoped that Milanovic's method can be applied to a longer time period since, in principle, it seems likely to give a more authoritative picture of global interpersonal distribution, although it requires an enormous data collection and homogenization process.

A Different Story: Ratios of Extremes

An integral measure of inequality is not necessarily a good estimator of social justice. What is received by the most and least economically privileged part of a population can be a much better indicator, even though it does not use all the data available on distribution among the population. It is quite possible for a Gini coefficient to improve, even though the ratio of incomes at the extremes worsens. At least, therefore, we need to look at indicators of inequality other than the integral measures.

The effects of doing so produce a strikingly different picture of recent developments from that produced by earlier estimates of the Gini coefficient. As a by-product of estimating the average incomes of deciles or quintiles of the population necessary for calculating global Gini coefficients, we can derive the ratios between the richest and poorest sections of the population.

Table 3.2 shows a comparison of global Gini coefficients with global ratios of extremes. Between 1980 and 2000, the ratio between the richer and poorer halves of the world's population (the 50/50 or 'Robin Hood' ratio), along with the richest/poorest 20 per cent and 10 per cent ratios, fell, repeating the fall in the Gini coefficient. However, at some point in this period, each of the ratios, except the 50 per cent one, began to move upwards: inequality grew between the richest and poorest 20 per cent and 10 per cent after 2000; it grew between the richest and poorest 5 per cent from 1990 onwards, and between the top and bottom 1 per cent all the time. The implication of this is that the roughly 60 million humans with the highest incomes in 1980 received 216 times as much as the 60 million with the lowest incomes; this immense divergence has grown ever since, and by 2003, had reached 564 times. This conclusion—that inequality, in this sense, has been increasing—emerges from exactly the same data used to suggest that inequality in another sense (the Gini coefficient) has

TABLE 3.2
Global Gini coefficients and percentile ratios, 1980–2003

Year	1980	1990	2000	2003
Gini coefficient	0.667	0.65	0.627	0.63
50/50 ratio	13.62	10.21	8.83	8.60
20/20 ratio	45.73	33.85	29.49	31.96
10/10 ratio	78.86	64.21	57.41	64.41
5/5 ratio	120.75	101.02	116.41	130.46
1/1 ratio	216.17	275.73	414.57	564.27

Sources: For 1980 to 2000, see Sutcliffe (2003) for an explanation of the method. For 2003, the author's calculations are based on data from World Bank (2005a).

Note: The last column is not strictly comparable with the previous ones, but following the earlier methodology would produce very similar results.

been declining. Very few commentators have emphasized this conclusion. An exception is Arne Melchior, using intercountry estimates (see Melchior, 2001; Melchior, Telle and Wiig, 2000; Melchior and Telle, 2001).

The groups which, according to this method, emerge as the richest 1 per cent of the world's population are the richest 10 per cent of the following economies: Australia, Austria, Belgium, Canada, Denmark, France, Germany, Hong Kong SAR, Ireland, Italy, Luxembourg, Netherlands, Norway, Singapore, Switzerland, UK and USA; and the poorest 1 per cent are composed of the poorest 40 per cent in Sierra Leone, the poorest 30 per cent in Malawi, the poorest 20 per cent in Burundi, Central African Republic, Guinea-Bissau, Madagascar, Niger, Nigeria, Tanzania and Zambia, and the poorest 10 per cent in Burkina Faso, Honduras, Kenya, Lesotho, Mali and Yemen (Afghanistan and Ethiopia would surely have been represented here, but there are no data for those countries). Of course, more detailed intracountry distribution figures would admit people from other countries to these extreme groups. While the estimates for 2003 in Table 3.2 are not strictly comparable to those for earlier years, they continue a trend which makes it clear that, if our criterion is the ratio of incomes of the very top and very bottom of the economic hierarchy, inequality has not ceased to grow.

There seems to me little room for debate over the fact that the relative difference between the very rich and the very poor has become worse; and the worsening is greater, the smaller is the extreme proportion compared. So, the immensely rich have done especially well in the last 25 years, while the extremely poor have done especially badly. The top one-tenth of US citizens now receives a total income equal to that of the poorest 2,200,000,000 citizens in the world.

The conclusion is consistent with what has recently become almost a new branch of inequality studies: the investigation of very high incomes in the

FIGURE 3.4
A visualization of global income distribution

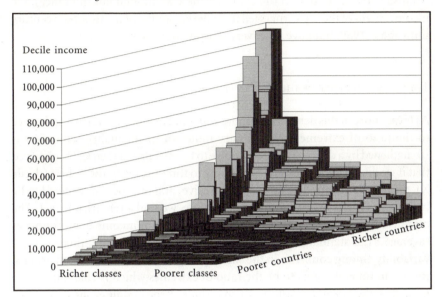

Source: Sutcliffe (2005).

FIGURE 3.5
Income shares by decile groups

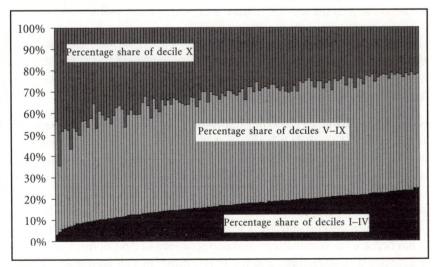

Source: Author's calculations based on data in World Bank (2005a); also see Palma (2003).

richest countries (for example, see Atkinson, 2005; and Krugman, 2002). Atkinson concludes that in the USA and the UK (though not in France), the income shares of the top earners fell from the beginning of the twentieth century until about 1980, but have risen very sharply since then.

THE CONSTANT SHARE OF THE MIDDLE GROUPS

As I read more of this debate, I am more and more inclined to attach importance to the ratio of extremes as a primary indicator of inequality. This view is strengthened by a discovery which we owe to Gabriel Palma (2003). He observed that if we divide the share of income going to three groups—the richest (decile X), the middle group (deciles V to IX inclusive) and the poorest (deciles I to IV inclusive)—for as many countries as possible, we find a remarkable fact. The middle group gets very nearly the same percentage of income in all countries (average 51.3; standard deviation 4.1), but at the same time, there is great variability among countries in the shares going to the top and bottom groups. Just as, in time, it seems to be the ratio of extremes which is changing much more than the integral measures which include all the middle groups, so, across space, virtually all the intercountry differences in internal income distribution are the result of differences in what the very rich and the poor get. The point is very clearly visible in Figure 3.5, in which each column represents one country and the countries are ordered from left to right according to the percentage received by the poorest group. The constancy of the middle groups and the variations among the top and bottom groups are plainly visible.

WEALTH, POVERTY AND INEQUALITY

What Has Happened to Egalitarianism?

So far, I may have given the wrong impression that inequality is a subject which is very widely discussed. It is true that in recent years, there has been some revival in the number of academics and researchers in international organizations who write about it. However, in the world as a whole, it would be truer to say that the subject of inequality is systematically avoided, in favour of something which may appear to be the same thing, but is not—namely poverty.

There is certainly no shortage of written and verbal attention given to poverty. It has become the dominating word in discussions of development within the international organizations and the governments of rich countries. The key objective of official development thinking is the reduction of poverty and 'pro-poor growth'. The central objective of the United Nations Millennium Development Goals is the elimination of poverty. It has also become the focus of large public humanitarian campaigns, such as the recent one around the slogan 'Make poverty history'. There is a kind of global unanimity on the subject. Nobody, other than a religious ascetic, would dare to say they are not against poverty.

A particular concept of poverty dominates these campaigns and pronounce-ments: it is poverty as absolute deprivation. It is usually measured by the value of real consumption, the two poverty thresholds being living on $1 a day (PPP dollars in 1990 prices) (extreme poverty) or $2 a day (poverty). The World Bank produces regular updates of the numbers of people living below these thresholds, and the Millennium Development Goals are designed in relation to these figures (one of them is to halve the proportion of people living on $1 a day by 2015).

There is in official discussions, however, another concept of poverty, that is, of poverty as relative deprivation. There is a long historic debate among social scientists about which of these is appropriate, but the point I wish to draw attention to here is that in virtually all the developed countries, it is the relative —and not the absolute—concept which is used to measure poverty. Most governments of rich countries define poverty as living on less than 50 per cent of the national median income.

However, the definition of poverty applied to poor countries is the absolute one. This has a major consequence: according to the World Bank's figures, poverty is being reduced. The number of people living on $1 a day fell from 1.2 billion in 1990 to 1.1 billion in 2001 (World Bank, 2005b). But what if the rich countries' definition of poverty—which is based on inequality, rather than an absolute level of consumption or income—was applied to the entire world population? The result would be that poverty is being reduced much less rapidly, and perhaps not at all. Some of the world's richest people were active supporters of the 'Make poverty history' campaign. I wonder if they would have been quite so enthusiastic about a 'Make inequality history' campaign.

Of course, it is statistically possible that less poverty and more equality can go hand in hand; but we have to examine very closely what are the political and ideological conditions in which that happens. The present fashion for 'pro-poor growth' does not involve any questioning of the centrepiece of today's economic orthodoxy, namely that growth comes largely from private sector (capitalist) investment, and that is not going to take place if the investors are not assured that they will gain from it. Will they invest if the poor gain more than they do?

Plans to reduce absolute poverty through minimum income guarantees or reduction in the number of people lacking basic necessities can be important;

but poverty always possesses a relative as well as an absolute constituent. It is a major weakness of the Millennium Development Goals, for example, that they propose halving the number of people in absolute extreme poverty without a single mention of inequality; and there is now a very active campaign by anti-egalitarian, pro-capitalist ideologues in favour of the complete separation of the two. That is wrong, not only because inequality is what partly defines poverty, but more importantly, because inequality and policies of poverty reduction should be inseparable. To separate them is to say that redistribution should not form part of the solution of poverty. Everyone is prepared, in some sense, to regard poverty as undesirable; but egalitarians see riches as equally pathological. The objective of reducing poverty is integrally linked to the objective of reduced inequality.

Summing Up the Evidence

My aim in this chapter has been not so much to find a definitive answer to the question of what has happened to inequality as to disentangle some of the confusing and contradictory conclusions which have been arrived at, to help them make a little more sense, to show how they are interconnected, and to evaluate some of the conclusions drawn from them. There is much we shall never know in detail, but also much which will still be discovered.

To questions about inequality, there are many answers, because there are many choices which make significant differences to the results. Some of them are obviously wrong; but when they have been eliminated, more than one answer will still remain, because there is more than one question. The reduction in Gini coefficients after 1980 in studies which use GDP figures by themselves or with quintile distribution figures does reflect the disproportionate rise in income of a few countries—especially China, but also other Asian countries—which has been sufficient to offset the statistical effect of countries— especially Africa—experiencing economic decline. Nonetheless, these results are conditionally contradicted by Milanovic's calculations based directly on household surveys which give more weight to internal differences. It is to be hoped that further research in this direction will clarify whether the same discrepancy exists for a longer period.

I have concluded that more attention should be devoted to what has happened to the ratios of extreme incomes. These may tell a more powerful story in relation to global social justice than the integral measures; and they highlight important changes hidden by integral measures of inequality such as the Gini coefficient. Whether or not the integral measures show convergence, the ratios of extremes reveal dramatically rising polarization between the top and bottom groups.

I am not at all persuaded that the addition of different variables, such as life expectancy, eliminates divergence between countries. The hypothesis is based on the idea that income and longevity are substitutes, so low welfare due to poverty can be compensated by being poor for a longer time. It is true that if you present almost any group of people with a choice, they will choose longer life; but it is not a real choice that anyone is able to make. Longevity does not change current economic welfare. In any case, at a global level, any tendency for the distribution of life expectancy to offset the tendency for the distribution of income no longer exists, due almost entirely to the HIV/AIDS epidemic. During the period 1990 to 2001, life expectancy figures show overall divergence between countries.

An important conclusion is that it is futile to summarize anything as complicated as world inequality in a single figure. The world is made up of innumerable specific inequalities; whenever anything changes, some of these get worse and some get better. This is not an argument against looking for integral measures; but they are not the end of the debate.

To get a more multidimensional picture of actually existing inequality, it is imperative to look at it from many angles, and that means to look at many different statistics. In particular, I have stressed the importance of observing not only the integrated measure, but also the movement of the extremes. When this is done, a different picture of the movement of inequality in the period begins to emerge: one in which not only those around the centre of the distribution are, to some extent, drawing together after centuries of increasing inequality, but where, at the same time, the extremes have been flying apart. This is not a step along a convergence process in which inequality may rise to begin with, as the late starters catch up one by one, but which mutates benignly into greater equality later on, as everyone finally arrives at higher levels of productivity and income (the scenario envisaged in the famous Kuznets curve). There is no sign at all that the malign processes of extreme impoverishment at the bottom or extreme enrichment at the top of the world distribution are coming to an end.

The debate is undoubtedly infected with a good deal of inequality denial. This is what is behind the considerable interest shown in suggestions that divergence has been replaced by convergence in the last two decades. Even if this were true, it is important to stress that there are signs that it will be short-lived, and world inequality, however measured, remains very close to its highest historical levels. The fact is that most calculations agree that the level of the Gini—calculated using PPP income and imputing income to population quintiles or deciles for all countries with published distribution figures—is about 0.63. With one exception, this is a higher level of inequality than for all countries of the world (including such emblems of inequality as Brazil and South Africa). The exception is Namibia, a country still showing the economic legacy of apartheid. The world ratio of the income of the top 10 per cent to the bottom 10 per cent is about 64. On this measure, only nine countries are more unequal than the world as a whole, including Brazil and South Africa. This appalling fact would remain true, even if the trends towards convergence discussed above continued for another 20 years.

Inequality and Globalization

Is it possible to see any relation between globalization and world inequality? Maddison's data show a continuous increase in population-weighted inter-country inequality from 1820 to 1980, seemingly not affected by fluctuations in the degree of globalization. Other studies have suggested that during the period of retreat from globalization between the two World Wars, convergence between the wage levels of the richer countries ceased or went into reverse; and yet others have stressed that during the same period, some of the less rich countries began to converge with the richer ones (an argument often made by dependency theories).

The problem, however, seems to be a long way from any kind of clear definition which would allow any empirical test. If the answer has to be a statistical correlation between a single variable which stands for globalization and another which stands for inequality, then the question is both conceptually and practically unanswerable.

Globalization is a concept which receives many definitions, some of them contradictory. The period since 1980 is widely seen as one of particularly strong globalization. However, does globalization include those aspects of the world economy which became more liberal and involved greater integration, or does it also include those aspects which were anything but liberal? In other words, is globalization loosely what happens during a period which has been widely called globalizing, or just those things which really did expand global interchanges of goods, capital and people? The amount of globalization in the second sense, during the present period of globalization in the first sense, has been greatly exaggerated (Sutcliffe and Glyn, 2003). Trade, international investment and international capital flows have, of course, all relatively expanded, but the expansion has been especially concentrated among the countries which were rich at the beginning of the period, and it has been limited by the maintenance of very high discriminatory protection in some sectors of rich country markets (especially agriculture).

In addition, political interest in systematic international redistribution in the form of development aid has sharply declined in the last two decades. Aid is now only about 0.2 per cent of the income of the donor countries, and the 2005 G8 meeting probably did not do much to change that. Considerably greater redistribution is effected by the repatriation of wages by immigrants from the South working in the North. In both cases, however, there is no correlation between the amount of aid or remittances which countries receive and their level of income per head. So, while these mechanisms may produce some specific redistributions, they are not responsible for any general redistribution.

Inequality has as many meanings as globalization. This chapter has reviewed integral measures of intercountry and global inequalities, but has also added some calculations of intermediate levels of distribution. It is striking that when we disaggregate income figures by continent, major differences emerge: the recent convergence of Asia contrasting sharply with the strong and continuous divergence of Africa and the less marked divergence of Latin America from the developed economies. Other disaggregations, either between countries or between classes within countries, or combining the two, as in the ratio of extremes measures, are necessary in order to appreciate the complex changes in inequalities which are taking place. A greater understanding of inequality involves also disaggregating countries and income groups into categories which can help to explain its causes: classes, gender, regions, age, health status, disability and many others.

Disaggregation can also be applied to the globalization side of the equation. Policies and tendencies which have enabled particular countries to benefit from increasing involvement in the world goods and capital markets can be identified. By a combination of high investment and the mobilization of competitively cheap labour, the countries of Asia have experienced historically unprecedented growth rates of the economy, industrial production and exports. Some of this growth has been aided by imports of foreign capital; but these, in common with the export of manufactures, have been very unequally distributed. In 2001, the population-weighted Gini coefficient of net inflows of foreign direct investment was 0.7, which makes it more unequal than any of the measures of world income distribution.

The integration of product and capital markets has, of course, been much smoother and more complete among developed countries than between them and developing countries, and this itself must have led to some negative effects of globalization on inequality. Nevertheless, a number of studies have tried to conclude that for poor countries, growth rates would benefit, and an improvement in their incomes (and consequently, a reduction in world inequality) would follow, from the market reforms almost universally promulgated during the last 20 years.

This conclusion, however, is increasingly contested; and it ignores the fact that integration into some world markets has not been under poor countries' control. This is particularly true of the world labour market, the global liberalization of which has never been part of the neoliberal prescriptions. In fact, most richer countries' immigration laws have been continuously tightened in the last 20 years, although sometimes, without the apparently intended results. Hatton and Williamson (1998) have argued that the freedom to migrate from Europe to the USA during the late nineteenth and early twentieth centuries reduced the intercountry distribution between the USA and Western Europe, and so mitigated the forces which were, at the same time, making for greater inequality on a global scale. As was seen in earlier sections, something of that pattern remains today.

A different question relating to the disaggregation of integral measures of distribution is the subject of vigorous debate (see Milanovic, 2005; Quah, 1996; Sala-i-Martin, 2002b). This question is not the overall measure of inequality, but the shape of international income distribution—in particular, if it is or is becoming uni-modal, or if it remains bi-modal, as it has been for a long time. The answer to this is crucial to finding the relationship between globalization and inequality. Different modalities in distribution correspond to different concepts of globalization. If the distribution is coming to resemble the uni-modal one, typical of a single country, this would not necessarily alter measures of inequality such as the Gini coefficient; but it could be taken as evidence that a unified capitalism was establishing itself on a global scale and that the international fissures in the system produced by imperialism were abating, a hypothesis which is frequently heard. However, if the world distribution remains strongly bi-modal, if countries still only very rarely evolve from the less privileged to the more privileged group, then this would be strong evidence that the obituaries of imperialism have been premature. Some might see such a result as an indication that globalization continues to be the agent of imperialism; on the other hand it might mean that today's imperialism is to be found less in globalization as such and more in its partial and biased nature. This latter interpretation would see actually existing globalization as being something of a mess, something of a myth, as well as something of a fraud.

Is there an Answer?

There is no yes-or-no answer to the question 'Is the world converging or diverging?'. As so often in any serious question relating to human society, the answer is a complex and contradictory mixture of yes and no. The most basic fact about world inequality is that it is monstrously large; and that result is inescapable, whatever the definition of it or the method used to arrive at it. As to its direction of change in the last 25 years, to some extent there are different answers to the same question; but also, there are different questions. Inequality is not a simple, one-dimensional concept which can be reduced to a single number. Single integral measures of world inequality (where all incomes are, in principle, taken into account) give a different result from measures of the relation of the extremes of income (the richest compared with the poorest). In the last 25 years, we find that the bottom half of world income earners seems to have gained something in relation to the top half (in this sense, less equality), but the bottom 10 per cent have lost seriously in comparison with the top 10 per cent (more inequality), and the bottom 1 per cent have lost enormously in relation to the top 1 per cent (much more inequality). None of these measures is a single real measure of inequality; they are all part of a complex structure of inequalities, some of which can lessen as part of the same overall process in which others increase.

More concretely, the gap between China and the rich countries is closing very rapidly. This produces convergence and is expressed in reductions in most calculations of intercountry and global coefficients of inequality. However, within China, inequality is growing fast, and millions are relatively, if not absolutely, left behind in its headlong growth. This growing inequality must reduce the contribution of China to the reduction of measures of inequality. In addition, the gap is widening between the richest countries and all the other major groups of countries, especially Africa and Latin America. In the case of Africa, poverty is growing and deepening, and there has been a sudden worsening in some other indices as well, such as life expectancy.

Everybody says they are against poverty, but few people examine the role of riches in the maintenance of poverty. Many things which make some people rich, make others poor. That was once more recognized than it is now, and resulted in the building of welfare states, strongly redistributive tax systems and plans for the systematic transfer of resources from rich to poor countries. There was never a golden egalitarian age, but these features of egalitarianism are currently under serious threat and, in some cases, are on the run. In the end, I believe that an answer to inequality will involve insisting on the importance of permanent, compulsory redistribution, rather than occasional charity, and recognizing that, if we are seeking justice, riches and privilege are as unacceptable as poverty and exclusion.

NOTES

[1] This paper draws heavily on Sutcliffe (2003; 2004).

REFERENCES

AFL-CIO, Executive PayWatch (2005). CEO pay widens the income gap. (http://www.aflcio.org/corporatewatch/paywatch/).

Atkinson, A.B. (2005). Top incomes in the UK over the 20th century. *Journal of the Royal Statistical Society: Series A (Statistics in Society)* 168 (2), March: 325–43.

Bourguignon, François, and Christian Morrisson (2002). Inequality among world citizens: 1820–1992. *American Economic Review* 92 (4), September: 727–44.

Deininger, Klaus, and Lyn Squire (1996). A new data set measuring income inequality. *The World Bank Economic Review* 10 (3), September. (http://www.worldbank.org/research/growth/dddeisqu.htm).

Firebaugh, Glenn (2003). *The New Geography of Global Income Inequality.* Harvard University Press, Cambridge, MA.

Forbes Magazine (2005). The World's Billionaires. (http://www.forbes.com/billionaires/).

Hatton, Timothy J., and Jeffrey G. Williamson (1998). *The Age of Mass Migration: Causes and Economic Impact.* Oxford University Press, New York.

Heston, Alan, Robert Summers and Bettina Aten (2002). *Penn World Table Version 6.1* (October). Center for International Comparisons, University of Pennsylvania (CICUP), Philadelphia.

Krugman, Paul (2002). For Richer. *New York Times Magazine*, 20 October.

Maddison, Angus (1995). *Monitoring the World Economy, 1820–1992.* OECD, Paris.

Maddison, Angus (2001). *The World Economy: A Millennial Perspective—Appendix tables.* Development Centre Studies, OECD, Paris.

Maddison, Angus (2003). *The World Economy: Historical Statistics.* Development Centre Studies, OECD, Paris.

Melchior, Arne (2001). Global income inequality: beliefs, facts and unresolved issues. *World Economics* 2 (3), July–September: 87–110.

Melchior, Arne, Kjetil Telle and Henrik Wiig (2000). Globalisation and Inequality: World Income Distribution and Living Standards, 1960–1998. Report 6B, Studies on Foreign Policy Issues. Royal Norwegian Ministry of Foreign Affairs, Oslo.

Melchior, Arne, and Kjetil Telle (2001). Global Income Distribution 1965–98: Convergence and Marginalisation. *Forum for Development Studies* 28 (1): 75–98.

Merrill Lynch and Capgemini (2005). *World Wealth Report, 2005.* (http://www.ml.com/media/48237.pdf).

Milanovic, Branko (2002). True world income distribution, 1988 and 1993: First calculation based on household surveys alone. *Economic Journal* 112 (476), January: 51–92.

Milanovic, Branko (2005). *Worlds Apart: Measuring International and Global Inequality.* Princeton University Press, Princeton, NJ.

Palma, Gabriel (2003). National inequality in the era of globalisation: What do recent data tell us? In Jonathan Michie (ed.). *The Handbook of Globalisation.* Edward Elgar, Cheltenham.

Quah, Danny (1996). Twin Peaks: Growth and convergence in Models of Distribution Dynamics. *Economic Journal* 106 (437), July: 1045–1055.

Sala-i-Martin, Xavier (2002a). The World Distribution of Income (estimated from individual country distributions). NBER Working Paper No. 8933, National Bureau of Economic Research, Cambridge, MA. (http://www.nber.org/papers/w8933).

Sala-i-Martin, Xavier (2002b). The Disturbing 'Rise' of Global Income Inequality. NBER Working Paper No. 8904, National Bureau of Economic Research, Cambridge, MA. (http://www.nber.org/papers/w8904).

Sutcliffe, Bob (2003). A more or less unequal world? *Indicators: the Journal of Social Health* 2 (3), Summer: 24–70.

Sutcliffe, Bob (2004). Globalization and inequality. *Oxford Review of Economic Policy* 20 (1), Spring: 15–37.

Sutcliffe, Bob (2005). *100 imágenes de un mundo desigual.* Icaria/Intermon, Barcelona (previous edition in English: *100 Ways of Seeing an Unequal World.* Zed Books, London, 2001).

Sutcliffe, Bob, and Andrew Glyn (2003). Measures of globalization and their misinterpretation. In Jonathan Michie (ed.). *The Handbook of Globalisation.* Edward Elgar, Cheltenham.

World Bank (2003). *World Development Indicators, 2003.* Online version. World Bank, Washington DC.

World Bank (2005a). *World Development Indicators, 2005.* Online version. World Bank, Washington DC.

World Bank (2005b). *Global Economic Prospects, 2005.* World Bank, Washington DC.

4

World Economic Growth and
Income Distribution, 1980–2000

ALBERT BERRY and JOHN SERIEUX

The huge gap between the world's rich and its poor[1] has made trends in world inequality a matter of much interest. That gap appears to have widened markedly during a period beginning in the early nineteenth century at the latest[2] and continuing until at least the middle of the twentieth. Since about 1950, it has been possible to follow the evolution of inequality with much more precision, given the availability of national accounts in all major countries and of intra-country inequality measures in an increasing share of them. Most prior studies have underscored three main points. First, the distribution of world income is highly unequal, considerably more so than that of any but the most inegalitarian countries (Whalley, 1979; Berry, Bourguignon and Morrisson, 1983; 1991). Second, when the measure of income is absolute purchasing power (in international prices), the bulk of world inequality comes from intercountry income differences rather than from intracountry differences. Finally, the level of world inequality did not change markedly, in either direction, between 1950 and the mid-1980s (Berry, Bourguignon and Morrisson, 1991; Bourguignon and Morrisson, 2002; Peacock, Hoover and Killian, 1988; Schultz, 1998).

Updated and wider-ranging analysis of recent patterns and trends of world inequality is warranted, partly because the period since about 1980 has brought a wave of historic changes in several regions of the world and in the character of the world economy, and partly because a variety of theories and pieces of factual information suggest that past distributional patterns might be changing. With such issues in mind, this chapter examines the evolution of world income and its distribution across regions, countries and individuals over the period 1980–2000. The next section examines the theoretical approaches to the issue of global income distribution since 1980 and the degree to which they inform current concerns. The following section presents estimates of the weighted average growth of the world economies from 1970 to 2000 and measures of the intercountry distribution of world income. The next three sections present estimates of the distribution of world income between persons (based on a methodology outlined in Berry and Serieux, 2005: Appendix C) followed by caveats and clarifications related to those estimates. The penultimate section presents data on changes in world poverty during the 1980–2000 period and the chapter concludes with a brief review of the issues, results and implications.

THE WORLD SINCE 1980

The 1980s and 1990s have seen several profound changes both in the nature of economic interaction between countries and in the economic and political fortunes of certain regions and countries. Prominent among these changes have been the break-up of the Soviet bloc and the transition of its former members toward the market system; accelerated growth and an increasing role of the market in the Chinese economy; the international debt crisis of the 1980s, that made this a 'lost decade' in South and Central America; a severe regional crisis in sub-Saharan Africa; and 'globalization'—the increasingly tight interaction among national economies, to the point where the economic raison d'être of the national state is increasingly called into question.

Viewing these changes along more 'systemic' lines, a number of authors have argued that the years around 1980 constituted a 'watershed' between a previous relatively successful phase of Third World growth, during which per capita output rose at a healthy rate (by about 2.2 per cent from the end of World War II until 1978, in Bairoch's [1997, vol. 3: 997–1000] periodization) that allowed some narrowing of the (intercountry per capita income) gap with the rich industrial world, and a subsequent period of slow and erratic growth, during which most of the Third World lost ground to the rich countries of the West. Arrighi (2002) attributes the transition to the fact that the United States of America, previously a major capital exporter, became a major importer of capital, leading to a rise in real interest rates, a shift to which many authors give great weight in explaining subsequent problems, including the debt crisis of the 1980s (Easterly, 2001; Galbraith, 2002). While a few developing countries did manage to achieve sustained growth over this period, it is often seen as one of bifurcation within the Third World, with the majority of countries doing badly in this most recent phase (Easterly, 2001; Milanovic, 2005).

Opinions vary widely on the implications of some of these events and trends. One prominent view, derived in part from trade theory, is that national economies which interact increasingly with each other will converge (Barro, 1991; Barro and Sala-i-Martin, 1992; Ben-David, 1993), either through a tendency for such interaction to equalize the returns to factors of production across countries and/or through technological diffusion, which suggests important advantages to being a follower, rather than a leader, and thus being able to borrow abroad to invest and to have low-cost access to the technological innovations made elsewhere. Much of the vast literature that relates overall economic growth in developing countries to export performance may be considered to fall broadly into this latter category (see the reviews in Bliss, 1989, and Evans, 1989). Similarly, the neoclassical growth model predicts convergence in per capita incomes among countries because poorer countries with higher marginal rates of return to capital will grow faster than (and attract capital from) richer countries with lower marginal rates of return (Solow, 1957). Approaches allowing for different steady states or augmenting the neoclassical model with human capital, and some specifications of new growth models, predict less strong or *conditional* convergence, which maintains the expected higher growth rate for poorer countries but allows for persistent differences due to varying rates of physical and human capital accumulation and population growth between countries (Mankiw, Romer and Weil, 1992).[3]

Counterpoised against these theories is the idea that there are powerful centrifugal forces in the world economy, ranging from the extreme case in which rich countries straightforwardly control and exploit the weaker through the use of power, to less directly power-related mechanisms, as in the core-periphery model, that nonetheless produce a similar outcome. Beyond these propositions, the majority of new growth models predict either sustained in-equality in mean country incomes or outright divergence. Several empirical studies have concluded that, at the world level, divergence among mean county incomes has been the prevailing pattern (Pritchett, 1995; UNCTAD, 1997) and hence that the world distribution of income has become substantially more unequal over the last few decades (Korzeniewicz and Moran, 1997; UNDP, 1999).

Whether the sources of convergence or of divergence have, on balance, been the stronger, the pattern is unlikely to have been a very simple one. During much of the twentieth century there was a partial convergence in the sense that the fastest growing countries were neither those at the top nor those at the bottom of the income hierarchy, but rather a subset of middle-income 'follower' countries, among which Japan and the Soviet Union were, for much of the period, the most prominent. While these countries were gaining on the leaders, the group of low-income countries below them was not. This pattern has changed since the late 1970s when China, a (then) low-income country with about a fifth of the world's population, began to register fast growth, thereby contributing to the equalization of world distribution. Since the early 1980s, India's growth has also accelerated, albeit less dramatically than China's. Two other large low-income countries, Indonesia and Pakistan, have (until recently) put in relatively strong growth performances. The poorer performing countries of Africa, a region yet to achieve a strong take-off and still experiencing rapid, though now falling, population growth, are home to an increasing share of the world's poor.

There is little overlap between theories that address the question of convergence among countries in per capita income and those which focus on intra-country distribution although, naturally, some of the same aspects of economic life are assumed to be at work in both cases (e.g., international trade, technological change). The benchmark theory with respect to intracountry distribution is Kuznets' (1955) idea that the level of inequality would first rise, then fall, over the course of development. That view has lost currency over the last few decades, and any current consensus on the long-term changes in internal distribution is probably limited to a few rather obvious points, e.g., that an equalization over time in the distribution of such important assets as agricultural land and human capital will tend to produce a more equitable distribution of income.

Whatever the expectations may have been for the pattern of intracountry distribution, the overall experience of the 1980s and 1990s is generally recognized to have been negative, in both developed and developing countries (Corry and Glyn, 1994; Berry and Stewart, 1997; Cornia, 2004). Increases in international trade and technological change have been cited as possible causes of the frequent episodes of increasing inequality within both developed and developing countries. In the United States, they are the main candidates discussed (Wood, 1994; Bound and Johnson, 1992). In developing countries, the analysis is less far advanced, but these phenomena are again among the suspects (Robbins, 1996).

Growth Trends and Changes in the Intercountry Distribution of Income

This chapter presents evidence on the world distribution of income among persons over the period 1980–2000, and notes some of the more obvious possible links to the monumental events of the last two decades. Of particular interest is the question of whether or not the impact of economic integration has been closer to the hopeful predictions of the optimists or the worrisome prognoses of the pessimists.

The period 1980–2000 was punctuated by economic crisis in many countries of the Third World, especially those of South and Central America, sub-Saharan Africa and most of the former Soviet bloc. However, this was also a period of continuing fast growth for most of East Asia (including China at an impressive 6–9 per cent per year), and of a stronger performance by the Indian subcontinent than had been the case during most of the post-colonial period, especially by India itself, with a rate of nearly 6 per cent per year. The developed countries of Europe and North America grew at 2 to 3 per cent per year, Japan decelerated substantially to a low of 1.6 per cent in the 1990s, and the former Soviet bloc countries underwent marked economic contractions in the early 1990s (Berry and Serieux, 2005: Table 1).

At the income-group level, the pattern of world growth was similarly complex (Table 4.1). Africa's weak performance notwithstanding, the per capita income in the poorest countries as a group (i.e., the World Bank's 'low income' category) grew faster than in the rich ones during both the 1980s and the 1990s, with an average gap of 0.6 per cent over the two decades. This differential would have been even wider, and contributed to a greater reduction in world inequality, had demographic trends been similar between these country groupings. With both the substantially faster population growth in the low-income countries taken into account and India excluded from that group, the result is slower per capita growth than in the high-income countries, creating a source of income divergence (Table 4.1). India's presence in the low-income group of countries can, therefore, be thought of as the source of convergence of that category towards the higher ones.[4]

In a departure from the pattern of the 1970s, when the middle-income countries as a whole substantially outgrew both the low-income and the high-income groups, this category suffered serious deceleration in the 1980s and

TABLE 4.1
Average annual rates of output growth by country income group, 1970–2000

Country income categories	Weighted country averages					
	Real GDP (Domestic currency)			Real per capita GDP (Domestic currency)		
	1970–1980	1980–1990	1990–2000	1970–1980	1980–1990	1990–2000
Low-income	3.58	4.87	4.66	1.08	2.49	2.59
Lower-middle income	4.87	3.42	1.32	3.05	1.85	0.23
Upper-middle-income	5.94	1.52	3.27	3.81	-0.31	1.87
High-income	3.14	2.75	2.42	2.35	2.16	1.74
Low-income without India	4.18	3.90	3.39	1.46	1.28	1.06
Lower-middle-income without China	5.23	2.55	-1.10	3.44	0.83	-2.23
China and India	3.74	6.32	6.85	1.72	4.57	5.46
World without China	3.78	2.69	2.14	1.91	0.92	0.63
World without China and India	3.82	2.58	1.96	2.05	0.91	0.53
World without Eastern Europe	3.64	3.03	3.18	1.68	1.24	1.67
World without China and Eastern Europe	3.60	2.84	2.86	1.59	0.94	1.20
World without China, India & E. Europe	3.63	2.71	2.70	1.71	0.90	1.08
World	3.81	2.86	2.47	1.94	1.16	1.06

Sources: Authors' calculations using data from the WDI (online), UN Common Database (UN) and the Penn World Tables—Mark 5.6 (CIC).

1990s (Table 4.1). In the 1980s, it was the upper-middle income countries that suffered the largest drop in output growth (from 5.9 to 1.5 per cent) as per capita growth became negative—a reflection of the crises in South and Central American economies. In the 1990s the lower-middle income group met this fate. Even with the impressive performance of China, that category showed almost zero growth in per capita income (0.23 per cent). Excluding China, the average decline in per capita income for that group was a dramatic 2.2 per cent per year—reflecting the near economic implosion that occurred in Eastern Europe and Central Asia.

The crucial role of China and India in determining changes in the intercountry pattern of distribution of world output since 1980, suggested by Table 4.1, is confirmed by the conventional measures of income inequality. The Gini, Theil and three Atkinson measures reported in Table 4.2 all indicate a moderate improvement in world intercountry inequality in each decade

TABLE 4.2
Intercountry income inequality measures

	Year	Gini	Theil	Atkinson (0.5)	Atkinson (1)	Atkinson (2)
All countries	1980	0.585	0.700	0.288	0.503	0.695
	1990	0.578	0.636	0.275	0.471	0.654
	2000	0.553	0.559	0.251	0.428	0.623
World without China	1980	0.537	0.622	0.247	0.463	0.695
	1990	0.558	0.629	0.258	0.467	0.688
	2000	0.567	0.630	0.264	0.467	0.685
World without India	1980	0.560	0.674	0.268	0.490	0.709
	1990	0.564	0.631	0.263	0.468	0.678
	2000	0.547	0.574	0.246	0.436	0.658
World without China and India	1980	0.473	0.512	0.198	0.401	0.680
	1990	0.510	0.572	0.224	0.436	0.706
	2000	0.541	0.634	0.249	0.469	0.730
World without Eastern Europe	1980	0.606	0.751	0.313	0.528	0.702
	1990	0.593	0.678	0.296	0.492	0.662
	2000	0.563	0.591	0.263	0.446	0.637

Contribution of China and India to world inequality (Theil coefficient-based analysis)

	1980	1990	2000
China's contribution to international inequality	11.1%	1.0%	-12.6%
India's contribution to international inequality	3.7%	0.8%	-2.6%
The combined contributions of China and India	26.9%	10.0%	-13.3%

Sources: Authors' calculations using data from the WDI (online), UN Common Database (UN) and the Penn World Tables—Mark 5.6 (CIC).

between 1980 and 2000.[5] However, when China and India are excluded, the pattern is reversed, with all measures indicating a deterioration in the distribution of world income, often of roughly comparable magnitude to the improvement that occurs when they are included. The exclusion of India alone does not reverse the trend. The exclusion of China alone does so for the Gini coefficient and to a lesser extent the Theil and Atkinson (0.5) measures as well, but the Atkinson (1) suggests no change and the Atkinson (2), which gives most weight to changes at the bottom of the income ladder, continues to suggest an improvement—an effect of the improving situation in India.[6] The exclusion of Eastern Europe alone generally reinforces the overall trend of improvement.

The dramatic effect of the growth performance of China and India on measures of intercountry income inequality is perhaps best illustrated by a disaggregation of the Theil coefficient, presented at the bottom of Table 4.2. In 1980, over a quarter of estimated intercountry income inequality could be attributed to the low income levels of China and India. In 2000, however, these countries' contribution to world inequality was negative, i.e., their presence made the intercountry distribution of world income more equal!

The Distribution of World Income among Persons

Although prior analyses concur on the conclusion that, at the world level, most of the inequality among persons is the result of differences in average incomes across countries, intracountry inequality is also significant and changes therein could have an important impact on the level of world inequality among people. The fact that many developing and most major developed countries suffered worsening income distribution during the 1980s (known, especially in the United States, as the 'greed decade') or the 1990s, makes this a possibility to be reckoned with.

Among the 25 large countries[7] for which reasonably comparable Gini coefficient estimates from the beginning and end of the 1980s are available (from the WIDER World Income Inequality Database and the 2001 World Development Indicators), 14 recorded increases in the Gini coefficient[8] (i.e., a worsening distribution of income) while 10 recorded decreases (i.e., improved distribution), and 1 saw no change.[9] In the 1990s, the general deterioration of intracountry income distribution appears to have been even more acute. Of 27 countries for which comparable Gini coefficient estimates were available, 18 suffered increasing inequality and only 8 recorded an improvement. In the 1990s, as they attempted the transition to capitalism, the great majority of the Eastern European and Central Asian countries with available data experienced worsening inequality. China, while going much less far along the path of economic reform than the former Soviet bloc countries, also appears to have experienced the negative effects of growing market forces on distribution.

With both intra- and intercountry income differences taken into account, our best estimate of the 1980 decile distribution of world income among individuals (ranked by per capita household income, and converted to current international dollars using purchasing power parity (PPP) rates) implies a Gini coefficient of 0.651, a Theil coefficient of 0.891 and a ratio of 73.7-fold between the average income of the top decile and that of the bottom one (Table 4.3).[10]

Between 1980 and 1990, all of the indicators we use suggest that the overall level of world inequality declined at least slightly. The Gini coefficient fell to

TABLE 4.3
Decile distribution of world income among persons, and associated inequality measures

Income shares by decile of world population (%)			Change in share of total world income	Annual income growth (1985 PPP value of income)	
1980	1990	2000	1980–2000	1980–1990	1990–2000
Decile 1	0.63	0.71	0.74	0.11	2.4%	1.8%
Decile 2	1.09	1.29	1.32	0.23	3.0%	1.6%
Decile 3	1.45	1.69	1.90	0.44	2.8%	2.5%
Decile 4	1.90	2.12	2.46	0.56	2.4%	2.9%
Decile 5	2.51	2.75	3.18	0.67	2.2%	2.8%
Decile 6	3.71	4.07	4.39	0.68	2.2%	2.1%
Decile 7	6.73	6.23	6.41	-0.32	0.5%	1.6%
Decile 8	12.34	10.89	10.19	-2.16	0.0%	0.7%
Decile 9	23.06	21.61	20.13	-2.93	0.6%	0.6%
Decile 10	46.57	48.64	49.28	2.71	1.7%	1.5%
World	100.00	100.00	100.00			

	Measures of inequality			20-year change in inequality measure	
Gini coefficient	0.651	0.648	0.639	-0.012	
Theil coefficient	0.891	0.845	0.802	-0.089	
Atkinson (0.5)	0.349	0.343	0.332	-0.017	
Atkinson (1)	0.590	0.570	0.552	-0.038	
Atkinson (2)	0.792	0.773	0.763	-0.029	
Ratio of top-to-bottom decile income	73.7	69.0	66.7		

Sources: Authors' calculations using data from the WDI (World Bank), UN Common Database (UN), Penn World Tables—Mark 5.6 (CIC) and WIID (WIDER).

0.648 (from 0.651) and each of the various Atkinson coefficients dropped a little (Table 4.3). The Theil coefficient fell more noticeably, from 0.891 to 0.845. Between 1990 and 2000, all of the indicators fell again, some by a bit more than in the 1980s and some by a bit less. The ratio of average top decile income to average bottom decile income fell from 73.7 in 1980 to 69.0 in 1990 and to 66.7 in 2000. Though all of the inequality measures we use indicate at least a mild improvement in the distribution of world income over the two decades, the 2000 distribution does not Lorenz dominate either the 1990 or 1980 distributions, nor does the 1990 distribution Lorenz dominate the 1980 distribution.[11]

All of the bottom six deciles gained in income share in both decades; the six combined moved up markedly from a share of 11.3 per cent in 1980 to 12.6 per cent in 1990 and 14.0 per cent in 2000. The losing deciles were 7, 8 and 9, their share falling sharply from 42.1 per cent in 1980 to 36.7 per cent in 2000, while the top decile gained over two percentage points, from 46.6 per cent in 1980 to 49.3 per cent in 2000. Much of the gain achieved by the bottom deciles reflects the fast growth in China and India. The fact that the deciles near the top were unable to hold on to their share was the combined result of poor growth of per capita income in the upper middle-income countries (South and Central America in the 1980s and Eastern Europe in the 1990s) and the widening income gaps within the high-income countries.[12] The world's poorest were, generally speaking, substantially better off in 2000 than in 1980. The bottom 20 per cent (40 per cent) enjoyed an income increase of 50 per cent (59 per cent) over the 20-year period. The temporal and geographic nature of that improvement will be discussed later.

What is perhaps most intriguing, and at first glance paradoxical, about the outcome for 1980–2000 is that, though no previous post-war period seems to have been characterized by as general a pattern of intracountry worsening of distribution as this one, the overall level of inequality has moved in the opposite direction, again in contrast to the previous tendency of near constancy over the preceding decades (Berry, Bourguignon and Morrisson, 1991: 73; Bourguignon and Morrisson, 2002: Table 4.1).

Among other studies using the same methodology (conversion among currencies by the International Comparison Programme (ICP) indices of the United Nations Statistics Division and the University of Pennsylvania, and national accounts-based figures for average income of each country), the finding of constancy or decline in global inequality over the past couple of decades appears to be the norm. Studies differ more in the absolute level of inequality that they report. This is not surprising, because most methodological differences are likely to lead to fairly systematic differences over time between any two studies. Judged by the Gini coefficients, whereas our figures indicate a very small decrease in inequality (from 0.651 in 1980 to 0.639 in 2000), Bhalla (2002: 84) finds a somewhat greater decline from a higher level (0.687 in 1979 to 0.676 in 1989 and 0.660 in 1999) while Sala-i-Martin (2002: 60) reports a decline from 0.638 in 1980 to 0.630 in 1990 and 0.609 in 1998. Perhaps the faster fall in inequality reported by these two studies than ours is substantially due to the fact that we adjusted the official Chinese data and they did not. When we used the unadjusted official figures, our Gini estimates also fell by one percentage point in the 1980s and two in the 1990s (Berry and Serieux, 2005: Table B2). If we include Bourguignon and Morrisson (2002) data for 1980 to 1992 (Ginis of 0.657 and 0.663, respectively) as approximating the story of the 1980s, all four studies come up with minimal change in the Gini coefficient over that decade (one percentage point or less), but Bhalla (2002) and Sala-i-Martin (2002) find larger declines of a couple of percentage points in the 1990s compared to our 0.9 percentage point. Milanovic (2005: 118) reports a decline

TABLE 4.4
Sources of world income inequality
(based on the additive separability property of the Theil coefficient)

Theil inequality measures	1980	%	1990	%	2000	%
As measured with only large-country inequality considered						
Interregional inequality	0.426	47.8	0.393	46.6	0.370	46.1
Average intraregional (intercountry) inequality	0.274	30.8	0.243	28.7	0.189	23.6
Total intercountry inequality	0.700	78.6	0.636	75.3	0.559	69.7
Average intracountry inequality (*when limited to large countries*)	0.191	21.4	0.209	24.7	0.243	30.3
World income inequality (As measured in this chapter)	0.891	100.0	0.845	100.0	0.802	100.0
Including small-country inequality						
Interregional inequality	0.426	46.1	0.393	44.6	0.370	43.7
Average intraregional (intercountry) inequality	0.274	29.7	0.243	27.6	0.189	22.4
Total intercountry inequality	0.700	75.8	0.636	72.2	0.559	66.1
Average intracountry inequality (*when extrapolated to all countries*)	0.223	24.2	0.245	27.8	0.287	33.9
World income inequality (implied)	0.923	100.0	0.881	100.0	0.846	100.0

Sources: Authors' calculations using data from the WDI (World Bank), UN Common Database (UN), Penn World Tables—Mark 5.6 (CIC) and WIID (WIDER).

Notes: The first part of the table presents inequality estimates (and percentage measures) derived directly from the data where large countries (those with populations of over 25 million and representing, roughly, 85% of world population) have been disaggregated into income groups but small countries have not and are thus not included. In the second part of the table, intracountry inequality is extrapolated to all countries (i.e., small countries are assumed to have average levels of inequality similar to those of large countries).

TABLE 4.5
Decile distribution of world income among persons when China is excluded

Income shares by decile of world population (%)				Change in share of total world income	Annual income growth (1985 PPP value of income)	
	1980	1990	2000	1980–2000	1980–1990	1990–2000
Decile 1	0.54	0.58	0.59	0.05	1.9%	1.0%
Decile 2	1.01	1.12	1.09	0.08	2.2%	0.6%
Decile 3	1.38	1.49	1.63	0.25	1.9%	1.8%
Decile 4	2.03	1.97	2.12	0.09	0.8%	1.6%
Decile 5	3.22	2.95	2.83	-0.39	0.2%	0.5%
Decile 6	5.50	4.71	4.32	-1.18	-0.5%	0.0%
Decile 7	8.88	7.95	6.88	-2.00	-0.1%	-0.5%
Decile 8	14.19	13.00	11.45	-2.73	0.2%	-0.4%
Decile 9	22.40	22.25	22.15	-0.26	1.0%	0.9%
Decile 10	40.86	43.98	46.95	6.09	1.8%	1.6%
World	100.00	100.00	100.00			

Measures of inequality				20-year change in inequality measure
Gini coefficient	0.612	0.630	0.644	0.033
Theil coefficient	0.826	0.842	0.865	0.039
Atkinson (0.5)	0.313	0.328	0.341	0.028
Atkinson (1)	0.562	0.569	0.579	0.017
Atkinson (2)	0.801	0.798	0.800	-0.001
Ratio of top-to-bottom decile income	76.2	75.8	80.0	

Sources: Authors' calculations using data from the WDI (World Bank), UN Common Database (UN), Penn World Tables—Mark 5.6 (CIC) and WIID (WIDER).

of 0.6 over the slightly different period 1988–1998 for a common sample of countries, a decline that might be a little bigger had he converted to a common currency only in one year, as we did. Overall then, in light of a variety of differences in details of the methodology, adjustment of official data made or not made, and decisions with respect to which source of intracountry inequality to accept, these modest differences in estimates and in trends are reassuring.

As noted, world inequality reflects, in large part, the huge differences in average income levels across countries. Expressed in terms of the Theil index, which has the advantage of being decomposable in a straightforward way, this factor accounted for over three-quarters (75.8 per cent) of overall world inequality in 1980, while just 24.2 per cent reflected intracountry inequality (Table 4.4). These proportions had changed to 66.1 per cent and 33.9 per cent respectively by 2000, reflecting the general deterioration of intracountry distribution evidenced by the rising Gini coefficients mentioned earlier, as well as the rapid decline of the intraregional between-country component of overall inequality over the period.

With its large share of world population, China's economic evolution is obviously important to what happens at the world level. Since its growth performance has substantially outpaced other countries' in the period under discussion, and since its economic system has unique features, it is of interest to ask what happened to distribution (and to growth) in the world outside China over these years. With China excluded, the Gini coefficient rises by about three percentage points, the Theil coefficient by about four points and Atkinson (0.5) by nearly three points, while the other two Atkinson indices show less or no significant change (Table 4.5). Thus, the presence of China significantly changes our estimated outcome over this twenty-year period from a modest, but clear, decrease in inequality to a worsening—at least as judged by most of the indicators. Interestingly, the pattern of change varies less than do the summary measures. Even with China excluded, the bottom four deciles gain in income share; meanwhile, the top decile records a dramatic gain of over six percentage points.

The inequality trend is affected further if India is excluded along with China (Table 4.6). For the remaining 62 per cent of the world population, there was a clear worsening of the distribution of income, as the Gini coefficient rose sharply from 0.559 to 0.621 between 1980 and 2000 and the ratio of average income of the top decile to that of the bottom rose from 61.5 to 85.2. With two of the fastest growing countries (as well as the two largest) excluded, average income per capita for the rest of the world grew at only 0.9 per cent per year between 1980 and 1990, and 0.5 per cent per year during the 1990s.

Although the bottom three deciles still recorded marginal income growth, the next four all lost in absolute terms; only the top two showed substantial income increases, with the share of the top decile rising sharply from 36.1 per cent in 1980 to 42.9 per cent in 2000 (about the same amount as in the case where only China is excluded). Though the biggest losers are in the middle deciles, the fall in the income shares of the bottom deciles, as well, exposes and highlights the fact that growth in China and India offset the poor economic performance of other low-income countries, particularly those in Africa.

The deterioration in the distribution of world income when China and India are excluded is more unequivocal than both the improvement when these countries are included and the deterioration when only China is excluded. There is no Lorenz dominance in either of the latter two cases but, when both China and India are excluded, the 1980 distribution of world income Lorenz

TABLE 4.6

Decile distribution of world income among persons when China and India are excluded

	Income shares by decile of world population (%)			Change in share of total world income	Annual income growth (1985 PPP value of income)	
	1980	1990	2000	1980–2000	1980–1990	1990–2000
Decile 1	0.59	0.54	0.50	-0.08	0.2%	0.1%
Decile 2	1.07	1.06	0.99	-0.08	0.9%	0.2%
Decile 3	1.78	1.56	1.52	-0.26	-0.3%	0.5%
Decile 4	2.83	2.46	2.21	-0.62	-0.4%	-0.2%
Decile 5	4.65	3.84	3.33	-1.31	-0.9%	-0.6%
Decile 6	7.05	6.16	5.13	-1.92	-0.3%	-1.0%
Decile 7	10.13	9.21	7.89	-2.25	0.1%	-0.7%
Decile 8	14.77	14.11	13.60	-1.17	0.6%	0.4%
Decile 9	21.00	21.45	21.92	0.92	1.3%	1.0%
Decile 10	36.13	39.62	42.90	6.77	2.0%	1.6%
World	100.00	100.00	100.00			

	Measures of inequality			20-year change in inequality measure	
Gini coefficient	0.559	0.591	0.621	0.062	
Theil coefficient	0.692	0.768	0.840	0.148	
Atkinson (0.5)	0.264	0.293	0.321	0.057	
Atkinson (1)	0.499	0.536	0.568	0.069	
Atkinson (2)	0.775	0.804	0.818	0.043	
Ratio of top-to-bottom decile income	61.5	73.2	85.2		

Sources: Authors' calculations using data from the WDI (World Bank), UN Common Database (UN), Penn World Tables—Mark 5.6 (CIC) and WIID (WIDER).

dominates both the 1990 and 2000 distributions and the 1990 distribution Lorenz dominates that for 2000.

Given the dramatic events befalling the former Soviet bloc, it is also of interest to see what effect they had on the trajectory of growth and inequality (Berry and Serieux, 2005: Table A4, Appendix A). During the 1990s, the world economy grew at just 2.5 per cent, while the world outside the former Soviet bloc grew at 3.2 per cent, highlighting the major impact of its collapse on world growth. However, the significant increase in inequality reported for most countries of the bloc, even when combined with the effect of their falling income on intercountry inequality, contributes only modestly to the pattern of world income distribution. Excluding the countries of the former Soviet bloc leads to a moderate exaggeration of the pattern of decreasing overall inequality. In the world outside the former Soviet bloc, the Gini coefficient fell by 0.017 points; with that bloc included, that decline was of 0.009 points. The world Theil coefficient fell by 0.043 points, while that of the world outside the former Soviet bloc fell by 0.055 points. Qualitatively similar stories emerge for the other indicators of inequality. Exclusion of this part of the world, however, does not lead to Lorenz dominance by later distributions over earlier ones.

Major Caveats

Given the number of data problems and possible methodological flaws in calculations like those reported above, it is a foregone conclusion that the results are, at best, approximations to the true reality. It is almost certain that the country-level figures in most developing countries understate inequality, mainly because of the incomplete reporting of capital incomes (especially large ones) relative to labour incomes,[13] but also because of the exclusion of income from asset appreciation. This creates a presumption that the estimates of world inequality are also downward biased, but since the methodological flaws involved in merging the data for different countries can create either upward or downward biases, this is less certain.[14]

Our main concern here, however, is with possible biases in the estimated trends in inequality. These are far too numerous to list; much additional research will be required to sort out their impacts and their relative import-ance.[15] Probably the two phenomena most capable of leading to significant bias are changes in the degree of under-coverage of capital incomes, already mentioned, and differences in the price trends for different income groups within countries. The latter relates to the fact that each datum on inequality is based on current prices. If, in a given country, prices rise faster for some income groups than for others, the changes in the distribution of purchasing power will be misestimated by the change in current price inequality. Under many circumstances there may be no reason to expect the income-group-specific price indices to move very differently over time, but in the context of major freeing of markets and the attendant, sometimes substantial, changes in relative prices, such an assumption is not so defensible. For example, countries of Eastern Europe which saw a reduction of the rationing systems and freeing of prices of staples may well have undergone differential price changes by group. The same goes for countries that have opened up quickly to international trade; in most developing countries, this has led to declines in the relative prices of a number of luxury goods (such as cars), which may mean that the relative cost of the market basket consumed by the rich has fallen vis-à-vis that of the poor.

Another concern, which may technically be viewed as a special case of the previous one, involves public consumption goods. All of the country distribution data used here refer only to private income; though everyone recognizes the need to also take account of the distribution of public good consumption, the practical difficulties have precluded it as a general practice.[16] Given the widespread decline in public expenditure in recent years, it is probable that distributional trends would look somewhat different, and very likely more negative, were public consumption included in the data, though the increase in targeting of certain services may have had a sufficiently strong, positive effect to prevent this outcome or even reverse it.

The above biases involve the estimation of inequality at the country level as opposed to the merging of country data for the world-level estimate. In both cases, there is a reasonable theoretical presumption (related to the processes of liberalization and globalization) that the bias will have risen since 1980, and a modest amount of empirical evidence has been brought forward in support of that conclusion (e.g., de Ferranti and others, 2004: 235). Allowing for these possible (or probable) biases might suggest a 'best guess' that the level of world inequality, instead of falling a little from 1980–2000, was very close to staying constant, or might even have risen a little. It is worth emphasizing that, although there has been a considerable convergence of results around the 'modest decline in world inequality' conclusion for at least the last two decades of the twentieth century, most of the major remaining possible biases in the estimates (especially the most glaring ones noted above) are common to all of the studies. Thus, it is quite possible that all of them are significantly off the mark in the same direction.

Milanovic (2002: 72), relying exclusively on household survey data for both mean income and its distribution, estimated that between 1988 and 1993, the Gini coefficient for the world income distribution had risen from 0.628 to 0.660 for a common sample of countries. This suggested that, if his methodology was indeed the correct one, not only was world inequality increasing, it was doing so very rapidly. The message contrasted significantly from that of the other available and comparable studies that, as noted above, pointed to a smallish decrease since 1980. In fact, the difference between the two approaches turns out to have been much less than first met the eye, since when Milanovic added 1998 estimates, these showed an inequality decline between 1993 and 1998 and hence a more modest increase from 1988 to1998 of 1.8 Gini percentage points, from 0.623 to 0.641 (Milanovic, 2005: 118). From 1990 to 2000, our estimated Gini coefficient fell from 0.648 to 0.639 (Table 4.3). Milanovic also undertook estimates using national accounts-based figures for mean per capita income of each country, and in that case found the Gini coefficient to fall from 0.641 in 1988 to 0.635 in 1998, figures almost identical to our own for 1990–2000. This suggests that the main difference between his preferred result and ours reflects the use of different figures for mean per capita income of countries, rather than a number of other differences of methodological detail or the fact that the end years are a little different. This leaves us with two interesting questions arising from Milanovic's results, where they contrast with others.

First, was there, in fact, a rather sudden increase in world inequality between 1988 and 1993 as his figures show (albeit less markedly in his 2005 publication than in that of 2002)? Sorting out this question would require an analysis of the statistical sources of that increase to discern whether they more likely reflected true trends or statistical error, and is well beyond the scope of this study.

Second, what can be said about the relative merits of using household survey-based estimates of per capita income in each country versus national accounts-based estimates? This is also a complicated matter that cannot currently be resolved on the basis either of theory or available empirical evidence. All approaches have to use distribution data from household surveys so the weaknesses of that information show up in all estimates. The difference between the two is the choice of the mean income measures. Milanovic's approach uses the mean per capita income measure derived directly from household surveys with its likely underestimation of true mean income (mainly because of the underreporting of capital income), while our method uses national accounts-based per capita income figures (which is not without its own measurement problems). However, it is not accuracy of measurement that is the critical issue here. The main argument for using national accounts estimates of per capita income is that the methodology is likely to produce less variability in the errors of observation over time than the household survey data. Given the underreporting of capital incomes in survey data, it is unclear how this effect plays out over time with respect to the distribution of global income. Capital incomes do vary over time and, at this point, our knowledge of the distribution of capital income in developing countries is too limited to allow more than conjecture as to patterns of change and consequent effects on income measures.

It should be emphasized that which methodology is best and which sources of bias are the most serious depends on exactly what one wants to learn from the data. One methodology may be better at approximating true inequality at a point of time but worse at identifying trends—our main interest here. One may be better at approximating the distribution of consumption expenditures and the other at approximating the distribution of income. If the former is one's main interest, household surveys (when there are enough of them and they are comparable enough) are likely to provide the better approach, since the capital income reporting problem becomes close to irrelevant. Meanwhile, studies of changing inequality in given countries do not confront many of the challenges involved in dealing with world inequality.

Our focus here is the direction of changes in world inequality among persons. For that purpose, we suspect that the use of national accounts-based per capita income measures is superior to the use of household survey-based figures. However, accepting that this is, nevertheless, debatable, it is somewhat reassuring that the apparent impact of that methodological choice is less than it appeared to be when Milanovic (2002) was published. From 1988 to1998, the measured changes in the Gini coefficient, according to Milanovic's (2005: 118) calculations, differ by 2.4 percentage points—a 1.8 percentage point increase using the survey-based means and a 0.6 point decrease using the national accounts-based means.

A Clarification with Respect to Studies Showing Increasing Inequality of World Distribution

Most of the confusion and ambiguity as to what has been happening to world inequality has been due, not to the methodological issues discussed in this chapter, but to two others: whether the individual person or the country is the unit of comparison and whether per capita incomes are converted to a common base using official or market exchange rates or using PPP conversion rates. All of the studies previously referred to in this chapter, with the exception of Korzeniewicz and Moran (1997), share with us the practice of converting national data to a 'common' base using PPP conversion ratios and using the individual as the basic unit of observation.

When the country rather than the individual is the unit of observation, one is, in effect, giving equal weight to each country; China with several hundred times more people than Costa Rica, is given the same weight as that country. This treatment inevitably means that what happens in the many small or relatively small countries becomes the main determinant of 'world inequality'. China and India, with between them around 40 per cent of the world's population, have only between 1 and 2 per cent of the weight in these calculations. If most countries fell in about the same size range, it would not matter much whether one weighted by population or did not; but in fact, countries vary enormously in size, as the just-cited figures indicate. Hence, it does matter. Among those who have focused on this 'unweighted' measure of world inequality is Castells (1993). The very widespread view that global inequality has been rising has been supported by these simple comparisons of growth rate in richer versus poorer countries and, ironically, has often been fuelled by statements coming from such establishment institutions as the World Bank and the IMF.[17] Milanovic (2005: 39–44) presents a time series covering 1950–2000 that shows a modest increase in unweighted intercountry inequality from a Gini coefficient of 0.44 in 1950 to about 0.47 around 1980, followed by a very sharp increase to about 0.54 at the end of the century. Over the fifty years as a whole, most of the increase comes from what happens in Africa (as one might guess from the fact that there are so many small countries there and they have done relatively badly compared to other developing countries), but the concentrated increase since 1980 does not have that origin; it is, instead, due mainly to events in Latin America and in the middle-income countries of Eastern Europe and the former Soviet Union.

Conclusions about world inequality trends are also very sensitive to whether conversion of national data to an international 'currency' takes the PPP route or uses official exchange rates.[18] The United Nations Conference on Trade and Development (UNCTAD) was one of the institutions, along with the United Nations Development Programme (UNDP) (1999) to report a major increase in inequality at some point in the last few decades, with the Gini coefficient rising from 0.66 in 1965 to 0.74 in 1990 and the ratio of the richest quintile to the poorest rising dramatically from 31.1 to 60.1 (UNCTAD, 1997: 81). The report drew on Korzeniewicz and Moran (1997). The authors were aware that the choice between market exchange rate conversion and PPP conversion matters. They judged that the latter was the more appropriate way to gauge relative welfare conditions but followed Arrighi (1991: 22–23) to the conclusion that exchange rates provide a better "indicator of the command that different countries have over the human and natural resources". However, most users of these estimates are basically concerned with the distribution of welfare and, by implication, access to locally available resources at domestic prices—suggesting the use of PPP exchange rates. Thus, as Firebaugh (2003: 37) puts it, "virtually all recent studies of between-nation or global income inequality use income data adjusted for purchasing power parity differences".

Poverty Trends and Patterns

Trends in the incidence of poverty naturally depend on where the poverty line is drawn. Rather than choosing one line, inevitably somewhat arbitrary, we estimate poverty incidence for three different levels: 500, 1,000, and 1,500 1985 international dollars (annually). We diverge from the standard $1 and $2-a-day poverty lines partly because ours are income-based poverty lines, in contrast to the consumption-based approach used by the World Bank and United Nations. Given average national levels of private consumption relative to total income, the $1-a-day (or $365 a year) consumption-based poverty line is likely to be fairly close to our $500 income poverty line.[19] In effect, then, our $500 and $1,000 poverty lines can be considered roughly comparable to those

$1 and $2-a-day consumption lines. Persons with income below $500 can be reasonably considered extremely poor, those with income of $500 or greater but less then $1,000, very poor; and those with income of $1,000 or greater but less than $1,500, moderately poor.

For the world as a whole, it is noteworthy that poverty, when measured by the 500-international-dollar poverty line, continued to decline rapidly during the 1980s, but the pace slackened markedly in the 1990s (Table 4.7). During the 1980s, the share of people below this line fell sharply in East Asia, mainly reflecting the growth of China, and also in South Asia, while remaining about constant in Africa (Table 4.8). In the 1990s, though it had already been lowered considerably, poverty by this definition was again roughly halved in East Asia. However, the rate of improvement fell sharply in South Asia due to increasing inequality in India (although per capita income growth increased slightly) and the fact that income groups were much less clustered close to that line than previously. Poverty incidence again held about constant in sub-Saharan Africa. Thus, these two decades saw modest poverty reduction (by this definition) in the world outside China, and very little indeed in the world outside China and India—from 12.1 in 1980 to 10.1 in 2000. In both these latter two cases, there was some reduction in the 1980s, followed by a loss of ground in the 1990s.

The distinction between the 1980s and the 1990s is dramatically different when the poverty line is set at $1,000. For the world as a whole and for the world minus China, the percentage point decline was greater in the 1990s and substantial in absolute terms (Table 4.7). For the world outside China and India, there was only a very marginal decline in each decade. This reflects the fact that in South Asia (and, more particularly, India), the worsening distribution of income that muted the effect of rising overall income for the lowest income groups had a less dramatic effect in this intermediate range, as well as the fact that fewer income classes were located near that poverty line in 1980 than in 1990.[20] Through both decades, the Middle East continued to record moderate declines in poverty, but in South and Central America, the retrogression of the 1980s was not erased in the 1990s (Table 4.8).

At the higher poverty line of $1,500 the pattern is again different. Poverty, by that definition, changes moderately for the world as a whole, only a little when China is excluded, and almost immeasurably over the two decades when both China and India are excluded. In terms of the regional distribution, only East Asia and the Middle East record large declines in poverty defined by this line, while South Asia recorded a moderate decline, and Africa, surprisingly, a modest decline as well. However, increasing proportions of the Eastern European and the South and Central American populations fell below that level over the two decades.

TABLE 4.7
World poverty incidence (alternative poverty lines, 1980–2000)

International poverty lines (in fixed 1985 international dollars)	% of total world population		
	1980	1990	2000
The World			
Income groups with average income of < $500	25.7	14.6	12.1
Income groups with average income of < $1000	53.8	43.6	28.5
Income groups with average income of < $1500	60.5	54.1	44.8
The World without China			
Income groups with average income of < $500	18.6	12.6	12.2
Income groups with average income of < $1000	40.4	35.9	27.1
Income groups with average income of < $1500	46.9	45.8	42.2
The World without China and India			
Income groups with average income of < $500	12.1	9.0	10.1
Income groups with average income of < $1000	26.7	24.4	20.2
Income groups with average income of < $1500	32.8	32.3	31.4
The World without Eastern Europe			
Income groups with average income of < $500	27.4	15.4	12.8
Income groups with average income of < $1000	57.3	46.2	29.7
Income groups with average income of < $1500	64.5	57.3	46.9

Sources: Authors' calculations using data from the WDI (World Bank), UN Common Database (UN), Penn World Tables—Mark 5.6 (CIC) and WIID (WIDER).

TABLE 4.8
Rates of poverty by region

Regions	Poverty lines (in 1985 international dollars)								
	$500			$1000			$1500		
	1980	1990	2000	1980	1990	2000	1980	1990	2000
Sub-Saharan Africa	56.9	57.5	58.0	74.8	75.3	71.4	85.2	85.8	80.8
East Asia	36.8	15.3	7.6	73.8	53.3	27.6	82.6	66.4	46.9
Eastern Europe & Central Asia	0.0	0.0	0.0	0.0	0.0	4.2	0.0	0.0	4.2
Middle East	3.3	3.1	0.0	30.2	20.0	13.2	40.4	29.8	23.1
North America	0.0	0.0	0.0	4.2	4.6	0.0	4.2	4.6	4.8
South Asia	36.1	21.3	20.0	80.0	67.5	46.0	88.0	81.0	72.1
South and Central America	0.0	0.0	0.0	15.4	17.3	17.3	21.8	31.6	32.8
Western Europe	0.0	0.0	0.0	2.7	0.0	0.0	5.4	3.2	0.0

Sources:Authors' calculations using data from the WDI (World Bank), UN Common Database (UN), Penn World Tables—Mark 5.6 (CIC) and WIID (WIDER).

The two regions with the largest poor populations in 1980 have been reducing poverty rapidly, while the third one has been going in the opposite direction. The net positive outcome—a significant decline in world poverty incidence— seems to have run out in the 1990s. An improvement on the performance of that decade, in particular in sub-Saharan Africa, and more equitable growth in South Asia will be necessary for poverty reduction to regain the momentum of the earlier decades.

SUMMARY AND CONCLUSIONS

In the light of divergent income trends across other regions, rapid and sustained expansion of the Chinese economy, and the more moderate, but consistent growth in India was critical to the modest expansion of the world economy during the 1980s and 1990s. World inequality among persons fell during both the 1980s and the 1990s, according to all of our indicators—marginally according to some (including the Gini coefficient) and more markedly according to others (including the Theil coefficient). Income share was transferred from the upper middle deciles seven to nine to the top decile and the bottom six. This outcome can be seen as the net result of two offsetting trends: falling intercountry inequality and rising intracountry inequality in wealthier countries and some of the developing ones (most prominently China). In fact, the observed improvement in the distribution of world income can be attributed entirely to the fact that the lessening of income gaps between countries was sufficient to offset the rising inequality within countries. As a result, the world's poor were, generally speaking, substantially better off in 2000 than in 1980 and, accordingly, world poverty incidence continued its long downward trend. The rate of poverty reduction (in the world as a whole) was brisk in the 1980s, continuing the pattern of the 1960s and 1970s, as East and South Asia (the home of the majority of the world's poor) expanded at a significantly faster rate than the rest of the world. However, despite continued growth in these regions in the 1990s, we see that increasing intracountry inequality (particularly in China and India) and the fact the most of the remaining poor had incomes well below the poverty line, combined with increasing poverty in Africa, led to a near cessation in the reduction of extreme poverty globally.

It might be argued that the overall pattern of world income distribution over the period 1980–2000 was one of convergence; but with such a finding resting largely on the performance of a single country (China), its meaning would be open to question. When India is excluded along with China, the pattern is unmistakably one of divergence. In the world outside those two countries, overall per capita economic growth fell by close to 50 per cent in each successive decade after the 1970s, the distribution of income became markedly more unequal and poverty levels were roughly unchanged. Thus, the two decades spanning the period 1980 to 2000 can be described as manifesting strong pressures towards divergence, offset plus a little by the rapid growth of the two largest low-income countries. In short, these two countries can be considered to have rescued the world from a dismal overall performance, on the equality front, in the closing decades of the twentieth century.

NOTES

[1] Poverty is defined here by per capita income of the family to which a person belongs, with the income data for each country converted to a common base (international dollars) in such a way as to imply that the poverty line involves the same 'purchasing power' in each country. The many methodological and data difficulties confronted in trying to achieve this goal are discussed below.

[2] Estimates by Bourguignon and Morrisson (2002) go only as far back as 1820, though Lindert and Williamson (2001) suspect that the widening may have been occurring for some time before that point.

[3] A more technical interpretation is that countries with different rates of accumulation are evolving to different steady states, and thus, convergence is *conditioned* on the steady state.

[4] Though China was also a low-income country through most of that period, it had graduated to the lower-middle income category by 2000 and is thus included in that group for these calculations.

[5] The Atkinson coefficients are implied welfare-based measures of inequality. As the number shown in brackets increases, income transfers near the bottom of the distribution have a stronger effect on the inequality measure. See Berry and Serieux (2005: Appendix C) for a more detailed description of these measures.

[6] Because this analysis excludes the effect of changes in intracountry distributions, it overstates the positive effect of China's rapid growth on world income distribution among persons, since the distribution of income within China was deteriorating during these periods.

[7] By our definition, those with populations of over 25 million.

[8] Gini coefficient estimates are considered comparable if they derive from similar enumeration and measurement approaches. Thus, income distribution estimates that use households as the enumeration and income as the measurement unit are not compatible with those that use persons as the enumeration unit or those that use expenditure as the measurement unit.

[9] Since very few countries have annual measurements of income inequality, the end/beginning of decade inequality measures had to be approximated in most instances from years close to the beginning or end of the decade. Thus, the 1980 distribution was often approximated by an estimate from the period 1978–1983; the 1990 distribution from measures from the period 1988–1992; and the 2000 estimate from the latest distribution beyond 1995.

[10] The methodology involved in including within-country income in our estimates is detailed further in Berry and Serieux (2005: Appendix C).

[11] One distribution is said to Lorenz dominate another one if the Lorenz curve corresponding to the former lies nowhere below and is at least sometimes above the Lorenz curve corresponding to the other distribution.

[12] In effect, these income groups consist largely of small, upper middle-income countries

and the middle classes of the large, upper middle-income countries, together with the lower income groups of the large wealthy countries.

[13] Altimir (1987) re-estimated inequality in several Latin American countries using plausible assumptions about the level and distribution of capital income; the adjusted Gini coefficients were typically 2–6 Gini points higher.

[14] It is also the case that the bias due to under-coverage of capital incomes in individual countries might have very little reflection at the global level if the problem mainly characterized middle-income countries—not impossible since data accuracy is generally higher in rich countries and the capital share itself may be lower in poor countries, in which case the biasing impact of its being underreported would also be muted.

[15] The list would include the possibility that inclusion of public goods would change the observed patterns of inequality change, that improvements to household surveys are making them more accurate as time goes on and that this leads to observed trends being different from actual trends, changes in the distorting effects of the way PPP conversion is carried out, and so on.

[16] Early important case studies were those of Selowsky (1979) for Colombia, and Meerman (1977) for Malaysia. For no country, to our knowledge, has an attempt been made to include public goods in the estimates of inequality on a continuing basis such as to allow one to see how their inclusion affects trends in inequality.

[17] Thus "The average income in the richest 20 countries is 37 times the average in the poorest 20—a gap that has doubled in the past 40 years" (International Monetary Fund, 2000: 50, cited in Firebaugh, 2003: 18).

[18] Although there are tricky issues within the broad PPP approach (see Milanovic, 2005; Dowrick and Akmal, 2001; Dowrick and Quiggin, 1997; and others), these appear to matter much less to most results than does the choice of any variant of this general approach as opposed to official exchange rates.

[19] Direct translation from consumption to income using the national average ratio between these two variables gives about $540 per year, but this would be an overestimate because people with lower incomes generally tend to consume a higher share of their income than do those with higher incomes.

[20] Essentially because some of the income groups in the upper part of this range in 1990 were less adversely affected by the worsening income distribution.

REFERENCES

Altimir, Oscar (1987). Income distribution statistics in Latin America and their reliability. *Review of Income and Wealth* 33 (2): 111–55.
Arrighi, Giovanni (1991). World income inequalities and the future of socialism. *New Left Review* 189: 39–65.
Arrighi, Giovanni (2002). The African Crisis: World Systemic and Regional Aspects. *New Left Review* 15 (May–June): 5–36.
Bairoch, Paul (1997). *Victoires et deboires. Histoire economique et sociale du monde de XVIe siecle a nos jours.* 3 volumes. Folio Histoire Gallimard, Paris.
Barro, Robert (1991). Economic growth in a cross section of countries. *Quarterly Journal of Economics* 106: 407–43.
Barro, Robert, and Xavier Sala-i-Martin (1992). Convergence. *Journal of Political Economy* 100: 223–51.
Ben-David, Dan (1993). Equalizing exchange: Trade liberalization and convergence. *Quarterly Journal of Economics* 108: 653–79.
Berry, Albert, Francois Bourguignon and Christian Morrisson (1983). Changes in the World

Distribution of Income Between 1950 and 1977. *Economic Journal* 93 (37): 331–50.

Berry, Albert, Francois Bourguignon and Christian Morrisson (1991). Global Economic Inequality and its Trends Since 1950. In Lars Osberg (ed.). *Readings on Economic Inequality.* M.E. Sharpe, New York.

Berry, Albert, and John Serieux (2005). Riding The Elephants: The evolution of world economic growth and income distribution at the end of the 20th century (1980–2000). UN/DESA Working Paper, Department of Economic and Social Affairs, United Nations, New York.

Berry, Albert, and Frances Stewart (1997). Market Liberalization and Income Distribution: the Experience of the 1980s. In Roy Culpeper, Albert Berry and Frances Stewart (eds). *Bretton-Woods: 50 Years Later.* Macmillan, London.

Bhalla, Surjit (2002). *Imagine there's no country: Globalization and its Consequences for Poverty, Inequality and Growth.* Institute for International Economics, Washington, DC.

Bliss, Christopher (1989). Trade and Development. In Hollis Chenery and T.N. Srinivasan (eds). *Handbook of Development Economics*, Volume 2. North Holland, Amsterdam.

Bound, J., and G. Johnson (1992). Changes in the Structure of Wages in the 1980s: An Evaluation and Alternative Explanations. *American Economic Review* 82 (3): 371–92.

Bourguignon, Francois, and Christian Morrisson (2002). Inequality among World Citizens, 1820–1992. *American Economic Review* 92 (4): 727–44.

Castells, Manuel (1993). The informational economy and the new international division of labor. In Martin Carnoy, Manuel Castells, Stephen S. Cohen and Jorge Enrique Cardoso (eds). *The new global economy in the information age.* Pennsylvania State University, University Park.

Cornia, Giovanni Andrea (ed.) (2004). *Inequality, growth, and poverty in an era of liberalization and globalization.* Oxford University Press, New York.

Corry, D., and Andrew Glyn (1994). Macroeconomics of equality, stability and growth. In Andrew Glyn and David Miliband (eds). *Paying for Inequality: The Economic Cost of Social Injustice.* IPPR/Rivers Oram Press, London: 1–23.

de Ferranti, David, Guillermo Perry, Francisco H. G. Ferreira and Michael Walton (2004). *Inequality in Latin America: Breaking with history?* Latin American and Caribbean Studies, World Bank, Washington, DC.

Dowrick, Steve, and Muhammed Akmal (2001). Contradictory Trends in Global Income Inequality: A Tale of Two Biases. Processed: Ecocomm.anu.edu.au/economics/staff/dowrick/dowrick.html

Dowrick, Steve, and J. Quiggin (1997). True measures of GDP and convergence. *American Economic Review* 87 (1): 332–41.

Easterly, William (2001). The Lost Decades: Developing Countries' Stagnation in Spite of Policy Reform, 1980–98. *Journal of Economic Growth* 6 (2): 135–57.

Evans, David (1989). Alternative Perspectives on Trade and Development. In Hollis Chenery and T.N. Srinivasan (eds). *Handbook of Development Economics.* Volume 2. North Holland, Amsterdam: 1241–1304.

Firebaugh, Glenn (2003). *The New Geography of Global Income Inequality.* Harvard University Press, Cambridge, MA.

Galbraith, James K. (2002). A Perfect Crime: Inequality in the Age of Globalization. *Daedalus* (Winter): 11–25.

International Monetary Fund (2000). How we can help the poor: Introduction. *Finance and Development* 37 (4): 2.

Korzeniewicz, R., and T. Moran (1997). World Economic Trends in the Distribution of Income, 1965–1992. *American Journal of Sociology* 102 (4): 1000–1039.

Kuznets, Simon (1955). Economic Growth and Income Inequality. *The American Economic Review* 45 (1): 1–28.

Lindert, Peter, and Jeffrey Williamson (2001). Does Globalization Make the World More

Unequal, *NBER Working Papers: 8228*. National Bureau of Economic Research, Cambridge, MA.

Mankiw, Gregory, David Romer and David Weil (1992). A Contribution to the Empirics of Economic Growth. *Quarterly Journal of Economics* 107 (2): 407–37.

Meerman, Jacob (1977). *The distribution of public expenditure for education and agriculture in Malaysia: Methodological issues and a new approach.* Oxford University Press, New York, for the World Bank, Washington, DC.

Milanovic, Branko (2002). True world income distribution, 1988 and 1993: First calculations based on household surveys alone. *Economic Journal* 112 (476): 51–92.

Milanovic, Branko (2005). *Worlds Apart.* Princeton University Press, Princeton, NJ.

Peacock, Walter G., Greg A. Hoover and Charles D. Killian (1988). Divergence and Convergence in International Development: A Decomposition Analysis of Inequality in the World System. *American Sociological Review* 53: 838–52.

Penn World Tables (PWT). Mark 5.6, University of Pennsylvania, Philadelphia PA: Center of International Comparisons.

Pritchett, Lant (1995). Divergence Big Time. Policy Research Working Paper No. 1522, World Bank, Washington, DC.

Robbins, D. (1996). Evidence on Trade and Wages in the Developing World. Technical Paper No. 119, December, OECD Development Centre, Paris.

Sala-i-Martin, Xavier (2002). The Disturbing 'Rise' of Global Income Inequality. NBER working paper no. 8904, National Bureau of Economic Research, Cambridge, MA.

Schultz, T. Paul (1998). Inequality in the distribution of personal income in the world: How is it changing and why? *Journal of Population Economics* 11 (3): 307–44.

Selowsky, Marcelo (1979). *Who benefits from government expenditure? A case study of Colombia.* Oxford University Press, New York, for the World Bank, Washington, DC.

Solow, Robert (1957). Technical Progress and the Aggregate Production Function. *Review of Economics and Statistics*, 39 (3): 312–20.

United Nations common database (UNCDB), New York, NY: United Nations Statistic Division. URL: http://unstats.un.org/unsd/cdb/cdb_help/cdb_quick_start.asp

UNCTAD (1997). *Trade and Development Report 1997: Globalisation, Distribution and Growth.* United Nations Conference on Trade and Development, Geneva.

UNDP (1999). *Human Development Report 1999.* Oxford University Press, New York, for the United Nations Development Programme, New York.

WIDER, World Income Inequality Database (WIID), Helsinki: United Nations University, World Institute for Development Economics Research, URL: http://www.wider.unu.edu/wiid/wiid.htm

Whalley, John (1979). The Worldwide Income Distributions: Some Speculative Calculations *Review of Income and Wealth* 25 (3): 261–76.

Wood, Adrian (1994). *North-South Trade, Employment and Inequality.* Oxford; Clarendon Press.

World Bank, World Development Indicators (WDI)—Online Version. Washington DC. http://publications.worldbank.org/register/WDI

5

Globalizing Inequality:
'Centrifugal' and 'Centripetal' Forces at Work[1]

JOSÉ GABRIEL PALMA[2]

"For unto every one that hath shall be given,
and he shall have abundance;
but from him that hath not shall be taken away,
even that which he hath."

Matthew 25:29

One of the main stylized facts of the era of globalization is that a remarkable increase in the levels of international trade has been associated in most countries with a significant deterioration of income distribution. This trend towards greater inequality at a time of a generalized increase in trade is far from the predictions of Samuelson's 1950s trade-related factor price equalization theorem. For him, an increase in trade would improve both the national and international distributions of income. This should happen because export expansion would increase the relative income of the (cheap) abundant factor and reduce that of the (expensive) scarce factor in each country. In fact, of all Samuelson's economic hypotheses, there is probably none that influences the foreign policy of the United States of America today as much as the one that postulates that increased trade between two countries should reduce the incentive for labour to move across frontiers. In the case of the US relationship with Mexico, for example, following the 1982 'debt crisis', the US—always frightened that worsening economic problems in Mexico could turn the flow of Mexican immigrants into a tidal wave—gave Mexican exports increasingly preferential access to its market, a process that led to the creation of the North American Free Trade Agreement (NAFTA).[3]

Therefore, the issues addressed by Samuelson as far back as the 1950s are still some of the most contested hypotheses in the debate on the effects that the globalization-induced increase in trade would have on national and international factor movements and income distribution.[4] As is well known, one major problem with this (or any other) debate on income distribution has been the difficulty of testing alternative hypotheses, especially time series formulations, due to the low quality of available income distribution data. However, household survey data have recently substantially improved allowing at least some robust testing of cross-sectional hypotheses. At the same time, some institutions—like the Organization for Economic Cooperation and Development (OECD) and the World Bank (WB)—have made sustained efforts to collect and process these surveys.[5] The relevant WB publication, for example, now provides a relatively homogeneous set of data on personal income distribution for 112 countries (World Bank, WDI, 2004). However, there are still some significant problems with the World Development Indicators data set. For example, although most data refer to income distribution, some still refer to consumption expenditure (particularly in Sub-Saharan Africa). This mix of data makes regional comparison more difficult, as the distribution of consumption tends to be more equal than the distribution of income (usually by a difference of about three percentage points on the Gini scale). The accuracy of these surveys is also still a problem.[6]

Another problem is that, rather surprisingly, the WDI data set still reports income (or consumption) distribution only in terms of quintiles; for deciles, it only reports the shares of deciles 1 and 10. Although this is a marked improvement over the WB's earlier Deininger and Squire (D/S) data set (Deininger and Squire, 1996)—which does not report data for a single income decile—it is clearly unsatisfactory. As will be discussed in detail below, crucial distributional information is lost when data are aggregated in quintiles (particularly in the top one). Meanwhile, the Research Department of the Inter-American Development Bank (IADB) has constructed a slightly more up-to-date income distribution data set for several Latin American countries; it uses the same methodology (primary household survey data) and data aggregation (quintiles and deciles 1 and 10) as the WDI (Székely and Hilgert, 1999b).

The main aim of this chapter is to use these new WB and IADB data sets to take another look at national income inequalities in this era of globalization. Throughout this chapter, unless otherwise stated, the IADB data set will be used for Latin America, and the WDI for the rest of the world. The total number of countries included in this study is 109.[7]

INEQUALITY RANKING

Figure 5.1 illustrates how these 109 countries are ranked according to their Gini indices of inequality in the second half of the 1990s. Of the many issues emerging from this graph, two stand out. First, in the second half of the 1990s, there was a particularly wide range of inequality across countries—from a very

FIGURE 5.1

Most recent data on Gini indices of personal income distribution in 109 countries

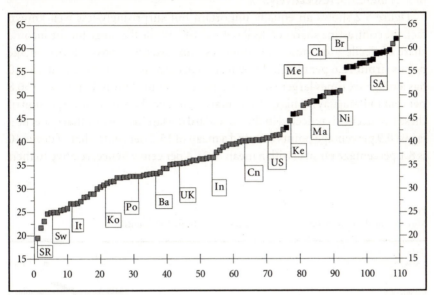

Notes: Countries are ranked according to their degree of inequality (1 to 109); Latin American countries are shown in black (this will also be the case in similar graphs below). Throughout this chapter, Gini indices are reported on a scale from 1 to 100.

Br = Brazil; Ch = Chile; Me = Mexico; SA = South Africa; Ni = Nigeria; Ma = Malaysia; Ke = Kenya; US = United States; Cn = China; In = India; UK = United Kingdom; Ba = Bangladesh; Po = Poland; Ko = Republic of Korea; It = Italy; Sw = Sweden; and SR = Slovak Republic.

Sources: World Bank, 2004.

low Gini index of 19.5 per cent (Slovak Republic) to a high of 62.3 per cent (Paraguay). Second, all Latin American countries were clearly grouped at the very top end of the inequality ranking—with a median Gini of 56.7 per cent and mean of 54.7 per cent. The degree of inequality in Latin America was well over half as much again as the median value for the rest of the sample (92 countries), and more than 40 per cent higher than that for the 'non-Latin American' developing countries (51 countries, excluding OECD and transition economies). In addition, among the 109 countries studied, the median country-inequality ranking for the 17 Latin American countries was 100 (see also UNCTAD, 1996).

There also seemed to be an extraordinary difference between English-speaking and non-English-speaking OECD countries, with the latter including continental Europe and Japan—with median Ginis of 36.0 and 27.1, respectively. The same contrast was found between the ex-communist countries of the former Soviet Union and those of Central Europe—with median Ginis of 34.4 and 27.5, respectively.

Figure 5.2 shows an equally important but surprisingly less well-known fact: the contrasting shares of deciles 9 and 10.[8] While the range for the income share of decile 9 in these 109 countries only extends across 5.6 percentage points (from 12.6 per cent in India to 18.8 per cent in South Africa), decile 10 has a range six times larger (from 18.2 per cent in the Slovak Republic to 50.8 per cent in Paraguay). This extraordinary difference between the dispersion of these two deciles is reflected in their standard deviations—while that of decile 9 is just 0.9 percentage points (around a mean of 15.2 per cent), that of decile 10 is 8.1 percentage points (with a mean of 31.4 per cent); hence, relative to their

FIGURE 5.2

Most recent data on income share of deciles 9 and 10 in 109 countries

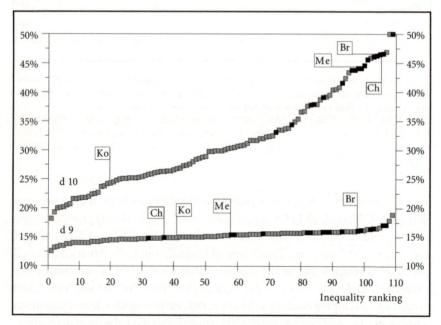

Notes: Each ranking is made independently from the other. Unless otherwise stated, this will be the case for all similar graphs in this chapter.

In this and other graphs below, the data for Brazil, Chile and Mexico will be highlighted, as these are the three Latin American countries that have the worst income distribution in terms of the relationship between income distribution and income per capita (see Figure 5.16 below). Data for the Republic of Korea are shown for comparison.

Br = Brazil; Ch = Chile; Ko = Republic of Korea; Me = Mexico.

Source: World Bank, 2004.

own means, the standard deviation of decile 10 is more than four times larger than that of decile 9.

This phenomenon is also corroborated by the fact that while the median values for the share of decile 9 in the Latin American and non-Latin American groups are quite similar (15.9 per cent and 15.4 per cent, respectively), those for decile 10 are very different, with the Latin American share more than half as much again as the median value for the rest of the sample (44.1 per cent and 28.4 per cent, respectively). In other words, one of the key elements (if not the key one) needed to understand the effects of globalization on national income distribution is the impact it has on the share of decile 10.[9]

Figures 5.3 and 5.4 indicate that the key characteristic of the income distribution of most Latin American countries is its shift towards a 'winner

FIGURE 5.3
Chile: income shares of deciles 9 and 10, 1957–99

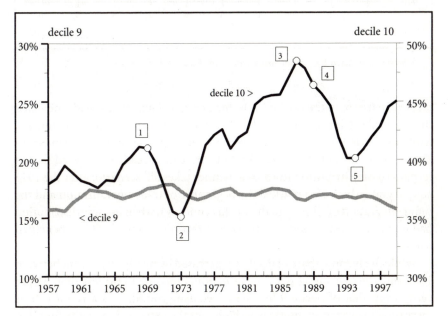

Notes: Three-year moving averages. [1] = election of President Allende; [2] = Augusto Pinochet's coup d'état; [3] = the year before President Pinochet's plebiscite (seeking a mandate to remain in power for another 8 years); [4] = first democratic government (centre-left coalition) after President Pinochet lost his plebiscite (and had to call for presidential elections); [5] = second democratic government (same political coalition, but a return to 'market-led' distributed policies). Decile 9 is shown on the left-hand axis, and decile 10 on the right-hand one.
Source: Ruiz-Tagle (2000). Unless otherwise stated, this is the source of all historical data for Chile.[10]

FIGURE 5.4
Chile: changes in income shares (%), 1972–1987

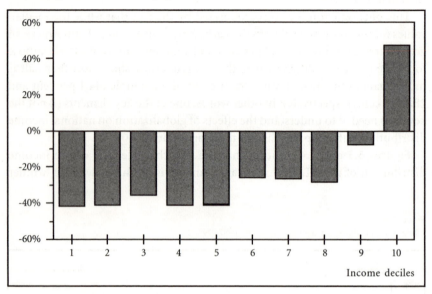

Source: Constructed by Author using data from Ruiz-Tagle (2000).

takes all' pattern. In the case of Chile, for example, Figure 5.2 already indicated that its decile 10 is ranked as the 104th most unequal among the 109 countries, while its decile 9 is only ranked 38th (its ranking is even better than South Korea's!). In turn, Figures 5.3 and 5.4 illustrate the already mentioned shift in its pattern of distribution towards a 'winner takes all' scenario: after the 1973 coup d'état (which also marked the beginning of trade liberalization and the rapid integration of Chile into the world economy), when income distribution had one of the fastest deteriorations ever recorded, only decile 10 benefited from it.

While the income share of decile 10 increased by nearly 50 per cent between 1972 and 1987 (from 34 per cent of national income to no less than 51 per cent), even that of decile 9 lost some relative ground.[11] As a result of this increasing polarization, one way to highlight the extreme inequality found in Latin America is to look at the ratio of the income shares of deciles 10 and 1.[12]

Figure 5.5 shows that there is a significant difference even between the ratios of deciles 10 to 1 and that of deciles 9 to 2. However, the huge difference is principally due to the last third of the sample—mainly comprising Latin American and Sub-Saharan African countries. The resulting ranges for both rankings are very different: while the ratio of deciles 10 to 1 ranges

FIGURE 5.5
Ratio of income shares of deciles 10 to 1, and 9 to 2, in 109 countries

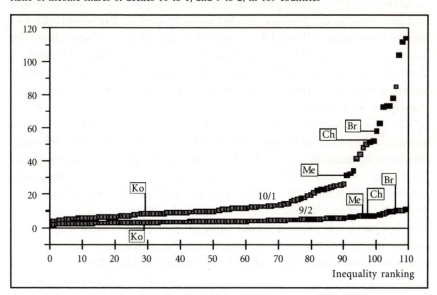

Notes: Br = Brazil; Ch = Chile; Ko = Republic of Korea; Me = Mexico.
Sources: World Bank, 2004; Székely and Hilgert, 1999b.

from 3.6 to 114, that of deciles 9 to 2 only extends from 1.9 to 10.9.[13]

Of the more straightforward statistics for measuring inequality, this probably best reflects the degree of income inequality found in Latin America, and the extraordinary degree of income polarization in the region. At a median value of 58.1, the Latin American ratio is 4.7 times the median value for the 51 non-Latin American developing countries, and more than 6 times the median value for the 92 non-Latin American countries in the sample (9.6). The statistics also differentiate most Latin American inequality from that of Sub-Saharan Africa (the latter's median value, at 19.3, is only one third that for Latin America).

Latin America's greater inequality, vis-à-vis other regions of the world, decreases rapidly for income groups closer to the middle of the distribution, i.e., between deciles 8 and 3. Yet, many theories purporting to explain Latin America's greater inequality refer to phenomena in the middle of the distribution, e.g., the import-substituting industrialization-related 'labour aristocracy' hypothesis of the 1960s, and the trade liberalization-related 'asymmetric demand for labour' proposition of the 1990s.

The first hypothesis, widely invoked during the 1960s and 1970s, particularly by those connected with the World Bank, argued that one of the main causes of inequality in Latin America during that period was the price distortions associated with import-substituting industrialization (ISI). These distorted the values of sectoral marginal productivities, causing artificially higher real wages in manufacturing, i.e., producing higher wage differentials than would otherwise exist in the economy (World Bank, 1987; Krueger, 1983). However, there was little then (as now) to differentiate Latin America from the rest of the world—developing and developed, ISI and non-ISI—in terms of the income distribution among groups that would include 'aristocratic' and non-'aristocratic' labour (say, quintiles 4 to 2, or 3 to 2).

The second proposition basically recycled the 'labour-aristocracy' hypothesis to explain the increased inequality in many Latin American countries following trade and financial liberalization. This increase in inequality, following greater integration into the world economy, contrasts not only with Samuelson's original expectations but also with the predictions of the 'Washington Consensus' before the implementation of these reforms (Lal, 1983). Hence, it is now argued that this previously unforeseen development took place because trade liberalization introduced new production techniques requiring more skilled workers, thus increasing wage differentials.[14] However, as is obvious from the previous graphs and Table 5.1, Latin American income inequality has been distinguished at the poles of the income distribution—hardly where either skilled or unskilled members of the formal labour force are located. Therefore, even if trade liberali-

TABLE 5.1
Regional median values for different income ratios

	d10/d1	d9/d2	q4/q2	q3/q2
Latin America	58.1	7.0	2.7	1.6
Non-LA Dev. Ctries	12.5	3.9	2.0	1.4
Sub-Saharan Africa	19.3	4.8	2.1	1.4
East Asia-2	15.9	5.1	2.3	1.5
Caribbean	13.8	4.3	2.1	1.4
OECD-2	11.8	4.0	2.0	1.4
North Africa	9.6	3.8	2.0	1.4
Ex-communist-2	9.6	3.7	1.9	1.4
South Asia	8.3	3.3	1.8	1.3
Ex-communist-1	6.2	2.8	1.7	1.3
East Asia-1	8.4	3.3	1.8	1.3
OECD-1	6.0	2.7	1.6	1.3
All	11.6	3.9	2.0	1.4
Developing Countries	14.2	4.7	2.2	1.5

Notes: Regions as in Appendix 5.1. Non-LA Dev. Ctries = non-Latin American developing countries (51 countries); d10/d1 = ratio of deciles 10 to 1; d9/d2 = ratio of deciles 9 to 2; q4/q2 = ratio of quintiles 4 to 2; and q3/q2 = ratio of quintiles 3 to 2.
Sources: World Bank, 2004; Székely and Hilgert, 1999b.

FIGURE 5.6
Chile: ratio of income shares of deciles 10 to 1, 9 to 2, and 5 to 3, 1957–1999

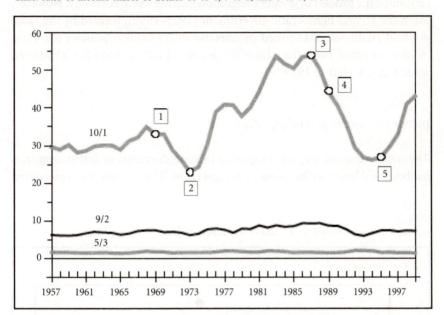

Notes: Three-year moving averages. [1] = election of President Allende; [2] = Augusto Pinochet's coup d'état; [3] = the year before President Pinochet's plebiscite (seeking a mandate to remain in power for another 8 years); [4] = first democratic government (centre-left coalition) after President Pinochet lost his plebiscite (and had to call for proper presidential elections); [5] = second democratic government (same political coalition).
Source: Ruiz-Tagle (2000).

zation introduced new production techniques with 'asymmetrical labour demand', it is unlikely that this would account for much of the region's increased income inequality; the case of Chile provides a good example of this.

Even though Chile implemented one of the most radical trade liberalization policies in the developing world, and in spite of the fact that this policy has now been in place for more than three decades, it seems to have had little effect on the relative income distribution between skilled and unskilled members of the formal labour force (proxied in Figure 5.6 by the ratio of deciles 9 to 2 and 5 to 3). This graph suggests that massive political upheavals, radical economic reforms and greater integration into the world economy have had significant effects at the extreme ends of the income distribution, but little effect in between.

The Chilean experience also indicates that 'policy matters'. Income distribution did improve significantly with the progressive distribution policies of the first post-Pinochet democratic government (1989–1993), even though it continued the process of greater integration into the world economy. However, when the second democratic government (1993–1999), formed by the same political coalition, abandoned progressive distributional policies for more 'market-oriented' ones, the ratio of deciles 10 to 1 returned to what it had been when Pinochet left in 1989.

INCOME INEQUALITY AND INCOME PER CAPITA

The most common way of comparing income distribution across countries has been in relation to the income per capita level. This approach was pioneered

FIGURE 5.7
Regional Gini indices and log of income per capita

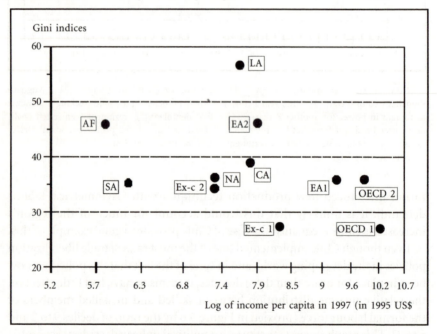

Notes: Regional figures are median values. LA = Latin America; AF = Sub-Saharan Africa; EA1 = 'first-tier' NICs; EA2 = 'second-tier' NICs; SA = large South Asia and low-income Southeast Asia; NA = North Africa; CA = Caribbean countries; OECD 1 = non-English-speaking OECD; OECD 2 = English-speaking OECD; Ex-C 1 = ex-communist countries of Central Europe; Ex-C 2 = ex-communist countries of the former Soviet Union. For countries within each region, see Appendix 5.1.
Sources: World Bank, 2004.

by Kuznets (1955) and has dominated distributional debates ever since. Figure 5.7 shows the regional averages for the whole sample.[15] The graph suggests four 'layers' of inequality across countries. First, a more equal layer containing the ex-communist countries of Central Europe and the non-Anglophone OECD; a second layer containing a great variety of regions, with more than three-quarters of the world's population; a third one including only Sub-Saharan Africa and the 'second-tier' newly industrialized countries (NICs) (East Asia '2'); and fourth, Latin America, with inequality well above every other region in the world, including those with similar income per capita, like North Africa, East Asia '2' and the Caribbean.

However, as discussed above, it is also important to look 'inside' the Gini ratio. As might have been expected, Figure 5.8 shows a particularly close correlation between regional Ginis and the income shares of decile 10. Of course, this strong correlation is the result of the way the Gini index is calculated.

Figure 5.9 shows the regional distribution pattern for deciles 1 to 4 mirroring that for decile 10. Therefore, the Ginis for regional inequality are reflected both at the very top and at the bottom of the distribution of income for the regions. However, when one looks in Figure 5.10 at the remaining 50 per cent of the

FIGURE 5.8
Regional income shares of decile 10 and log of income per capita

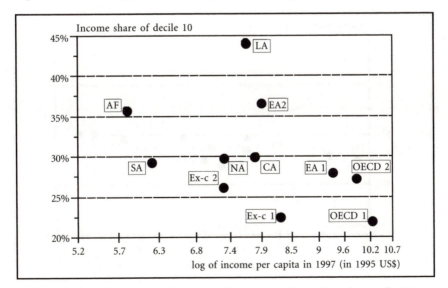

Notes: Regional figures are median values. Regions as in Figure 5.7 and Appendix 5.1.
Source: World Bank, 2004.

FIGURE 5.9
Regional income shares of deciles 1 to 4 and log of income per capita

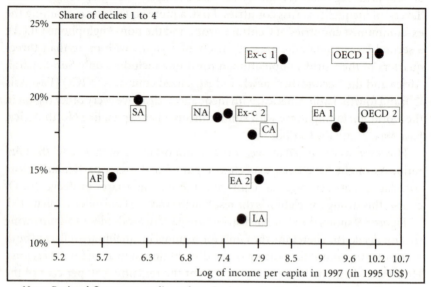

Notes: Regional figures are median values. Regions as in Figure 5.7 and Appendix 5.1.
Source: World Bank, 2004.

FIGURE 5.10
Regional income shares of deciles 5 to 9 and log of income per capita

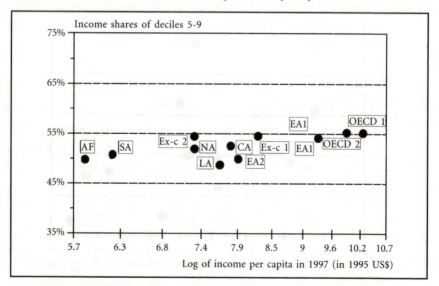

Notes: Regional figures are median values. Regions as in Figure 5.7 and Appendix 5.1.
Source: World Bank, 2004.

FIGURE 5.11
Regional income shares of deciles 7 to 9 and log of income per capita

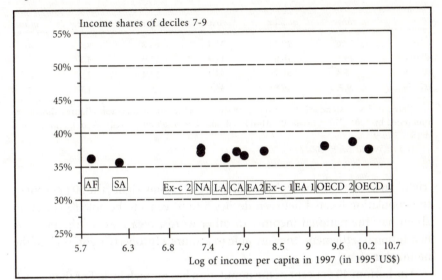

Notes: Regional figures are median values. Regions as in Figure 5.7 and Appendix 5.1.
Source: World Bank, 2004.

population, the 'middle classes' (sometimes also called the 'administrative classes' in institutional economics) located between deciles 5 to 9, the regional distributional picture changes from one of huge variation to remarkable similarity. This similarity is even more surprising for the 'upper middle' 30 per cent of the population (deciles 7, 8 and 9), as shown in Figure 5.11.

Table 5.2 presents statistics for the whole sample, emphasizing the remarkable contrast between the distributional heterogeneity at the top and bottom of the income distribution and the homogeneity in the middle. Of all the statistics in Table 5.2, the coefficient of variation best shows this distributional contrast—the figures for both decile 10 and deciles 1 to 4 are nearly four times greater than those for deciles 5 to 9. Furthermore, they are nearly *seven* times larger than for deciles 7 to 9. The 50 per cent of the population located between deciles 5 to 9 seems to be able to count on about half the national income. This suggests that 'middle classes' across the world, particularly the 'upper middle classes', seem to be able to benefit from a distributional 'safety net', i.e., regardless of the per capita income level of the country, the characteristics of the political regimes, the economic policies implemented, the structure of property rights, or whether or not they belong to countries that managed to get their prices

TABLE 5.2
Measures of centrality and spread for income groups (whole sample)

	range	median	mean	variance	st dev	c of var
d10	32.6	29.4	31.4	64.8	8.1	26
d1-d4	19.8	18.0	17.4	21.9	4.7	27
d5-d9	15.4	51.7	52.4	11.4	3.9	7
d7-d9	9.7	36.8	36.6	2.7	1.7	4

Notes: st dev = standard deviation; c of var = coefficient of variation (figures shown are multiplied by 100); d10 = decile 10; d1-d4 = deciles 1 to 4; d5-d9 = deciles 5 to 9; and d7-d9 = deciles 7 to 9.
Source: World Bank, 2004.

'right', their institutions 'right', or their social capital 'right', the 50 per cent of the population located between deciles 5 to 9 seems to be able to count on about half the national income. In other words, regardless of the political institutional settlement, they are able to acquire a 'property right' on half the national income.

The bottom 40 per cent of the population has no such luck. For them, such policy and institutional variations make the difference between getting as much as one-quarter of national income (as in the non-English speaking OECD or the ex-communist countries of Central Europe), or as little as 10 per cent (as in Latin America). As far as the top income decile is concerned, the sky is (almost) the limit.

In other words, the regional distributional pattern suggested by the Gini index only reflects the income disparities of *half* the world's population, i.e., those at the very top and at the bottom of the distribution, and does not reflect the distributional homogeneity of the other half. This is a rather important phenomenon from a statistical point of view, raising serious questions about the usefulness of the Gini index as an indicator of overall income inequality. Analytically, economic reforms, trade and financial liberalization, globalization, changing property rights as well as other recent economic and political developments seem to have been associated with two very different distributional dynamics across regions in the world: a (better known) 'centrifugal' one in the income shares of the top and bottom deciles (decile 10 and deciles 1 to 4), and a (lesser known) 'centripetal' movement in the income shares of deciles 5 to 9.

Regional distributional homogeneity in the middle (especially upper-middle) of the distribution casts doubts on the 'human capital' theory of income distribution. According to this theory, the level of education is a crucial—if not *the* most crucial—variable in the determination of income inequality (Neal and Rosen, 2000). However, in all regions of the world (developed and developing, Latin American and non-Latin American), the top income decile is made up of individuals with relatively advanced levels of education, while those in the bottom four deciles have relatively low levels of formal education—either relatively little schooling, or (in the more advanced countries), schooling of rather doubtful quality. So why do these two relatively homogeneously educated groups have such great distributional diversity? In turn, if significant educational diversity is found among the population in deciles 5 to 9—e.g., in terms of the share of the population with secondary and (especially) tertiary education—why does one find such extraordinary *similarity* in the shares of national income of this educationally highly *heterogeneous* group?

Obviously, more research needs to be done on the forces shaping the national income shares of different deciles along such different paths (particularly in such opposite 'centrifugal' and 'centripetal' directions). Remarkably, this simple observation does not seem to have been emphasized before. Also, it seems odd that much of the recent literature on income 'polarization' has produced indices to emphasize distributional changes around the *middle* of the distribution,

FIGURE 5.12
Regional ratios of deciles 10 to 1 and log of income per capita

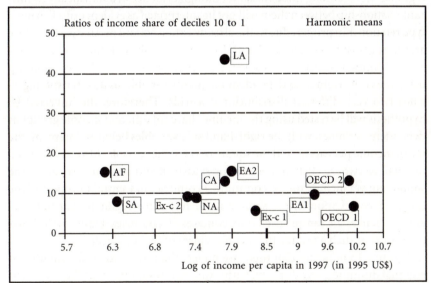

Notes: Regional figures are harmonic means for the ratios of the income share of deciles 10 to 1, and arithmetic means for the log of income per capita. Regions as in Figure 5.7 and Appendix 5.1.

Sources: World Bank, 2004; Székely and Hilgert, 1999b.

where there has, in fact, been far greater distributional homogeneity.[16] In fact, the higher degree of heterogeneity at the very top and bottom of the income distribution makes income ratios, such as those of deciles 10 to 1, highly sensitive statistical indicators of distributional disparities across the world, particularly highlighting Latin America's greater income polarization. From this perspective, Figure 5.12 shows that Latin America seems to be living in a distributional world of its own—as if on a different planet!

Testing for Regional Effects in a Cross-Section Framework

As is well known, the Kuznets 'inverted U' framework is the most commonly used hypothesis for testing the relationship between income inequality and income per capita, both in a time series and in a cross-section framework. However, in doing so, one has to distinguish crucially between two factors: first, whether there is a statistical relationship of this kind between these two variables, and second, how to interpret this relationship analytically; i.e., if the test shows a significant relationship of this kind, the Kuznets 'structural change' hypothesis is just one of several possible interpretations of the nature of this relationship.

Here, I am going to use the traditional econometric specification test for regional effects among these variables, though evidence of a statistically significant relationship between them will not be interpreted as evidence of a Kuznets-type relationship proper, due to the already extensive and persuasive literature arguing against this (Kanbur, 2000). In view of the above finding (of a homogeneous 'middle' versus heterogeneous 'poles'), I shall not test this rela-tionship using the Gini 'average' as dependent inequality variable, as this statistic aggregates two very different distributional worlds. Therefore, the 'inverted U' hypothesis will be tested using the income shares of different income groups as dependent variables, with the right-hand side variables being an intercept, the log of income per capita, and the square of the same variable. Also, as discussed in detail elsewhere (Palma, 2002c), for statistical and analytical reasons, one should not yet include the ex-communist countries of Central Europe and the former Soviet Union in the sample to be tested for regional distributional effects. Hence, the sample used only contains 90 countries. Figure 5.13 shows the results of such a test for the income shares of the top decile.[17]

Figure 5.13 indicates that there are no less than five statistically significant regional dummies: one dummy, Latin America, is significant at the 1 per cent level, and the other four at the 5 per cent level; all other parameters and the F test are significant at the 1 per cent level. The adjusted R^2 is 74 per cent. In fact, the only regions where the dummies were not significant at the 5 per cent level

FIGURE 5.13
Income shares of decile 10 and log of income per capita

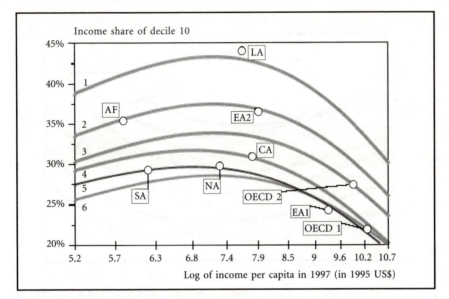

Notes: 1 = the regression with an intercept-dummy for Latin America; 2 = with an intercept-dummy for Sub-Saharan Africa; 3 = base regression; 4 = with a dummy in the square of income per capita variable for the non-English-speaking OECD; 5 = with a dummy on the income per capita variable for South Asia and low-income South East Asia; and 6 = with an intercept-dummy for North Africa.[18]

For the summary statistics of the regressions, see Appendix 5.2.

Regional figures are median values. Regions as in Figure 5.7 and Appendix 5.1.

Source: World Bank, 2004.

were East Asia, the Caribbean and the English-speaking OECD (14 countries in all); therefore, these countries are included in the base regression together with the eight countries not classified in any of these regions (see Appendix 5.1).

Figure 5.14 shows again the converse relationship between the share of the top decile and that of the bottom four deciles. This regression is also highly significant, with all eight parameters (including all five dummies) and the F test significant at the 1 per cent level. The R^2 is 64 per cent.

However, not surprisingly, the regionally homogeneous 'middle' (deciles 5 to 9) shows no significant regional effects for this half of the population. Finally, strong regional effects are again found when an 'inverted U' specification is tested with the ratio of deciles 10 to 1 as the dependent variable, as in Figure 5.15.

Again, this regression is highly significant; four of the dummies are significant at a 1 per cent level, and all other parameters (except for the intercept) are

FIGURE 5.14

Income shares of deciles 1 to 4 and log of income per capita

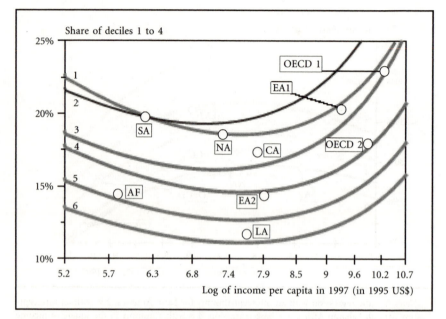

Notes: 1 = the regression with a dummy for North Africa; 2 = with a dummy for South Asia and low-income Southeast Asia; 3 = with a dummy for the non-English-speaking OECD; 4 = base regression; 5 = with a dummy for Sub-Saharan Africa; and 6 = with a dummy for Latin America.

For the summary statistics of the regressions, see Appendix 5.2.

Regional figures are median values. Regions as in Figure 5.7 and Appendix 5.1.

Source: World Bank, 2004.

significant at 5 per cent. The R^2 is 71 per cent. This is the specification of the regional distributional effects, in which the 'excess' degree of Latin American inequality is shown in more extreme form. In general, the Latin American intercept dummies are significant at the 1 per cent level in all three specifications of the dependent variable (decile 10, deciles 1 to 4, and the ratio of deciles 10 to 1). There seems to be particularly strong statistical evidence that towards the end of the 1990s, Latin American countries developed a higher degree of inequality vis-à-vis their middle-income level.[19]

However, as there is no Latin American country with high income per capita, this sample provides no information as to what could happen to this higher inequality as such countries reach higher income levels.[20] Furthermore, as

FIGURE 5.15
Income ratios of deciles 10 to 1 and log of income per capita

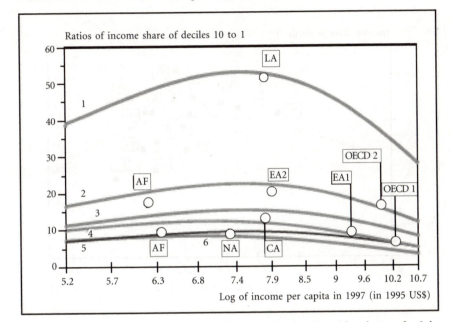

Notes: 1 = the regression with a dummy for Latin America; 2 = with a dummy for Sub-Saharan Africa; 3 = base regression; 4 = with a dummy for the non-English-speaking OECD; 5 = with a dummy for South Asia and low-income Southeast Asia; and 6 = with a dummy for North Africa.

For the summary statistics of the regressions, see Appendix 5.2.

Regional averages in this graph are geometric means for the ratios of the income shares of deciles 10 to 1, and arithmetic means for the log of income per capita. Regions as in Figure 5.7 and Appendix 5.1.

Sources: World Bank, 2004; Székely and Hilgert, 1999b.

Figure 5.16 shows, towards the end of the 1990s, as per capita income increased in Latin America, the distributional dispersion among countries in the region also increased rapidly.

The five countries with the highest per capita incomes in the region— Uruguay, Chile, Brazil, Venezuela and Mexico—have a large range of income shares for decile 10. In fact, the two countries with the highest income per capita, Uruguay and Brazil, have the lowest and the second highest income shares for this decile: 33.1 per cent and 46.5 per cent, respectively. Also, at the end of the 1990s, in Brazil, Chile and Mexico, income inequality was actually growing as per capita income increased, moving therefore in the opposite direction shown by the inverted 'U' curve.

FIGURE 5.16
Latin America (17): income share of decile 10 and log of income per capita

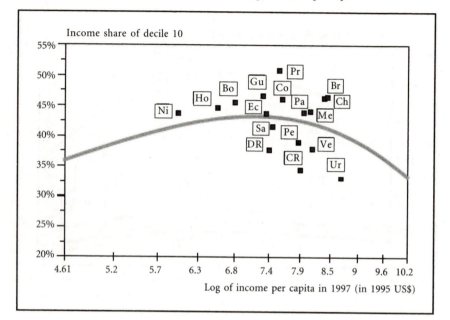

Notes: Ni = Nicaragua; Ho = Honduras; Bo = Bolivia; Gu = Guatemala; Pr = Paraguay; Ec = Ecuador; Sa = El Salvador; Co = Colombia; Pa = Panama; Br = Brazil; Ch = Chile; DR = Dominican Republic; Pe = Peru; Me = Mexico; Ve = Venezuela; CR = Costa Rica; and Ur = Uruguay.

The regression for Latin America is as in Figure 5.13. For summary statistics of this regression, see Appendix 5.2.

Source: World Bank, 2004.

THE MEXICAN EXPERIENCE

A brief analysis of Mexico could help us understand why increased integration into the world economy, after economic reform in general and trade and financial liberalization in particular, has increased the gap between the top and the bottom of the distribution. Although political reform began in Mexico during the presidency of Lopez Portillo (1976–1982), trade liberalization began with President de la Madrid, who took office in the midst of the 1982 debt crisis. Mexico has never looked back in terms of growth of manufacturing exports—in constant US dollar terms, manufactured exports (including those from so-called 'maquila' enterprises) grew from US$8 billion in 1981 to US$150 billion in 2004 (in 2000 US$ values)—a figure similar to South Korea's manufacturing exports. This 19-fold increase (equivalent to an average annual growth rate of 14 per cent) increased the share of manufactures in the country's total goods exports to 80 per cent from less than 10 per cent in 1981.[21]

Even though Mexican history shows that proximity to the US is a mixed blessing at best, as far as goods exports are concerned, few developing countries have such a geographical advantage, augmented by preferential access to the US market (via NAFTA).[22] Nevertheless, even considering the help provided by the related flood of foreign direct investment (FDI),[23] the growth of Mexican manufactured exports in this period has been truly exceptional. Yet, this export expansion has had a far more complex, and weaker, impact than expected on the Mexican economy as a whole, especially on growth, investment, productivity and wages. In particular, it has been associated with both a collapse of the export multiplier and the de-linking of the export sector from the rest of the economy; this has produced a situation in which increasing export competitiveness has had little effect on growth and living standards.[24]

Figure 5.17 shows the trademark of the 'liberalization package' in Mexico (as in the rest of Latin America): a fall in the share of wages and salaries in gross domestic product (GDP). In Mexico, over just two six-year presidential terms (1976–1982, 1982–1988) and one economic crisis, the share of wages and salaries in GDP fell by no less than 14 percentage points. In the last presidency of the 1990s (which saw yet another economic crisis), the share of wages in GDP fell by a further 8 percentage points. In all, the share of wages fell from 40 per cent of GDP in 1976 to just 18.9 per cent in 2000.

Figure 5.18 shows the root cause of this fall in the share of wages in GDP: the emergence of a new 'scissors' effect between wages and productivity after political and economic reforms. One can identify three distinct periods over the second half of the 20th century. First, up to the Echeverría Government (1970–1976), one can see the essential characteristic of the traditional Partido Revolucionario Institucional (PRI) distributive policy: wages were able to grow at a pace similar to productivity growth, i.e., increased bargaining power in a corporatist environment enabled labour to gain the 'property right' to share in the benefits of economic growth.

In the second period, during Lopez Portillo's term of office (between 1976 and 1982), marking the beginning of political-ideological change in Mexico, economic policy led to progressive stagnation of wages, despite massive new oil riches.[25] Then, when economic crisis struck Mexico in 1982, and with the ascendance to power of President de la Madrid and his economic reform team, a third period started, characterized by a rapidly growing gap between productivity and wages. By 2000, two presidents and another economic crisis later, this gap had reached approximately 30 percentage points. Figures 5.19 and 5.20 show

FIGURE 5.17
Mexico: wages as a share of GDP, 1950–2000

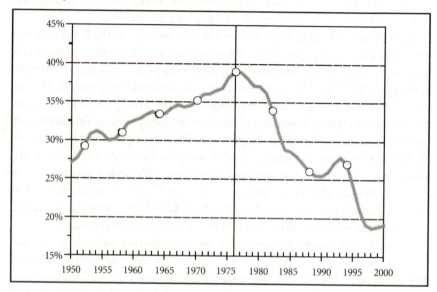

Notes: Wages, salaries and employers' contributions. Intervals between circles correspond to presidential periods.
Source: Palma (2005).

FIGURE 5.18
Mexico: average real wages and productivity, 1950–2000

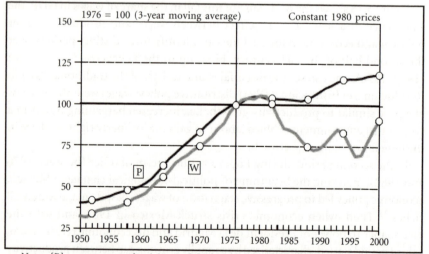

Notes: [P] = average productivity; and [W] = average real wages, salaries and employers' contributions.
Source: Palma (2005).

FIGURE 5.19

Mexico: wages and productivity in the manufacturing sector, 1970–1999

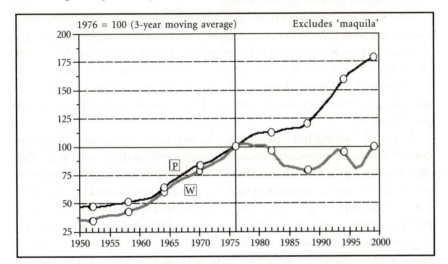

Notes: [P] = average productivity; and [W] = average real wages, salaries and employers' contributions.

Source: Palma (2005).

FIGURE 5.20

Mexico: wages and productivity in the non-tradable sector, 1950–1999

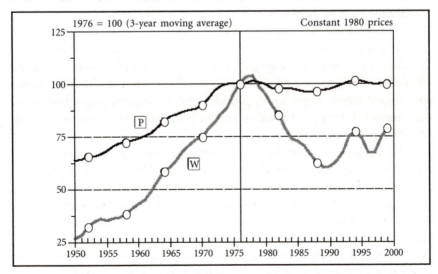

Notes: [P] = average productivity; and [W] = average real wages, salaries and employers' contributions.

Source: Palma (2005).

that the gap between productivity and wages took a different form for manufacturing than for non-tradables.

Prior to 1976, there was a relatively stable relationship between productivity growth and wage growth in manufacturing; this pattern subsequently changed due to a sharp break in the trend of wage growth. In fact, by the end of the 1990s, the average wage was only just recovering to its 1976 level, while productivity had increased by about 80 per cent in the meantime—a clear case of a shift towards a new 'winner takes all' pattern of distribution with greatly increased profit margins.

As Kalecki would have predicted, the two crises (1982 and 1994) also contributed to the new distributional environment, by drastically weakening the bargaining power of labour. However, as Prebisch and Singer would have predicted, as soon as manufacturing became export-oriented—particularly with capital increasingly mobile and labour relatively immobile—it began to behave as if it were a traditional primary commodity sector: wages immediately stagnated, and all productivity growth was either captured by capital or transferred to consumers in the North (in this case, to the US) via lower prices. In fact, wages were not able to grow in any significant way even in the motorcar industry—which was the most successful activity within manufacturing during this period—despite a 330 per cent productivity growth (Palma, 2005). Mexico's experience, in this respect, is certainly closer to the predictions of Prebisch and Singer than to those based on Samuelson's theorem of trade-related wage equalization across the world.

What about the relationship between wages and productivity in a sector unable to deliver productivity growth? Figure 5.20 indicates a similar gap between productivity growth and wage growth in non-tradables, but one moving in a different direction—i.e., a similar 'scissors' pattern, but this time with a downward trend. Here, given productivity stagnation, wages had to fall substantially for the gap to emerge and for profit margins to increase as in the rest of the economy.

This decline in wages in non-tradable sectors (services, utilities and construction, accounting for about two-thirds of GDP) contrasts sharply with the situation before 1976, when there was another gap (then in favour of labour), with wages growing *faster* than productivity. This was one characteristic of the previous 'corporatist' structure of property rights in the labour market: wages in *manufacturing* (which grew at a rate roughly similar to productivity growth) set the pace for wage growth in the non-manufacturing sector of the economy, even in sectors where productivity growth was slower than in manufacturing.

In this way, a new pattern of accumulation emerged with economic reform in Mexico (as in the rest of Latin America). If there is productivity growth, the new pattern is one of a shift towards a 'winner takes all' scenario (increasing profit margins a la Prebisch-Singer); if there is none, capital can still increase its profit margins, via the contraction of wages (à la Arthur Lewis, because institutional changes in the labour market allow capital to squeeze wages towards their subsistence level).[26] In this way, even if productivity growth is disappointing (mainly as a result of particularly poor investment effort), the stagnation of wages in some activities, and their decline in others, have proved to be an effective compensatory mechanism for capital to increase profit margins in this era of globalization.

CONCLUSIONS

Although the ('average') Gini picture of the income distribution for different regions of the world clearly shows four 'layers' of distribution across the world, this phenomenon only reflects what happens to half the world's population—those at the very top and those at the bottom of the distribution. The other half—in the middle and upper-middle deciles (5 to 9) of the distribution—offers a rather different picture, of extraordinary homogeneity. This is a truly remarkable fact that has not been properly emphasized in the literature so far. Clearly, more research is needed on the forces behind these opposite 'centrifugal' and 'centripetal' movements.

The similar income shares of the middle and upper-middle deciles across regions raise some doubts about distributional theories that give pride of place either to education or to trade-related wage differentials as the main determinants of income distribution. Groups with the highest degree of heterogeneity in distributional terms are more likely to have higher degrees of homogeneity in educational terms, and vice versa. Looking at trade-related wage differentials, there does not seem to be much distributional variance in the middle part of the distribution where 'skilled' and 'unskilled' labour are most likely to be found. In general, political-institutional factors seem to have greater influence on the determination of income distribution than purely economic ones.[27]

The sample also shows a significant distributional difference between English-speaking and non-English-speaking OECD countries; the same phenomenon is found among the ex-communist countries (the difference between those countries that used to belong to the Soviet Union and those in Central, formerly Eastern Europe).

Finally, in terms of the relationship between income distribution and income per capita in the era of globalization—and taking into account all the necessary econometric caveats on cross-sectional regressions of this nature, problems with the quality of the data, and the fact that, in many countries (especially in Sub-Saharan Africa), the data refer to expenditure, not income—the relevant regressions seem to support the following three hypotheses. First, statistically, the 'inverted U' and 'U' cross-section relationship still applies in the case of the distributional diversity at the very top and at the bottom of the income distribution; second (and in analytical terms, far more important), within these relationships, (much more homogeneous) regional effects clearly dominate; and third, Latin America has, so far, had the largest 'excess' inequality of any region in the world vis-à-vis its income per capita. In fact, Latin America seems to be in a distributional league of its own.[28] While political oligarchies all over the Third World would be very happy to appropriate such high shares of national income, the question remains why only in Latin America they manage to get away with it!

Appendix 5.1

- LA (Latin America) = Bolivia, Brazil, Chile, Colombia, Costa Rica, Dominican Republic, Ecuador, El Salvador, Guatemala, Honduras, Mexico, Nicaragua, Panama, Paraguay, Peru, Uruguay and Venezuela.
- AF (Sub-Saharan Africa) = Burkina Faso, Burundi, Cote d'Ivoire, The Gambia, Ghana, Guinea, Guinea-Bissau, Kenya, Lesotho, Madagascar, Mali, Mauritania, Mozambique, Niger, Nigeria, Rwanda, Senegal, South Africa, Swaziland, Tanzania, Uganda, Zambia and Zimbabwe.
- EA1 ('first-tier' NICs) = The Republic of Korea.[29]
- EA2 ('second-tier' NICs) = Malaysia, Philippines and Thailand.
- SA (large South Asia and low-income Southeast Asia) = Bangladesh, China, India, Indonesia, Lao PDR, Pakistan, Sri Lanka and Viet Nam.
- NA (North Africa) = Algeria, Egypt, Jordan, Morocco and Tunisia.
- CA (Caribbean countries) = Guyana, Jamaica, St. Lucia and Trinidad and Tobago.
- OECD1 (non-English-speaking OECD) = Austria, Belgium, Denmark, Finland, France, Germany, Greece, Italy, Japan, Luxembourg, Netherlands, Norway, Portugal, Spain and Sweden.
- OECD2 (English-speaking OECD) = Australia, Canada, Ireland, New Zealand, United Kingdom and United States.
- Ex-C1 (ex-communist countries of Central Europe) = Bulgaria, Croatia, Czech Republic, Hungary, Poland, Romania, Slovak Republic and Slovenia.
- Ex-C2 (ex-communist countries of the former Soviet Union) = Belarus, Estonia, Kazakhstan, Kyrgyz Republic, Latvia, Lithuania, Moldova, Russian Federation, Turkmenistan, Ukraine and Uzbekistan.
- Not classified = Cambodia, Ethiopia, Israel, Mongolia, Nepal, Papua New Guinea, Turkey, Switzerland and Yemen.

APPENDIX 5.2
Parameters' point estimation

	Reg. d10	Reg. d1–d4	Reg. d10/d1
Intersect	2.0484	4.8866	-0.6353
Ln Y pc	0.4222	-0.5541	0.9062
Ln Y pc sq	-0.0288	0.0354	-0.0610
LA dummy	0.2462	-0.3118	1.2329
AF dummy	0.1016	-0.2317	0.3822
SA dummy	-0.0196	0.0286	-0.0846
NA dummy	-0.1717	0.1963	-0.4801
OECD1 dummy	-0.0013	0.0019	-0.0041

Notes: The first regression corresponds to Figure 5.13; the second, to Figure 5.14; and the third, to Figure 5.15. Ln Y pc = log of income per capita; Ln Y pc sq = square of the log of income per capita; for dummy specifications see Figure 5.13.

't' values

	Reg. d10	Reg. d1–d4	Reg. d10/d1
Intersect	5.05	7.95	-0.46
Ln Y p c	3.74	-3.50	2.48
Ln Y pc sq	-3.99	3.61	-2.63
LA dummy	5.17	-4.87	7.45
AF dummy	2.07	-2.89	2.22
SA dummy	-2.02	3.37	-4.73
NA dummy	-2.45	2.97	-2.98
OECD1 dummy	-2.32	3.92	-3.22

Notes: 't' statistics (and the 'p' values below) are based on 'White's heteroscedasticity adjusted standard errors'. Ln Y pc = log of income per capita; Ln Y pc sq = square of the log of income per capita; for dummy specifications see Figure 5.13.

'p' values

	Reg. d10	Reg. d1-d4	Reg. d10/d1
Intersect	0.000	0.000	0.650
Ln Y pc	0.000	0.001	0.015
Ln Y pc sq	0.000	0.001	0.010
LA dummy	0.000	0.000	0.000
AF dummy	0.042	0.005	0.029
SA dummy	0.047	0.001	0.000
NA dummy	0.016	0.004	0.004
OECD1 dummy	0.022	0.000	0.002

Notes: Ln Y pc = log of income per capita; Ln Y pc sq = square of the log of income per capita; for dummy specifications, see Figure 5.13.

(contd)

APPENDIX 5.2 (*contd*)
Regression statistics

	Reg. D10	Reg. d1–d4	Reg. d10/d1
R-bar-sq	0.74	0.64	0.71
se y	0.13	0.19	0.47
F	32.7	20.5	28.2
'p' of F	0.000	0.000	0.000

Notes: R-bar-sq is the adjusted coefficient of determination; se y is the standard error for the 'y' estimate; F is the F statistic; and 'p' of F is the 'p' value of F.

NOTES

[1] This chapter draws heavily on Palma (2002b; 2003).

[2] Tony Atkinson, Stephany Blankenburg, Rodrigo Caputo, Jayati Ghosh, Andrew Glyn, Daniel Hahn, K.S. Jomo, Richard Kozul-Wright, Ugo Pagano, Guillermo Paraje, Hashem Pesaran, Guy Standing, Fiona Tregenna and especially Bob Sutcliffe made very useful suggestions. Participants at conferences and seminars in Bangkok, Chennai, Geneva, Kuala Lumpur, Santiago, Siena and Sydney also made helpful comments. The usual caveats apply.

[3] At the time of the creation of NAFTA, there were already well over 10 million Mexicans living in the US.

[4] For a comprehensive analysis of this literature, see Kanbur (2000). See also Sutcliffe (2004), Atkinson (1997), Aghion, Caroli and Garcia-Peñaloza (1999), IADB (1999) and UNCTAD (1996, 2002).

[5] For the OECD's Luxembourg Income Study (LIS), see http://www.lis.ceps.lu. The WB's basic income distribution information is published regularly in its World Development Indicators (WDI). See also WIDER (2000).

[6] The Sierra Leone survey, for example, undertaken in the midst of a rather brutal civil war, claims to have 'national' coverage! In the case of Latin America, a critical review of the quality of household surveys can be found in Székely and Hilgert (1999a).

[7] Following advice from WB staff, data from Sierra Leone and the Central African Republic are excluded from the sample due to inconsistencies.

[8] This is just one of the many instances of loss of information when data is only available in terms of quintiles.

[9] In fact, as discussed elsewhere, decile 10 also tended to have significant internal dispersion; and the real concentration of income is found within the first five percentiles of income recipients (see Palma, 2002a). This point is also clear from some country studies; see, for example, Ferreira and Litchfield (2000) for Brazil, Panuco (1988) for Mexico, and Paraje (2004) for Argentina. Consequently, one should focus on the effects of globalization on the income share of the top 5 per cent of the population; however, this is not possible with the available data.

[10] Chile is only one of a few developing countries for which there is relatively systematic income distribution data for a good length of time. See Ruiz-Tagle (2000) for a detailed discussion of the quality of the data (relating to 'Greater Santiago', all of which have the same source and methodology), and of the work by this author to improve their consistency.

[11] Moreover, later on, when the second democratic Government in Chile (1994–1999) abandoned the progressive distributive policies of the first, and the income share of decile 10 recovered all the ground lost since 1989 (6 percentage points of national income), the share of decile 9 again dropped.

[12] The broad range of income shares of decile 1 across countries is almost as remarkable as that found in decile 10—from 5.1 per cent in Belarus and the Slovak Republic (and 4.8 per cent in Japan), to just 0.5 per cent in Guinea-Bissau (and 0.6 per cent in Guatemala, and 0.7 per cent in Paraguay). Again, Latin American countries were at the unequal end of the ranking; while the median value of the income shares for decile 1 for all countries was 2.6 per cent, that for Latin America was just 0.8 per cent (only about a third that for the non-Latin American countries).

[13] The range for the ratio of deciles 10 and 1 extends from 3.6 in the Slovak Republic (and 3.9 in Belarus, 4.4 in Austria, 4.5 in Japan and 5.1 in Finland), to no less than 114 in Bolivia (and 112 in Honduras and 104 in El Salvador).

[14] See, for example, Juhn, Murphy and Pierce (1993); Revenga (1995); Cline (1997; this book has a very useful survey of the literature); Haskel (1999); and Melendez (2001). For critiques of this literature, see Krugman and Lawrence (1993), Robbins (1996) and Atkinson (1997).

[15] In this section, data from Hong Kong SAR and Taiwan Province of China are added to that for South Korea to form an enlarged EA1. The data for these countries, not available in the WDI database, were obtained from Deininger and Squire (1996). However, these two countries are not included in the regressions of the fourth section, as the data there are from a different source.

[16] Wolfson (1994), for example, started the recent 'polarization' literature by developing an index that cuts the Lorenz curve right in the middle! For a discussion of this point, see Palma (2002b).

[17] For a discussion of the econometric issues raised by cross-section regressions like these, see Pesaran, Haque and Sharma (2000); see also Palma (2002c). In particular, one has to understand that these regressions are simply a cross-sectional *description* of cross-country inequality differences, categorized by income per capita; i.e., they should not be interpreted as 'predictive', because there are a number of difficulties with a curve estimated from a single cross-section—especially regarding the homogeneity restrictions that are required to hold. This is one reason why the use of regional dummies is so important, because they bring us closer to the required homogeneity restrictions for prediction. Nevertheless, there is no obvious way of knowing if we are close enough to be able to predict with reasonable confidence. The jury is, therefore, still out regarding the predictive capacity of such regressions. Moreover, in any classification of this type, there is a 'pre-testing' danger, as there are many ways to define regions.

[18] Dummies for each region were selected according to the Akaike Information Criterion. The same dummies were used in the regressions below.

[19] This statement can be confirmed, for example, by testing the Latin American dummy vis-à-vis the Sub-Saharan African one; in all four specifications, the null hypothesis that both are not significantly different is easily rejected at the 1 per cent level.

[20] In any case, as discussed above, even if there were such information, in order to be able to use regressions like these for prediction purposes, one would require strong 'homogeneity restrictions' to hold.

[21] In 2000, Mexico's manufacturing exports were 3.5 times greater than those of Argentina and Brazil taken together. In terms of overall merchandise exports, Mexico's share in the Latin American total doubled from just under one-quarter to about one-half.

[22] As Mexicans like to say, their country is doubly cursed—so far from God, but so close to the US.

[23] In US$ of 2000 value, between 1982 and 2000 Mexico received US$200 billion in net inflows of FDI (Palma, 2005).

[24] For a detailed analysis of the Mexican economy after trade liberalization, see Palma (2005).

[25] Wages stagnated at a time of economic euphoria in Mexico, with the new oil industry coming on stream at a time of particularly high oil prices. This mania reached such heights that

the previous President had declared at the end of his term in office that from then on, 'economic policy in Mexico was no longer an issue of allocation of scarce resources among multiple needs, but one of the distribution of abundance'. This 'abundance' clearly did not reach wages!

[26] This 'centrifugal' force was so powerful that in real terms, if the level of the minimum wage is set at 100 in (the peak year of) 1976, by 1994, it had fallen to just one-third of that value, and by 2000, to a remarkable low of one-fifth! See Palma (2005).

[27] This issue is discussed in more detail in the Latin American context in another paper (Palma, 2002a). See also Krugman and Lawrence (1993).

[28] Brazil, Chile or Mexico may be characterized as middle-income countries, but the top 10 per cent are able to live the equivalent of a modern European lifestyle, thanks mainly to the fact that the bottom 40 per cent are still living the equivalent of a medieval European lifestyle.

[29] As mentioned above, in graphs where regional averages are shown, data from Hong Kong SAR and Taiwan Province of China were added to that for South Korea to form an enlarged EA1. However, these two countries are not included in the regressions of the third section, as their data are from a different source (Deininger and Squire, 1996).

REFERENCES

Aghion, Philippe, Eve Caroli and Cecilia García-Peñaloza (1999). Inequality and economic growth: The perspective of the new growth theories. *Journal of Economic Literature* 37 (4): 1615–660.

Atkinson, A.B. (1997). Bringing income distribution in from the cold. *The Economic Journal* 107 (441): 297–321.

Atkinson, A.B., and François Bourguignon (2000). *Handbook of Income Distribution, Vol. 1.* North-Holland, Amsterdam.

Cline, William (1997). *Trade and Income Distribution.* Institute for International Economics, Washington, DC.

Deininger, Karl, and Lyn Squire (1996). A new data set measuring income inequality. *The World Bank Economic Review* 10 (3), September: 745–65. http://www.worldbank.org/research/growth/dddeisqu.htm

Ferreira, Francisco, and Julie Litchfield (2000). Desigualdade, pobreza e bem-estar social no Brasil: 1981/95. In R.E. Henriques (ed.). *Desigualdade e Pobreza no Brasil.* Instituto de Pesquisa Econômica Aplicada (IPEA), Rio de Janeiro: 45–84.

Haskel, J.E. (1999). The trade and labour approaches to wage inequality. Working Paper No. 405, Queen Mary and Westfield College, University of London, London.

IDB (1999). *Economic and Social Progress in Latin America.* Inter-American Development Bank, Washington, DC (www.iadb.org/oce/ipes).

Juhn, C.K., Kevin M. Murphy and B.R. Pierce (1993). Wage inequality and the rise in returns to skill. *Journal of Political Economy* 101 (3): 410–42.

Kanbur, Ravi (2000). Income distribution and development. In A. B. Atkinson and François Bourguignon (eds). *Handbook of Income Distribution, Vol. 1.* North-Holland, Amsterdam: 791–841.

Krueger, Anne (1983). *Trade and Employment in Developing Countries, Vol. 3: Synthesis and Conclusions.* National Bureau of Economic Research, Cambridge, MA.

Krugman, Paul, and Robert Lawrence (1993). Trade, jobs, and wages. NBER Working Paper No. 4478, September, National Bureau of Economic Research, Cambridge, MA.

Kuznets, Simon (1955). Economic growth and income inequality. *American Economic Review* 45: 348–62.

Lal, Deepak (1983). *The Poverty of 'Development Economics'.* Institute of Economic Affairs, London.

Melendez, J.L. (2001). The structure of wages under trade liberalization: Mexico from 1984 to 1998. Processed, Universidad Nacional Autónoma de Mexico (UNAM), Mexico.

Neal, D., and S. Rosen (2000). Theories of the distribution of earnings. In A. B. Atkinson and François Bourguignon (eds). *Handbook of Income Distribution, Vol. 1.* North-Holland, Amsterdam: 379–427.

OECD. Luxembourg Income Study (LIS). Organization for Economic Cooperation and Development, Paris. http://www.lis.ceps.lu

Palma, José Gabriel (2002a). Property rights, institutional constraints and distributional outcomes: Why does Latin America have the worst income distribution in the world? Processed, Faculty of Economics, Cambridge University, Cambridge.

Palma, José Gabriel (2002b). New indices of income polarization: What do they tell us? Processed, Faculty of Economics, Cambridge University, Cambridge.

Palma, José Gabriel (2002c). The Kuznets Curve revisited. *International Journal of Development Issues* 1 (1): 69–93.

Palma, José Gabriel (2003). National inequality in the era of globalization: What do recent data tell us? In Jonathan Michie (ed.). *The Handbook of Globalisation.* Edward Elgar, Cheltenham: 104–35.

Palma, José Gabriel (2005). The seven main stylised facts of the Mexican economy since trade liberalization and NAFTA. *Journal of Industrial and Corporate Change* 14 (6), December: 1–51.

Panuco, Humberto (1988). Economic policy and the distribution of income in Mexico: 1984–1992. PhD thesis, University College, University of London, London.

Paraje, Guillermo (2004). Inequality, welfare and polarization in the greater Buenos Aires, 1986–1999. PhD thesis, Faculty of Economics, Cambridge University, Cambridge.

Pesaran, Hashim, N.U. Haque and S.E. Sharma (2000). Neglected heterogeneity and dynamics in cross-country savings regressions. In J. Krishnakumar and E. Ronchetti (eds). *Panel Data Econometrics: Future Directions.* Elsevier Science and Technology, Amsterdam: 52–82.

Revenga, Ana (1995). Employment and wage effects of trade liberalization: The case of Mexican manufacturing. Policy Research Working Paper 1524, World Bank, Washington, DC.

Robbins, D.J. (1996). HOS hits facts: facts win; Evidence on trade and wages in the developing world. Development Discussion Paper No. 557, Harvard Institute for International Development, Harvard University, Cambridge, MA.

Ruiz-Tagle, Jaime (2000). Chile: 40 años de desigualdad de ingresos. Processed, Departamento de Economía, Universidad de Chile, Santiago.

Sutcliffe, Bob (2004). World inequality and globalization. *Oxford Review of Economic Policy* 20 (1), Spring: 15–37.

Székely, Miguel, and M.A. Hilgert (1999a). What's behind the inequality we measure: An investigation using Latin American data. Research Department Working Paper No. 409, Inter-American Development Bank, Washington, DC.

Székely, Miguel, and M.A. Hilgert (1999b). The 1990s in Latin America: Another decade of persistent inequality. Research Department Working Paper No. 410, Inter-American Development Bank, Washington, DC.

UNCTAD (1996). *Trade and Development Report, 1996.* United Nations Conference on Trade and Development, Geneva.

UNCTAD (2002). *Trade and Development Report, 2002.* United Nations Conference on Trade and Development, Geneva.

WIDER (2000). *World Income Inequality Database.* (www.wider.unu.edu/wiid).

Wolfson, Michel (1994). When Inequalities Diverge, *American Economic Review* 84: 353–58.

World Bank (1987). *World Development Report, 1987.* World Bank, Washington, DC.

World Bank (2004). *World Development Indicators, 2004.* World Bank, Washington, DC.

6

Growth Is Failing the Poor:
The Unbalanced Distribution of the Benefits and
Costs of Global Economic Growth[1]

DAVID WOODWARD and ANDREW SIMMS

This chapter questions an idea which has become almost unquestionable in mainstream economics—that a growing global economy is the indispensable foundation for solving all with regard to reducing poverty. The Governments of the world have committed themselves to meeting the Millennium Development Goals (MDGs), the first of which, MDG1, is to halve the proportion of the population of developing countries living below the $1-a-day poverty line from its 1990 level by 2015.

How can this best be achieved? The answer, we are told, is growth. Poverty reduction, according to the orthodoxy, requires rapid economic growth in developing countries; economic growth in developing countries in turn requires rapid growth in the global economy; therefore, poverty reduction requires the fastest possible growth in the global economy. If this creates environmental problems, conventional wisdom puts faith in technology to reduce the damage.

However, the rate of technological improvement is much too slow, given the severity of current environmental problems, such as climate change, and their impact, which is greatest on the poorest. This appears to give rise to serious tension between the objectives of human development and poverty reduction, on the one hand, and environmental sustainability, on the other. Is this tension inevitable, however, or does the world view underlying it rest on false logic?

The extreme inequality in the global distribution of income and assets seriously undermines the effectiveness of global growth in reducing poverty. The corresponding inequality in the use of natural resources, particularly energy, is one of the biggest barriers to progress on international environmental issues. Based on statistics from the International Energy Agency, the average resident of the United States generates as much of the chief greenhouse gas, carbon dioxide, in a single day as someone in China does in more than a week, while the average Tanzanian takes about seven months to generate the same amount.

This chapter, therefore, considers the extent of the inequality in the distribution of the benefits of growth and the possibility of resolving the tensions between human development and environmental objectives by shifting the focus from growth to income distribution at the global level.

THE GROWTH DILEMMA: POVERTY REDUCTION VERSUS THE ENVIRONMENT?

The two greatest challenges facing the global economy are eradicating poverty and achieving environmental sustainability. Even on the basis of World Bank data, 45 per cent of the world's population—some 2.8 billion people—live below the "$2-a-day" poverty line; and more than 1.1 billion—more than the total population of the developed world—below the "$1-a-day" line.

Since the $1-a-day line is based on purchasing power parity (PPP), in principle, it represents the level of consumption of a single earner in the United Kingdom at the minimum wage, with 36 dependents paying tax but receiving no benefits (and in most contexts, with no access to free health care or education) (Woodward and Simms, 2006: box 1).

The interquartile range of child mortality rates at the $1-a-day line is one in six to one in twelve, and that for the rate of stunting in survivors between one third and one half. In Niger, the under-five mortality rate at the $1-a-day line is more than one in three (Wagstaff, 2003). This compares with an overall rate in developed countries of around one in one hundred and fifty. That nearly half the world's population should live in the twenty-first century in such poverty that up to one third of their children die before they reach the age of five, at a time of unprecedented wealth among the world's rich, can only be described as a moral outrage.

If poverty reduction is a moral imperative, resolving our current environmental crises is, in many respects, a practical necessity. The concentration of greenhouse gases in the atmosphere has been rising steadily since the Industrial Revolution as a direct consequence of burning fossil fuels to power economic activity. Emissions have risen dramatically as the global economy has grown over the last few decades (see Figure 6.1).

According to UK Prime Minister Tony Blair's International Climate Change Task Force (2005), the growth rate of greenhouse gas concentrations associated with current economic growth rates could, within a decade, lead to a level commensurate with environmental feedbacks that, in turn, could make the process irreversible. Even current levels of warming can seriously undermine the livelihoods of the poorest people (Simms, 2005).

Poverty, we are told, can only be reduced through continued—and ideally faster—growth of the global economy. This message, often linked with

FIGURE 6.1
World GDP and fossil fuel carbon emissions, 1960–2002

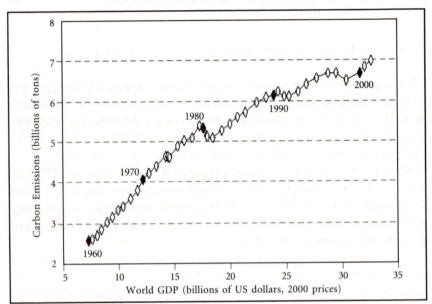

Sources: Marland and Boden (2005), World Bank (2005a).

injunctions to follow orthodox economic policies, has become a mantra of the international financial institutions: "No country has achieved the sustained rapid growth needed to reduce poverty without opening up its trade with the rest of the world.... Economic growth is the principal route to lasting poverty reduction" (Krueger, 2004a); "Of course, the poor have yet to benefit as much [from growth in India] as they—or we—would like.... But the solution is more rapid growth—not a switch of emphasis towards more redistribution. Poverty reduction is best achieved through making the cake bigger, not by trying to cut it up in a different way" (Krueger, 2004b).

At the same time, however, there are serious and growing concerns about the effects of global economic growth on the environment, particularly in terms of climate change, but also with regard to the exhaustion of natural resources. Paradoxically, the latter concern applies particularly to oil, whose rising price undermines the economies of oil-importing poor countries—although our current closeness to key climatic thresholds and the plentiful availability of other fossil fuels means that oil depletion will not resolve climate change.

Assessing the literature on growth and environmental degradation, the World Bank (2000) concluded that "A growing economy imposes even greater demands on natural resources and makes management interventions crucial." It is sometimes argued that, beyond a certain point, increasing income turns from worsening to improving environmental conditions such as air and water quality. However, relying on this is dangerous because "many developing countries cannot reach the turnaround income level for decades". Moreover, as the Bank also observes, any growth rate leads to an absolute depletion of natural resources, such as forestry, fisheries, soil and the natural capital of coastal regions. Thus "neither rapid nor slow growth is an automatic ally of natural capital", and fast growth especially creates pressure causing a decline in its "quality".

WHO'S COSTING THE EARTH, AND WHO'S PAYING THE PRICE?

According to the most recent assessment of humanity's ecological footprint, in 2002, human demands on the planet, transmitted through our growth-based economies, exceeded the biosphere's regenerative capacity by more than 20 per cent. While nature can tolerate certain degrees of overexploitation, persistent overburdening leads to the collapse of ecosystems and natural resource availability. Diamond (2005) attributes historical collapses of civilizations to human inability to identify the stage at which societies pass the ecological point of no return.

Our environmental demands are also very unevenly distributed. The world's total available biocapacity consists of 11.5 billion hectares of biologically productive space—grassland, cropland, forests, fisheries and wetlands. Since there are approximately 6.4 billion people on the planet, this gives an average of 1.8 hectares of "environmental space" per person. Europe, on average, requires 4.7 global hectares to produce the resources it consumes and absorb the wastes it generates—a figure which has nearly doubled since 1961 (Global Footprint Network, 2005). Since it only has 2.3 global hectares available per person, more than half its footprint effectively falls outside its borders. Based on 2002 data, the figure is even higher in the UK (at 5.4 global hectares per person), only slightly lower in Japan and twice as much in the US (EEA, forthcoming; Wackernagel and others, 2005).

As the world economy grows, so does its footprint, taking us ever further away from living within our environmental means and the target of real sustainability. In per capita terms, the footprint of the developed countries has grown much faster than that of the developing countries. The footprint per person in the former grew from 3.8 global hectares per person in 1961 to 5.4 in 1981 and 6.4 in 2001—an overall increase of 68 per cent. In developing countries, the increase over the same period was just 7 per cent—one tenth as

FIGURE 6.2
Average environmental footprint per person, 1961–2001

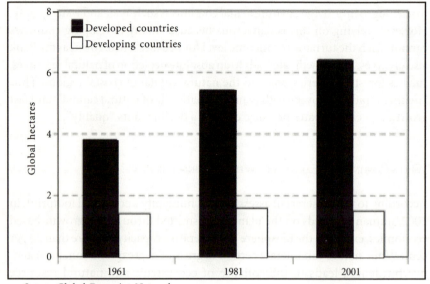

Source: Global Footprint Network

much—from 1.4 global hectares per person in 1961 to 1.5 in 2001; the footprint actually *decreased* between 1981 and 2001 (Wackernagel and others, 2005; see Figure 6.2).

Moreover, increasing consumption in Europe and the US sets an aspirational model for the rest of the world to follow. However, for everyone on Earth to live at the current European average level of consumption, more than double the bio-capacity actually available would be required—the equivalent of 2.1 planets the size of our Earth; for everyone to consume at the US rate, five would be required.

While rich countries are disproportionately *causing* environmental problems, however, it is the poor countries—and especially the poorer people within them—who suffer the most serious consequences. The problem is one of inverse dynamics: while the poorest receive very little of the benefit of global growth, as discussed below, they bear a disproportionate share of its costs—for example, the consequences of global warming.

As a result, the pursuit of poverty reduction through a strategy based primarily on global economic growth quickly becomes perverse: the already wealthy become both relatively and absolutely wealthier, while the poorest both slip further behind economically and have their well-being and prospects further undermined by environmental degradation.

The Climate Barrier

Recent US research has shown that, in the second half of the twentieth century (with some variation), "the Sahel, the transition zone between the Saharan desert and the rainforests of Central Africa and the Guinean Coast ... experienced a severe drying trend." The models used by the researchers predict a drier Sahel in future, primarily due to human-caused rising greenhouse gas emissions, with "far-ranging implications for the economy and ecology of the region" (Held and others, 2005). Research from the US National Oceanic and Atmospheric Administration describes a 20 per cent drop in rainfall in drought-prone southern Africa in the second half of the last century and predicts "much more substantial ongoing drying" (Marty Hoerling, quoted in BBC Online (2005).

The potential consequences of such trends are indicated by recent experiences in the region. Since 2001, consecutive dry spells in southern Africa have led to serious food shortages. According to the United Nations Office for the Coordination of Humanitarian Affairs, the drought of 2002–2003 resulted in a food deficit of 3.3 million tonnes, with an estimated 14.4 million people in need of assistance (IRIN, 2005).

Globally, natural disasters, most of which are related to the earth's hydrological cycle and are therefore directly affected by climate change, devastate the lives of the poorest people most, according to the World Bank Hazard Management Unit. The poor are more likely to occupy dangerous and vulnerable sites, such as flood plains, river banks, steep slopes and reclaimed land. According to the Red Cross *World Disasters Report*, the frequency and cost of natural disasters will increase due to a combination of environmental degradation, climate change, urban population growth and economic globalization (IFRC, 1999). Of all deaths from natural disasters, 96 per cent occur in developing countries (World Bank, 2004).

No Quick Fix: Why Technology Isn't the Answer

It is clear, therefore, that we need to resolve our environmental crises but that we also have a moral obligation to eradicate poverty. However, if eradicating poverty requires economic growth, and economic growth will make our environmental problems still more insoluble, how can we achieve both? To the extent that this question is even asked at present, the answer proposed is to seek a technological fix—to develop new technologies which will enable us to go on growing by reducing the environmental impact of each $1-worth of goods and services we produce and consume.

Globally, real GDP grew at 3.0 per cent per year over the period 1980 to 2001 (World Bank, 2005a), while energy consumption grew at 1.7 per cent per year (EIA, 2004). Although the rates of growth differ, the two are clearly linked (Figure 6.1). If the link between growth and rising emissions could be severed to such an extent that the change in emissions not only slowed substantially but became sufficiently negative, the clash between growth and global warming could potentially be reconciled. This would require a carbon Kuznets curve[2] showing greenhouse gas emissions sufficiently delinked from global economic growth to prevent greenhouse gas concentrations passing about 450 ppmv (parts per million by volume) of CO_2 equivalent—the level at which irreversible feedback effects could well occur.

However, there are several reasons to doubt that this scenario is likely or even possible. First, there are technical criticisms of the possibility of the neat hill-shaped relationship hypothesized by the carbon Kuznets curve, showing income and emissions rising together before emissions drop off (Müller-Fürstenberger and others, 2004). Second, while economists tend to assume that increases in economic growth are limitless, there are strict limits, governed by the laws of thermodynamics, on efficiency increases in how we burn fossil fuels.

While fuel efficiency has increased substantially over the course of the last century, driven by technological development, there are serious questions about how much further it can go. Even in the most optimistic scenario—a global political consensus on action, immediate and comprehensive application of the most efficient technologies available and a massive shift towards the least polluting fossil fuel (natural gas)—the result would be a delay of only 24 years in reaching a given higher concentration of greenhouse gases in the atmosphere. In a more probable and recognizable political future, with continued economic growth, fuel efficiency measures could deliver only negligible delays in higher concentrations (di Fazio, 2000). As a result, none of the standard International Panel on Climate Change (IPCC) scenarios for the emissions arising from global economic activity show their concentrations being restrained to anything like the degree sufficient to prevent dangerous human interference in the climate system (Intergovernmental Panel on Climate Change, 2001).

Regardless of how reliable or reckless such technological optimism may be, those who appeal for a purely technological solution are asking the wrong question. Development of new technological solutions could be pursued equally in contexts of rapid, slow, zero or even negative growth. Rapid growth may generate more resources for investment, but it also creates a greater need for those resources to be invested in increasing the volume of production to meet growing demand. This means that its effect on the availability of resources for investment in environmentally friendly technologies is ambiguous.

Moreover, given the scale of impending environmental disasters such as global warming, the rate at which we are approaching them, the limited scope for resolving them with a purely technological approach and the long time lags inevitably entailed, it seems clear that we need *both* slower growth *and* as much technological progress as we can achieve. Technological improvement is necessary, but alone it represents no more than a small step in the right direction. It does not offer a viable solution to the growth dilemma.

Growth and Poverty Reduction: A Necessity or a Diversion?

If attempts to delink environmental damage from growth do not provide an answer, could delinking poverty reduction from growth then provide a more viable alternative? Because, strange as the proposition may sound to economic orthodoxy, poverty can indeed be reduced without growth.

Changes in the incomes of poor households can be seen as a product of two variables: economic growth (increasing overall income) and changes in the share of poor households in total income (distribution of income). It would thus be entirely possible to offset a slower rate of growth—or even a decline in total income—by increasing the share of poor households in total income. There is growing recognition that distribution is important to poverty reduction as well as growth. For example, Wade (2001) noted that:

> "It is remarkable how unconcerned the World Bank, the IMF and other international organisations are about these trends [towards increasing polarization of global incomes]. The Bank's *World Development Report* for 2000 even said that rising income inequality 'should not be seen as negative' if the incomes at the bottom do not fall and the number of people in poverty falls. Such lack of attention shows that to call these world organisations is misleading."

Perhaps stung by such criticisms, the World Bank has recently increased its attention to distributional issues, devoting its 2006 flagship *World Development*

Report 2006 to "equity and development" (World Bank, 2005b). However, it insists that "from an equity perspective, the distribution of *opportunities* matters more than the distribution of *outcomes*" (p. 4) and appears concerned with equity primarily because a) "with imperfect markets, inequalities in power and wealth translate into unequal opportunities, leading to *wasted productive potential* and to an *inefficient allocation of resources*" (p. 7), and b) because "unequal power leads to the formation of institutions that perpetuate inequalities in power, status and wealth—and that typically are also *bad for investment, innovation and risk-taking that under-pin long-term growth*" (pp. 8–9). In short, while paying lip-service to "intrinsic motives" for promoting equity, the Bank's main concern is with the possibility of inequity undermining economic growth. When it comes to substance, there is no sign, as yet, of any concern with equity being translated into changes in the economic policies pressed on developing country Governments. Thus, the Epilogue to the 2006 *World Development Report* says "recognizing the importance of equity… implies the need to *integrate and extend existing approaches* [to development]" (emphasis added) (World Bank, 2005b: 226).

However, there is a fundamental logical problem in this whole approach. The conceptual separation of income growth and the income distribution on which it rests assumes, often implicitly, that growth and distributional change occur independently of each other, so that growth can be pursued with one set of policies, leaving distribution to be adjusted by a separate set of redistributive measures. This is conceptually incoherent. Economic changes (including policies) act on individual incomes in different ways, according to how each person earns and spends his or her income. Average income and income distribution are two ways of summarizing the same set of variables—the individual incomes of the population—so, if one changes, the other will almost certainly change too. Moreover, how distribution alters will be critically dependent on the policies implemented in pursuit of growth.

In 2000, the World Bank published a paper by David Dollar and Art Kraay, entitled "Growth is Good for the Poor". This purported to prove statistically that the income of the poor (defined as the poorest fifth of the population) increased one-for-one with overall income and that standard "pro-growth" policies and openness to trade were therefore beneficial for the poor. However, the paper— as well as subsequent versions (Dollar and Kraay: 2001; 2002)—has been robustly criticized, and its findings (particularly on policy and trade openness) are widely seen as discredited by serious flaws in methodology, compounded by the inevitable problem of data quality (Oxfam, 2000; Weisbrot and others, 2001; Amman and others, 2002). In another, much less publicised, World Bank paper using the same data set as Dollar and Kraay, Lopez (2006), found that faster growth was associated with a faster increase in inequality in the 1990s, though not in the 1970s or 1980s.

In any case, to investigate the relationship between growth and distribution, or even to make assumptions about it, is to ask the wrong question. The question is not whether *growth* affects distribution (or *vice versa*), but whether *economic policies designed to promote growth* affect distribution. The worst outcome of all, in terms of poverty reduction, is to pursue policies which sacrifice distribution to prioritize growth but which in practice fail to generate faster growth. This has been the story of most developing countries for most of the last 25 years (Weisbrot and others, 2001).

Ironically, free-market economists are among the first to assert the existence of a connection, albeit a negative one, between growth and policies designed to promote redistribution. For example, they argue that tax/transfer-based redistribution measures weaken growth by undermining incentives—even though economic theory is ambiguous on this and the evidence is inconclusive (Klasen, 2003). To say that policies for redistribution impede growth, however, is inconsistent with asserting that policies to promote growth do not affect distribution—particularly as these may include the reversal of policies designed to effect redistribution.

Economic Growth: The Wrong Measure

In light of these considerations, there is no fundamental reason to pursue economic growth as a primary objective of policy, or indeed, to consider it as the key indicator of economic performance. Economic growth does not, in itself, make people's lives any better or necessarily reflect changes in well-being.

Generally speaking, growth takes account only of paid work (with some exceptions, notably subsistence agriculture). The exclusion of unpaid work within the home, in particular, is a major distortion: though contributing considerably to well-being, it is not considered production. Suppose, for example, that Parent A takes a paid job looking after the children of Parent B and in turn pays Parent B the same amount to look after his/her children. Both incomes will then add to national income, and to economic growth, even though nothing additional is being produced and no one is any better off financially. Thus a shift away from self-reliance generates economic growth without necessarily reflecting any increase in well-being. In countless, more complex, real-life examples, from household maintenance and decorating to cooking and cleaning, this scenario is played out over and over again.

National income accounts do not take account of non-financial aspects of well-being, such as working time, either. Thus if production were increased by 10 per cent as a result of everyone working 10 per cent longer, people would not be 10 per cent better off, because of the extra time they were working. The measured growth rate is the same, however, whether working time is increased or not. Similarly, no account is taken of the effects of changes in uncertainty or financial insecurity. Equally, in the childcare example, neither the immediate social and psychological costs of separating young families nor any longer term effects, e.g., on crime or health, are counted.

National accounts also include defensive consumption, without taking account of the social problems which give rise to it. Thus, the additional spending required to clean up pollution, to maintain security in the face of increasing crime or social unrest or to ensure national defence in response to increasing international tensions all *add* to national income and growth.

Most importantly in the present context, growth calculations take no account of the distribution of income. National accounts treat $1 of income identically, whoever receives it. This is clearly unrealistic and counter-intuitive: the effect of an additional $100 on the well-being of a household with an income of $100 is clearly far greater than for a household with an income of $1 million. As a result, the effect of a given change in aggregate income on well-being is critically dependent on *whose* income is increased.

This means that from a well-being perspective, the incomes of the rich are systematically overvalued at the expense of the incomes of the poor. If we set economic growth, rather than well-being, as our policy objective, it institutionalizes this serious distortion, so that policies will inevitably result in a lower level of well-being than could otherwise be reached by biasing policies towards the worse off.

The Myth of "Pro-Poor Growth"

The World Bank has responded to distributional concerns by shifting its language from growth promotion to the promotion of "pro-poor growth". One might reasonably conclude that this change represents a step towards increasing emphasis on poverty reduction and greater efforts to ensure that the poor benefit more from growth—a rather overdue change of focus given the Bank's self-proclaimed mission to reduce poverty. The term is potentially misleading, however, as the shift in language is greater than the shift in the underlying reality.

There are two main contenders for the definition of pro-poor growth:
- that the percentage increase in the income of the poor should be no less, on average, than that of the non-poor—that is, that growth should not

be accompanied by a reduction in the income share of the poor (Baulch and McCulloch, 1999; Kakwani and Pernia, 2000; White and Anderson, 2001); or

- that growth should result in some increase in the incomes of the poor, however small (Ravallion and Chen, 2003; Ravallion, 2004; DFID, 2004).

The latter definition makes the term "pro-poor growth" extremely misleading, as it considers economic growth that is accompanied by a considerable increase in inequality as pro-poor. For example, to define growth as "pro-poor" when the annual income of the average rich person increases from $10,000 to $11,000, while that of the average poor person rises from $100 to $100.01, would seem to render the term virtually meaningless.

However, even the first of the definitions seems unduly lax. At first sight, it might seem reasonable to consider growth as "pro-poor" if the incomes of the poor rise at least as much as those of the rich. However, the criterion is the *percentage* change in income, not the *absolute* change. This means only that the share of the poor in the proceeds of growth should be no less than their initial share in income—which, by definition, is relatively small.

Even in a relatively less unequal society such as the UK, the share of the poorest 10 per cent of the population in income—or pro-poor growth—is only 2.8 per cent, while that of the richest 10 per cent is 28 per cent—ten times as much (ONS, 2005). This means that, even by the stronger definition, "pro-poor" growth may benefit the richest 10 per cent ten times as much as the poorest 10 per cent. In many other countries—the US as well as most developing countries—inequality is much greater, and so, therefore, is the pro-rich bias of "pro-poor" growth.

This suggests a serious discrepancy between the rhetoric of pro-poor growth and the reality. This arises because the language of pro-poor growth presupposes a growth-focused strategy. As a quantifiable target of policy to be maximized, the increase in the overall incomes of the poor may be appropriate (although it would be desirable to temper this, e.g., by taking account of income distribution *among* the poor, effects on non-financial well-being, etc.). However, the phrase "pro-poor growth" implies that the question being asked is how pro- (or anti-) poor a given rate of growth is in a particular context, and this definition is entirely incapable of addressing that question.

This raises the question of why the concept of maximizing the increase in the incomes of the poor should be termed "pro-poor *growth*" when it is quite conceivable that it could best be achieved in some contexts through policies which entail *negative* growth, with substantial redistribution. In other words, referring to this concept as pro-poor *growth* (rather than, for example, income poverty reduction) implies, quite erroneously, that it necessarily *requires* growth.

The discrepancy also arises partly because of the implicit assumption that it is only the *absolute* incomes of the poor which matter. Absolute changes in income are undoubtedly much more important at the bottom of the global income distribution than they are to the majority of the population of developed countries. In the latter case, around 85 per cent of people live above the level at which absolute income ceases to affect well-being. Even among the poor, however, the effect of relative incomes (e.g., through effects on social status and self-worth) may also be significant.

What increases the importance of relative incomes immeasurably, however, is the very considerable *cost* attached to growth, in a world which is approaching—and may even have reached—certain environmental constraints. This applies particularly to limits on carbon emissions, which, if transgressed, will rebound most devastatingly on some of the world's poorest people. In this real-world context, the question of how much poverty reduction is achieved *relative to overall economic growth* becomes a critical consideration.

This is illustrated in table 6.1 for a selection of developing countries with different levels of income per capita and inequality. For the countries with the highest overall income levels—the World Bank upper-middle-income category—poor households account for no more than 3.5 per cent of national income. This means that, even if inequality does not increase, it takes between $29 and $125 of economic growth, with all the associated environmental costs, to achieve each $1-worth of poverty reduction.

For the middle-income group (the World Bank lower-middle-income

TABLE 6.1
Growth required for poverty reduction in selected developing countries

Income	Inequality		Population below $2/day poverty line (percentage)	Share of poor households in income/ growth (percentage)	$ growth required per $ of poverty reduction
Low	High	Central African Rep.	82.5	24.0	4.16
Low	Medium	Cameroon	50.6	9.6	10.38
Low	Low	Kyrgyzstan	27.2	12.3	8.10
Medium	High	Namibia	53.9	4.5	22.39
Medium	Medium	Philippines	46.9	7.3	13.65
Medium	Low	Ukraine	21.5	3.5	28.45
High	High	Botswana	45.0	3.5	28.85
High	Medium	Malaysia	32.1	2.5	39.92
High	Low	Latvia	9.2	0.8	124.67

Sources: Authors' estimates, based on World Bank (2005a) and PovCalNet.

category) the share of the poor in income is only 3.5–7.5 per cent. In that case, $14–$28 of growth is required per $1 of poverty reduction. Even in the poorest and most unequal country in the group, the Central African Republic, where more than 80 per cent of the population lives below the $2-a-day poverty line, the poor receive less than one quarter of the income or the benefits of growth.

Thus, a third definition of "pro-poor growth" is required:

- that the poor should have a greater-than-average share in the additional income generated by growth *in absolute terms.*

Although this represents a better intuitive interpretation of the concept of pro-poor growth, it is generally ignored or explicitly discounted as unrealistic, principally because it would require the incomes of the poor to grow much faster in percentage terms than those of the rich (White and Anderson, 2001; Klasen, 2005).

However, if our objective is to reduce poverty while remaining within environmental constraints, this is precisely what we want to measure—how much of the absolute increase in production and consumption associated with growth actually contributes to poverty reduction? Concerning ourselves only with the share of the poor in the benefits of growth *relative to their already seriously inadequate share in income* becomes an irrelevance.

This logic becomes considerably more compelling if we extend it to the global level. The combination of inequality *within* countries with the extreme inequality *between* countries gives rise to a quite extraordinary degree of inequality among the population of the world as a whole (see Figure 6.3). In fact the world distribution of income is substantially more unequal than even the most unequal country. The highest Gini coefficient recorded by the World Bank for any country is 74.3 percent, for Namibia in 1993 (World Bank, 2005a), compared with 80 per cent for the world as a whole (Milanovic, 1999).

In 1993, the poorest 10 per cent of the world's population accounted for just 0.8 per cent of world income, compared with 50.8 per cent for the richest 10 per cent. The richest 1 per cent alone accounted for 9.5 per cent, implying an average income for this group some 120 times the average for the poorest 10 per cent (Milanovic, 1999). This means that the average benefit of global growth to someone in the richest 1 per cent of the population could be 120 times more than that of someone in the poorest 10 per cent, and yet it would still be considered "pro-poor" even by the more progressive of the two definitions. This is, to say the least, counter-intuitive.

In fact, even this figure understates the scale of the difference. Any increase in global inequality since 1993 will have widened the gap still further, as would using market exchange rates. Extrapolating the trend from 1988 to 1993 (an annual increase of 2.8 per cent) would increase the ratio to around 170 in

FIGURE 6.3

World income distribution, 1993

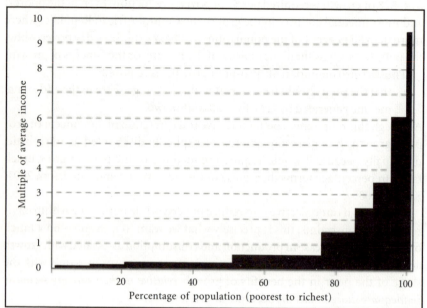

Sources: Milanovic (1999).

2006, and the differences between market and PPP exchange rates in low-income countries (typically a factor of between 2 and 5 (World Bank 2005a)[3]) would increase the ratio by a factor of around 3. Combining these effects could potentially increase the ratio to around 500.

Comparing Growth and Poverty Reduction

If we line up the population in order of income from the poorest (on the left) to the richest (on the right), and measure their incomes, we get a picture such as the curve in Figure 6.4. Superimposing the poverty line, the total income of poor households is the shaded area below the curve.

As incomes increase, so the income line rises, as shown in Figure 6.5. Comparing the income of the poor as defined in each year is misleading, as the incomes of those who escape poverty will then appear as a reduction in the income of the poor. Partly due to the form in which the data are provided by the World Bank, we therefore include increases in the incomes of those escaping poverty up to, but not beyond, the poverty line—that is, the shaded area in Figure 6.5. By comparing this with the total increase in income (the total gap

FIGURE 6.4
The income of the poor

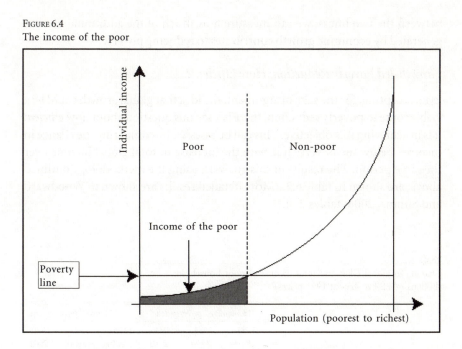

FIGURE 6.5
Growth and the income of the poor

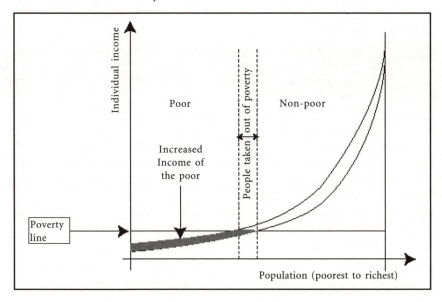

between the two lines), we can measure how much of the additional income generated by economic growth contributes to reducing poverty.

Growth-led Poverty Reduction: How Efficient?

Even accepting, for the sake of argument, the idea that global growth could be a viable route to poverty reduction, there is a serious question about how *efficient* it is in achieving this objective. This can be assessed by comparing the change in incomes below the poverty line with the increase in total global income over the same period. The results of this analysis, using the methodology outlined above, are shown in table 6.2. (More detailed results are shown in Woodward and Simms, 2006: tables 2–4.)

TABLE 6.2
Changes in global GDP and total income of poor households
(billions of PPP dollars at 1993 prices)

		"$2-a-day" poverty line			"$1-a-day" poverty line		
		1981–2001	1981–1990	1990–2001	1981–2001	1981–1990	1990–2001
WITHOUT population adjustment	Poverty reduction	786	371	388	278	151	95
	Change in GDP	18,691	7,512	11,179	18,691	7,512	11,179
	Poverty reduction as % of change in GDP	4.21	4.94	3.48	1.49	2.01	0.85
	Income of poor as % of GDP	4.35	4.35	3.94	1.80	1.80	1.18
	Ratio of share in growth to share in GDP	0.97	1.13	0.88	0.83	1.12	0.72
WITH population adjustment	Poverty reduction	335	187	148	104	76	28
	Change in GDP	8,160	3,443	4,717	8,160	3,443	4,717
	Poverty reduction as % of change in GDP	4.11	5.45	3.13	1.28	2.20	0.60
	Income of poor as % of GDP	4.35	4.35	3.94	1.80	1.80	1.18
	Ratio of share in growth to share in GDP	0.94	1.25	0.80	0.71	1.22	0.51

Source: All figures are calculated from Woodward and Simms (2006: tables 2 and 3).

Between 1981 and 2001, world GDP (PPP in 1993 prices) increased by $18,691 billion. Of this, only $786 billion, or 4.2 per cent, went to poverty reduction as defined by the $2-a-day poverty line—slightly *less* than the share of the poor in GDP at the beginning of the period (4.35 per cent)—even though the poor represented the majority of the world population. These figures are potentially misleading, however, as a substantial part of both the change in GDP and the change in the total income of the poor reflect the increase in the world population rather than increased output and income per person. Adjusting for this reduces the proportion of GDP contributing to poverty reduction slightly further to 4.1 per cent.

While the $2-a-day level may be a more realistic, if still very low, definition of poverty, attention currently focuses on the $1-a-day line, which provides the basis for MDG1. Almost inevitably, the extent of poverty reduction based on the $1-a-day poverty line between 1981 and 2001 was even smaller than that below the $2-a-day line, at $278 billion—just 1.5 per cent of GDP growth. More worryingly, it was also five times further below the share of the poor in GDP in 1981 than on the basis of the $2-a-day line (one sixth less, as compared with one thirtieth). Again, adjusting for population growth makes the situation substantially worse, reducing the share of GDP growth contributing to poverty reduction to just 1.3 per cent, between one quarter and one third less than the share of the poor in GDP.

To put it another way, of every $100 of growth in income per person in the world as a whole between 1981 and 2001, just $1.30 contributed to reducing poverty as measured by the $1-a-day line and a further $2.80 to reducing poverty between $1-a-day and $2-a-day lines. The remaining $95.90 went to the rest of the world population above the $2-a-day line.

Is it Getting Better?

The 1980s were widely described as "the lost decade for development", especially for Latin America and Africa. Much of the developing world was plagued by the debt crisis; interest rates were exceptionally high; commodity export prices collapsed; aid fell ever further below the 0.7 per cent of national income level to which developed countries had committed themselves in 1970; and most developing countries were going through the most painful initial phase of structural adjustment. It seemed things could hardly get worse.

The 1990s should have heralded a much more favourable environment for development. Aid levels were expected to benefit from a peace dividend following the end of the cold war; the debt crisis was over in most middle-income countries; and debt cancellation was increasingly available for poor countries. Interest rates had fallen back to more normal levels, and, after a decade of structural adjustment, developing countries should have been poised to enjoy the promised economic recovery meant to result from their painful sacrifices in the 1980s. The World Trade Organization was established in 1993 to create the more open international trading system seen as necessary for growth, and the World Bank rediscovered its mission to reduce poverty. Markets were freer and more deregulated, States were smaller, economies were more open and macroeconomic policies were tighter. All in all, if the mainstream economic story is to be believed, the stage was perfectly set for growth-led poverty reduction.

The reality, however, was very different: performance in terms of growth-led poverty reduction was much worse in almost every respect in the 1990s than in the 1980s. In PPP terms, global growth actually *fell* slightly, from 1.7 per cent per annum in 1981–1990 to 1.6 per cent per annum in 1990–2001 (Figure 6.6). While PPP data are not available prior to 1980, global growth at market exchange rates had already slowed down by nearly half, from 3.2 per cent per annum to 1.7 per cent per annum between 1960–1970 and 1970–1981, slowing further to 1.5 per cent per annum in 1981–1990, and still further to just 1.3 per cent per annum in 1990–2001 (World Bank, 2005a).

Worse still, global growth also appears to have become much *more* anti-poor between the 1980s and the 1990s. Based on the $2-a-day poverty line, the proportion of growth contributing to poverty reduction fell from nearly 5 per cent in the 1980s to just under 3.5 per cent in the 1990s. This represents a decline from one eighth *more* than the initial share of the poor in GDP to one eighth *less*. Adjusting for population growth further worsens performance in the 1990s and accentuates the deterioration between the 1980s and the 1990s. By this measure, the share of poverty reduction in growth fell from 5.5 per cent (one quarter *more* than the share of the poor in initial GDP) to 3.1 per cent (one fifth *less*) (see Figures 6.7 and 6.8).

Based on the $1-a-day line, poverty reduction fell still more sharply, from $151 billion (2.0 per cent of the increase in GDP) in the 1980s to $95 billion (0.8 per cent) in the 1990s. The latter figure is one quarter less than the initial share of the poor in world GDP, compared with one eighth more in the 1980s. Again, adjusting for population growth makes the picture still worse. The contribution of per capita growth to poverty reduction fell from $76 billion to $28 billion—from 2.2 per cent of the population-adjusted increase in GDP to just 0.6 per cent, barely half the initial share of the poor in GDP. This means that in the 1990s it took $166 of global per capita growth, with all the associated environmental costs, to achieve just $1 of progress towards MDG1.

FIGURE 6.6
Growth of global GDP per capita, 1960–2001

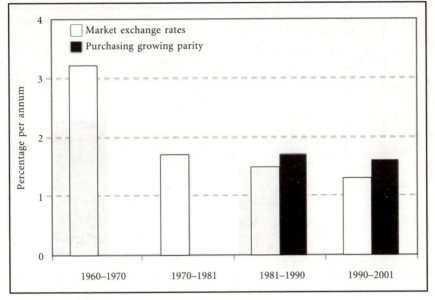

Source: World Bank (2005a).

FIGURE 6.7
Share of the poor in per capita growth, 1981–2001

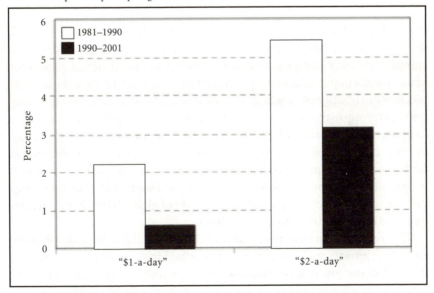

Source: Table 6.2.

FIGURE 6.8
Share of the poor in per capita growth, relative to initial share in income, 1981–2001

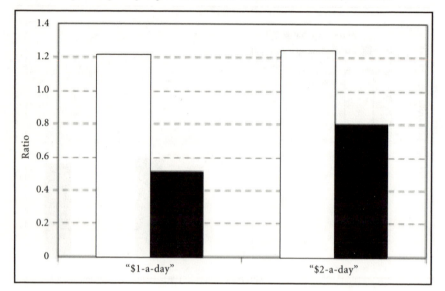

Source: Table 6.2.

GROWTH AND DISTRIBUTION: A COMPARISON

If global growth is an inefficient and environmentally dangerous solution to the problem of global poverty, how does changing the distribution of income compare? Redistributing just 1 per cent of the income of the richest 20 per cent of the world's population to the poorest 20 per cent would benefit the latter as much as distributionally equal growth of around 20 per cent. Even expanding the target group to the poorest 50 per cent of the world's population—equivalent to a poverty line of around $2.50 per day at 1993 prices—and the source group to 25 per cent (roughly the level at which the well-being literature indicates that further increases in income cease to raise well-being), a 1 per cent redistribution is equivalent to economic growth of 7.4 per cent. This is more than four times the average 1.7 per cent per capita growth rate of global GDP (in PPP terms) since 1981 (Woodward and Simms, 2006).

The argument that poverty should or could be tackled through redistribution, rather than growth, tends to be dismissed by orthodox economists on the grounds that redistribution is unsustainable. Redistribution, they argue, can only continue for a limited period, as incomes will be equalized, so that there is no further scope for redistribution. By contrast, they contend, growth can continue indefinitely.

Apart from the fallacy of the contention that growth can be sustained indefinitely, a simple analysis demonstrates the invalidity of this argument, at least at the global level. The total amount going to poverty reduction below the $2-a-day line between 1981 and 2001 (population-adjusted) came to $335 billion in real PPP terms. Based on the estimated global distribution of income in 1993, the income of the richest 10 per cent of the world's population was $14,543 billion.

This means that the rate of poverty reduction achieved between 1981 and 2001 could have been achieved through the redistribution annually of just 0.12 per cent of the income of the richest 10 per cent of the world's population. This rate of transfer could be sustained for 300 years before the world as a whole even reached the average level of inequality in European Union countries.

Why Growth? The "Positive-Sum Game" Fallacy

If growth is so meaningless as an objective and so inefficient in reducing poverty, and if it gives rise to such serious tensions between poverty reduction and environmental sustainability, why is it so prominent in the economics discourse?

Trying to reduce poverty through redistribution of income alone in a no-growth global economy is, by its nature, a zero-sum game in terms of its financial effects. The incomes of the poor can only be increased by the same amount as those of the rich are reduced. Growth, on the other hand, means that there is more income available in total, so that the rich can get richer even as the poor get less poor. Moreover, since the rich are generally more powerful than the poor (World Bank, 2005b)—globally as well as at the country level (Jubilee Research, 2005)—this is seen as presenting a more politically feasible approach than redistribution.

However, there are three fundamental problems with this argument. First, looking beyond the financial effects to take account of environmental impacts means that growth is no longer necessarily a positive-sum game. Every $1 of growth comes with an environmental price tag, so $1 of extra income generated through growth brings less than $1 in actual benefits.

Second, as noted earlier, the benefits associated with an extra $1 of income depend critically on who receives it. Thus looking at effects on economic and social rights and well-being—which are objectives in their own right—rather than at financial effects—which are only a means to an end—redistribution *is* a positive-sum game. By taking $1 away from a millionaire and giving it to a pauper, we have no perceptible effect on the rights or well-being of the millionaire, but a much greater effect on the life of the pauper. While *income* may be no higher as a result, well-being and the fulfilment of rights are improved—without necessarily generating additional consumption or production which might have environmental costs.[4]

Thirdly, the zero-/positive-sum game argument is based on a false dichotomy between growth and *redistribution*—in effect, returning to the conceptual separation between the average level and the distribution of income. In practice, the question is not whether our policy objective should be economic growth or no growth, or whether we should or should not take steps to redistribute the income arising from this growth. Rather, the question is whether economic policies should aim to maximize *total* income in the hope that poverty will fall as a by-product, or whether they should aim more specifically to increase the incomes of poorer households and treat *growth* (or the lack of it) as a by-product—that is, whether distributional effects should be integrated into the design of economic policies as a whole.

POLICY IMPLICATIONS

If growth does not offer the prospect of reconciling poverty reduction and environmental sustainability, then what is the alternative? While a greater emphasis on redistribution policies as an add-on to growth-oriented policies would help at the country level, it is insufficient to resolve a problem which arises at least as much from inequalities *between* countries as from inequalities *within* them.

Intercountry inequality has been recognized as a fundamental problem since the colonial era, giving rise to the developed country Governments' 1970 pledge to provide 0.7 per cent of their national income in aid. However, this commitment has failed miserably: the shortfall of aid from this target was $140 billion in 2004.

World Bank analysis suggests that each extra $1 billion of aid provided by the International Development Association (IDA) in 1997–1998 lifted 434,000 people permanently out of poverty, as defined by the $1-a-day line (Goldin, Rogers and Stern, 2002). On this basis, if all the OECD countries had met the 0.7 per cent target in every year since 1970, and the additional aid had had a similar poverty-reduction effect, this would, in principle, have been sufficient to eradicate poverty below the $1-a-day line in 1999—the very year the MDGs were adopted.

Moreover, despite their failure to deliver more than a fraction of the promised aid, the developed country Governments have extracted a considerable price for what they have provided. They have used aid to prop up sympathetic, but undemocratic, deeply unpopular and often corrupt Governments, to secure policy changes that favour their national and commercial interests at the expense of the population of the recipient country and to persuade Governments to sign up to international agreements which bind them and their successors to flawed policies for the indefinite future.

Patronage aid thus confers power on the developed country Governments and international institutions like the World Bank and the IMF, thus helping to entrench the inequitable structures of the global economic system which underlie the more fundamental problem. It is the products of this power imbalance—the continuation of the debt crisis in many of the poorest countries for nearly 25 years, the imposition of neo-liberal policies across the developing world, the chronic decline in commodity export prices and international trade agreements which lock developing countries into an unbalanced market paradigm—which reinforce and exacerbate global income inequality.

The alternative is to move decisively away from the current top-down approach, in which policies are largely determined at the global level, ostensibly, at least, to promote global growth. Instead, we need to move definitively towards a system in which national policies are designed explicitly and directly to achieve social and environmental objectives; and in which the global economic system is designed to promote, foster and support such policies, treating *growth* as a by-product, and putting the interests of the poor majority of the world's population first. In short, we need to move definitively away from what is, in effect, no more than a global variant of the long-discredited idea of "trickle-down" to a concept of income "bubbling up" from poverty reduction.

This might include the generation of additional resources for development at the global level, through, for example:

- introducing international taxation (for example, on foreign exchange transactions, air travel and transport, fuel, etc.);
- assigning countries tradable, revenue-raising entitlements to emit greenhouse gases on a globally equal per capita basis; and
- introducing a new global currency, so that money creation generates new public resources at the global level (also limiting the potential for financial instability arising from irresponsible economic policies in the US).

It might also entail international collaboration, for example:

- to promote local investment, strengthen public finances and allow more progressive tax systems, e.g., through coordinated measures to control capital flight, tax havens and tax competition;
- to limit the supply of agricultural commodities produced primarily by developing countries, so as to reverse the long-term decline in prices;

- to ensure that royalties and other payments from extractive industries reflect the full cost of natural resource depletion, by increasing transparency and controlling competition between countries; and
- to focus research and development investment on developing technologies which fulfil social and environmental needs, rather than those which maximize corporate profits.

At the country level, as well as implementation of such collaborative measures, it might mean, for example:

- using resources generated at the global level and strengthened public finances to provide high-quality, free and universal education and basic health services; pensions, child benefits and social safety nets; and the infrastructure needed for the development of micro, small and medium enterprises;
- favouring local suppliers in low-income areas in procurement for these and other public programmes;
- targeting income-generation programmes so that the additional production generated broadly matches the increase in demand resulting from the associated poverty reduction (based on consumption patterns revealed by household expenditure surveys); and
- strengthening agricultural extension programmes, focusing particularly on crops consumed locally by low-income consumers (so that the price effects of increased supply will contribute to poverty reduction as well as the income effects).

Without such changes, it appears extremely unlikely that we can reconcile substantial poverty reduction—let alone eradication—with the need for environmental sustainability. However, any significant progress will require two further fundamental changes:

- a change in the way we think about and discuss economic issues, allowing us to break out of the confines of mainstream economic discourse; and
- a shift in power relations, both globally and nationally, to move power from developed countries, elites and commercial interests to the majority of the world's population who still live on less than $2.50 per day (at 1993 PPP).

CONCLUSION

We have, in recent years, become fixated on economic growth. This is partly just one component of a broader fixation on the macroeconomy and partly a result of the tyranny of numbers—a growing obsession with quantifiable indicators of policy performance and a failure to make what is important measurable, rather than making what is measurable important.

It is also partly a product of political pragmatism, on the grounds that the rich are too powerful to allow redistribution of their income or wealth. While this may have some justification, it is noteworthy that the economists, politicians and opinion makers who express this view are themselves among the elite to which they ascribe such power—and not generally at the forefront of efforts to rectify the imbalance of power at the global level. It is difficult to escape the conclusion that there is more than a little self-interest in such arguments.

More generally, the pro-growth view is critically dependent upon a number of implausible or counter-intuitive assumptions: that it is aggregate income that matters, rather than people's quality of life; that growth and distribution are separable, both conceptually and practically; that economic growth has no unmanageable environmental costs; and that power relations are immutably fixed. In other words, this view is critically dependent on the mindset of orthodox economics.

Our analysis indicates that global economic growth is an extremely inefficient and environmentally dangerous way of achieving poverty reduction—particularly MDG1—and is becoming even more so. Between 1990 and 2001, for every $100 worth of growth in the world's income per person, just $0.60 contributed to reducing poverty below the $1-a-day line, 73 per cent less even than in the lost decade for development, the 1980s. Each $1 of poverty reduction thus requires $166 of additional global production and consumption, with all its associated environmental impacts which adversely affect the poorest most.

This suggests that reconciling the objectives of poverty reduction and environmental sustainability requires a decisive shift away from the blind pursuit of global economic growth and the fallacious economic orthodoxy and grossly skewed global governance structures which underlie it. In effect, the global growth model amounts to sacrificing the environment on which we all depend for our very survival to give yet more to those who already have too much, in the hope that a few more crumbs will fall from the rich man's table. The scale of growth this model would require to eradicate poverty—surely our ultimate goal—would generate unsupportable environmental costs, which would fall disproportionately and counterproductively on the poorest, rendering the process self-defeating.

In the growth debate, for all its theoretical sophistry, orthodox economics repeatedly falls back on a few tried and tested metaphors to defend its growth obsession—that a rising tide lifts all boats, or that it is better to bake a larger cake than to cut the existing one more equally. Ironically, however, sea levels really are rising, as a result of the global warming driven by economic growth itself, and millions of the poor have no boats to rise in, literally or metaphorically. As for the cake analogy, even the massed ranks of orthodox economists have yet to find either the recipe or the ingredients to bake a spare planet to share among the world's population.

If we are serious about increasing well-being and eradicating poverty within our environmental constraints, then it is our progress towards doing so, not growth of aggregate income, for which we should design our economic policies and institutions and by which we should judge our progress. This means designing national policies to achieve our ultimate social and environmental objectives and changing the global economic system, not only to accommodate, but to foster and promote, these policies. Maximizing economic growth, and hoping that we will make some progress towards our ultimate objectives as a by-product, has not, will not, and cannot work.

NOTES

[1] This paper is based on Woodward and Simms (2006), to which readers are referred for more detailed results and some additional analysis. Except where otherwise specified, all poverty data are taken from the World Bank's PovCalNet computational tool, accessible at http://iresearch.worldbank.org/PovcalNet.

[2] By analogy with the Kuznets hypothesis on the relationship between income inequality and overall income levels in the course of development, a Kuznets carbon curve hypothesizes that carbon emissions rise with increasing income up to a certain level of income, but decline as income rises beyond this point.

[3] The Gini coefficient for the global economy in 1993 was estimated at 80 per cent at market exchange rates, but at only 60 per cent at PPP rates (Milanovic, 1999).

[4] While the change in the patterns of consumption and production associated with changes in the distribution of income may have environmental effects, these may be either positive or negative.

REFERENCES

Amann, E., N. Aslanidis, F. Nixson and B. Walters (2002). Economic growth and poverty alleviation: A reconsideration of Dollar and Kraay. Paper presented at the Annual Conference of the Development Studies Association, University of Greenwich, 9 November.

Baulch, R., and N. McCulloch (1999). Tracking pro-poor growth. *ID21 Insights* 31. Institute of Development Studies, Sussex. September. http://www.id21.org/insights/insights31/insights-iss31-art03.html

BBC Online (2005). Climate change will dry Africa, 29 November. http://news.bbc.co.uk/2/hi/science/nature/4479640.stm

DFID (2004). What is Pro-poor Growth and Why Do We Need to Know? Pro-Poor Growth Briefing Note 1, Policy Division, Department for International Development, London.

di Fazio, A. (2000). *The Fallacy of Pure Efficiency Gain Measures to Control Future Climate Change.* Astronomical Observatory of Rome and Global Dynamics Institute, Rome.

Diamond, Jared (2005). *Collapse: How Societies Choose to Fail or Survive.* Penguin/Allen Lane, London.

Dollar, David, and Aart Kraay (2000). Growth is good for the poor. Development Research Group, World Bank, Washington, DC.

Dollar, David, and Aart Kraay (2001). Growth is good for the poor. Policy Research Working Paper 2587, World Bank, Washington, DC.

Dollar, David, and Aart Kraay (2002). Growth is good for the poor. *Journal of Economic Growth* 7: 195–225.

EEA (2006). *The European Footprint: How the Planet and the World's Largest Economy Interact.* Forthcoming, European Environment Agency, Copenhagen.

EIA (2004). World energy use and carbon dioxide emissions. Energy Information Administration, US Department of Energy, Washington, DC. http://www.eia.doe.gov/emeu/cabs/carbonemiss/chapter1.html

Global Footprint Network (2005). *Ecological Footprint Assessment.* www.footprintnetwork.org

Goldin, Ian, H. Rogers, and Nicholas Stern (2002). The Role and Effectiveness of Development Assistance: Lessons from World Bank Experience. Processed, 18 March, World Bank, Washington, DC. http://siteresources.worldbank.org/DEC/Resources/roleofdevelopment.pdf

Held, I.M., T. Delworth, J. Lu, K. Findell, and T. Knutson (2005). Simulation of Sahel drought in the 20th and 21st centuries. *Proceedings of the National Academy of Sciences*, 102, 1 December: 17891–896.

IFRC (1999). *World Disasters Report 1999.* International Federation of Red Cross and Red Crescent Societies, Geneva.

International Climate Change Taskforce (2005). *Meeting the Climate Challenge.* International Climate Change Taskforce, London. www.ippr.org.uk

InterGovernmental Panel on Climate Change (2001). *Third Assessment Report: Climate Change 2001.* Cambridge University Press, Cambridge.

IRIN (2005). Rising Indian Ocean temperatures will bring escalating drought. 25 May, Integrated Regional Information Networks, UN Office for the Coordination of Humanitarian Affairs, Johannesburg.

Jubilee Research (2005). Physician, heal thyself! The World Bank's *World Development Report, 2006: Equity in Development.* 27 September. www.jubileeresearch.org/analysis/articles/worldbank280905.htm, 27 September.

Kakwani, Nanak, and E. Pernia (2000). What is pro-poor growth? *Asian Development Review* 18 (1): 1–16.

Klasen, S. (2003). In search of the Holy Grail: How to achieve pro-poor growth. In B. Tungodden, N. Stern and I. Kolstad (eds). *Toward Pro-poor Policies: Aid, Institutions and Globalization. Proceedings of the Annual Conference on Development Economics Europe Conference 2003.* World Bank, Washington, DC: 63–92.

Klasen, S. (2005). Economic Growth and Poverty Reduction: Measurement and Policy Issues. Working Paper No. 246, September, Development Centre, OECD, Paris.

Krueger, Anne (2004a). Expanding trade and unleashing growth: The prospects for lasting poverty reduction. Remarks at the IMF Seminar on Trade and Regional Integration, 6 December, Dakar, Senegal. http://www.imf.org/external/np/speeches/2004/120604.htm

Krueger, Anne (2004b). Letting the future in: India's continuing reform agenda. Keynote speech to Stanford India Conference, Stanford University, Stanford, CA, 4 June. http://www.imf.org/external/np/speeches/2004/120604.htm

Lopez, Humberto (2006) Did Growth Become Less Pro-Poor in the 1990s? Policy Research Working Paper 3931. World Bank, Washington D.C., June.

Marland, Gregg, and Tom Boden (2005) Global CO2 Emissions from Fossil-Fuel Burning, Cement Manufacture, and Gas Flaring: 1751–2002. Carbon Dioxide Information

Analysis Center (CDIAC), Oak Ridge, Tennessee. http://cdiac.esd.ornl.gov/ftp/ndp030/ global. 1751_2002.ems

Milanovic, Branko (1999). True World Income Distribution, 1988 and 1993: First Calculations, Based on Household Surveys Alone. Policy Research Working Paper 2244, November, World Bank, Washington, DC.

Müller-Fürstenberger, G., M. Wagner, and B. Müller (2004). *Exploring the Carbon Kuznets Hypothesis.* Oxford Institute for Energy Studies, Oxford.

ONS (2005). *Social Trends 2005.* Office for National Statistics, London.

Oxfam (2000). *Growth with Equity is Good for the Poor.* Oxfam, Oxford.

Ravallion, Martin (2004). Pro-poor Growth: A Primer. Policy Research Working Paper 3242, World Bank, Washington DC.

Ravallion, Martin, and Siaohua Chen (2003). Measuring pro-poor growth. *Economics Letters* 78 (1): 93–99.

Simms, Andrew (2005). *Africa—Up in Smoke? The Second Report from the Working Group on Climate Change and Development.* New Economics Foundation and International Institute for Environment and Development, London.

Wackernagel, M., D. Moran, S. Goldfinger, C. Monfreda, A. Welch, M. Murray, S. Burns, C. Königel, J. Peck, P. King and M. Ballasteros (2005). *Europe 2005: The ecological footprint.* Global Footprint Network and WWF. www.footprintnetwork.org

Wade, Robert (2001). Winners and losers. *The Economist,* 26 April.

Wagstaff, A. (2003). Child health on a dollar a day: Some tentative cross-country comparisons. *Social Science and Medicine* 57: 1529–38.

Weisbrot, Mark, Dean Baker, Robert Naiman, and Gila Neta (2001). *Growth may be Good for the Poor—but are the IMF and World Bank Policies Good for Growth?* Center for Economic Policy Research, Washington, DC.

White, H., and A. Anderson (2001). Growth vs. redistribution: Does the pattern of growth matter? *Development Policy Review* 19 (3): 167–289.

Woodward, David, and Andrew Simms (2006). Growth isn't working: The unbalanced distribution of benefits and costs from economic growth. New Economics Foundation, London. January.

World Bank (2000). *The Quality of Growth.* World Bank, Washington, DC.

World Bank (2004). Natural disasters: Counting the cost. 2 March. World Bank, Washington, DC. www.worldbank.org

World Bank (2005a). *World Development Indicators Online.*

World Bank (2005b). *World Development Report, 2006: Equity and Development.* World Bank, Washington, DC.

7
Inequality Trends in Some Developed OECD Countries

JOHN WEEKS

The current discourse on inequality within countries, and especially within the developed market economies of the OECD, must be placed in historical context. A long period of the growth of international trade within a laissez faire framework and colonial expansion characterized the second half of the nineteenth century, with the United Kingdom the dominant country, being overtaken by a group of later developers, principally the United States of America, Germany, and France. This period of relative peace among the advanced countries came to an end in 1914, with the outbreak of the First World War (or, 'the Great War', as it was called at the time).

The thirty years that followed brought a series of disasters to the developed world: hyper-inflation in Germany, the Great Depression, and a second global war. Almost without exception, the leadership of the mainstream parties in the developed countries, from Christian Democrats through the various Socialist parties, concluded that these disasters resulted from instabilities inherent in market economies. In particular, there arose a consensus that the two great authoritarian political systems of the century, fascism and communism, had in no small part arisen from the consequences of those instabilities.

In the academic literature, the prominent British economist K. W. Rothschild made this connection in what was perhaps the profession's leading periodical, the *Economic Journal* (Rothschild, 1947). Discussing the tendency towards concentration of economic power in major international markets, Rothschild referred to "the most violent aspect of the oligopolistic struggle, the attempts of the biggest oligopolistic groupings to regroup their forces on a world scale" (Rothschild, 1947: 318). He argued that a characteristic of this regrouping on a world scale was the anti-social effect of oligopolistic competition: "there is no fundamental difference between 'economic activities like cut-throat pricing' and 'modern wars and armed interventions'" (Rothschild, 1947: 317). He went on to conclude, "that Fascism...has been largely brought into power by [the] struggle...of the most powerful oligopolists to strengthen through political action, their position in the labour market and vis-à-vis their smaller competitors, and finally to strike out in order to change the world market situation in their favour" (Rothschild, 1947: 318).

At the beginning of the twenty-first century it is startling to read such strong political conclusions anywhere, much less in a major economics journal. That such views would be held by a mainstream economist, and published in a leading technical journal, reflects the generally accepted view of the time that two wars, a disastrous depression, and the rise of two authoritarian systems were evidence of something fundamentally amiss with competitive capitalism that was insufficiently regulated and contained—fundamental problems that went well beyond 'market failures'. Many of the institutions established in the last years of the Second World War, in San Francisco, Washington, D.C. and Bretton Woods, were designed to limit the working of markets mechanisms at the international level.

In 1944, the Declaration of the International Labour Organization had affirmed, with more hope than likelihood, that 'labour is not a commodity'. In 1945, the International Monetary Fund was created with two main purposes that seem quite extraordinary at the beginning of the twenty-first century: maintaining economic prosperity among countries and strictly limiting the market in currencies through a fixed exchange rate system. Fixed exchange rates, based on a US dollar with a fixed gold price, were designed to end 'competitive devaluations' ('beggar thy neighbour' devaluations), the purpose of which was to 'export unemployment'. So far is current thinking from the concerns of sixty years ago that these phrases, which to contemporaries encapsulated the lessons of catastrophic experience, seem quaint and absurd.

The commitment of post-war leaders to preventing the international rise of uncontrollable corporate power had its domestic aspect, which was pursued with even greater zeal. Along with the concern that the rise of corporate power was a threat to democratic institutions went the closely linked view that excessive concentrations of private income and wealth were a manifestation of that threat at the household and individual levels. The broad political support for policies to restrict the concentration of wealth and income came from strong trade union movements in most of the countries, which, again, at the beginning of the twenty-first century seems an anachronism. The growing international rivalry between the United States and the then Soviet Union reinforced the political commitment in the 'free world' to policies of limiting inequality, with the political leadership in Washington recognizing a need to demonstrate the superiority of the market system in providing for the welfare of its citizens.

It is the argument of this chapter that income inequality has increased in several, but not all, developed countries over the last twenty years. The increase in some countries supports the conclusion that the deregulation of markets, resulting in the concentration of economic power, is the fundamental cause as well as the gross manifestation of inequality of both income and wealth. The argument is developed as follows. The next section presents the abstract analytics of income distribution, to demonstrate that theoretical inconsistencies in the neoclassical framework lead to the conclusion that the functional distribution of income, and, therefore, the size distribution, is indeterminate without considering bargaining power. The following section reviews the movements in income inequality in seventeen OECD countries, which produce a clear distinction between 'the Anglo-Saxon four' and the other thirteen. The penultimate section considers causation, using a simple statistical exercise to support the argument that where income inequality has increased, it resulted from the imbalance in bargaining power resulting from deregulation of markets. The concluding section proposes a change in the economic and political agendas in which the central task of policy is to reverse the measures which have caused the imbalance in bargaining power.

Analytical Framework

The orthodox argument against interventions to reduce inequality derives from an analysis that concludes that income distribution arises from the production technology of an economy, and that the resulting distribution is technically determined, economic efficient, and unique given that technology. It follows, therefore, that inequality reflects the distribution of assets, including so-called human capital,[1] and the efficient return to those assets. In the context of globalization, this argument is extended to maintain that if it is the case that globalization has been associated within increased inequality, this results from irresistible technological and demographic factors that cannot be countered; or, if attempts are made to counter them, the result is to foster inefficiency and undermine competitiveness.

However, this argument, that distribution is technically determined, is logically flawed. It derives from an analysis based upon the concept of a unique aggregate production function that dictates aggregate distribution, whose validity was refuted in the famous Cambridge Controversy (Robinson, 1969; Harcourt, 1972). The refutation begins with a simple two-commodity economy in which there is one output, one input, and the input is completely used in each period (capital has a life span of one period). To produce the commodities, there is a range of methods with fixed coefficients, and capitalists choose the most profitable given the factor prices that they face. The combined methods for the two commodities, one an input into the other, constitute the technology of the economy. The production conditions for the economy using a technology designated as A, with 1 standing for the output and 2 for the input, can be written as follows (for greater detail, see Weeks, 1989):

(unit capital cost)$_1$ + (unit labour cost)$_1$ + (unit profit)$_1$ = (price)$_1$
(unit capital cost)$_2$ + (unit labour cost)$_2$ + (unit profit)$_2$ = (price)$_2$

The terms on the left sum to the aggregate value added of the economy. In more detail, this can be written as:

$$P_{(a2)}k_{(a1)} + P_{(a1)}wl_{(a1)} + (profit)_{(a1)} = P_{(a1)}$$
$$P_{(a2)}k_{(a2)} + P_{(a1)}wl_{(a2)} + (profit)_{(a2)} = P_{(a2)}$$

Where the p's are prices, k's are the unit capital inputs, w is the amount of the output workers consume, and the l's are unit labour inputs, for technology A. If we omit the technology symbols, set the prices of the output to unity (so that $p = p_2/p_1$), and define r as the profit rate on capital, one obtains:

$$[1 + r]pk_1 + wl_1 = 1$$
$$[1 + r]pk_2 + wl_2 = 1$$

These two equations can be solved simultaneously for the profit rate. This allows the profit rate to be expressed as a function of the wage rate and technical parameters:

$$r = [1 - wl_1], [k_2 + w(k_2l_1 - k_1l_2)]$$

The neoclassical term for this equation is 'factor price frontier' (FPF). It gives the profit rate implied by any real wage. If it is a straight line (linear), then the real wage and profits are determinate when one adds a neoclassical labour market: equilibrium in the labour market determines w,[2] and w implies r. When the wage rises, firms switch to a more capital intensive technique, and when the wage falls, to a more labour intensive one. However, inspection of the equation shows that the factor price frontier will be a straight line if and only if $k_2l_1 = k_1l_2$,[3] that is, if the input and the output have the same factor intensity. In general, the factor price frontier will be convex (input more capital intensive) or concave (output more capital intensive). If the factor price frontier is non-linear, it implies that FPFs for different technologies can intersect twice. This analysis results in an extremely important theoretical prediction: when the real wage goes up, prompting a capitalist to change technology, he/she may find it profitable to choose a more *labour* intensive one, and vice versa. In other words, clearing of the labour market no longer produces a unique profit rate, even if technological possibilities remain constant.

We can now summarize the practical implications of this apparently arcane analysis. The labour market does not produce a unique distribution between wages and profits on the basis of technical parameters, because there are many possible market-clearing wage and profit combinations. It is a trivial extension of this analysis to include additional factors of production, such as labour of different skills, and convert the discussion from the functional to the size distribution of income. Which general equilibrium is realized, and its associated distribution, will be determined in part by the relative bargaining power of the various economic agents. Economic theory concludes that within a broad range of outcomes, distribution results from relative bargaining power. This is the analytical framework we use to consider actual changes in distribution, after reviewing the empirical evidence.

TRENDS IN INEQUALITY

In anticipation of the presentation of the empirical evidence, a brief discussion of measures of inequality is necessary. Many measures are used in empirical work, and our presentation restricts itself to the Gini coefficient, not because of its superiority over other calculations of inequality, but because of the frequency of its use. It assigns diminishing weights as incomes rise, which can be seen as an advantage if one is inequality-averse. Its major drawback is that it is relatively insensitive to changes in the middle range of a distribution. As a result, two distributions can yield the same index, though their income frequencies differ— a special case of the general problem of Lorenz curves crossing.

In this section we review the changes in inequality in the major industrial countries with the purpose, first, of identifying trends, and, second, of drawing conclusions about the major forces underlying those changes. In the previous section it was demonstrated that income distribution cannot be determined technically even in the abstract. However, this conclusion need not in itself undermine the apologies for globalization-driven inequality, which can be defended by various ad hoc arguments. In particular, we inspect the hypothesis that increases in inequality reflect characteristics of the economic forces determining growth in the late twentieth century, forces allegedly inherent in that growth, beyond the power of policy to influence or arrest. In other words, increases in equality represent an irresistible development driven by fundamental technological and demographic forces. This is not a difficult hypothesis to test. Were it true, one would expect a general tendency across countries, manifest in varying degrees, for inequality to increase.

With this hypothesis in mind, we can inspect Table 7.1, which shows the average Gini coefficients for seventeen developed OECD countries for four decades (see also Figures 7.1–7.3). The countries divide into three groups: 1) those with a rising trend in inequality, all of which, except Canada, are the so-called Anglo-Saxon countries (four: Australia, New Zealand, the United Kingdom, and the United States of America); 2) those with a falling trend (again, four: Canada, Italy, Norway and Spain); and 3) those showing no trend (nine: Austria, Belgium, Denmark, Finland, France, Germany, Japan, Netherlands and Sweden).[4]

The absence of a global pattern is strong prima facie evidence that trends and non-trends reflect policies, not inexorable forces beyond the influence of governments. First, it should not be controversial that the four countries with trends towards greater inequality are those which pursued a broadly similar policy programme that has come to be called 'neo-liberal'.[5] Second, without exception, the rising inequality manifested itself in the four countries during the years when that broadly similar policy agenda was pursued most vigorously, especially the 1980s, but also the 1990s. In each of these countries, the decade average inequality for the 1980s and 1990s was higher than in the pre-liberalization 1960s and 1970s. Finally, while the Governments of the other thirteen countries introduced policy changes that may have reduced the social protection associated with the welfare state, none consistently pursued neo-liberal policies.

Thus, two conclusions derive from Table 7.1, which are beyond challenge. First, in the vast majority of countries there was no trend increase in inequality. This alone prompts one to reject the hypothesis that inherent in the global economy in the last decades of the twentieth century were inequality increasing forces. Second, the small number of countries that exhibit significant increases in inequality followed broadly similar economic and social policies, with labour market deregulation perhaps being the most important.

The increases in inequality for the Anglo-Saxon 'neo-liberal four' are striking for the dramatic and historical change that they represent. In the 1950s, Simon Kuznets famously argued that income inequality, across countries and over time in most countries, follows an inverted 'U' pattern with respect to per capita income: after an initial tendency for inequality to rise at low levels of per capita income, this tendency would reverse itself (Kuznets, 1955). This hypothesis implies that the inequality indices of the high-income countries would be found well below the medium value for all countries (since most countries with distributional data are middle-income).

TABLE 7.1
Gini coefficients by decade, 17 OECD countries

		1960s	1970s	1980s	1990s	last year	Coef var	Trend
1. Australia		32.0	37.3	37.3	41.7	1990	.097	rising
	n=	1	4	5	1	11		
2. Austria		na	25.3	25.5	26.1	1991	.031	none
	n=		8	10	2	20		
3. Belgium		na	28.3	26.3	27.1	1995	.031	none
	n=		1	3	2	6		
4. Canada		31.5	31.6	31.5	28.9	1994	.053	falling
	n=	4	6	9	3	22		
5. Denmark		na	31.0	32.0	33.0	1992	.039	none
	n =		1	2	2	5		
6. Finland		na	28.7	25.5	26.1	1996	.059	none
	n=		2	5	8	15		
7. France		na	36.2	37.2	36.0	1994	.041	none
	n=		3	2	3	8		
8. Germany		30.9	31.3	30.6	28.2	1994	.066	none
	n=	2	2	4	3	11		
9. Italy		na	37.4	33.4	33.3	1993	.072	falling
	n=		6	8	2	16		
10. Japan		35.2	34.1	35.2	35.0	1990	.038	none
	n=	3	10	5	1	19		
11. Netherlands		na	28.4	28.6	29.4	1991	.033	none
	n=		3	8	1	12		
12. N Zealand		na	30.7	35.3	40.2	1990	.084	rising
	n=		4	7	1	12		
13. Norway		36.0	37.4	31.6	33.3	1992	.083	falling
	n=	1	2	4	1	8		
14. Spain		na	37.1	25.7	32.5	1990	.159	falling
	n=		1	6	1	8		
15. Sweden		33.4	31.6	31.6	32.1	1993	.046	none
	n=	1	2	9	3	15		
16. UK		25.0	24.3	27.3	32.5	1990	.115	rising
	n=	9	10	10	1	30		
17. USA		35.7	35.8	38.5	41.4	1996	.061	rising
	n=	10	10	10	7	37		

(contd)

TABLE 7.1 *(contd)*

	1960s	1970s	1980s	1990s	last year	Coef var	Trend
No. of countries, highest value	2	7	1	7			
Lowest average	25.0	24.3	25.5	26.1	*Trends:*		
country	UK	UK	Finland	Austria	rising		4
Highest average	35.7	37.4	38.5	41.7	falling		4
country	USA	Italy	USA	Australia	none		9

Notes: na = not available or not consistent with other years

n = number of observations per decade, with total under 'last year'

boxed = by country, highest average for the four decades

coef var = coefficient of variation (standard deviation divided by the average)

Earlier decades

Canada: 1950s, 32.3 (1951 & 1957)

USA: 1940s, 37.5 (1947–1949); 1950s, 36.3 (all years)

High-income OECD countries not included: Greece, Luxembourg, Portugal, and Switzerland. While there are some variations in definitions among the countries, with few exceptions, the measures are for gross personal income before taxes.

Sources: Austria: Gusenleitner, Winter-Ebmer & Zweimuller (1996)

Germany: Becker & Hauser (2002); All others: Dollar & Kraay or WIDER.

FIGURE 7.1

USA, Canada and UK: Gini coefficients, 1940s through 1990s

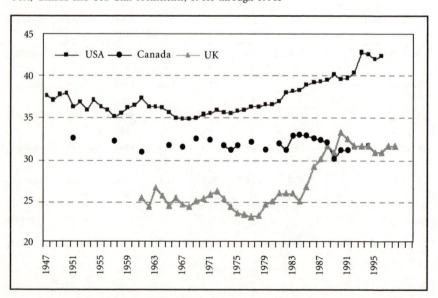

FIGURE 7.2
Gini coefficients for Japan, 1960s through 1990

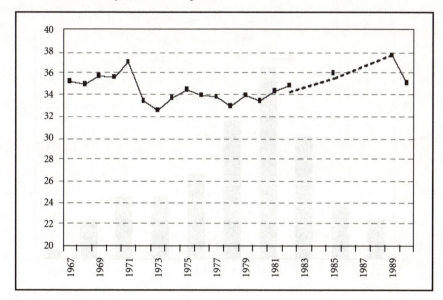

FIGURE 7.3
Gini coefficients for Australia, the Netherlands, New Zealand and Sweden, 1960s through 1990s

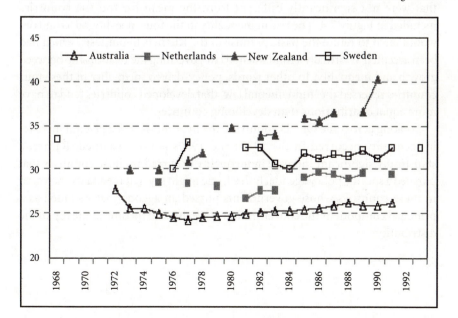

FIGURE 7.4
Distribution of Gini coefficients, 104 countries, 1990s

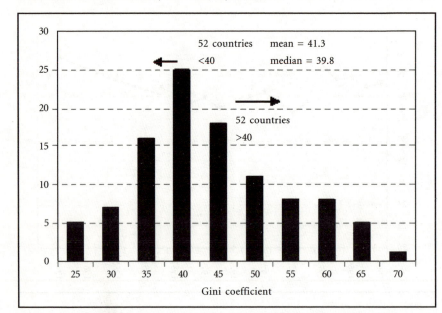

However, for the 1990s, all of the 'liberalizing four' had Gini coefficients that were not significantly different from the mean for the 104 countries included in Figure 7.4. The rise in inequality in the four 'neo-liberal' countries would seem to refute the basic premise of the Kuznets hypothesis, which had been accepted as virtually a fundamental law governing the relationship between growth and inequality. In other words, policy-driven inequality in these four countries reversed the 'fundamental law' that developed countries tend to have more equal distributions than developing countries.

Looking across the OECD countries, the hypothesis that a general increase in inequality occurred in the 1980s and 1990s is not sustained. Rather, a statistically significant increase in inequality occurred in those countries that pursued a specific policy agenda. Indeed, one might say that inequality increased in those countries whose governments pursed an agenda that included as a principal component the concentration of wealth and income at the top of the distribution.

ACCOUNTING FOR THE CHANGES

In the four OECD countries in which inequality significantly increased, the proximate causes are clear. Reference to demographic changes, changes in the sectoral composition of output, and technological impact on skilling have their place in a longer-term analysis, but the sudden and dramatic increase in inequality in these countries has less subtle and more obvious causes.

1. Reduction in the progressivity of national tax structures, including a shift from direct to indirect taxes (from corporate and personal income taxes to sales, or VAT, taxes), a fall in the average income tax rates by reducing taxes at the top of the distribution, and reduction in corporate taxes and taxes on unearned income;

2. Reductions in expenditures on universal social programmes (e.g., unemployment compensation and old age pensions), resulting in declines in transfers from the public budget to low-income households;

3. Increasing unemployment, which overwhelmingly affects those at the lower end of the income distribution;

4. Elimination of the basic elements of the regulation of the financial sector, generating a shift in the distribution of national income from profits to revenues and rents derived from financial speculation; and

5. Declines in the strength of trade unions, especially in the United Kingdom and the United States, leading to a fall in the share of national income going to labour.

The last effect, a fall in labour's share, represents, as in the case of the Kuznets hypothesis, a change in what previously had been considered a fundamental parameter of developed countries, the distribution of factor shares.[6]

As listed above, the major instruments for restricting the accumulation of wealth and income in a few hands were progressive taxation, universal entitlement programmes (i.e., not targeted), and collective bargaining (especially when it was conducted at a national level). These instruments mediated the link between labour and product market competition and the distribution of income, such that measures of inequality varied relatively little during the 1950s and 1960s. Collective bargaining established a wage structure within industries such that relative wages and salaries remained relatively unchanged as the general level of income rose. This system came to be described in various terms, such as 'social contract' or, by left wing 'regulationist' writers as 'the system of capitalist regulation', with the latter based on what they called 'Fordism' (Aglietta, 1976).

Following from the theoretical analysis in the second section, we argue that the basis causal mechanism for all of these proximate causes is the relative bargaining power of capital and labour, which, with the technical and social parameters of a country, determines the functional distribution of income. On the basis of this theory, we construct a simple model and apply it empirically. Increasing inequality works through long-term and short-term mechanisms. The major long-term mechanism is the net distributional impact of the public sector. While the trade movement working through the political process is an important factor influencing progressive distributional policies, this occurs with a lag determined by country specific conditions and the specificity of the redistributive mechanisms. The introduction of progressive mechanisms may occur only after a long period of union pressure, and persist in legislation after that pressure has waned. Therefore, this long-term mechanism will enter the model in its proximate form rather than as a function of its underlying cause. On the basis of the distinction between long and short-run factors, we specify inequality to be the result of the progressiveness of the public budget and the bargaining power of non-capitalists:

$G_t = G_t (\Delta_t, B_t)$
Where:
G_t = inequality, measured by the Gini coefficient
Δ_t = progressive distributional effect of government expenditure and taxation
B_t = bargaining power of trade unions

Due to lack of data on the net incidence of taxation and expenditure, the share of current expenditure in GDP serves as a proxy variable for the progressiveness of the public budget. There are two aspects to this proxy. If the net progressive impact of all budgets were the same, then the share of expenditure would be an exact proxy were budgets always balanced, or the deficit or surplus did not change. This is unlikely, either within or across countries. However, cross-country and intra-country experience suggests that the larger public expenditure is in GDP, the more progressive the net impact of the budget. This is because important categories of public expenditure that have little or no distributional impact are viewed as irreducible—military expenditure being an example. More straightforward is the bargaining power of organized labour, measured by the share of wage employees that are in trade unions, mediated by the unemployment rates, which indicates the 'tightness' of the labour market.

$\Delta_t = \Delta_t(E_t)$
$B_t = B_t(U_t, TU_t)$
E_t = the share of government current expenditure in GDP
U_t = the national unemployment rate

TU_t = share of wage employees in trade unions, 'union density'

The relationship is assumed to take a multiplicative form. Substituting and using logarithms, the estimating equation becomes:

$$\ln[G_t] = a_0 + a_1\ln[U_t] + a_2\ln[E_t] + a_3\ln[TU_t] + a_4C_1 + \ldots + a_nC_n + \varepsilon$$

This is an equilibrium model, in that it assumes that inequality in each year completely adjusts to the value implied by the behavioural variables. The terms $C_1 \ldots C_n$ are dummy variables accounting for so-called fixed affects across countries. The coefficient on the unemployment variable is predicted to be positive, because it reduces the bargaining power of organized labour. Also, there is a direct distributional effect because involuntary cyclical and structural unemployment is suffered disproportionately by the lower and middle classes, and hardly at all by the wealthy. The government expenditure variable is predicted to be negative, because of 'entitlement' programmes in current budget outlays. Trade union density is predicted negative, for reasons discussed above.

The model is tested with data from seven countries: Australia, Canada, Germany, Japan, Sweden, the United Kingdom and the United States, for 1980–1998. The results of the cross-section, time series estimation are shown in Table 7.2. Because the Gini coefficient is a summary measure of inequality, it is difficult to interpret the absolute value of the coefficients on the behavioural variables, except to note that they all have their predicted signs and are statistically significant at less than a five per cent level of the probability that their true value is zero. The model accounts for almost ninety per cent of the variation in Gini coefficients over time and across countries. It should be noted that the most statistically significant variable is trade union membership.

Because cross-country regression should always be treated sceptically, we also apply this model to two countries for which there are sufficient annual data, the United Kingdom and the United States. It is unfortunately the case that consistent data on trade union membership dates from the 1980s, providing a rather short time series. Nonetheless, the results for both countries support our argument that organized labour played a major role in reducing inequality. The results of the two country estimations are shown in Table 7.3. For the United Kingdom, the longer time series that omits trade union membership yields the predicted signs for unemployment and government expenditure, with both highly significant. For the shorter time series that includes trade union membership, unemployment and government expenditure are intercorrelated, and neither significant. However, trade union membership is significant, at the .04 level of probability (see Figure 7.5). In the case of the

TABLE 7.2

Cross-country, time series estimation of the Gini coefficient of inequality, seven countries, 1980–1998

Variable	Coeff	Std Error	t value	Sig.
(Constant)	5.234	.232	22.57	.000
ln(unemp)t	.067	.023	2.06	.044
ln(GovCurrExp)t	-.356	.199	-2.99	.004
ln(TUD)t	-.236	.032	-7.24	.000
1. Australia	.274	.031	8.88	.000
2. Germany	-.198	.037	-5.35	.000
3. Sweden	.427	.057	7.42	.000
4. UK	-.036	.020	-1.82	.074
Summary:				
Adj R Sq =	.870			
F Stat =	52.75	sig @	.000	
DF =	47			

Sources: See Table 7.1 for Gini coefficients; other variables: World Bank, *World Development Indicators, 2003*; ILO, *International Labour Statistics* (website).

Notes: For fixed effects, the USA is the omitted country. Coefficients for Canada and Japan were non-significant and are not included.

Years of coverage (total 61): 1. Australia: 1981, 1984, 1986, 1988, 1990, 1992, 1994, 1996–98 (10). 2. Canada: 1981–91, 1994 (12). 3. Germany: 1994, 1998 (2). 4. Japan: 1980, 1982, 1985, 1989–90 (5). 5. Sweden: 1989, 1991, 1993 (3). 6. UK: 1982, 1985–98 (15). 7. USA: 1983–96 (14)

TABLE 7.3

United Kingdom and United States: Time series estimation of the Gini coefficient of inequality

Statistics	United Kingdom		United States
	(1971–98)	(1980–98)	(1960–96)
[constant]	7.256	4.583	4.775
	(.000)	(.000)	(.000)
ln(unemployment)t	.208	.190	
	(.000)	(nsgn)	
ln(TU density, prv)t		-.235	-.130
		(.040)	(.000)
ln(Gov Curr Exp)t	-1.443		-.268
	(.000)		(.002)
Adjusted R Square =	.594	.572	.899
F-Statistic =	20.79	11.71	162.78
	(.000)	(.000)	(.000)
Durb-Wat =	1.468	1.520	1.800
DF =	25	14	34

Note: Numbers in parenthesis are the probabilities associated with the T-statistics (probability that the coefficient is zero).

FIGURE 7.5
UK: trade union density and Gini coefficient, 1980–1998

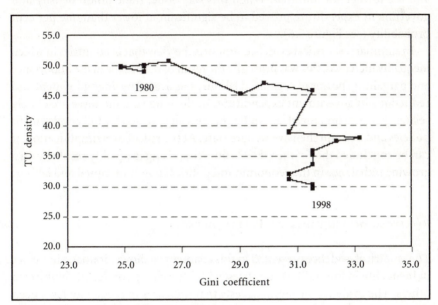

FIGURE 7.6
USA: trade union density and Gini coefficient, 1960–1998

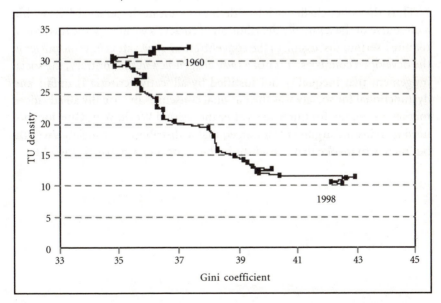

United States, unemployment and trade union membership are intercorrelated, and the former was omitted. When this was done, trade union density and government expenditure proved to be significant at lower than one per cent probability (see Figure 7.6).

In summary, statistical evidence supports the view that in countries in which inequality increased, this was primarily the result of the decline in the importance and bargaining power of organized labour, aggravated by unemployment and reductions in government expenditure. In the long run, the three are closely related, because organized labour has historically pressed for full employment policies and a comprehensive welfare state. At the risk of oversimplification, it can be concluded that in the OECD countries, rising inequality results from a growing imbalance in the economic and political power of capital and labour.

REDEFINING THE INEQUALITY AND POVERTY AGENDA

The empirical evidence presented in this chapter has shown dramatic increases in inequality in four OECD countries, with little change or decline in thirteen others. The evidence strongly suggests that increases in inequality have been the result of policies, most importantly, policies that have weakened the power of organized labour. Reductions in government social expenditure and abandoning full employment as a policy goal have also played a substantial role.

Thus, the policy challenge is to redefine or relocate the policy debate within a discourse of the equitable distribution of society's wealth. While this would require a serious discussion of the concentration of private economic power in the developed countries, it is not a radical agenda. On the contrary, the social judgement that inequality not justified by allocative criteria is unfair and dysfunctional for society was the national consensus in virtually all advanced market economies for thirty years after the Second World War. One does not need to 'reinvent' arguments for an equitable distribution of society's wealth, but merely to invoke that consensus in the context of a globalizing world.

NOTES

[1] So-called because the concept lacks one of the central characteristics of capital: vendibility. 'Human capital' refers to the enhancement of the skills of a person, usually acquired through education of some sort. While the labouring time of the skilled person can be sold, the asset in question, being skilled, cannot be sold, except in a slave society. An asset which cannot be bought and sold is not capital.

[2] More precisely, equilibrium in the labour market produces the money wage, $p_1 wl_1$, as part of a general equilibrium system in which prices, outputs and the real wage are determined simultaneously.

[3] In this special case, the equation becomes $r = 1 - w(l/k)$.

[4] For discussions of inequality in some of these countries, see Atkinson (1995, comparison of the United States and European countries), Becker and Hauser (2002, Germany), Burniaux and others (1998, OECD countries), Cornia (2004, developed countries), Cornia, Addison and Kiiski (2004, developed countries), Jantti (1997, US and European), Piketty (2001, France), and Saunders (2003, Australia).

[5] For a theoretical model of why inequality differs across countries, see Benabou (2000).

[6] On what was then an apparent long-term stability in income distribution in the United States, see Kravis (1959; 1960), and Goldsmith and others (1954).

REFERENCES

Aglietta, Michel (1976). A Theory of Capitalist Regulation. Monthly Review Press, New York.
Atkinson, A.B. (1995). Income Distribution in Europe and the United States. Working Paper nos 13 and 103, Nuffield College, Oxford.
Becker, Irene, and Richard Hauser (2002). Anatomie der personellen Einkommens—und Vermögensverteilung—Ergebnisse der Einkommens—und Verbrauchsstichproben 1969–1998. Edition Sigma, Berlin.
Benabou, Roland (2000). Unequal societies: Income distribution and the social contract. American Economic Review 90 (1): 96–129.
Burniaux, Jean-Marc, Thai-Thanh Dang, Douglas Fore, Michael Förster, Marco Mira d'Ercole and Howard Oxley (1998). Income Distribution and Poverty in Selected OECD Countries. Economics Department Working Paper No. 189, Organization for Economic Cooperation and Development (OECD), Paris.
Cornia, G.A. (2004). Inequality, Growth, and Poverty: An overview of changes over the last two decades. In G.A. Cornia (ed.). Inequality, Growth, and Poverty in an Era of Liberalization and Globalization. Oxford University Press, Oxford: 3–25.
Cornia, G.A., Tony Addison and Sampsa Kiiski (2004). Income Distribution Changes and their Impact in the Post World War II Period. In G.A. Cornia (ed.). Inequality, Growth, and Poverty in an Era of Liberalization and Globalization. Oxford University Press, Oxford: 26–56.
Goldsmith, Selma, George Jaszi, Hyman Kaitz and Maurice Liebenberg (1954). The Size Distribution of Income since the mid-Thirties. Review of Economics and Statistics 36 (1): 1–32.
Harcourt, Geoffrey (1972). Some Cambridge Controversies in the Theory of Capital. Cambridge University Press, Cambridge.
Jantti, Markus (1997). Inequality in five countries in the 1980s: the role of demographic shifts, markets and government policies. Economica (New Series), 64 (255): 415–40.
Kravis, Irving (1959). Relative income Shares in fact and Theory. American Economic Review 49 (5): 917–49.

Kravis, Irving (1960). International Differences in the Distribution of Income. *Review of Economics and Statistics* 42 (4): 408–16.

Kuznets, Simon (1955). Economic Growth and Equality. *American Economic Review* 45 (1): 1–28.

Piketty, Thomas (2001). Income Inequality in France, 1901–1998. Discussion Paper No. 2876, Centre for Economic Policy Research, London.

Robinson, Joan (1969). *The Accumulation of Capital*. Macmillan, London.

Rothschild, K. W. (1947). Price Theory and Oligopoly. *Economic Journal* 57 (227): 299–320.

Saunders, Peter (2003). Examining Recent Changes in Income Distribution in Australia. Discussion Paper No. 130, Social Policy Research Centre, Sydney.

Weeks, John (1989). *A Critique of Neoclassical Macroeconomics*. Macmillan, London.

8

Unequal Fortunes, Unstable Households: Has Rising Inequality Contributed to Economic Troubles for Households?

HEATHER BOUSHEY and CHRISTIAN E. WELLER

For the better part of the past three decades, the U.S. economy has been characterized by a growing income disparity. Rising inequality has taken two forms. The share of national income that has gone to employee compensation has tended to decline, and the distribution of this shrinking share of the pie has become more unequal.

Rising inequality may also have impacted the economy in the aggregate. While the link between rising inequality and productivity growth is hard to substantiate, the connection between greater inequality and aggregate demand finds more support. However, despite rising inequality demand growth has remained relatively strong. One resolution to this ambiguity may have been a rise in more consumer borrowing, especially for low income households. In turn, this may have increased economic distress for households, particularly if economic mobility was limited.

The rest of the chapter proceeds as follows. In the next section, we present background data on inequality as well as on household indebtedness and household economic distress. In the following section, we discuss the causes of the rising inequality in the U.S., followed by an overview of the macro economic consequences of rising inequality. After that, we discuss the evidence on the link between inequality and innovation and aggregate demand. The penultimate section presents our evidence on the link between inequality, consumer indebtedness and economic distress. Concluding remarks follow.

INEQUALITY TRENDS

Inequality between capital and labour and within labour has been on the rise in the U.S. over the past decades. A striking characteristic of the last economic recovery in the U.S. was a rapidly growing gap between supply and demand. Economic growth and employment diverged because historically weak demand growth did not keep pace with productivity growth[1], resulting in rising profits and laggard employee compensation (Figure 8.1) (Bivens and Weller, 2004a; Weller, 2004a). In response, households borrowed more to maintain their consumption (Weller, 2004a) and businesses, not expecting strong sales growth, did not ratchet up investment quickly (Weller, Bivens and Sawicky, 2004; Weller, 2004b). Instead, much of the additional resources went for uses other than productive investments, such as share repurchases and dividends (Bivens and Weller, 2004a).

The 'job loss' recovery, though, was the culmination of long-run trends. Since the mid-1970s, productivity growth has outpaced compensation growth (Figure 8.2). Over the period from 1947 to the middle of 1975, productivity and real hour compensation grew apart by a total of 6.0 per cent. From the middle of 1975 to early 2004, productivity grew 25.7 per cent faster than real compensation. Consequently, profits rose, too. While the profit share on average was quite similar between the earlier period, from 1947 to 1975, compared to the later period—6.7 per cent as compared to 6.5 per cent, respectively—the profit share grew more rapidly in the latter period than in the former (Bivens and Weller, 2004b; Wolff, 2003). After-tax profit rates and shares, including net interest earnings, already saw the strongest growth, compared to other profit measures in the earlier periods (Table 8.1).[2] The trends of profit shares are reflected in the trends of labour shares. Although the averages do not differ or are even greater in the latter period, the trends tell a different story. Regardless of how the labour share is measured, it declined in the latter period, whereas it grew in the earlier period. The declines were especially pronounced after 2001 (Table 8.1).

Since the 1970s, inequality within the distribution of labour income has also increased, regardless of how it is measured, relatively or absolutely. We focus first on wage inequality because wages and salaries make up the bulk of family income. However, research has found that shifts in the distribution of earnings are not necessarily the most important factor in explaining changes in the income distribution. Over the past 25 years, changes in the distribution of other kinds of income (interest, dividends, and rent) have played just as an important role. The severity of the inequality problem is heightened by decreases in economic mobility at the same time.

Overall, the past few decades have seen a dramatic shift of income away from labour and away from low-wage earners and low-income families. The sharpest increases occurred during the 1980s: from the economic peak in 1979 to the next peak in 1989, workers in the bottom 10th percentile saw their wages fall by 14.1 per cent while those in the 95th percentile saw their wages rise by 8.1 per cent. Inequality also increased between workers at the median and those at the top, as wages for the median worker did not grow at all (0.0 per cent growth)

FIGURE 8.1

Components of US national income growth over 8 quarters, 1949–2001

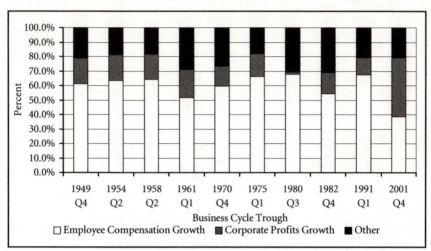

Notes: The figures are calculated as the difference in national income components relative to the difference in national income.

Source: BEA (2004), authors' calculations.

FIGURE 8.2

US productivity vs. compensation, 1947–2004

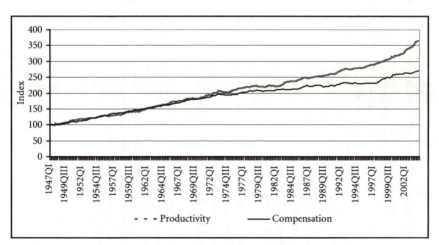

Notes: Productivity refers to output per hour in the non-farm business sector and compensation is real hourly compensation in the non-farm business sector.

Source: BLS (2004a), authors' calculations.

TABLE 8.1
USA: levels and changes of profit shares and labour shares of national income

	After tax profit share with net interest	After tax profit share without net interest	Before tax profit share with net interest	Before tax profit share without net interest	Compensation share	Compensation and proprietors' income share
Average—earlier period	9.3	6.7	14.2	11.6	62.9	73.2
	(1.4)	(1.0)	(1.1)	(1.4)	(1.82)	(1.14)
Average monthly rate of change (percentage points)—earlier period	0.05	0.01	0.03	-0.01	0.05	0.00
Average—later period	13.6	6.4	16.7	9.5	65.6	73.3
	(1.2)	(1.0)	(1.0)	(1.2)	(0.88)	(0.88)
Average monthly rate of change (percentage points)—later period	0.04	0.04	0.03	0.03	-0.02	-0.01
Average—2002 to 2004	14.4	8.3	16.7	10.6	65.2	73.7
	(0.7)	(0.9)	(0.8)	(1.0)	(0.71)	(0.58)
Average monthly rate of change (percentage points)—2002 to 2004	0.17	0.23	0.23	0.29	-0.18	-0.17

Notes: All figures are in per cent. Figures in parentheses are standard errors. The entire sample for profit shares spans from 1947 to the first quarter of 2004 and is split at the second quarter of 1975.
Source: Bivens and Weller (2004a).

over that same period (Mishel, Bernstein and Boushey, 2003). The overall trend was for the top and bottom to pull away from each other, while the middle saw little change.

Over the 1990s, the growth in wage inequality slowed. Between 1989 and 2000, wages increased by 13.1 per cent for those in the bottom 10th percentile and increased by 16.6 per cent for those in the 95th percentile. Inequality between the top and the middle increased more so than between those at the top and bottom, as the median worker saw their wages rise by only 5.9 per cent. Much of the slowing of inequality occurred during the latter half of the 1990s, as unemployment dipped below 5 per cent. Between 1995 and 2000, those at the bottom of the wage distribution saw their wages rise faster than those at the top for the first time in decades (Mishel, Bernstein and Boushey, 2003).

If overall inequality rose primarily because of across-group inequality, then it would be due to factors specific to particular groups, such as discrimination or increasing returns to skills. But if inequality has been primarily driven by within-group differences, then the problems are more generalized and cannot be evaluated with microeconomic, human capital based models. The general consensus is that there has been an increase in both across and within-group inequality. While across-group inequality has increased in terms of educational attainment, it has not increased substantially across African Americans and whites, and gender inequality has actually attenuated.

Across-group wage inequality declined among male and female workers over the past three decades, mostly because male wages fell during the 1970s and 1980s. Over the period from 1975 to 1996, average male wages stagnated, while average female wages rose by about one-fifth. Even once wages are regression-adjusted to control for education and experience, the gender gap closed from 47 per cent in 1975 to 27 per cent in 1993. However, since 1993, the gender pay gap has remained unchanged, hovering at around 25 per cent (Gottschalk and Danziger, 2003).

The inequality gap between African-American and white workers stayed relatively constant over the past three decades. Controlling for personal characteristics, among women, the black/white gap was virtually non-existent in the late 1970s, however it increased to 4 per cent by 2001. Among men, the black/white gap was 14 per cent in 1975, rising to about 20 per cent in the early 1980s. It came back down to 15 per cent by 2001.

Inequality has increased, however, across educational attainment levels. Economists think that human capital, that is, the education and training experiences of the worker, is correlated with a worker's productivity, which, in turn, determines their wage. Thus, there is an expectation of inequality across educational attainment levels. However, there is not an expectation of an increase in this inequality over time, which is what has happened. In 2003, college-educated men earned 41.5 per cent more than high-school-educated men, compared to a college premium of only 25.3 per cent in 1973. For women, the increase was less dramatic: in 2003, college-educated women earned 46.1 per cent more than high-school-educated women, compared to a 37.7 per cent premium in 1973 (Mishel, Bernstein and Allegretto, 2005). Most of the increase in educational inequality occurred between the late 1970s and the early 1990s. Since 1992, the gap between high-school and college-educated workers has been relatively flat among both men and women, although there is slight upward trend, more so for men than women (Gottschalk and Danziger, 2003).

Another way of evaluating wage inequality is to examine the within-group differences. Changes in within-group inequality indicate that something has fundamentally changed about the economy that affects all kinds of workers, rather than only affecting some workers based on their educational attainment level or other identifying characteristics. Over the past few decades, this kind of inequality has increased alongside across-group inequality. As with across-group inequality, the largest increases in within-group inequality occurred during the 1970s and 1980s. Among both men and women, the residual wage inequality in hourly wages at the 10th percentile fell precipitously between 1975 and the late 1990s. A person at the 10th percentile of the distribution—where 10 per cent of households have income below that level and 90 per cent have income above that level—in the late 1980s had earnings roughly 25 per cent lower than a similar person in 1975. For individuals at the 90th percentile, wages were about 10 per cent higher in the mid-1980s, compared to 1975, but stopped increasing during the 1990s (Gottschalk and Danziger, 2003).

Since most American families derive the majority of their income from wages, trends in income inequality closely mirror wage inequality. During the period 1947 to 1979, annual growth in inflation-adjusted family income was similar across quintiles. However, from 1979 to 2003, those in the top quintile, and in particular the top 5 per cent, saw their family income grow significantly faster than those in the lower-income quintiles (Figure 8.3).

As with wage inequality, the largest increases in income inequality occurred in the 1980s. Between 1979 and 1989, rising inequality was the result of large increases in income among high-income families and declining income among lower-income families. In the 1990s, income among lower-income families started to rise, but incomes of higher-income families rose even faster. Between 1989 and 2000, among married families with children, incomes of those in the bottom fifth of the income distribution rose by 8.8 per cent, compared to 14.1 per cent among those in the top fifth (Mishel, Bernstein and Allegretto, 2005).

Analysis of percentiles does not allow us to see just how much those at the

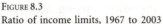

FIGURE 8.3
Ratio of income limits, 1967 to 2003

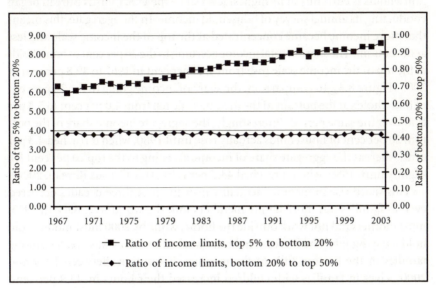

Source: Census (2004a).

very top of the income distribution have gained over the past three decades. To see this, we need to look at data on tax returns that does not top-code the incomes of those at the very top. Top-coded data has all values over a certain threshold recoded as a common number in order to protect the privacy of the very wealth. Recent research using tax returns has found that between 1973 and 2000, the average real income of the bottom 90 per cent of American taxpayers fell by 7 per cent while the income of the top one per cent grew by 148 per cent (Piketty and Saez, 2001).

While the top has pulled away from the bottom, the top has also been pulling away from the middle. Households at the 80th percentile now have over twice the income (2.01 times) of households at the 50th percentile. Back in 1967, this ratio was only 1.66. The gap between households at the bottom and middle has remained relatively constant, at 0.42 in both 1967 and 2003. Similarly, the ratio of the income limit for the top 5 per cent of income earners to the bottom 20 per cent rose from 6.3 in 1967 to 8.6 in 2003 (Figure 8.3). Also, the annual increases almost doubled after 1980. From 1967 to 1980, the ratio of income cut-offs increased annually by 0.6 per cent, whereas it rose by 1.0 per cent on average each year from 1980 to 2003. In comparison, the ratio of the income limits for the bottom 20 per cent to the middle percentile stayed fairly constant at about 0.42 (U.S. Census Bureau, 2004).

As a result of unequal growth in incomes, inequality among American households is currently at its highest level since the U.S. Census Bureau began conducting its annual survey of household income. In the aggregate, this means that more income became concentrated at the top of the income scale and less at the bottom. The share of total income accruing to the 20 per cent of households at the top of the income scale rose from 43.8 per cent in 1967 to 49.8 per cent in 2003 (Figure 8.4). In comparison, the share of income going to the 20 per cent of households at the bottom of the income scale fell from 4.0 per cent to 3.4 per cent over the same period. Interestingly, the aggregate income share of the bottom 20 per cent of households actually rose until 1980, when it reached 4.3 per cent, whereas the aggregate share of income accruing to the top 20 per cent fell slightly until 1980, when it reached 43.7 per cent (U.S. Census Bureau, 2004).

This sharp rise in income inequality over the past three decades occurred even as families put more family members into the workforce. Back in 1973, most mothers did not work outside the home, while by 2000 most mothers did hold a paying job. The increase in hours worked by wives was greater among families in the bottom fifth of the income distribution. Between 1979 and 2000, wives in families with children increased their hours by 43.9 per cent, compared to a 27.4 per cent increase in hours among wives in families in the top fifth. Within married families with children, inequality would have increased even more without the contribution of wives' income. Between 1979 and 2000, among families in the bottom fifth, income would have fallen by 13.9 per cent without the earnings of wives, rather than rising by 7.5 per cent; among families

FIGURE 8.4
Aggregate shares of US income, 1967–2003

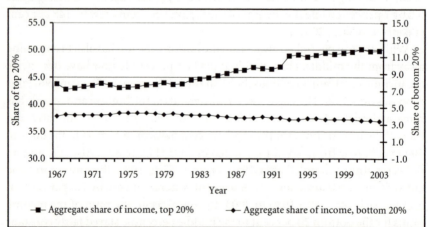

Source: Census (2004a).

TABLE 8.2
USA: decomposition of changes in coefficient of variation

	Family income	Head earnings	Other's earnings	Government	Other (rent, dividend, interest)
1975	0.588	0.407	0.157	-0.025	0.049
2001	0.737	0.433	0.208	0.000	0.096
Change	0.148	0.025	0.051	0.025	0.047

Source: Gottschalk and Danziger (2003)

in the top fifth, income would have increased by 51.5 per cent, rather than 63.0 per cent (Mishel, Bernstein and Allegretto, 2005).

The increase in working wives also contributed to rising inequality. Both the growth in non-head's earnings and unearned income (from rents, dividends, or interest) contributed twice as much to the rise in income inequality from 1975 to 2001 (Table 8.2). At the same time, the government sector in the United States has ceased to work to close the inequality gap: in 1975, government taxes and transfers reduced inequality, but by 2001, they had no net effect on family income inequality.

If wage and income inequality were counterbalanced by the potential for economic mobility, then greater inequality would not require that some stay at the bottom (or at the top). This would be especially true if inequality was the result of immigration as new immigrants enter at the bottom and then move up. However, this is not the case. In the 1970s, 50.7 per cent of families who began the decade in the bottom quintile and 49.1 per cent of families who began the decade in the second bottom quintile moved into a higher quintile over the decade. However, in the 1990s, only 46.8 per cent of families who began the decade in the bottom quintile and 37.9 per cent of families who began the decade in the second bottom quintile moved into a higher quintile (Bradbury and Katz, 2002).

Wysong and others (2004) found that class matters now more than ever. Sons from the bottom three-quarters of the socioeconomic scale were less likely to move up in the 1990s than in the 1960s. By 1998, only 10 per cent of sons of fathers in the bottom quarter (defined by income, education, and occupation) had moved into the top quarter, whereas by comparison, by 1973, 23 per cent of lower-class sons had moved up to the top. Thus, there is a smaller chance that a low-income family will move up the income ladder over time.

The labour force participation of wives has been critical to the story of mobility. Recent research has found that families where wives had high and rising employment rates, work hours, and pay were more likely to move up the income ladder or maintain their position, rather than fall down the ladder (Bradbury and Katz, 2004). But, even the large increase in the labour supply of women (and mothers, in particular) has not been sufficient to counterbalance declining mobility overall.

Even though wages account for most of family income, other factors are important, too. Capital income as a share of personal income doubled from 7.1 per cent in early 1947 to 14.1 per cent in the second quarter of 2004 (BEA, 2004). However, the assets underlying these income streams are fairly unequally distributed. For instance, Wolff (2002a) reported that the bottom 40 per cent of households had negative financial net worth in 1998, and that they had little total net worth. Further, Wolff (2004) reported that wealth inequality rose from 1998 to 2001 for total net worth.

Macro-Economic Background

With income growth lagging, households increased their consumption by saving less and borrowing more.[3] The personal savings rate declined from an average high of 9.7 per cent in the early 1970s to 4.7 per cent in the 1990s and to 2.2 per cent in the latest business cycle (Table 8.3). Simultaneously, consumer debt, especially mortgage debt, rose from 63.7 per cent of disposable income in the early 1970s to over 100 per cent in the most recent business cycle.

At the same time, the economic distress of households increased. From 2001 through mid-2004, households dedicated at least 13 per cent of their dis-posable income to service their debts—the largest share in twenty years (Figure 8.5). Charge-off rates have also been high with, for instance, credit card charge-off rates above 5 per cent of all loans since 2001 (BOG, 2004a). In addition, personal bankruptcies have risen so that the share of households that declared bankruptcy reached an estimated record 1.5 per cent in 2003 (Figure 8.6).

While households borrowed more to make ends meet, firms used their additional profits for uses other than productive investments. Specifically, firms increased their share repurchases and dividend pay-outs. While in the 1970s, corporations used 10.7 per cent of their resources for these purposes, this share grew to more than 30 per cent since the 1980s as capital expenditures simultaneously declined (Table 8.4).

Despite laggard investment, productivity accelerated. Compared to other early recovery periods, this was the first time during which productivity growth actually outpaced aggregate demand growth in the first two years of a recovery (Figure 8.7). Measured as business cycle averages, productivity growth in 2002

TABLE 8.3
USA: savings and consumer debt, business cycle averages

Business cycle dates	Personal savings rate	Total consumer debt as share of disposable income	Mortgages as share of disposable income	Consumer credit as share of disposable income
1949:IV–1953:II	7.4	38.2	23.1	11.6
1953:III–1957:III	7.9	47.3	29.1	13.9
1957:IV–1960:II	7.9	55.0	35.0	15.0
1960:III–1969:IV	8.4	65.4	41.0	17.7
1970:I–1973:IV	9.7	63.7	38.2	18.1
1974:I–1980:I	9.5	65.2	41.0	17.6
1980:II–1990:III	8.9	73.4	47.0	17.9
1990:IV–2001:I	4.7	91.7	61.3	20.0
2001:II–2004:I	2.1	109.0	74.3	23.9

Notes: All figures are in per cent. Mortgages comprise both traditional mortgages and home equity loans. Consumer credit refers to revolving consumer credit, such as credit card debt, and non-revolving credit card debt, such as car loans.
Source: Bivens and Weller (2004a).

TABLE 8.4
USA: selected use of non-financial corporate resources, business cycle averages

Business cycle dates	Financial uses as share of total internal resources			Productive uses as share of total internal resources
	Total	Dividend payouts	Net equity issues	Capital expenditures
1953:III–1957:III	17.9	23.3	-5.4	79.1
1957:IV–1960:II	17.9	22.3	-4.5	74.6
1960:III–1969:IV	20.1	21.8	-1.7	83.1
1970:I–1973:IV	10.7	20.0	-9.3	101.2
1974:I–1980:I	14.8	17.2	-2.5	106.4
1980:II–1990:III	31.4	18.5	12.9	95.1
1990:IV–2001:I	32.0	25.2	6.8	88.3
2001:II–2004:I	30.8	25.4	5.4	76.7

Notes: All figures are in per cent. Total internal resources are defined as after tax profits plus inventory valuation adjustments and capital consumption allowance. Net equity issues, originally a source of funds, are multiplied by minus one to make them comparable with other uses of funds. Figures do not add to 100 per cent since other sources, especially borrowing of funds, are excluded.
Source: Bivens and Weller (2004a).

FIGURE 8.5
US household debt service ratio (DSR), 1980Q1–2004Q1

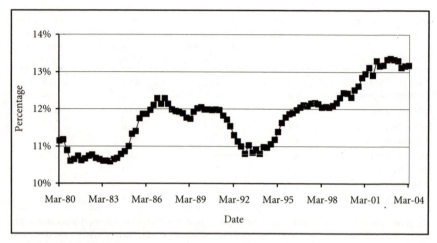

Source: BOG (2004b).

FIGURE 8.6
Personal bankruptcy filings as share of households

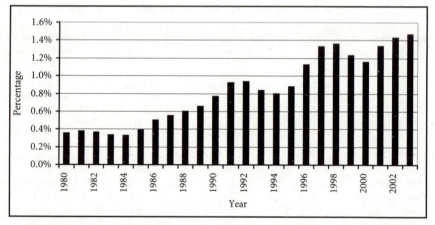

Notes: Total number of households is assumed to be equal to 1/1.1 times the number of housing units.

Sources: ABI (2004), Census (2004b) and authors' calculations. Figures for 2003 are based on estimates for total number of households.

TABLE 8.5
USA: select macroeconomic measures, business cycle averages, 1948 to 2003

Business cycle dates	Share of income of bottom 20%	Share of income of top 20%	Ratio of income limits of 95th to 50th percentile	Productivity growth	Real GDP growth	Real consumption growth	Growth contribution, consumption & residential fixed investment	Consumption as share of GDP	Consumption as share of disposable income
1948–1952	n.a.	n.a.	n.a.	3.55	4.75	4.77	-37.49	63.73	91.42
1953–1957	n.a.	n.a.	n.a.	1.96	2.90	2.92	6.91	62.25	90.34
1958–1959	n.a.	n.a.	n.a.	2.92	2.93	2.96	6.02	63.05	90.12
1960–1969	4.10	43.20	2.61	2.67	4.33	4.33	64.41	61.83	89.49
1970–1979	4.13	43.58	2.69	1.15	2.93	2.92	205.69	62.15	87.87
1980–1990	4.35	43.48	2.82	1.44	2.90	2.89	25.65	62.63	88.22
1991–2000	3.66	48.67	3.36	2.00	3.23	3.22	83.01	67.26	91.82
2001–2003	3.47	49.87	3.56	3.68	1.88	1.86	144.96	70.17	94.52

Notes: All figures are in per cent. Starting date for inequality data is 1967.
Sources: BEA (2004a), Census (2004a), and BLS (2004a).

FIGURE 8.7
Difference between US growth and productivity in recoveries,
eight quarters after the start of the recovery, 1949–2003

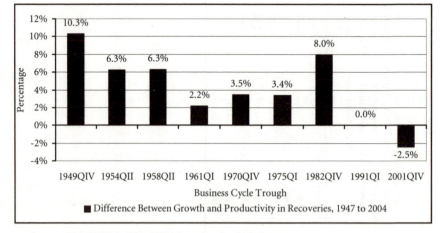

Sources: BLS (2004a), BEA (2004a), authors' calculations.

and 2003 was higher than in previous business cycles, although the economy
sustained productivity growth that was almost as high for a period of four years
in the late 1940s (Table 8.5).

Reflecting the weakness in demand and the divergence between supply and
demand, consumption growth has slowed since 2001 (Table 8.5). For 2002 and
2003, average real consumption growth was 1.9 per cent, compared to 3.2 per
cent in the 1990s—the slowest consumption increase of any post-war business
cycle. However, consumption never slowed during the most recent recession
and consumer spending on new homes and home renovations accelerated
more than it had in prior recoveries. Thus, consumer spending contributed
more to growth than the actual growth rate, reflecting the continued trade
deficits and the slowdown in investment (Table 8.5) (Weller, Bivens and
Sawicky, 2004).

EXPLAINING THE RISE IN INEQUALITY

A number of factors contributed to the rise in inequality between capital and
labour. The two most convincing explanations are increasing trade intensity
and changes in the institutional make-up of U.S. corporations that gave more
power to institutional investors and managers and reduced the influence of

labour unions (Bivens and Weller, 2004a; Lazonick and O'Sullivan, 2000).

Increased trade, especially in manufactured goods, is a non-negligible factor in explaining the rise in inequality. About a third of the loss of manufacturing jobs that occurred from the end of 2000 to the end of 2003—the largest driving force of the 'job loss' recovery—can be attributed to rising trade deficits in manufactured goods (Bivens, 2004; Atkinson, 2004). This result is consistent with standard trade theory. The predicted structure of trade for a nation like the U.S.—labour-intensive imports and capital-intensive exports—implies that trade should lead to a decline in the demand for labour and rise in the demand for capital, moving wages (down) and profit rates (up) accordingly.

During the 1970s and 1980s, the main distributional impact of trade seemed to be on the distribution of *wages*; as trade raised the return to skilled labour and lowered the return to unskilled labour (Cline, 1997). The relative lack of a capital/labour income dimension of trade was consistent with what economists dubbed 'Leontief's Paradox': the finding that U.S. exports were not notably capital-intensive, nor were U.S. imports labour-intensive. What really seemed to distinguish U.S. trade in the 1970s and 1980s was that it was particularly biased against blue-collar workers (Borjas and Ramey, 1996). That is, for most of the period that we are interested in, trade can explain an increase in the within labour inequality, but not a rise in the inequality between labour and income.

Another factor that explains the divergent trends between capital and labour is a rising imbalance in the corporate governance realm. Specifically, a growing concentration among institutional shareholders and rising power of managers in deciding corporate resource allocations was juxtaposed with a declining unionization rate.

A greater reliance on managed assets in household savings led to a rising concentration of shares in the hands of mutual funds, brokers, public and private pension funds and insurance companies. In 1952, institutional investors owned less than 10 per cent of outstanding equities, and in 2004, it surpassed 50 per cent for the first time (BOG, 2004c).

Also, institutional investors had growing incentives to use this opportunity to allocate resources towards capital. Starting in the 1970s, institutional changes, such as the Employee Retirement Income Security Act (ERISA) of 1974 and the introduction of 401(k) plans, gave fund managers and households a common interest in maximizing asset returns (Bivens and Weller, 2004a). This altered the way corporations were run, creating a new class of professional managers that enjoyed greater freedom in allocating corporate resources towards a strategy of rent extraction, including downsizing, outsourcing, and restructuring, as well as a reorientation towards financial service activities, away from actual production (Lazonick and O'Sullivan, 2000; O'Sullivan, 2000). Consequently, labour compensation declined, along with union representation as jobs especially in manufacturing were lost. Thus, the allocation of corporate resources towards faster profit growth proceeded with less opposition than in the past. Profits in turn were increasingly used for dividend pay-outs and share repurchases, which directly benefited executives, whose compensation was dependent on the performance of a company's share value.

Corporate governance changes explain the rise in income inequality in important ways. For one, they explain a growing emphasis of profit generation, thus shrinking the allocation of corporate resources towards labour. They also explain the growing inequality within labour as a result of more rent extracting activities and executive compensation contingent on share price performance. Finally, the latter aspect also explains the growing share of personal income that is derived from assets, which in turn contributes to the rise in income inequality due to the unequal distribution of household wealth.

Because inequality has risen along so many dimensions, the reasons for its expansion are not easy to pinpoint on a single source or in a single regression. The concentration of financial market power, combined with declining bargaining power—decline in unionization, deregulation and privatization, assaults on social programs, a lack of increase in the minimum wage, and an inequitable distribution of health care—all contribute the power imbalance of workers with respect to employers and the state.

The level of unemployment is critical in explaining changes in inequality—higher unemployment leads to inequality growth and inequality tends to shrink during periods of tight labour markets. This is because unemployment affects the fortunes of those at the bottom of the labour market more than those at the top. Individuals with limited education or who earn in the bottom of the wage distribution are more likely to lose a job when unemployment rises. The mechanisms through which unemployment affects wages are not always direct, but, at their core, they are related to the relative power of labour and capital within the U.S. economy. If workers are fearful of losing their job, because of high levels of unemployment, they will be less likely to bargain hard for higher wages and less able to search for a new position at a higher wage (or benefit) level.

Structural changes in the U.S. economy are also implicated in inequality's growth. The decline in unionization, the lessoning of labour market regulation, changes in the industrial and occupation mix of jobs, and globalization have all contributed to growing inequality. A declining real minimum wage and de-unionization can explain about one-third of the growth in wage inequality, while globalization—immigration, trade, and capital mobility—can explain another one-third of inequality's rise (DiNardo, Fortin and Lemieux,

1996; Gottschalk 1997; Lee; 1999; Card, Lemieux and Riddell, 2003).

Growing inequality is also the result of a lack of a broad-based social insurance system. Once an American becomes poor, it is exceedingly difficult to rise back up into the middle class. The Organisation for Economic Cooperation and Development (OECD) has found that in the U.S., there are not only more poor families, but they are less likely than the poor in other countries to 'exit' from poverty. For example, while 41.1 per cent of poor Germans exit poverty each year, only 29.5 per cent of poor Americans do. Because income transfers are so small, the only way out of poverty is earnings or marriage; this has left U.S. poor people more likely to exit poverty through earnings than in other OECD nations. Yet, because of limited growth in wages among low-wage workers over the past few decades (up until the late 1990s), this led to lower poverty exit rates in the U.S. Thus, the U.S. social welfare state does not help to reduce inequality through helping families back into the middle class; further, the U.S. has more wage and income inequality than any other OECD country (Mishel, Bernstein and Boushey, 2003).

In general, the U.S. labour market has become an increasingly insecure place for workers. As they emerged from the stagflation of the 1970s, U.S. firms made the case to government and to workers that they needed more control over workers and that could not afford to compete internationally while paying decent wages and benefits. Much of the blame for stagflation was placed on labour's 'unreasonable' demands. The plant closings and outsourcing that happened over the next decade—the decimation of manufacturing and the unions—scared policymakers as well as labour unions. For example, one trend in the U.S. has been for cities and states to compete with one another to reduce taxes to lure and keep employers in their locality, often without requiring any-thing of the firms in exchange. At the same time, the responsibility for ensuring a living wage has fallen more to the government than to low-wage employers, as low wages are supplemented by the Earned Income Tax Credit, even as the inflation-adjusted minimum wage declined markedly. Further, no longer can a worker assume that they will stay in a job for their career. Internal labour markets are increasingly a thing of the past.

INEQUALITY AND THE MACRO-ECONOMY

If the rise in the profit share translates into an increase in the profit rate, it may result in more investment and potentially more growth since greater profits provide firms with more incentives to invest, particularly if tax policy supports the increase in the profit rate (Bivens and Weller, 2004b; Palomba, 2002).

However, a greater profit rate may also attract more entrants into an industry and reduce the rate of profit below what was originally expected (Peretto, 1995). In addition, profit rate gains may have been generated by reducing wage growth, which may suppress demand growth and thus profit growth over time (Palley, 1996). Furthermore, through rent extraction, many core activities of a firm are abandoned. This may impede organizational learning and thus innovation and growth (Lazonick and O'Sullivan, 2000; O'Sullivan, 2000). These concerns, though, do not necessarily contradict the original notion that a higher profit rate will lead to more investments. They do suggest, however, that over time countervailing forces will gain ground and weaken the link. This may explain why there is little empirical evidence for profit led growth (Stockhammer and Onaran, 2005).

A positive link between inequality and innovation has been suspected, particularly because inequality may imply a greater wage premium on skills. The opposing view, though, contends that rising inequality leads to growing political instabilities, and thus to disincentives for accumulation, followed by reduced innovation (Alesina and Perotti, 1996; Larrain and Vergara, 1997; Rodriguez, 2000). There may be a threshold below which inequality fosters growth, but above which political instability considerations outweigh skill development effects (Benhabib, 2003; Chen, 2003).

Patterns of wage growth do not suggest a connection between inequality and skill development (Mishel, Bernstein and Schmitt, 2001; Mishel, Bernstein and Allegretto, 2005; Appelbaum and Weller, 2001). From the late 1970s to the mid-1990s, wages declined, especially for young high school graduates. By the late 1990s, they had not recovered to the levels of the late 1970s. Also, entry-level wages among male college graduates were stagnant from 1973 to 1989 and fell 9.9 per cent from 1989 to 1995. However, between 1995 and 1999 among young college graduates, real wages rose 14.9 per cent for men and 9.4 per cent for women. Wage inequality rose fastest in the 1980s, yet productivity growth was slower than during the 1970s, when wage inequality did not rise. When productivity growth accelerated in the 1990s, there was no matching inequality increase, thus there is no direct connection between productivity and growth in wage inequality (Mishel, Bernstein and Schmitt, 2001; Mishel, Bernstein and Allegretto, 2005). Most of what explains the rise in wage inequality is a pulling away of the top 10 per cent of wage earners in the 1990s, while the differential between low and middle wage earners was stagnant (Mishel, Bernstein and Schmitt, 2001; Mishel, Bernstein and Allegretto, 2005). Finally, the occupations that account for the largest education wage differentials were managers and sales workers, not technical professions (Mishel, Bernstein and Schmitt, 2001).

Additional findings are largely inconclusive as to the effect of inequality on innovation. Some researchers have found a positive, albeit small effect of inequality on growth (Scully, 2002), while others found a negative relationship between the two (Alesina and Perotti, 1996; Panizza, 2002; Rodriguez, 2000; Rupasingha, Goetz and Freshwater, 2002). The findings of a link between inequality and growth, though, appear to be sensitive to the empirical model's specification (Crafts, 1992; Panizza, 2002). Also, the contention that income inequality in the U.S. has resulted in greater productivity growth due to better skill development does not seem to enjoy empirical support (Appelbaum and Weller, 2001; Osberg, 2003; Mishel, Bernstein and Schmitt, 2001; Mishel, Bernstein and Allegretto, 2005).

Even though a link does not seem to exist between inequality and aggregate supply, there may be a connection between inequality and demand. If the labour share of national income declines, aggregate demand could fall as consumption growth slows. This effect could be exacerbated if inequality within labour rises, too. A greater concentration of total income among higher income earners may reduce aggregate demand growth as higher income earners have a lower marginal propensity to consume and thus are more prone to save than lower income households (Keynes, 1936).

On the face of it, the figures do not necessarily support the notion that rising inequality can lead to declining consumption. For instance, the share of consumption relative to disposable income, one of the measures that should decline with inequality actually increases as inequality rises (Table 8.4). Also, research based on micro data appears to be somewhat ambivalent. Specifically, savings incentives should be relatively most effective for high income earners and least effective for low income earners. An analysis using micro data to study the effectiveness of savings incentives, such as 401(k)s and IRAs, tend to find that savings incentives seem to be more effective in raising savings for low income earners and not for high income ones (Engen and Gale, 2000).

A number of studies, though, based on macro data suggest that there is a negative connection between inequality and aggregate demand (Arestis and Howell, 1995; Brown, 2004; Pressman, 1997). It is possible that the gap between income and consumption has been filled by consumer debt.

INEQUALITY, CONSUMER DEBT, AND FINANCIAL DISTRESS

As inequality rose, consumption should have declined without compensating increases in consumer debt (Brown, 2004). Some researchers have argued that in fact the rise in inequality has given way to an endogenous development of credit markets, increasing the credit supply in response to rising inequality (Kruger and Perri, 2002).

The credit supply rose for a number of reasons and its expansion was most notable among low-income households. First, the standardization of mortgages and the introduction of mortgage backed securities took shape in the 1960s with the creation of Ginnie Mae under the Housing and Urban Development Act of 1968, the creation of Freddie Mac, the engagement of Fannie Mae in the pass-through market under the Emergency Home Finance Act of 1970, and tax advantages for mortgages under the 1986 Tax Reform Act (Vandell, 2000). These innovations helped to reduce the risks for mortgage lenders and lowered the costs of mortgages (Figure 8.8) (Van Order, 2002). Pearce and Miller (2001) estimated that the costs savings to consumers amounted to somewhere between $8.4 billion to $23.5 billion.

Second, financial innovation increased credit supply. The Tax Reform Act of 1986 phased out the deductibility of most non-mortgage interest and introduced new marginal tax rates that reduced the tax advantage of all types of debt. This led to a shift of consumer debt towards mortgages and home equity lines (Figure 8.9) (Dunsky and Follain, 2000; Stango, 1999). Stango (1999) estimates that by 1991 aggregate mortgage debt was over one percent higher, credit card debt approximately 14 per cent lower, and auto loan debt

FIGURE 8.8
US mortgage rates, 1971–2003

Notes: Real mortgage rates are the difference between the nominal mortgage rates and the year-on-year change in the consumer price index (CPI).
Sources: BLS (2004b), BOG (2004d), authors' calculations.

FIGURE 8.9
US home equity lines, 1990–2002

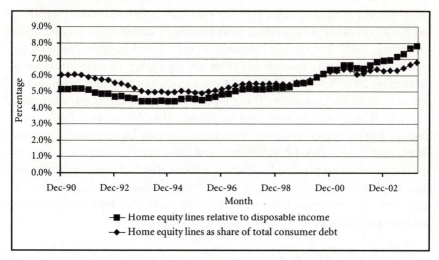

Sources: BOG (2004c), authors' calculations.

FIGURE 8.10
US credit card debt, 1968–2004

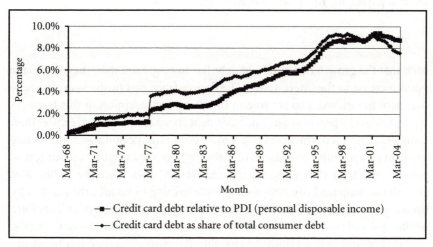

Notes: Credit card debt refers to revolving consumer credit.
Sources: BOG (2004c, 2004e), authors' calculations.

approximately 9 per cent lower than they would have been without these changes.

Third, increased financial competition raised the credit supply. Specifically, competition among credit card providers gave financial institutions incentives to offer credit cards to clients that were previously underserved (Figure 8.10) (Manning, 2000). The relative increases of credit card debt appear to be larger among lower income households than among higher income households (Manning, 2000; Yoo, 1996). In addition, non-bank credit also expanded in response to rising inequality. These types of loans, including payday loans, pawn-broking, rent-to-own and appliance title loans, and tax refund anticipation loans grew and were concentrated among low-income customers (Barr, 2001; CFA, 1998, 1999; Stegman and Faris, 2003).

Greater credit supply should offset the adverse effects of rising inequality on consumption. Higher debt service costs, though, could outweigh the added impulse to consumption from more debt. In particular, household sources have to equal their uses:

$$\Delta C_t + \Delta Tr_t + \Delta I_t + \Delta A_t = \Delta Y_t + \Delta D_t \tag{1}$$

The change in consumption, C, is thus equal to the change in disposable income, Y, plus the change in debt, D, minus the change in net transfers, Tr, minus the change in assets, A, minus the change in interest payments, I. Assuming that borrowing is the only thing that keeps consumption going, consumption can increase as long as new debt is larger than the increases in interest payments. Increases in interest payments are:

$$\Delta I_t = \Delta r_t * D_{t-1} \tag{2}$$

such that the growth of household debt has to be greater than the percentage point increase in the interest rate. The figures from past business cycles show that debt has played a larger role in financing consumption in this business cycle than in any previous ones and that debt changes were indeed greater than changes in interest payments (Table 8.6).[4] Specifically, personal income became a negative contributor to changes in consumption, meaning that consumption growth was larger than personal income growth. Also, since the 1980s, debt growth has outpaced consumption growth helping to finance the gap left by slower income growth. Yet, despite faster debt growth, interest payments were unchanged and even declined relative to consumption spending since the 1980s.

For debt and consumption to rise simultaneously, income has to go up, interest rates have to go down, or both. Debt and consumption grew at the same time, while income growth has been lagging at least behind consumption growth

TABLE 8.6
USA: sources and uses of household finances

Business cycle dates	Change in disposable income relative to consumer spending	Change in financial assets to consumer spending	Change in interest payments to consumer spending	Change in transfer payments to consumer spending	Change in debt to consumer spending
1954:3–1957:3	0.74	-7.93	0.31	0.00	-1.28
1957:3–1960:2	-1.78	2.79	0.16	-0.13	1.68
1960:2–1969:4	3.91	-0.55	0.49	0.13	-2.14
1969:4–1973:4	2.76	4.11	-0.05	0.11	3.11
1973:4–1980:1	-1.74	-0.40	0.22	-0.11	1.56
1980:1–1990:3	-0.94	-0.18	0.47	0.41	-2.44
1990:3–2001:1	-5.91	-6.91	0.00	0.39	0.22
2001:1–2004:2	-2.18	2.97	-0.77	0.13	5.14

Notes: All figures are in per cent. Totals do not add to zero due to statistical discrepancies. Disposable income refers to personal income minus taxes plus net investments in consumer durables and consumption of fixed capital minus all new spending on consumer durables, government insurance and pension reserves, and net capital transfers. Consumer spending refers to personal consumption expenditures plus capital expenditures on real estate.
Sources: BOG (2004c) and BEA (2004).

(Table 8.6). At the same time, though, interest rates have been falling in nominal and real terms (Figure 8.8). Thus, declining interest rates have allowed households to sustain their consumption.

Inequality and Consumer Debt

We can estimate the effect of inequality on the credit supply since under credit rationing, realized credit is equal to the credit supply (Stiglitz and Weiss, 1980). Credit supply is measured as credit relative to disposable income. Its explanatory variables are standard measures of collateral—expected income gains—and interest that we supplement with measures of inequality. Specifically, we use real disposable income lagged once and the real mortgage rate. In addition, we use the labour share of national income as a measure for inequality between capital and labour. To account for within labour inequality we use two measures, one for wage inequality and a proxy for wealth inequality and thus capital income inequality. Our wage inequality measure is Atkinson's inequality measure with a calibration factor of 0.5. As proxy of wealth inequality, we use the ratio of the stock market index to the housing price index (Wolff, 2002b):

$$\frac{D}{Y}_t = \beta_0 + \beta_1 (\sum_{i=t-4}^{t} \frac{LI}{NI}_i) / 4 + \beta_2 (\sum_{i=t-4}^{t} Atkinson05_i) / 4 + \quad (3)$$

$$\beta_3 (\sum_{i=t-4}^{t} \frac{SP500}{HPI}_i) / 4 + \beta_4 y_{t-1} + \beta_5 r_t + \varepsilon_t$$

where LI is labour income, NI is national income, $Atkinson05$ is Atkinson's inequality measure calibrated with a parameter of 0.5, $SP500$ refers to the S&P 500 index and HPI to the housing price index, y is real disposable income, r is the real mortgage rate, and e is a randomly distributed error term.

Data for labour income, national income, and disposable income come from BEA (2004a); data for the Atkinson's inequality measure is from CEPR (2004); data for the S&P 500 is from Yahoo! Finance (2004); data for the Housing Price Index is from OFHEO (2004); and interest rate data are from BOG (2004d). Income inequality is likely to affect debt over the course of some time, so that we use the average of the four quarters ending in the current quarter for all of our inequality measures[5]. In each case the natural logarithm is used.

Table 8.7 presents our results for the determinants of total debt. The first regression presents our baseline results with the expected positive signs for the explanatory variables. In regression (2), we add our measure for inequality between capital and labour. We would expect this measure to have a negative sign indicating that a greater distribution of national economic resources towards labour is less likely to give rise to endogenous credit expansions and thus less likely to lead to an increase in the credit supply, ceteris paribus. This measure is statistically insignificant. In regression (3), we add our two measures for income inequality. Again, neither one is statistically significant. Regression (4) introduces an alternative measure for inequality between capital and labour. Now, we consider proprietors' income as part of total labour compensation. This generates a statistically significant, yet positive correlation between inequality and the amount of debt. One explanation for this unexpected sign may be that more labour income may also constitute more collateral for households to borrow against. In regressions (5) and (6) we test the robustness of our results with respect to within labour inequality. In regression (5), we replace the Atkinson measure with the 0.5 calibration factor with the Atkinson measure with a 1.0 calibration factor. The results essentially remain the same. One problem with our labour income inequality measures may arise from the fact that both are highly correlated. To circumvent this problem, we combine both measures using factor analysis. We first standardize both variable and then calculate the principal factors. We use only the first factor to generate a new variable 'labour inequality', which is a linear combination of the two

TABLE 8.7
USA: regression results for determinants of household debt, 1980 to 2003

Explanatory variables	(1) Baseline	(2) Between inequality	(3) Within inequality	(4) Alternative between inequality	(5) Alternative within inequality	(6) Combined labour inequality
y_{t-1}	0.47#	0.56#	0.62#	0.64#	0.61#	0.59#
	(010)	(0.10)	(0.10)	(0.09)	(0.11)	(0.11)
r_t	-0.05*	-0.04	-0.04	-0.04	-0.04	-0.04
	(0.02)	(0.03)	(0.03)	(0.03)	(0.03)	(0.03)
LI/NI_t		0.72	0.81		0.78	0.78
		(0.51)	(0.52)		(0.52)	(0.52)
LPI/NI_t				1.01@		
				(0.51)		
$Atkinson05_t$			-0.14	-0.11		
			(0.14)	(0.13)		
$Atkinson10_t$					-0.13	
					(0.16)	
$SP500/HPI_t$			0.01	0.01	0.01	
			(0.03)	(0.03)	(0.03)	
$LIneq_t$						-0.01
						(0.02)
constant	-4.14#	-4.56#	-5.42#	-5.60#	-5.23#	-4.80#
	(0.90)	(0.85)	(1.00)	(0.89)	(0.98)	(0.91)
n	93	93	93	93	93	93
Adj. R-squared	0.23	0.25	0.45	0.65	0.44	0.33
Durbin-Watson	1.86	1.86	1.88	1.86	1.87	1.88

Notes: In each case, a Prais-Winsten regression is used. LPI refers to labour income plus proprietors' income and Atkinson10 refers to the Atkinson inequality measure with 1.0 parameter instead of 0.5. LIneq refers to the combined labour inequality measure derived by using the first factor. All inequality measures refer to the four quarter average ending in the current quarter. Figures in parentheses are standard deviations.
* denotes significance at the 5 per cent-level, and
# denotes significance at the one per cent-level.

separate variables and explains 89 per cent of the variance of both variables. Using this new variable instead of two separate measures for labour inequality generates regression (6). The results are again largely robust.

So far, we do not find a link between inequality and household debt. One explanation may be that total household debt is too broad a category to be affected by inequality. Borrowing by high and low-income households in response to rising inequality may have had offsetting effects. Specifically, higher-income earners are more likely than lower-income households to own a home and thus be able to borrow against their real estate (Wolff, 2002b, 2004). Income inequality rose because incomes of higher-income earners pulled away from the middle. Thus, households that were more likely to own their residence also had more collateral to borrow against, but less need to borrow additional money. In comparison, lower income households saw below average income gains as inequality rose, but also had fewer opportunities to borrow against their own homes. As they had a greater need to borrow, but less collateral, the literature suggests that a cycle of endogenous credit expansion took place, which may have manifested itself in a disproportionate increase in credit card debt among low income households. Thus, we estimate our results separately for mortgages (Table 8.8) and credit card debt (Table 8.9)[6].

Table 8.8 presents our results for mortgage debt. We find a consistent positive and statistically significant relationship between the labour share of national income and mortgage debt, suggesting that less labour income allowed fewer households to buy a home and borrow against the value of their real estate than otherwise would have been the case. A one per cent decline in the four quarter average of labour's share of national income translated into a one per cent decrease in the ratio of mortgage debt to disposable income. The results also show that the rising inequality in the distribution of wage earnings had an adverse effect on mortgage debt. A rise in earnings inequality translated into less mortgage debt as well. Thus, our results suggest that the increasing unequal distribution between capital and labour away from labour and the rising inequality of labour income lowered the amount of mortgage below where it otherwise would have been.

Our results on mortgage debt stand in contrast to our results on credit card debt (Table 8.9). We find no connection between an increasingly unequal distribution between capital and labour and the amount of credit card debt, but we find that greater inequality within labour results in more credit card debt, regardless of which measure is used. For instance, a one per cent increase in wage inequality has typically resulted in a 0.5 per cent increase in credit card debt relative to disposable income. For the period from 1980 to 2003, our inequality measure had a standard deviation that was 6.5 per cent of its mean. Thus, a one standard deviation increase would explain a 3.2 per cent increase in debt relative to disposable income. This is a small fraction of the total increase in credit card debt relative to disposable income as it rose almost fourfold over the period from 1980 to 2003. In comparison, a one per cent increase in our capital income proxy translated into an increase of 0.1 per cent in the ratio of credit card debt to disposable income. The standard deviation of our capital income inequality proxy was 56 per cent of its average, which would have meant a 5.6 per cent increase in the ratio of credit card debt to disposable income.

TABLE 8.8
USA: regression results for determinants of mortgage debt, 1980 to 2003

Explanatory variables	(1) Baseline	(2) Between inequality	(3) Within inequality	(4) Alternative between inequality	(5) Alternative within inequality	(6) Combined labour inequality
y_{t-1}	0.51#	0.59#	0.66#	0.63	0.65#	0.66#
	(0.11)	(0.16)	(0.12)	(0.11)	(0.12)	(0.12)
r_t	-0.05*	-0.03	-0.03	-0.03	-0.03	-0.03
	(0.03)	(0.03)	(0.03)	(0.03)	(0.03)	(0.03)
LI/NI$_t$		0.95*	1.13@		1.09@	1.13@
		(0.51)	(0.51)		(0.51)	(0.51)
LPI/NI$_t$				1.30@		
				(0.53)		
Atkinson05$_t$			-0.27*	-0.24*		
			(0.14)	(0.14)		
Atkinson10$_t$					-0.27*	
					(0.16)	
SP500/HPI$_t$			-0.03	-0.03	-0.03	
			(0.03)	(0.03)	(0.03)	
LIneq$_t$						-0.03@
						(0.02)
constant	-4.82#	-5.12#	-6.31#	-6.10#	-6.12#	-5.68#
	(0.98)	(0.97)	(1.09)	(1.05)	(1.08)	(0.98)
n	93	93	93	93	93	93
Adj. R-squared	0.35	0.41	0.45	0.50	0.46	0.25
Durbin-Watson	1.37	1.39	1.50	1.51	1.48	1.98

Notes: In each case, a Prais-Winsten regression is used. LPI refers to labour income plus proprietors' income and Atkinson10 refers to the Atkinson inequality measure with 1.0 parameter instead of 0.5. LIneq refers to the combined labour inequality measure derived by using the first factor. All inequality measures refer to the four quarter average ending in the current quarter. Figures in parentheses are standard deviations.

    * denotes significance at the 10 per cent-level,

    @ denotes significance at the 5 per cent-level, and

    # denotes significance at the one per cent-level.

TABLE 8.9

USA: regression results for determinants of credit card debt, 1980 to 2003

Explanatory variables	(1) Baseline	(2) Between inequality	(3) Within inequality	(4) Alternative between inequality	(5) Alternative within inequality	(6) Combined labour inequality
y_{t-1}	1.19#	1.18#	0.99#	1.06#	0.98#	0.99#
	(0.22)	(0.24)	(0.23)	(0.22)	(0.23)	(0.23)
pr_t	0.001	-0.01	-0.02	-0.01	-0.02	-0.02
	(0.04)	(0.04)	(0.04)	(0.04)	(0.04)	(0.04)
LI/NI_t		-0.81	-1.28		-1.23	-1.28
		(1.05)	(1.04)		(1.04)	(1.04)
LPI/NI_t				-0.86		
				(1.08)		
Atkinson05$_t$			0.51*	0.46*		
			(0.28)	(0.28)		
Atkinson10$_t$					0.61*	
					(0.33)	
SP500/HPI$_t$			0.12*	0.11*	0.11*	
			(0.06)	(0.06)	(0.06)	
LIneq$_t$						0.08@
						(0.03)
constant	-13.21#	-12.91#	-10.78#	-11.22	-10.83#	-11.97#
	(1.92)	(1.96)	(2.15)	(2.11)	(2.11)	(1.92)
n	93	93	93	93	93	93
Adj. R-squared	0.78	0.85	0.85	0.85	0.85	0.84
Durbin-Watson	1.48	1.93	1.93	1.92	1.93	1.93

Notes: In each case, a Prais-Winsten regression is used. Credit card debt refers to the share of revolving credit out of total household debt. LPI refers to labour income plus proprietors' income and Atkinson10 refers to the Atkinson inequality measure with 1.0 parameter instead of 0.5. LIneq refers to the combined labour inequality measure derived by using the first factor. All inequality measures refer to the four quarter average ending in the current quarter. Figures in parentheses are standard deviations.

   * denotes significance at the 10 per cent-level,

   @ denotes significance at the 5 per cent-level, and

   # denotes significance at the one per cent-level.

TABLE 8.10
USA: regression results for determinants of debt composition, 1980 to 2003

Explanatory variables	(1) Baseline	(2) Between inequality	(3) Within inequality	(4) Alternative between inequality	(5) Alternative within inequality	(6) Combined labour inequality
y_{t-1}	0.34#	0.59#	0.44#	0.53#	0.44#	0.44#
	(0.23)	(0.17)	(0.16)	(0.16)	(0.16)	(0.16)
pr_t	0.04	0.01	0.0005	0.01	0.004	0.001
	(0.03)	(0.03)	(0.03)	(0.03)	(0.03)	(0.03)
LI/NI_t		-1.53@	-2.08#		-2.00#	-2.08#
		(0.76)	(0.72)		(0.71)	(0.71)
LPI/NI_t				-1.79@		
				(0.75)		
$Atkinson05_t$			0.66#	0.60#		
			(0.20)	(0.20)		
$Atkinson10_t$					0.76#	
					(0.22)	
$SP500/HPI_t$			0.11@	0.10@	0.10@	
			(0.04)	(0.04)	(0.04)	
$LIneq_t$						0.10#
						(0.02)
constant	-687.39#	-8.60#	-5.86#	-6.52#	-6.06#	-7.43#
	(317.39)	(1.46)	(1.49)	(1.48)	(1.46)	(1.32)
n	93	93	93	93	93	93
Adj. R-squared	0.03	0.78	0.90	0.89	0.90	0.90
Durbin-Watson	1.50	1.45	1.75	1.73	1.74	1.75

Notes: In each case, a Prais-Winsten regression is used. LPI refers to labour income plus proprietors' income and Atkinson10 refers to the Atkinson inequality measure with 1.0 parameter instead of 0.5. All inequality measures refer to the four quarter average ending in the current quarter. Figures in parentheses are standard deviations.

  * denotes significance at the 10 per cent-level,
  @ denotes significance at the 5 per cent-level, and
  # denotes significance at the one per cent-level.

One way to combine the results on mortgage debt and credit card debt is to use the share of credit card debt out of total debt as the dependent variable (Table 8.10). The results show that the trend towards rising inequality between labour and capital and within labour has resulted in a larger share of credit card debt relative to total household debt over the period from 1980 to 2003. As the labour share of national income has trended downward, households increasingly shifted their borrowing towards credit card debt, possibly because it was more accessible than mortgage debt. A one per cent decrease in the labour share of national income resulted in a 2 per cent increase in the relative borrowing from credit cards. Also, increasing inequality within labour led to a growing share of credit card debt relative to total debt. A one per cent increase in wage inequality, averaged over four quarters, translated into an increase of 0.6 per cent in the relative size of credit card debt and a one per cent increase in capital income inequality translated into a 0.1 per cent increase in the share of credit card debt. The size of the effects is comparable to their impact on the volume of credit.

Inequality and Household Economic Distress

The rise in consumer debt could also have given rise to household economic distress if it was more pronounced for lower income households (Iyigun and Owen, 1997). The increase in debt levels, caused by a growing disparity between labour and capital, should increase financial distress. So should the rise in within labour inequality as more costly credit card debt disproportionately increases among lower income earners. Already, the largest increases in consumer default exist with respect to credit card debt. The charge-off rate on credit card loans increased almost threefold from 2.0 per cent in 1985 to 5.9 per cent at the end of 2003, while it only doubled on other consumer loans and declined on real estate loans (residential and commercial combined) (BOG, 2004a).

The rise in economic distress measures is somewhat surprising given the fundamental characteristics of household finances. Importantly, the debt service burden rose from an average of 11.9 per cent in the early 1980s to 13.0 per cent since 1999, a 9 per cent increase (Figure 8.11). At the time, though, household debt relative to disposable income rose from 78.0 per cent to 105.8 per cent, or a 36 per cent increase (Figure 8.11). Moreover, calculations based on data from the Fed (BOG, 2004c) show that household wealth relative to disposable income grew at the same time, too. Thus, as households borrowed more, their assets increased even faster, while the burden of repaying the debt rose much more slowly.

FIGURE 8.11
US debt and debt service relative to disposable Income, 1985–2001

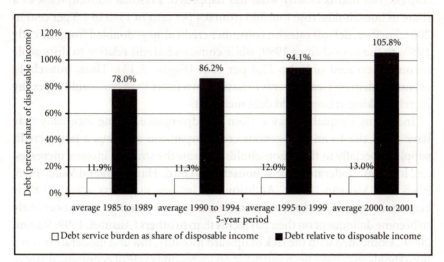

Sources: BOG (2004a, 2004c), authors' calculations.

FIGURE 8.12
Amount and charge-off rates of consumer credit, 1985–2001

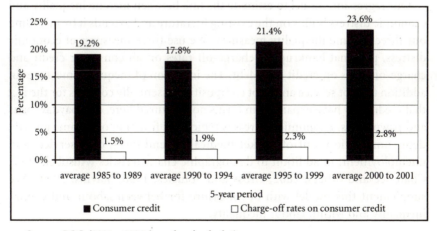

Sources: BOG (2004a, 2004c), authors' calculations.

Based on these figures, one would not necessarily expect a rise in economic distress, but that is exactly what has happened. Personal bankruptcies, as a share of households, rose fourfold from 0.4 per cent in 1980 to 1.5 per cent in 2003. Further, default rates on consumer credit almost doubled from the early 1980s to the period since 1999, while consumer credit relative to disposable income increased only by 23.4 per cent (Figure 8.12). Thus, household economic distress clearly seems to have grown faster than one would expect by merely looking at household debt measures.

Increasing inequality may explain this divergence. Rising inequality may have given rise to an endogenous credit expansion and thus a larger credit supply, especially to those households that saw the smallest income increases, i.e., low and moderate income households (Bird, Hagstrom and Wild, 1998; Black and Morgan, 1999). Additionally, lenders may have screened their customers carefully and offered worse terms to customers that were more likely to become delinquent on their payments than to others (Ausubel, 1999; Stavins, 2000). Combined with the lack of upward mobility, low and moderate income households may have been caught in an increasing cycle of economic distress, caused by the combination of low income growth, high debt growth, and high debt costs. Thus, both types of inequality may have contributed to a rise in economic distress due to the ensuing demand for credit and the extension of rising, and more costly credit, such as credit card debt (Chatterjee and others, 2002; Gross and Souleles, 1998; Stavins, 2000).

Our regression model to estimate the link between income inequality and economic distress builds on the existing literature and extends it by including our three income inequality measures. We use three measures of economic distress, personal bankruptcy, charge-off rates on all consumer credit and charge-off rates on credit card debt. The inclusion of inequality measures in addition to debt service and debt composition essentially controls for the fact that credit may have expanded in forms not captured here, e.g., payday loans and pawnshops. Economic distress is typically a function of income growth, debt composition, out-of-pocket medical expenditures, debt service, and unemployment, in addition to demographic characteristics (Ausubel, 1997; Chaterjee and others, 2002; Gross and Souleles, 1998; Stavins, 2000). We supplement this model with our measure for between labour and capital inequality and within labour inequality:

$$\frac{BR}{HH}_t = \beta_0 + \beta_1 UR_t + \beta_2 \frac{MEX}{Y}_t + \beta_3 \frac{y_t - y_{t-1}}{y_{t-1}} + \beta_4 \frac{CCR}{TC}_t + \beta_5 \frac{DS}{Y}_t$$

$$+ \beta_6 (\sum_{i=t-4}^{t} \frac{LI}{NI}_i)/4 + \beta_7 (\sum_{i=t-4}^{t} Atkinson05_i)/4 + \beta_8 (\sum_{i=t-4}^{t} \frac{SP500}{HPI}_i)/4 + \varepsilon_t \qquad (4)$$

Where BR refers to the total number of quarterly bankruptcy cases, at an annualized rate, HH refers to the total number of households[7], MEX to total medical expenditures, CCR to credit card debt, TC to total household credit, and DS to debt service ratio. The source for medical expenditures is BEA (2004a), the source for the unemployment rate is BLS (2004c), and the source for debt service is BOG (2004b). To make the results comparable for both our economic distress variables, we estimate the regression for the period from 1985 to 2003[8].

Table 8.11 summarizes our regression results for all of our economic distress variables, personal bankruptcies and charge-off rates.[9] All explanatory variables either have the expected sign or are statistically insignificant. Regression (1) presents our baseline results for personal bankruptcies. The share of households declaring bankruptcy in a given year is negatively related to income growth, and positively to medical expenditures, to the composition of debt and to debt service. Also, inequality between labour and profits does not affect the bankruptcy rate as regression (2) shows. However, inequality within labour, especially arising from wealth inequality, results in a higher personal bankruptcy rate as our results in regression (3) suggest. Using our combined labour inequality measure in regression (4) does not change the results materially. A rise in labour inequality by one per cent results in a rise in the personal bankruptcy rate by 0.2 per cent. Thus, a one-standard deviation increase in labour inequality, which equals 217 per cent of the average labour inequality, would result in a 39 per cent increase in the personal bankruptcy rate. In comparison, though, the personal bankruptcy rate rose by 473 per cent from 1985 to 2003. Thus, rising inequality within labour has significantly contributed to the increase in personal bankruptcies, but it does not explain the majority of the increase. Again, it is important to keep in mind that this is an average effect that ignores the fact that slow income growth at the bottom of the income scale went hand-in-hand with a disproportionate increase of credit card debt, non-bank loans and economic distress among lower-income households. Thus, the effect is likely more pronounced by income.

The results differ somewhat for the regressions on charge-off rates on consumer credit and credit card debt (Table 8.11). For instance, the unemployment

TABLE 8.11
USA: regression results for economic distress measures

Explanatory variables	(1) Baseline	(2) between inequality	(3) within inequality	(4) combined labour inequality	(5) within inequality	(6) combined labour inequality	(7) within inequality	(8) combined labour inequality
	Personal bankruptcy rate				Charge-off rate, consumer credit		Charge-off rate, credit cards	
$(y_t-y_{t-1})/y_{t-1}$	-0.02*	-0.02*	-0.02*	-0.02*	-0.01	-0.01	-0.01	-0.01
	(0.01)	(0.01)	(0.01)	(0.01)	(0.01)	(0.01)	(0.01)	(0.01)
UR_t	-0.03	-0.03	0.24	0.13	0.49@	0.35	0.72#	0.67@
	(0.02)	(0.17)	(0.19)	(0.19)	(0.24)	(0.23)	(0.24)	(0.25)
$(MEX/Y)_t$	1.80#	1.81#	1.79#	1.84#	0.66	0.80	0.13	0.80
	(0.43)	(0.44)	(0.41)	(0.44)	(0.58)	(0.59)	(0.49)	(0.63)
$(CCR/TC)_t$	0.64@	0.64@	-0.02	0.17	-0.08	-0.25	0.77	-0.09
	(0.30)	(0.31)	(0.40)	(0.40)	(0.60)	(0.61)	(0.51)	(0.68)
$(DS/Y)_t$	0.96*	0.96*	0.95*	0.87	1.76@	1.92@	1.69#	1.73@
	(0.52)	(0.53)	(0.48)	(0.53)	(0.75)	(0.77)	(0.57)	(0.79)
LI/NI_t		-0.08	-2.47	-2.47	-0.64	-1.70	1.76	-2.16
		(2.69)	(2.85)	(2.99)	(3.42)	(3.47)	(3.51)	(3.63)
$Atkinson05_t$			0.60		0.38		-0.70	
			(0.78)		(0.87)		(0.99)	
$SP500/HPI_t$			0.40#		0.44		0.31*	
			(0.15)		(0.15)		(0.18)	
$LIneq_t$				0.18*		0.21@		0.21@
				(0.10)		(0.09)		(0.10)
N	76	76	76	76	76	76	76	76
R-squared	0.96	0.96	0.96	0.96	0.13	0.08	0.25	0.11
Durbin-Watson	1.78	1.78	1.81	1.80	2.08	1.96	1.97	1.96

Notes: In each case, a Prais-Winsten regression is used. All inequality measures refer to the four quarter average ending in the current quarter. Figures in parentheses are standard deviations.
* denotes significance at the 10 per cent-level,
@ denotes significance at the 5 per cent-level, and
# denotes significance at the one per cent-level.

rate, instead of personal income growth, is a significant indicator of default. Higher unemployment rates raise the rate of default, which may be a reflection of the fact that unemployment rates are more volatile among low and middle-income households, where the expansion of credit card debt has been more pronounced. However, health care expenditures did not play a significant role in determining default rates, which may reflect the fact that health care coverage and thus out of pocket medical expenditures are unequally distributed. Further, the debt service burden has a much more pronounced effect on default rates than on personal bankruptcies as the size of the effect almost doubles. A 1 per cent increase in the debt service burden raises the default rate by 1.7–1.9 per cent as regressions (5) through (8) show. The effect of the within labour inequality on charge-off rates is similar to that on personal bankruptcy rates as they also rose fourfold from 1985 to 2003.

CONCLUSION

In this chapter, we look at the macro economic effects of rising inequality in the U.S. The distribution of national income between capital and labour has become more unequal as has the distribution within labour. At the same time that inequality rose, consumer debt and household economic distress grew, too. The evidence on a positive link between rising inequality and innovation is not supported by the data. The data either suggest no connection or a potential negative link.

In comparison, the link between growing inequality and aggregate demand is somewhat ambiguous since macro economic data show a negative connection that is not supported by the micro data. One way to clarify this ambiguity is the possibility that debt has increased and that it has increased more among low-income households. This seems to be the effect, especially when considering more costly forms of debt, such as credit cards and non-bank credit. We find that credit card debt is especially sensitive to changes in inequality and that rising inequality may thus have contributed to the stark increases in personal bankruptcies in the US. However, while our results show that rising inequality has played a non-trivial role in the expansion of some forms of credit and that it has contributed to the large increases in economic distress over the past two decades, it explains only a small part of the overall increases in debt levels and in economic distress. Yet, a look at aggregate data ignores the fact that changes in inequality, consumer credit and economic distress likely affected lower income households more than others.

NOTES

[1] All comparisons are for nine quarters or 28 months after the start of the recovery.

[2] All differences were statistically significant at least at the 5 per cent-level.

[3] Simultaneously, labour income became more unequally distributed, exacerbating the trends discussed here.

[4] For ease of comparison, all figures are divided by consumer spending.

[5] All series are non-stationary, integrated at the first degree, and co-integrated at the one per cent-level.

[6] Credit card debt refers to revolving consumer credit (BOG, 2004e).

[7] The total number of households is calculated by dividing the number of housing units by 1.1.

[8] Our previous results on debt levels are unaffected by the choice of time period.

[9] The results remain robust if the bankruptcy rate is calculated separately for Chapter 7 and Chapter 13 filings. They also are robust if the between inequality measure includes proprietors' income and the Atkinson10 measure instead of Atkinson05 measure is used for wage inequality.

REFERENCES

Alesina, A., and R. Perotti (1996). Income Distribution, Political Instability, and Investment. *European Economic Review* 40 (6): 1203–28.

American Bankruptcy Institute (2004). Non-Business Bankruptcy Filings by Chapter, 1990–2004, per Quarter. American Bankruptcy Institute, Alexandria, VA.

Arestis, P., and P. Howell (1995). Changes in Income Distribution and Aggregate Spending: Constraints on Full-Employment? *Review of Political Economy* 7 (2): 150–63.

Atkinson, R. (2003). *The Bush Manufacturing Crisis*. Policy Report, Progressive Policy Institute, Washington, DC.

Ausubel, L. (1997). Credit Card Defaults, Credit Card Profits, and Bankruptcy. *American Bankruptcy Law Journal* 71, Spring: 249–70.

Barr, M. (2001). Five Opportunities for the Bush Administration and the 107th Congress. Center on Urban and Metropolitan Policy, The Brookings Institution, Washington, DC.

Benhabib, J. (2003). The Tradeoff between Inequality and Growth. *Annals of Economics and Finance* 4 (2): 491–507.

Bird, E.J., P.A. Hagstrom and R. Wild (1999). Credit Card Debts of the Poor: High and Rising. *Journal of Policy Analysis and Management* 18 (1): 125–33.

Bivens, L. (2004). Shifting Blame for Manufacturing Job-loss: Effects of Rising Trade Deficits Can't be Ignored. Briefing Paper, Economic Policy Institute, Washington, DC.

Bivens, J., and Christian Weller (2004a). Causes of the 'Job Loss' Recovery. *Challenge* 48 (3): 23–47.

Bivens, J., and Christian Weller (2004b). Institutional Shareholder Concentration, Corporate Governance Changes, and Diverging Fortunes of Capital and Labour. Paper presented at the conference 'Pension Fund Capitalism and the Crisis of Old-Age Security in the United States', Center for Economic Policy Analysis (CEPA), New School University, New York, September.

Black, S., and D. Morgan (1999). Meet the New Borrowers. Current Issues in Economics and Finance, Federal Reserve Bank of New York, February.

Board of Governors, Federal Reserve System (2004a). Charge-Off and Delinquency Rates on Loans and Leases at Commercial Banks. Board of Governors, Federal Reserve System, Washington, DC.

Board of Governors, Federal Reserve System (2004b). Household Debt Service and Financial Obligations Ratios. Board of Governors, Federal Reserve System, Washington, DC.

Board of Governors, Federal Reserve System (2004c). Release Z.1 Flow of Funds Accounts of the United States. Board of Governors, Federal Reserve System, Washington, DC.

Board of Governors, Federal Reserve System (2004d). Release H.15 Selected Interest Rates. Board of Governors, Federal Reserve System, Washington, DC.

Board of Governors, Federal Reserve System (2004e). Release G.19 Consumer Credit. Board of Governors, Federal Reserve System, Washington, DC.

Borjas, G., and V. Ramey (1996). Foreign Competition, Market Power, and Wage Inequality. *Quarterly Journal of Economics* 110 (4), November: 1075–1110.

Boushey, Heather (2004). The Slow Road Down. *TomPaine.com*, August 27.

Bradbury, Katherine, and Jane Katz (2002). Are Lifetime Incomes Growing More Unequal? Looking at New Evidence on Family Income Mobility. *Regional Review* 12 (4): 2–5.

Bradbury, Katherine, and Jane Katz (2004). Wives' Work and Family Income Mobility. Public Policy Discussion Paper No. 04–03, Federal Reserve Bank of Boston.

Brown, C. (2004). Does Income Distribution Matter for Effective Demand? Evidence from the United States. *Review of Political Economy* 16 (3): 291–307.

Bureau of Economic Analysis (2004). *National Income and Product Accounts*. Bureau of Economic Analysis, Washington, DC.

Bureau of Labour Statistics (2004a). *Productivity.* Bureau of Labour Statistics, Washington, DC.

Bureau of Labour Statistics (2004b). *Consumer Price Index.* Bureau of Labour Statistics, Washington, DC.

Bureau of Labour Statistics (2004c). *Unemployment Rate.* Bureau of Labour Statistics, Washington, DC.

Card, D., T. Lemieux and W.C. Riddell (2003). Unionization and Wage Inequality: A Comparative Study of the U.S., the U.K., and Canada. NBER Working Paper No. 9473, National Bureau of Economic Research, Cambridge, MA.

Chaterjee, S., D. Corbae, M. Nakajima and J. Rios-Rull (2002). A Quantitative Theory of Unsecured Consumer Credit Risk with Default. Working Paper No. 02–6, Federal Reserve Bank of Philadelphia.

Chen, B. (2003). An Inverted-U Relationship between Inequality and Long-Run Growth. *Economics Letters* 78 (2): 205–212.

CEPR (2004). CPS ORG Uniform Data Files Version 0.9.3. Center for Economic and Policy Research, Washington, DC.

Cline, William (1997). *Trade and Income Distribution.* Institute for International Economics, Washington, DC.

Consumer Federation of America (1998). *The Growth of Legal Loan Sharking: A Report on the Payday Loan Industry.* Consumer Federation of America, Washington, DC.

Consumer Federation of America (1999). *Safe Harbor for Usury: Recent Developments in Payday Lending.* Consumer Federation of America, Washington, DC.

Crafts, N. (1992). *Was the Thatcher Experiment Worth It? British Economic Growth in a European Context.* CEPR Discussion Paper No. 710, Centre for Economic and Policy Research, London.

DeNavas-Walt, C., B.D. Proctor and R. J. Mills (2004). *Income, Poverty, and Health Insurance Coverage in the United States: 2003.* Current Population Reports, P60-226, U.S. Census Bureau, Washington, DC.

DiNardo, John, Nicole M. Fortin and Thomas Lemieux (1996). Labour Market Institutions and the Distribution of Wages, 1973–1992: A Semiparametric Approach. *Econometrica* 64 (5): 1001–1044.

Dunsky, R., and J. Follain (2000). Tax-Induced Portfolio Reshuffling: The Case of the Mortgage Interest Deduction. *Real Estate Economics* 28 (4): 683–718.

Engen, E., and W. Gale (2000). The Effects of 401(k) Plans on Household Wealth: Differences across Earnings Groups. NBER Working Paper No. 8032, National Bureau of Economic Research, Cambridge, MA.

Galbraith, James (1998). *Created Unequal: The Crisis in American Pay.* Century Foundation Press, New York.

Gottschalk, P. (1997). Inequality, Income Growth, and Mobility: The Basic Facts. *Journal of Economic Perspectives* 11 (2): 21–40.

Gottschalk, P., and S. Danziger (2003). *Wage Inequality, Earnings Inequality, and Poverty in the U.S. Over the Last Quarter of the Twentieth Century.* Boston College, Boston.

Gross, D., and N.S. Souleles (1998). An Empirical Analysis of Personal Bankruptcy and Delinquency. Financial Institutions Center Working Paper No. 98-28-B, The Wharton School, University of Pennsylvania, Philadelphia, PA.

Iyigun, M., and A. Owen (1997). Income Inequality and Macroeconomic Fluctuations. FEDS Working Paper No. 1997-586, Board of Governors of the Federal Reserve System, Washington, DC.

Krueger, D., and F. Perri (2002). Does Income Inequality Lead to Consumption Inequality? Evidence and Theory. NBER Working Paper No. 9202, National Bureau of Economic Research, Cambridge, MA.

Larrain, F.B., and R.M. Vergara (1997). Income Distribution, Investment, and Growth. Harvard

Institute for International Development Working Paper, Harvard University, Cambridge, MA.

Lazonick, William, and Mary O'Sullivan (2000). Maximizing Shareholder Value: A New Ideology for Corporate Governance. *Economy and Society* 29 (1): 13–35.

Lee, David S. (1999). Wage Inequality in the United States during the 1980s: Rising Dispersion of Falling Minimum Wage? *Quarterly Journal of Economics* 114 (3): 977–1023.

Manning, R. (2000). *Credit Card Nation: The Consequences of America's Addiction to Credit.* Basic Books, New York.

Mishel, Lawrence, Jared Bernstein and S. Allegretto (2005). *The State of Working America 2004–05.* Cornell University Press, Ithaca, NY.

Mishel, Lawrence, Jared Bernstein and Heather Boushey (2003). *The State of Working America 2002–3.* Cornell University Press, Ithaca, NY.

Mishel, Lawrence, Jared Bernstein and J. Schmitt (2001). *The State of Working America 2000–01.* Cornell University Press, Ithaca, NY.

OECD (2001). *Employment Outlook.* Organisation for Economic Cooperation and Development, Paris.

Office of Federal Housing Enterprise Oversight (OFHEO) (2004). *Housing Price Index,* Office of Federal Housing Enterprise Oversight, Washington, DC.

Osberg, Lars (2003). Understanding Growth and Inequality Trends: The Role of Labour Supply in the US and Germany. *Canadian Public Policy* (January Supplement): S163–S183.

O'Sullivan, Mary (2000). *Contests for Corporate Control.* Oxford University Press, New York.

Palley, T.I. (1995). Inside Debt, Aggregate Demand, and the Cambridge Theory of Distribution. *Cambridge Journal of Economics* 20 (4): 465–74.

Palomba, G. (2002). Firm Investment, Corporate Finance, and Taxation. IMF Working Paper No 02/237, International Monetary Fund, Washington, DC.

Panizza, U. (2002). Income Inequality and Economic Growth: Evidence from American Data. *Journal of Economic Growth* 7 (1): 25–41.

Papke, L. (1999). Are 401(k) Plans Replacing Other Employer-Provided Pensions? Evidence from Panel Data. *Journal of Human Resources* 34 (2): 346–68.

Peretto, P. (1995). Sunk Costs, Market Structure, and Growth. Department of Economics Working Paper 95–34, Duke University, Durham, NC.

Pearce, J., and J. Miller (2003). Freddie Mac and Fannie Mae: Their Funding Advantage and Benefits to Consumers. Federal Reserve Bank of Chicago Proceedings, March.

Piketty, Thomas, and Emmanuel Saez (2001). Income Inequality in the United States. NBER Working Paper No. 8467, September, National Bureau of Economic Research, Cambridge, MA.

Pressman, S. (1997). Consumption, Income Distribution and Taxation: Keynes' Fiscal Policy. *Journal of Income Distribution* 7 (1): 29–44.

Rodriguez, C. (2000). An Empirical Test of the Institutionalist View on Income Inequality: Economic Growth within the United States. *American Journal of Economics and Sociology* 59 (2): 303–13.

Rupasingha, A., S. Goetz and D. Freshwater (2002). Social and Institutional Factors as Determinants of Economic Growth: Evidence from United States Counties. *Papers in Regional Science* 81 (2): 139–155.

Scully, G.W. (2002). Economic Freedom, Government Policy and the Trade-off between Equity and Economic Growth. *Public Choice* 113 (1–2): 77–96.

Stango, V. (1999). The Tax Reform Act of 1986 and the Composition of Consumer Debt. *National Tax Journal* 52: 717–39.

Stavins, J. (2000). Credit Card Borrowing, Delinquency, and Personal Bankruptcy. *New England Economic Review* July/August: 15–30.

Stegman, M.A., and R. Faris (2003). Payday Lending: A Business Model That Encourages Chronic Borrowing. *Economic Development Quarterly* 17 (1): 8–32.

U.S. Census Bureau (2004). Households and Housing Units Estimates. U.S. Census Bureau, Washington, DC. http://www.census.gov/popest/housing/

Vandell, K. (2000). Securitization of the U.S. Mortgage Market: Progress and Pitfalls, with Lessons for Japan. Seventh Annual International Land Policy Forum, October 31.

Van Order, R. (2002). The Structure and Evolution of American Secondary Mortgage Markets, with Some Implications for Developing Markets. In T. Yasui (ed.). *Housing Finance in Transition Economies.* Organization of Economic Cooperation and Development, Paris.

Weller, Christian (2004a). *Reversing the Upside-Down Economy.* CAP Policy Brief, Center for American Progress, Washington, DC.

Weller, Christian (2004b). *Lagging Investment: The Cost of the Upside-Down Economy.* CAP Policy Brief, Center for American Progress, Washington, DC.

Weller, Christian, J. Bivens and M. Sawicky (2004). Macro Policy Lessons from the Recent Recession. *Challenge* 47 (3): 42–72.

Wolff, Edward (2002a). Is the Equalizing Effect of Retirement Wealth Wearing Off?. Unpublished manuscript, New York University, New York.

Wolff, Edward (2002b). *Top Heavy: A Study of Increasing Inequality of Wealth in America.* Newly updated and expanded edition. The New Press, New York.

Wolff, Edward (2003). What's Behind the Rise of Profitability in the U.S. in the 1980s and 1990s?. *Cambridge Journal of Economics* 27 (4): 479–99.

Wolff, Edward (2004). The Unraveling of the American Pension System, 1983–2001. In N. Ganesan and T. Ghilarducci (eds). *In Search of Retirement Security: The Changing Mix of Social Insurance, Employee Benefits and Personal Responsibility.* National Academy of Social Insurance, Washington, DC.

Earl Wysong, Robert Perrucci, and David Wright (2004). Organizations, Resources, and Class Analysis: The Distributional Model and the U.S. Class Structure, Indiana University Working Paper. Yahoo! Finance (2004). S&P 500 index data. www.yahoo.com.

Yoo, P. (1996). Charging up a Mountain of Debt: Households and Their Credit Cards. Working Paper 96-015A, Federal Reserve Bank of St. Louis.

9
Poverty and Inequality in Eastern Europe and the CIS Transition Economies

MIHALY SIMAI

In Eastern Europe and the Commonwealth of Independent States (CIS), which replaced the former Soviet Union, changes in the distribution of income and wealth associated with globalization, the restoration of the market system, the growing income gap in the former socialist countries, and the rise of the nouveau riche have brought issues of inequality into national politics. The economic, political and many of the social implications are country specific—as the countries are extremely diverse in terms of size, level of development, historical background, as well as social and political structure—and are related to the characteristics of the regimes.[1]

This chapter deals with certain aspects of the transition. The statistical data in this chapter cover countries that differ in terms of development level, size of the economy and population, degree of marketization and integration into global markets, and social costs of transformation. Of all the indicators for

TABLE 9.1
Classification of transition countries by income

Low income	Middle income		High income
	Lower	Higher	
Armenia	Albania	Croatia	Slovenia
Azerbaijan	Belarus	Czech Republic	
Georgia	Bosnia and Herzegovina	Estonia	
Kyrgyzstan	Bulgaria	Hungary	
Moldova	Kazakhstan	Poland	
Tajikistan	Latvia	Slovak Republic	
Turkmenistan	Lithuania		
Ukraine	FYR of Macedonia		
Uzbekistan	Romania		
	Russian Federation		
	Yugoslavia		

Source: World Bank (2000: 334–35).

showing differences, per capita gross domestic product (GDP) is the most widely used.

Due to the level of development and the speed of institutional reform in Central Asian countries, the transition to a market-based system over the past decade and a half has been much more difficult there than in the countries of the European part of the CIS or of Central Europe. Economic contraction in the Central Asian countries and the related growth in poverty and unemployment have lasted longer and been greater in magnitude. During the first half of the 1990s, real GDP of these countries fell by more than 50 per cent, while poverty and inequality increased substantially. Although growth resumed in the latter part of the 1990s, the output of most economies in Central Asia in 2002 remained around 25 to 30 per cent below their 1989 levels, while poverty and unemployment persisted.

This chapter has five sections. The first section provides an overview of the social consequences of the transformation, including the consequences of the disintegration of the Soviet Union, and of privatization and liberalization of the external sector. The second section deals with changes in the labour market and some consequences of unemployment, while the third section analyses poverty. The fourth section addresses changing social stratification, and the fifth section reviews certain social policy issues.

Social Dimensions of the 'Transition'

Most international organizations and social sciences have taken a rather simplified approach to the process known as 'transition', particularly during the first half of the 1990s. While international and national debates have emphasized the policy and institutional aspects of the changes, they have practically overlooked the mentality of the people and neglected the effects of transition on their welfare.

Some neoliberal gurus and many experts on transition assumed that the relatively low levels of poverty and inequality, together with the safety nets provided under the socialist system, would make the social costs of transition tolerable for the transition economies. They also anticipated that reintegration into global markets would provide historically unprecedented opportunities for these countries to accelerate economic modernization, with positive welfare effects. Many Western economic advisers to the new regimes suggested that rapid liberalization was the remedy for curing the economic ills of the transition countries, and would assist in rapidly increasing their export potential.

These assumptions were mainly based on mainstream economic theories, rather than on actual experience, e.g., the socioeconomic changes following decolonization. In addition, unrealistic expectations were raised about the degree of external assistance available and the likelihood of rapid improvement of the situation. By the mid-1990s, it had become apparent that the reality was quite different. In fact, the analysis and objectives offered by the 1995 World Summit for Social Development and the social goals of the Millenium Declaration concerning poverty, among other issues, are clearly relevant for many former socialist countries.

Social Dimensions of the Transformation

The transformation process has included three types of changes, each with profound social consequences. The first type of change was the disintegration of the Soviet Union. States built upon the ruins of the Union had new economic boundaries, institutions and government bureaucracies, which implied new currency, tax, price and market systems. The second was the collapse of the etatist-socialist regimes, resulting in new institutions with market economy characteristics, such as unsubsidized market prices and employment insecurity. The third transformation was the change in social structure, with the old structures being replaced by new ones resembling those of middle or low-income capitalist societies. In many ways, these changes were interrelated and reinforced one another.

The disintegration of the Soviet Union had significant economic implications for its former members. The division of labour was drastically changed, which deprived some republics, like Ukraine and Belarus, of oil and other sources of energy. The other republics no longer supplied Russian manufacturers with raw materials or semi-finished products. Some Central Asian republics lost the subsidies they had received from Moscow, while most non-Soviet Central and Eastern European countries lost markets as the Soviet economy disintegrated. All this resulted in substantial economic decline, hyperinflation, unemployment and government fiscal crises.

Independence left many CIS countries bereft of resource transfers, external markets, and many of the institutions necessary for running a modern economy. Tax and fiscal administrations are particularly relevant examples. In addition, as in all transition countries, many state-owned enterprises collapsed when they were cut off from their traditional markets or had to confront world energy prices. To prevent public enterprises and public services from failing, Governments borrowed heavily, thereby reducing some of the initial social costs associated with the transition. Much of the subsequent external debt crisis developed from these early borrowings. In many cases, the economic disruptions created by the break-up of the former Soviet Union were compounded by shocks, including armed conflicts and massive terms-of-trade changes. Adjustment to world prices has been estimated to be equivalent to terms-of-trade shocks of up to 15 per cent of GDP. Large fiscal deficits emerged, which initially could only be met by nonpayment of existing obligations and external borrowing.

The collapse of the Soviet market had an adverse economic effect on the countries in the bloc, particularly the former members of the Soviet Union. National economies emerged, and many industries lost their markets. Trade within the old Soviet Union became foreign trade with many new impediments. GDP declined on a scale unprecedented during peacetime. The cumulative loss of output and incomes during 1991–2001 was equivalent to about three years of GDP of the former Soviet Union, although the distribution of these losses among the affected countries and social groups was not, of course, equal.[2]

Analysis of the factors responsible for the diversity in GDP decline lies beyond this chapter. However, it is necessary to highlight two factors that influenced the social situation, namely the impact of the decline on different sectors and on national policies. Industrial and agricultural output declined very rapidly, due to the collapse of the Eastern markets, the unavailability or loss of means which made important inputs unaffordable, the crowding-out effects of imports and shrinking domestic purchasing power. Output and income losses were much greater and more sustained than those in the United States of America and Germany during the Great Depression of the thirties. Although there was an initial belief that the richer countries and their institutions would help moderate the social consequences of the transformation, this only occurred on a very small scale.

The social consequences of economic decline were aggravated by the well-known 'conditionalities' demanded by the Washington Consensus policies shared by the World Bank, the International Monetary Fund (IMF) and Western-educated advisers. These policies included fiscal and monetary austerity measures, trade liberalization, free capital movements, exchange-rate unification and devaluation, increased interest rates, removal of subsidies on food and other prices, large-scale privatization, tax reforms and other measures. While some countries tried the gradual approach, others introduced radical 'shock treatment'. In certain cases, these policies had favourable effects, resulting in macroeconomic stability, fiscal consolidation, new economic activities, and the development of basic institutions required for the efficient functioning of market economies. However, the human consequences of the transition process were generally neglected.

Global Market Integration

The reintegration of the countries into global markets exposed them to the forces of globalization, which included the various forces of global competition. This integration implied three major changes. First, it led to the development or reform of institutions, which paved the way for new regulation of external economic relations, and the establishment of tariffs and other instruments of market-oriented trade policy. The main trend was the liberalization of factor movements, the dismantling of the state's foreign trade monopoly and the privatization of the foreign trade system, the establishment of convertible currency, and the introduction of new migration regimes. The second was the countries' participation in a multilateral trading system and financial institutions, resulting in the need to fulfil certain conditions required by those institutions. The third change was related to the disintegration of the Soviet Union and the dissolution of the Council for Mutual Economic Assistance (COMECON). Relations with new external partners, both countries and transnational corporations, had an important influence on the process, speed and character of reintegration.

The processes have been difficult and unequal, often with painful economic and social consequences. The patterns and forms of competition and the institutions of the global market system, shaped mostly by strong corporations and developed industrial countries, have also made the reintegration process more difficult for the transition economies. Among the CIS countries, Armenia, Azerbaijan, Georgia, Kyrgyzstan and Moldova have shown the greatest degree of external sector liberalization, while the least liberal economies are those of Belarus, Turkmenistan and Uzbekistan. Countries on the lower level of development with few export industries, e.g., Georgia, Kyrgyzstan and Moldova, have liberalized their trade more than those that sought to protect their industries. There are also differences between raw material exporting countries and the rest. All the countries have different non-tariff barriers. Capital account liberalization and foreign direct investment (FDI) flows have occurred in varying degrees.

The reintegration has brought both economic and social benefits and costs. Even though it is virtually impossible to quantify the effects of reintegration on income distribution, one may come to certain conclusions. The growing and practically uncontrolled exports of oil, diamonds and different raw materials facilitated capital flight, which provided enormous benefits to the new business elite in the resource-rich countries. The growth of FDI had a positive effect on the income of those working in foreign-owned firms. The rapid growth of indebtedness of a number of countries in the region increased the debt-servicing burden and constrained public expenditure for health and education.

On the macro level, due to the absence of data, it is impossible to isolate the implications of domestic marketization and reintegration with the global markets. The two are, in many ways, interrelated and interconnected. The influence of trade on income and employment is more direct in the case of raw material and semi-finished product exporters and this has a positive regional effect in Kazakhstan and Russia, as unemployment in import-substituting and inter-industry trade sectors were high (Yudaeva, 2002). So far, foreign direct investment has had little impact on employment in general, but regions in the CIS countries, particularly Russia, have attracted far more foreign investments than others; such regions have also attracted mostly skilled labour from other regions. However, their effect on social institutions cannot be evaluated on the basis of existing data.

The marketization process and reintegration with global markets have necessitated the restructuring of uncompetitive industries. Some of these changes have been taking place with the help of FDI, which implies lay-offs and repatriated profits. The restructuring process with national capital is still at a relatively early stage in most countries such as Kazakhstan, the Russian Federation, Ukraine, Bulgaria and Romania. Available facilities for the support of dismissed workers and their families remain limited.

The integration of the CIS countries into the global information system has important implications, as it can reduce the information gap between different groups of a society, thus contributing to the reduction of inequality. The use of the Internet is spreading very fast in the Russian Federation and has been growing by 20 to 25 per cent annually since 2001. However, Russia is still among the countries at the lower middle level of Internet users. Other CIS countries also still lag behind.

The United Nations, particularly the Economic Commission for Europe (ECE) and the United Nations Development Programme (UNDP), has been addressing the social consequences of the transformation. The Social Summit in Copenhagen in 1995 drew attention to the social problems faced by the former socialist countries. A publication of the World Bank in 1996 highlighting the consequences of policies advocated by the Bretton Woods Institutions had little immediate influence on the development of new policies. Meanwhile, not one of the countries in the region has achieved the targets set forth by the Copenhagen Summit or the Millennium Declaration.

The Erosion of Human Capital and Social Support Systems

CIS countries and other countries like Bulgaria and Romania inherited a relatively large human capital stock from the socialist period, due to relatively large investments in education, and relatively well-developed and comprehensive systems of pre-primary, primary, secondary and university education. They also established research infrastructure that was more developed and sophisticated than those of market economies at similar development levels. After the changes, the quality of state-financed education deteriorated quickly, and a large number of research institutes ceased to exist, as tens of thousand of scientists, researchers and engineers emigrated.

The introduction of market institutions from 1991 onward, and the transformation recession, also seriously undermined the social support system of the socialist period (based on low, administered prices for food, rent, household utilities and other basic goods and services, along with the virtual guarantee of a job). Expenditure on health amounted to around 5 per cent of GDP, as did expenditure on education, before the changes in the former Soviet Union. By the end of the 1990s, expenditure on education declined to 4.2 per cent of GDP, and in low-income CIS countries, to 3.8 per cent. Health expenditure went down to 3.4 per cent of GDP, and in low-income CIS countries, to 2.7 per cent (UNDP, 2003).

Before the transition, education used to be essentially free for all. Enrolment ratios for girls at all levels were high, and the quality of education was relatively high. Over the years, the situation has deteriorated. By the beginning of the new millennium, the school systems in general had deteriorated due to budgetary constraints and neglect. While the share of public education expenditure averaged around 5 per cent of GDP in CIS countries at the beginning of the 1990s, it had declined to around 4.0 to 4.2 per cent of a smaller GDP by the end of the decade. According to a UNICEF-Innocenti report, the average share of education in terms of GDP in the low-income CIS countries is still higher than the world average of low-income states, but with much greater dispersion. In Armenia, Georgia and Tajikistan, it was below 2 per cent of GDP (UNICEF, Innocenti Research Centre 2002: 14). Moreover, social stratification of the educational system is on the rise, resulting in a deteriorating outlook for low-income people that will contribute to inferior employment opportunities and marginalization.

The health situation has deteriorated in all the CIS countries, with an increase in inequality of access to services. In some of the CIS countries, mortality is rising or has ceased to decline, the incidence of serious diseases (e.g., tuberculosis) has increased, and some infectious diseases (e.g., malaria) have reappeared.

In the Russian Federation, the accumulation of unfavourable changes in the population's health, the unsatisfactory development of basic medicine, and the inaccessibility of highly effective treatment methods have further aggravated the dynamics of morbidity and resulted in a rise in the disablement level among the population. The deterioration can be viewed through the fast spread of 'social diseases'. Since 1992, the annual increment in the number of people suffering from tuberculosis has been 10 to 15 per cent. Among those registered for the first time, there was an increase in the share of people with neglected or destructive forms of the disease. The incidence of syphilis registered in 2000 was 31 times higher than that registered in 1990. In addition, the rise in the HIV morbidity is evidence of the rapid spread of the HIV epidemic in the country. With the emergence of privately-financed (out-of-pocket) and unregulated health care, access to health care services by the poor has diminished.

The inherited structure of social benefits, comprising both social insurance (pensions and unemployment benefits) and social assistance programmes (including family allowances), is inadequate to deal with the needs created by the transition. Social insurance is largely financed through payroll taxation and federal budgetary funds, whereas social assistance is largely the responsibility of local authorities, who also finance and deliver the bulk of education and health services and subsidize housing and domestic utilities. Enterprises still provide a wide array of social benefits for their workers and local communities, encompassing housing, health care and childcare. An in-depth analysis of these trends shows not only the gap between expectation and reality, but also an increasingly unequal distribution of economic gains and losses, both within countries and among them.

New Growth

Since the late 1990s, GDP has been growing in nearly all 14 countries in the CIS region as well as in Bulgaria and Romania, for reasons which are beyond the scope of this chapter. Although economic growth in these countries cannot compensate for the losses suffered during the 1990s, it at least contributes to some improvement in the standard of living of a large segment of the population, particularly in some of the oil producing countries of the region. In 2003 and 2004, the upturn in the largest countries—Kazakhstan, the Russian Federation and Ukraine—benefited the whole region. Growth was driven by the expansion of private consumption, investments and oil exports. While there was some improvement, mainly in the capital cities and larger towns, most of the adverse social consequences of the changes remained, with high incidences of poverty and unemployment in small towns, one-industry towns and villages.

The balance of this chapter reviews some of the fundamental social problems which have contributed to increasing inequality: the labour market situation, the causes and consequences of poverty, and the new social stratification, among others. The character and effectiveness of some aspects of certain social policies will also be discussed.

THE EVOLVING LABOUR MARKET

Of the three main markets (the market for goods, capital and labour), the most sensitive and difficult in the transformation process has been the labour market. It has been most directly connected with political and institutional changes. In Kazakhstan, the Russian Federation and Ukraine, it has been simultaneously internationalized and de-internationalized, and has been influenced by ethnic diversity, exclusion and discrimination. The economic consequences of the transformation include unemployment, de-skilling[3], privatization and job insecurity. The relationship between urban and rural areas and the increase of regional differences also influence the evolving structure and institutions of the labour market.

Social Implications of the Labour Market

The establishment of labour markets in the former socialist countries had limited success in reducing poverty, providing employment, increasing labour mobility, and facilitating market-oriented wage determination. Most of these countries developed institutions for implementing both active and passive labour market policies and introduced unemployment benefits, retraining institutions and job counseling. The labour markets are interrelated with each of the other major markets as well as with important demographic and social processes, such as health, education, and the age structure of the population.

In the past, central planning offered job security, guaranteed benefits, employment, and high labour force participation (Barr, 1994: 122–123). While the central allocation of labour was abolished in most countries even before the systemic changes began, certain elements survived in the form of wage rigidities, which only allowed narrow differentials and little open unemployment. Labour hoarding that was encouraged by the system resulted in a highly inefficient use of the workforce. In a number of countries, skilled workers earned more than engineers, and in some cases, semi-skilled workers earned more than skilled workers. Labour mobility was restricted by legal measures and the socioeconomic effects of the system.

The development of labour market institutions in the Western region of Central and Eastern Europe was relatively fast. However, it was slower and more difficult in the CIS countries, where specific problems emerged. The full employment commitment of the socialist Governments—achieved by huge state-financed investments in labour intensive sectors of the economy—was gone. Unemployment grew in both open and hidden forms because of the obsolescence of skills. However, the decline in employment was much smaller than the decline of output, as firms adapted to their problems with lower or unpaid wages rather than with unemployment. As a result, there was an increase in the number of low paid jobs, which was a factor in growing inequalities among the working population.

Persistent Structural Unemployment or Temporary Lay-offs?

Unemployment statistics do not accurately reflect the actual situation since many of the unemployed (according to statistics in the CIS countries, between 50 to 80 per cent) do not register in labour offices, given the lack of benefits and services provided. In Russia and Ukraine, where output declined during 1990–1994 by 50 per cent, registered unemployment remained below 5.0 per cent. By 1997, when statistical data became more reliable, the figure rose to 11.8 per cent, but employment started growing again a few years later.

Some experts considered unemployment as a positive factor in promoting structural transformation (Jackman, 1999). However, this was not the case. Transnational corporations investing in the region and the new private firms recruited mainly from those already employed in the state sector or in other private firms. This was likely due to the fact that most of the unemployed had lower skill or educational levels, or that they were older people, i.e., over 45. There has been a decline in the participation rate, partly because of shrinking employment opportunities for women, which is not well reflected in the statistics on unemployment.

Small Entrepreneurs, the Informal Sector and Rural Problems

The rapid increase in the number of small entrepreneurs was another important indicator of the changing patterns in the labour markets. While a great number of people became self-employed after losing their jobs, the increased number of small firms failed to create more employment opportunities.

Another important area has been the growing informal or parallel sector, which has created new jobs and absorbed part of the displaced labour force. Although many job seekers find this source of income degrading, since informal activities do not correspond to their education level or income expectations, they turn to it for part-time work to supplement their incomes. Unfortunately, there is little information on the types of employment available and the incomes earned in this sector. It is therefore difficult to evaluate with objectivity the growing informal sector's role in increasing wage inequality.

Another source of new employment opportunities is the service sector, which was previously underdeveloped, except for social services, health care, education, science, and culture. As the statistics for these occupations were missing or included in earlier labour statistics under 'other economic activities', they were drastically underestimated. The previously poorly developed activities in the trade, catering, banking and insurance, communications and real estate industries, have boomed with the transition in all the former socialist countries. Of course, wages differ according to the type of services.

Employment in agriculture fell faster than total employment. Large-scale agriculture in the form of collective or state farms and agro-industrial complexes used to be one of the major employers in Central and Eastern Europe, particularly for unskilled rural labour. The transition from collective farming into private farming, the loss of state subsidies and guaranteed markets, and falling domestic demand significantly reduced labour demand and employment in this sector. According to many analysts, the rural population, comprising the largest group of the poor in certain regions of the Russian Republic, in the Caucasus and Central Asia, were disproportionably affected by the hardships of the transition (Mikhalev, 2000: 40). However, the number of small farmers increased substantially, which may become an important problem in the future, due to the low level of competitiveness of small-scale farming. The agricultural population has been one of the main losers in the transformation process. The large state and collective farms have either been dissolved or have gone bankrupt. In most cases, they have been replaced by subsistence farming, similar to those in developing countries.

The increase in unemployment not only resulted in the loss of income but also in the deterioration of the social status of individuals and their families, as well as in growing job insecurity. Unemployment trends depend not only on the prospects for economic growth but also on structural changes and the demand for skills. The Ministry of Labour in the Russian Federation projects a considerable growth of unemployment in the near future. Reforms in the power industry, public utilities, railway and metallurgy sectors will deprive hundreds of thousands (if not millions) of Russian people of their jobs. "It goes without saying that no population employment departments (not to mention small business or shadow economy) will be able to cope with such a huge mass of people. All these things will eventually result in the fact that the human labour price will drop considerably in Russia as a whole. The supply will exceed the unbalanced employment demand by several-fold. Hundreds of thousands of people will remain unemployed" (*Pravda*, 18 February 2003).

Problems of Youth and Women

One of the most difficult problems in the former Soviet republics and in the region in general is youth unemployment. Unemployment rates for those under 25 are almost twice as high as the general unemployment rate. Some documents issued by international organizations emphasize that one of the problems for young people is their lack of work experience. Another problem is the inferior education of these young people due to the fact that they were educated at the time when the transition resulted in greater differentiation and, in many cases, a marked deterioration in the quality of education.

Neglect and homelessness among children and young people have become alarming characteristics of Russian society. This social phenomenon is a consequence of the current socioeconomic and moral situation in Russia, engendered by a whole complex of factors behind the decline in living standards of a substantial part of the population, including, a deterioration in the mental health of the adult population, the spread of child abuse both in the family and in orphanages, a distancing of the school from children in difficulties, destruction of the traditional system of child upbringing, a fall in the moral standards of the population, and the growth of crime.[4]

Unemployment among women and youth is a particularly difficult issue in the Central Asian republics. In Tajikistan, for example, of the total number of women and young people aged 15–29 years in the labour force in 2002, some 53 per cent and 66 per cent, respectively, were unemployed.

The disintegration of many families and the breakdown of family ties are closely interconnected with the problems of young people. This problem is also related to the increase of poverty in the region, particularly in the urban areas of Belarus, the Russian Federation and Ukraine. There has been a growth in the divorce rate, a decline in marriages and an increase in the number of children born out of wedlock. The growth in the number of teenage mothers has also become an acute problem.

POVERTY AND INEQUALITY

While unemployment, changes in the labour markets and poverty are in many ways interrelated, poverty should be dealt with as a separate issue since it is an indicator and a major factor in growing inequality. The reduction of poverty is a major precondition for the economic and social strengthening of the region.

Who Are the Poor?

Poverty in this region is not new and has existed even before the transition. Most of the countries began their transformation with extensive hidden unemployment and at least one-tenth of its population below the then subsistence level (based on a 'social minimum' consumption basket). The growth of poverty has not been a consequence of the transition crisis, as it has been growing since the early 1980s due to economic difficulties, external indebtedness and mismanagement.

Poverty statistics are seldom exact or reliable. They depend on the concept being scrutinized and the method of measurement used. One common approach in poverty measurement is to define the 'poor' as those persons living in households with income or expenditure significantly below the average in their country. The rationale for this definition of relative poverty is that people whose living standards (as measured by their income or expenditure) fall far below the average are at risk of being excluded from the advantages and benefits considered normal in society. Where poverty is measured according to a relative criterion, a rise in inequality will cause the number of people in relative poverty to increase. When inequality declines, the number of relatively poor people will also decline. An alternative approach to poverty measurement involves calculating the cost of a minimum 'basket' of goods that people would need to survive. Globally, the absolute poverty threshold has been defined as two dollars income per day. According to the two dollars threshold, there were about 50 million people living in poor families in the former socialist countries at the end of the 1990s, mostly in the CIS countries.

Since then, however, the number of poor households has risen. By 1993, some 32 per cent of the population in Russia was living below the revised official poverty line. At that time, some 12 per cent of the Russian population was very poor (below 50 per cent of the poverty line). In early 1994, an estimated 26.8 per cent were poor, and 10.4 per cent were very poor. Real earnings have been halved since their end-1991 peak and remain somewhat lower than the 1987 level. Reductions in work hours have been widespread; workers have been placed on short-time work status or had to fake involuntary leave.

In the Russian Federation during 1993 and 1994, only 40 per cent of the workforce was paid fully and on time. High inflation has adversely affected the poor, especially those who rely on modest pensions and unemployment benefits. Earlier poverty indicators were based on income data, which are problematic (especially during high inflation), and rely on unrepresentative survey sources.

TABLE 9.2
Trends in real wages in the region, 1989–2001

Countries	1989	1995	2001
Bulgaria	100	60	51
Romania	100	74	71
Armenia	100	5	11
Azerbaijan	100	14	50
Georgia	100	12	40
Kazakhstan	100	23	36
Kyrgyzstan	100	21	26
Moldova	100	25	32
Russian Fed.	100	36	52
Tajikistan	100	5	7
Ukraine	100	44	46

Source: UN Economic Commission for Europe (2002: 167).

A two-year analytical study—by Russian and international experts on 'enhancing the measurement, monitoring and analysis of poverty'[5]—is probably the most comprehensive work on the problems of poverty in Russia. According to the Report (World Bank, 2005), the national incidence of poverty is close to 20 per cent. The rural population has the highest rates of poverty (30.4 per cent), while the urban population has a poverty rate of 15.7 per cent. The majority of the poor, close to 60 per cent, live in urban areas. The poverty rate is high in small and remote towns, particularly in depressed regions. The unemployed and many of the 30 million pensioners belong in the poor category. A large group of impoverished Russians is made up of able-bodied women and men in their 30s and 40s with primary education, who are marginalized by the market economy and hence operate in the urban 'black' or informal economy. Millions of others in this group are trapped in remote industrial small towns where manufacturing has collapsed. Many of them live in the far north where job opportunities have dried up. The situation of those who have some jobs is often aggravated by the fact that wages in the unregulated labour market are often far less than the subsistence minimum and are sometimes withheld for months.

In Russia and other CIS countries, the working poor predominate. About half of the poor live in households where the head of household is employed. The largest subgroup is composed of households with children, including single-parent and young households. Generally, the younger and more numerous the children, the more likely the family is poor. Nearly 62 per cent of families with three or more children fewer than six years old are poor. Single-parent households are much more likely to be poor compared to other types of families. More than 90 per cent of such households are headed by women.

Poverty among some of the ethnic minorities, particularly the Roma (gypsy) population, is one of the acute problems in some of the CIS countries, Bulgaria and Romania. The Roma population in these countries represents the real 'underclass' who are excluded from the mainstream of society because of their ethnicity and status.

The poor are not a stagnant group of people. Some of the poor households rose above the poverty level during 1992–1993, even while poverty was increasing as a whole. Nearly one-half of Russian households that were very poor in 1992 were not considered as such a year later, while a quarter of nonpoor households became poor over the same period. Regional differentiation of welfare indicators dramatically increased during the period. Of course, one must differentiate between countries at the middle level and low level of economic development. Russia, Romania and Ukraine are generally considered middle-level countries. Poverty is more widespread in some CIS countries, which are classified as low-income countries.[6] These poorest CIS countries show many characteristics of developing nations and need substantial international assistance to foster economic and human development. The external sources of funds have been relatively small, compared with the losses in GDP and the burden of debt service. During the 1990s, poverty and income inequality increased to very high levels in Central Asian republics.

Physical indicators of poverty have steadily worsened and social safety nets have deteriorated greatly, mainly owing to the limited resources available for poverty reduction and the absence of income and employment generation programmes. For example, about 50 per cent of the population in Kyrgyzstan lived below the poverty line in 2002. During the 1990s, the population of Tajikistan increased by 14 per cent, reaching 6.5 million in 2002, while GDP fell by 64 per cent, resulting in growing poverty. The majority of the 7.6 million people of Azerbaijan, 3 million of whom are children, live in poverty (an estimated 60 per cent of the population), in spite of the country's rich oil resources. Although privatization of collective farms and state-owned enterprises and the development of the petroleum industry are expected to have positive social implications, they have yet to benefit vulnerable population groups. Poverty is also a grave problem in Bulgaria, especially among rural households and families with children. In addition, the Roma community, which comprises around 7 per cent of the population, is reported to be 10 times poorer than other groups (World Bank, 2001).

Since the mid-1990s, there has been some improvement in most of the CIS countries and also in Bulgaria and Romania in poverty reduction, mainly due to economic growth. Reforms in the social sector are well under way in practically all of these countries, although they may not yet provide equal access to all groups or offer the range of services previously provided. The decentralization of most social services to local governments is not yet matched by the availability of skilled personnel and financial resources; the proportion of people in absolute poverty has fallen even in some of the poorest countries. However, the number of people living in poverty remains substantial. In 2001, half the population in Armenia, Georgia, Kyrgyzstan and Moldova was living below national subsistence levels. In the Russian Republic, real wages were only 53 per cent of those in 1989 (UNICEF Innocenti Research Centre estimates). Unemployment, lower average income and the growing inequality in the distribution of national income and wealth are the most important factors in the growth of poverty in the region. The Gini coefficient[7] for household income per capita rose from 0.26 to 0.43 in the CIS countries between the late 1980s and 1990s.

The lack of resources, unemployment and income inequality have created particularly grave social problems in other low-income CIS countries. Socioeconomic hardships have weakened the health and educational system, while drop-out rates have increased. The poor quality of education, low morale among teachers and chronic underfunding of schools pose many problems for the rural areas. In many cities, drug abuse, prostitution and juvenile delinquency are rapidly increasing, as are the numbers of children living or working on the street. In addition, the growing social inequity facing women in many of these countries may deteriorate and create additional problems.

GROWING INEQUALITY AND THE NEW SOCIAL STRATIFICATION

Clearly, the transition process and its main factors increased inequality in all the former socialist countries, particularly those of the former Soviet Union.

Prior to the transition, the social system in these countries was not egalitarian. Instead, it was the kind of society characterized in the West as 'meritocratic'. Even within the group characterized as the 'nomenclature', there were differences based on a subgroup's role in the party or state hierarchy, and the degree of that subgroup's decision-making power and control over the allocation of resources. These differences were not only 'status differences' but were expressed in the subgroup's standard of living and access to certain goods and services. The top political elite, the leading echelon of the technocrats, and the top managers of the state-owned enterprises belonging to the 'nomenclature' controlled the allocation and distribution of resources. Professionals also enjoyed a higher status in society. Blue-collar workers, particularly skilled workers, had job security and more privileges than did the peasantry.

The Winners and the Losers

The transformation process had a profound effect on the structure of society. In every society there are winners and losers. The normal functioning of a market system results in some gaining more income and wealth, while others lose their former economic and social advantages. Similarly, the transformation process in the former socialist countries brought about radical and unprecedented social changes. The winners were the young, the well-educated, the well-connected and the entrepreneurial, especially those privileged enough to be able to acquire assets of the state-owned firms. On the other hand, the losers were more numerous and diverse, comprising the old, pensioners in general, the less educated, women, those with little or no skills, rural people living in remote regions or in small towns, and those belonging to certain ethnic groups. The decline of GDP, 'informalization', liberalization (which included the cessation of the subsidized price system), inflation and unemployment hit all wage earners. Those with little or no savings had to sell their assets in order to survive. Income disparities in the Russian Federation during the years of the transition are reflected in Table 9.3.

It may be evident from this 'social balance sheet' that the concept of inequality must be understood from a multidimensional perspective. In addition to the same factors as in other transition countries, the increase in inequality in

TABLE 9.3
Income shares in the Russian Federation by quintiles, 1975–2001

Years	Poorest 20%	Second	Third	Fourth	Richest 20%	Total
1975	9.5	14.8	18.6	23.3	33.8	100
1980	10.1	14.8	18.6	23.1	33.4	100
1985	10.0	14.6	18.3	23.1	34.0	100
1990	9.8	14.9	18.8	23.8	32.7	100
1991	11.9	15.8	18.8	22.8	30.7	100
1992	6.0	11.6	17.6	26.5	38.3	100
1993	5.8	11.1	16.7	24.8	41.6	100
1994	5.3	10.2	15.2	23.0	46.3	100
1995	5.5	10.2	15.0	22.4	46.9	100
1996	6.2	10.7	15.2	21.5	46.4	100
1997	6.0	10.2	14.8	21.6	47.4	100
1998	6.1	10.4	14.8	21.1	47.6	100
1999	6.1	10.5	14.8	20.8	47.8	100
2000	6.1	10.6	14.9	21.2	47.2	100
2001	5.9	10.1	14.6	21.1	48.3	100

Source: Goskomstat, 2002.

Russia has an important territorial dimension, due to its size, geography and heterogeneity. The Russian Federation, with its climatic, ethnic and economic variety, had a relatively higher level of inequality right from the beginning. The regions, even during the pretransition era, were diverse in their level of economic development, density of transport, and consequently in mean real incomes. Although there was convergence during the Soviet period, this could not eliminate the differences in income levels. Political and socio-economic changes further increased divergence across regions. The income distribution between population groups and regions has also widened in other republics.[8]

The New Middle Class and the New Rich

Almost all the protagonists of the changes emphasized the necessity of developing a new 'middle class' to be the new owners of privatized state property, which was deemed necessary for the creation of a well-functioning economy. In the economic history of the Western world, the development of property owners or a capitalist class was a long-term process. This was also the case in the pre-socialist period in the Central and Eastern European countries as well as in Russia.

Privatization was considered to be the main instrument for developing a new middle class. It had two dimensions: the 'organic development' of private ownership and the transfer of wealth from state ownership into the hands of domestic or foreign individuals or firms. The latter has resulted in a radical shift in income distribution and has become the most important source of income inequalities. One of the consequences of restitution, voucher privatization, public auctions or direct sales of state property has been the increasing importance of capital income, directly related to ownership, among the sources of income. Of course, this is received by a small minority of the population. The idea of worker privatization, a popular concept during the early stages of the changes, as a more egalitarian form of private ownership, has been more or less forgotten in the process.

There are significant differences among the respective countries concerning the relative importance of the different forms of capital income. The role of dividends is relatively small, while the concentration of larger assets (and corresponding larger capital income) in the hands of the few is greater in countries where the legal framework is less developed.

Privatization has also involved small and medium-sized enterprises. Capitalists in these small and medium-sized enterprises comprise about 90 per cent of the entrepreneurial middle class. More than half of them had lost their jobs and concluded that starting some business became the only means of making a living. These small entrepreneurs include micro-entrepreneurs of

234 • Flat World, Big Gaps

the informal sector, similar to the 'barefoot-capitalists' of developing countries. Most of the small entrepreneurs are in commerce, handicrafts and services. While their total number is relatively large, they represent a rather small proportion of capital incomes. In Russia, their share is around 15–18 per cent.

Although ways of becoming very rich within a relatively short period of time might frequently have been immoral in some countries, they were a mixture of legal and illegal activities in others. The following patterns could be observed (with varying levels of importance in individual states):

1. Trade opportunities: the market evolved in certain new segments or niches (such as banks, foreign exchange, information technology, car imports, industrial consumer goods) as a result of liberalization, and large fortunes were obtained through the trading system.

2. Insider privatization or buying out (using the privileged position of being a top manager): state-owned production firms were pushed into bankruptcy and purchased for low prices, often with borrowed money, or by restructuring, or through the sale of parts for much higher prices. Sometimes investments in other branches were made, or parts of the originally purchased firms were modernized. This method was often combined with the active participation in the stock and currency ex-changes, often using insider information.

3. Control over resources: In Russia and some of the CIS countries with important raw materials or oil, certain political or government elites gained control over these resources, resulting in large monopolies, particularly in the extracting industries. The number of billionaires in the Russian Federation is only second to the United States. The largest private owners account for 42 per cent of employment and 39 per cent of sales (*Beyond Transition*: 3). The external revenues facilitated large foreign investments and other operations abroad.

4. Patent technology: Patents on important inventions and defense-related technology which had not been properly valued and utilized by the state-owned enterprises were obtained and commercialized, mainly through finding a foreign partner with whom joint ventures could be established.

5. Exploiting the system: This form opened the door to criminal elements on an unprecedented scale. Exploiting the loss of government control or special connections in the administration, some gained access to important assets in several sectors, particularly hotels, restaurants, commerce and banking. The lawless system, often characterized as a 'kleptocracy', was brought under control only after the end of the 1990s (*Beyond Transition*: 6).

The upper class in the CIS countries includes the political elite, top bureaucrats, and army leaders. The most recent changes in the political power structure have involved many from the middle echelon of the former party and the state and army bureaucracies; these groups are called 'silniki', meaning 'power-people'. Top managers in foreign-owned and large private firms enjoy high salaries and represent the most 'globalized' part of the elite. The evolving middle class includes the small businessmen, professionals, those in science and education, and the middle and lower-level staff in public administration.

According to some estimates, about two-thirds of the population in Russia (and a much greater proportion in the other CIS countries) belong to the lower-income group. Table 9.4 reflects the degree of inequality in the respective countries. As far as occupational status and sectoral characteristics are concerned, the lower-income group is extremely diverse in the countries of Eastern Europe and the CIS. The transformation process has had an adverse effect on their status and material situation. The decline of their real income has been quite substantial, and they have become vulnerable and exposed to the adverse effects of the changes, while enjoying few positive effects compared to the middle class or the new political and economic elite. The majority of the peasantry belongs to this group and constitutes a relatively large share of the population in some CIS countries, Bulgaria and Romania.

The lower-income groups are quite heterogeneous, divided by gender, skill

TABLE 9.4
Inequality in income or consumption around 2000

	Year	Share of income or consumption (%)				Inequality measures		
		Poorest 10%	Poorest 20%	Richest 20%	Richest 10%	Richest 10% to poorest 10%	Richest 20% to poorest 20%	Gini index
Armenia	1998	2.6	6.7	45.1	29.7	11.5	6.8	37.9
Azerbaijan	2001	3.1	7.4	44.5	29.5	9.7	6.0	36.5
Belarus	2000	3.5	8.4	39.1	24.1	6.9	4.6	30.4
Bulgaria	2001	2.4	6.7	38.9	23.7	9.9	5.8	31.9
Kazakhstan	2001	3.4	8.2	39.6	24.2	7.1	4.8	31.2
Romania	2000	3.3	8.2	38.4	23.6	7.2	4.7	30.3
Russian Fed.	2000	1.8	4.9	51.3	36.0	20.3	10.5	45.6
Tajikistan	1998	3.2	8.0	40.0	25.2	8.0	5.0	34.7
Ukraine [U]	1999	3.7	8.8	37.8	23.2	6.4	4.3	29.0
Uzbekistan	2000	3.6	9.2	36.3	22.0	6.1	4.0	26.8

Note: U – Data refers to urban areas only.
Source: UNDP (2003).

TABLE 9.5
Gender income differentials, 2001

	Estimated earned income (PPP US$)		Female to Male (%)
	Female	Male	
Armenia	2 175	3 152	69.0
Bulgaria	5 484	8 378	65.5
Kazakhstan	5 039	8 077	62.4
Romania	4 313	7 416	58.2
Russian Fed.	5 609	8 795	63.8
Tajikistan	891	1 451	61.4
Ukraine	3 071	5 826	52.7
Uzbekistan	1 951	2 976	65.6

Source: UNDP (2003).

level, sector, geography and ethnicity. Many of them belong to the category of the working poor. About one-third of all the workers in the Russian Federation belong in the low-paid category, receiving less than two-thirds of the median earnings. About 12 per cent belong to the 'very low-paid' category, earning less than one-third of the median earning (Goskomstat, 2002).

In view of the causes and consequences of the changes and the growing inequality, government policies—which can moderate the adverse social effects and consequences of unemployment, de-skilling and other forms of degradation—have special importance in these countries. Furthermore, the necessity of policies for poverty alleviation is unquestionable. The increasing inequalities, the impoverishment of large numbers of people, and the conspicuous gap between the rich and the poor may create social tensions that may even explode in violence. To what extent are these policies already in place? Are the governments able or ready to reduce the adverse effects of the transition? What priorities should be embodied in these policies? The answers to these questions require a much more thorough and detailed analysis of the economic conditions and the new political and economic power structures in the countries, which goes beyond the scope of this chapter.

CHALLENGES FOR NATIONAL SOCIAL GOVERNANCE

Most of the international organizations are recommending to the transition countries the 'standard trio' of priorities for the development of their social policies: social protection (safety net), health and education. The national and international programmes for good governance include growth and employment-oriented national policies, and democratic participation.[9] Major investments in education and health, and policies to provide people (especially the young) with skills, are probably the most important long-term goals in all the countries.

Practically all the countries in the region have some form of social safety net, like unemployment benefits which, in principle, should provide some support to the most needy and most vulnerable citizens. In practice, these benefits are very small (e.g., around 20 per cent of the average wage in Russia) and very few of the unemployed receive them.

The rise in poverty levels and the initiatives of some intergovernmental organizations have led the countries to critically re-examine their policies and to adopt some form of poverty-reduction measures. Poverty-monitoring procedures by investigating the incidence of poverty by gender, region and ethnic group have improved. Using available data and monitoring systems, the countries have begun to analyse the poverty impact of their policies and of exogenous shocks, and to formulate approaches to increase the pro-poor focus of these policies. The poverty reduction strategies are closely related to reforms in the labour markets, which include the development or improvement of labour legislation and the creation of new employment opportunities. For example, Azerbaijan adopted programmes for training and retraining employees and established an information system for labour markets. A similar information system was developed in Tajikistan to monitor labour markets and improve systems for job searching, particularly in the private sector. Governments of Central Asian countries have also introduced income generation policy reforms aimed at increasing the general wage level and improving payment systems.

Anti-poverty initiatives in low-income countries like Armenia, Azerbaijan, Georgia, Kyrgyzstan, Moldova, Tajikistan and Uzbekistan are particularly important due to the high incidence of poverty and deprivation in these countries, aggravated by a large debt. Much of the public debt, which accumulated during the early 1990s in the poorest CIS countries, was taken on to bolster day-to-day government spending after the breakup of the Soviet Union. Some of the poorest countries are paying a considerable sum—2 to 4 per cent of their national incomes—to service external public debt. In certain cases, this is more than what they spend on education or health care, which has declined to historically low levels, putting the long-term well-being of an entire generation of children at risk.

National strategies have been stimulated by some international initiatives. In 2002, the World Bank and other international financial institutions launched the CIS-7 Initiative with Governments of seven of the poorest countries in the

TABLE 9.6
Public spending priorities, 1990–2000

	Public expenditure on education (as % of GDP)		Public expenditure on health (as % of GDP)		Military expenditure (as % of GDP)		Total debt service (as % of GDP)	
	1990	2000	1990	2000	1990	2001	1990	2001
Armenia	7.0	2.9	–	3.2	–	3.1	–	2.6
Azerbaijan	–	4.2	2.7	0.6	–	2.6	–	2.4
Belarus	4.9	6.0	2.5	4.7	–	1.4	–	1.9
Bulgaria	5.2	3.4	4.1	3.0	3.5	2.7	6.6	10.1
Kazakhstan	3.2	–	3.2	2.7	–	1.0	–	14.9
Romania	2.8	3.5	2.8	1.9	4.6	2.5	(.)	6.7
Russian Fed	3.5	4.4	2.5	3.8	12.3	3.8	2	5.6
Tajikistan	9.7	2.1	4.9	0.9	–	1.2	–	7.6
Ukraine	5.2	4.4	3.0	2.9	–	2.7	–	6.0
Uzbekistan	–	–	4.6	2.6	–	1.1	–	7.4

Source: UNDP Human Development Report, different years.

region. Their recommendations contain strategies that go well beyond the social sphere. It has become increasingly clear that reduction of poverty cannot be achieved only through social transfers, but also requires sustained economic growth, employment-generating economic policies, a high and sustained level of public expenditure in health and education, and structural reforms in taxation. Together, these measures will be able to moderate the adverse social consequences of inequality in income and wealth, and to promote social mobility.

CONCLUSIONS

This chapter has dealt mainly with the problems of inequality and poverty in the countries east of the European Union's frontiers. Poverty and inequality have emerged as adverse consequences of the post-Soviet transition. In spite of some economic improvements, these problems persist in most CIS countries.

Different dimensions of the transformation process, including integration with global markets and the spillover effects of globalization, have resulted in growing inequality, de-industrialization, de-modernization, and widespread impoverishment. The evolving capitalist economy remains dominated by a few politically-connected financial-industrial groups (oligarchs) and mainly involves the exploitation of raw materials. The small and medium-sized enterprise sector remains relatively small and non-dynamic. The outcome of the transition has been described by some authors as a 'great leap backward'.

As a result of the adverse consequences of the changes, some countries are now closer to the developing world than to the economically advanced regions. The upper class, particularly the new bourgeoisie in Russia and the other CIS countries, seems to more closely resemble rent-seeking parasitic capitalists than a modern entrepreneurial class. Without major changes in economic and social policies, inequality and the erosion of human capital will worsen in most of these countries. In order for such changes to happen, there must be a radical change in the current power structure.

The main causes of poverty and inequality in these countries include output decline, hyperinflation, unemployment and macroeconomic stabilization policies. They also include such factors as the disintegration of the Soviet Union and the redistribution of productive assets in favour of a powerful minority. Although the tasks of employment creation, poverty reduction and social consolidation are formally similar to those in other semi-developed regions of the world, the required policies must take into account the specific characteristics of the countries, which are at various stages of overcoming the transition crisis. Many labour market problems are of a long-term, structural nature, involving de-skilling and new relations with global markets.[10]

The inequalities in income, wealth and consumption will have long-term impacts, especially on marginalized groups, and government intervention is necessary to avoid tension and conflict. The process of social degradation, without effective countervailing social and educational policies, may be irreversible. It is evident from ongoing trends that economic growth without redistribution is not enough to moderate the impact of inequality of ownership patterns. The degree of poverty and inequality that is sustainable or tolerable in these countries, with deeply-rooted egalitarian values, is an important issue.

In most Central and Eastern European and CIS countries, there have been three or more consecutive years of positive economic growth, and the pre-1989 level of GDP has been recently restored in most countries. However, social improvements have been much slower and more uneven, due to the increasing inequality of income distribution and structural problems of poverty. In some countries, living standards are rising and poverty levels are falling. In others, particularly the poorer CIS countries, the turnaround from the difficulties of the 1990s is still elusive. A relatively high level of poverty remains in areas outside the capital cities, partly due to structural and institutional problems.

There are different recommendations for reforms which could lead to higher tax revenues, increased public expenditure for health and education, unemployment benefits and other efficient active labour market measures, such as retraining and subsidized job creation. Although the introduction of these reforms will not be easy, they are not beyond reach. Warnings about the potential political consequences of rising inequality are increasingly voiced by academics, political opposition leaders and representatives of some NGOs, all of whom emphasize the importance of adopting appropriate measures to maintain the peace and security of the region.

NOTES

[1] There are complex interactions between past and present, and between the diverse political, economic and social processes, cultural values, national as well as external factors and institutions. The etatist-socialist regimes collapsed in different ways, creating the present spectrum of regimes with varying levels of progress made in terms of marketization, liberalization, and economic and social development.

[2] Calculated by the author on the basis of World Bank statistics.

[3] De-skilling refers to strategies used by employers to reduce the skills of their labour force, often occurring alongside the introduction of new technological processes in the work place.

[4] The current generation of young people has lived through a period of extraordinary change and uncertainty. The availability of age-appropriate services and information and any real understanding of their needs both remain very limited. Risky behaviour, reflecting the stresses they are under, leads to very high rates of accidental death, suicide, and alcohol and drug abuse. Trafficking of young women is a serious problem in the Russian Federation, Belarus and Ukraine. Rates of sexually transmitted infections (STIs) among young people in the Russian Federation and Belarus have doubled in the last decade. Closely connected with risky behaviour, the rapid growth of HIV is concentrated among young people. Currently, Ukraine and the Russian Federation have the fastest-growing epidemics in the world; in the Russian Federation, the number of officially registered HIV cases doubled during 2001. Over 70 per cent of new infections are among young people aged between 15 and 29 years. While the epidemic began among intravenous drug users, its spread into the mainstream population is already apparent. The transmission of HIV from mother to child is a new and growing phenomenon in the three countries. At least 20 per cent of children born to HIV-infected mothers are abandoned, and many spend extended periods in maternity hospitals because of lack of alternative solutions.

[5] This has been a collaborative project by the World Bank, the United Kingdom Department for International Development (DfID), the Russian Ministry of Labour and Social Development, the 'Goskomstat', the Russian Statistical Office, the Ministry of Labour and Social Development and Trade and the Ministry of Finance.

[6] Armenia, Azerbaijan, Georgia, Kyrgyzstan, Moldova, Tajikistan and Uzbekistan are the poorest countries in the CIS, and their transition to becoming market-based economies over the past decade has been extremely difficult.

[7] The Gini coefficient is a measure of inequality which is commonly used to measure income inequality, but can be used to measure any form of unequal distribution.

[8] The following quotation by the President of Kazakhstan in reference to the situation in his country is also relevant for the majority of the Central Asian CIS countries:

"The society is fully aware that the above gap exceeds the admissible limits. If Kazakhstan is a state of a thin layer of the well-off, then, by virtue of too low vitality, instability both within and without, it will be doomed to vegetative existence at best. We have already been a state of the poor though not in its pure form... Domestic political stability and development would rest on all the three classes: the rich, the middle and the poor. The society needs all of them, though naturally—in a normal civilized proportion.

"Polarization acquired a graphic manifestation in the relations established between the city and the countryside. In both cases we witness a global process of social differentiation with the gap there between growing steadily. Within the nearest decade the country-side must become a priority area from the point of view of giving an additional impetus to market transformations, to emphatic settlement of social problems and development of infrastructure.

"We are to expect considerable rejection of a free labour force in the country-side, significant migration to the city from the country-side and ever developing processes of urbanization. The country-side of today has become an epitome of major social problems: nonpayment of wages and pensions, backwardness, poverty and unemployment, poor ecology, poor infrastructure, education and health care. Meanwhile the country-side manifests the highest demographic potential". (Embassy of Kazakhstan document, February 2005).

[9] Among his stated second-term priorities (after winning re-election on 14 March 2004), President Vladimir Putin identified numerous stepped-up social programmes and mechanisms for the purposes of sustaining rapid economic growth, boosting the country's GDP and sharply cutting poverty.

[10] De-skilling implies that existing skills are less required.

REFERENCES

Barr, Nicholas (ed.) (1994). *Labour Markets and Social Policy in Central and Eastern Europe: The Transition and Beyond*. Oxford University Press, Oxford.

Beyond Transition, 15 (1), October–December 2004: 4 (The Russian Oligarchs).

Goskomstat [Russian Statistical Office] (2002). Russian Longitudinal Monitoring Survey, 2000: Microdata. University of North Carolina, Chapel Hill.

Jackman, Richard (1999). Unemployment and Restructuring. In Peter Boone, Stanislaw Gomulka and Richard Layard (eds). *Emerging from Communism: Lessons from Russia, China and Eastern Europe*. MIT Press, Cambridge, MA: 123–52.

Mikhalev, Vladimir (2000). *Inequality and Transformation of Social Structures in Transitional Economies*. Research for Action series No. 52, UNU/WIDER, Helsinki.

Pravda (2003). On the Edge of Unemployment Disaster, 18 February. *Market Bolshevism against Democracy*. United States Institute of Peace Press, Washington, DC.

UN Economic Commission for Europe (2002). *Poverty in Eastern Europe and the CIS*. UN Economic Commission for Europe, Geneva.

UNDP. *Human Development Report*. Various years. Oxford University Press, New York, for United Nations Development Programme, New York.

UNICEF Innocenti Research Centre (2002). Poverty in the Transition: Social Expenditures and the Working-Age Poor. Innocenti Working Paper No. 91, March, Innocenti Research Centre, Florence.

UNICEF. *International Child Development Centre Regional Monitoring Report*. Innocenti Research Centre, Florence. Various volumes.

World Bank (1996). *Development Report: From Plan to Market*. World Bank, Washington, DC.

World Bank (1999). *World Development Indicators, 1999*. CD-ROM. World Bank, Washington, DC.

World Bank (2000). *World Development Report 2000/2001: Attacking Poverty*. Oxford University Press, New York.

World Bank (2001). *Poverty Assessment Report, 2001*. World Bank, Washington, DC.

World Bank (2002). *World Development Indicators, 2002*. CD-ROM. World Bank, Washington, DC.

World Bank (2005). *Russian Federation: Reducing Poverty through Growth and Social Policy Reform*. Report Number: 28923-RU, 8 February, World Bank, Washington, DC.

Yudaeva, Ksenia (2002). Globalization and Inequality in CIS Countries: The Role of Institutions. Center for Economic and Financial Research (CEFIR), Moscow.

10

Equity in Latin America since the 1990s

PEDRO SÁINZ[1]

This paper analyses the evolution of equity and inequality in Latin America from the 1990s until 2003 in the context of growing liberalization and globalization. The first section reviews recent economic changes and their social repercussions, and includes a description of macroeconomic policies and reforms. The second section examines social policy objectives since the 1990s, with close attention to changes in orientation resulting from the reforms. The third section evaluates the status of poverty and equity during recent political changes.

OPENNESS, ECONOMIC CHANGE AND EQUITY

During the 1980s and 1990s, Latin America underwent profound economic changes, caused mainly by external influences. Multinational banks had played a major role in the indebtedness of the 1970s, while the Bretton Woods institutions and some developed countries, especially the United States of America, led the process of renegotiation of countries' external debt during the 1980s. These same actors strongly promoted institutional and macroeconomic reform during the 1990s, which lay at the core of the major economic transformation that replaced the previous government-led industrialization with a new system based on the dominant role of transnational corporations (TNCs).[2] This economic transformation cannot be explained without reference to recent policies associated with the present international economic order.[3]

Macroeconomic Features

During the 1990s, external capital movements, growth instability and the stagnation of per capita income since over two decades converged to decrease equity and increase poverty in Latin American economies.

Since the oil crisis in 1973, the region has experienced massive changes in its balance of payments. From the middle of the 1930s up to that time, the current account approach had been dominant, but after the crisis, capital account transactions became more frequent. This had significant macroeconomic consequences. Foreign trade was, on many occasions, responsive to situations associated with capital movements, e.g., increased imports with strong capital inflows, fixed exchange rates and easy access to credit for consumers.

From 1975 to 1981, the Latin American region became heavily indebted and funds were often misused, leading to the crisis of 1981–1982. The 1980s saw huge negative transfers effected to pay off national debts, with consequent negative growth rates in per capita income. From 1990 to 2001, there were again net capital inflows, with larger shares of foreign direct investment (FDI). In many cases, such investments were used to buy existing assets, not to increase fixed capital. Investment made recovery possible, albeit at slow growth rates, and was a significant factor in bringing about economic change. From 1998 to 2003, the region suffered from stagnation, as net capital inflows became negative again; the cumulative net transfer out of the region between 1975 and 2003 was $62 billion.

Macroeconomic policies were constrained by the restrictive conditions associated with freer capital movements. On many occasions, governments and other actors became highly indebted, which in turn limited their options for action. For example, in 2003, the high level of government indebtedness in Argentina and Brazil created economic and social complications, and limited government freedom to expand social policies, although these were urgently needed.

The long-term outcome of the reforms was disappointing. From 1980 to 2003, per capita GDP in the region (in 1995 US dollars) increased by only 3.4 per cent. Also, vulnerability, instability, limited economic policy instruments, and long-term economic stagnation had an adverse affect on equity and deepened poverty, especially during periods of crisis.

New Actors and Asset Distribution

The debt crisis of the 1980s and the reforms of the 1990s led to economic chan-ges and redistribution of assets. Since the beginning of the 1980s, external capital movements have had a significant effect on the economic health of enterprises. The devaluations that followed the debt crisis forced heavily indebted enterprises into bankruptcy, particularly those that had been borrowing during the 1970s, when access to foreign financial resources had been easy (see ECLAC, 1984). The reduction of domestic demand to improve the trade balance following the 1981–1982 crisis compounded these difficulties. These circumstances allowed foreign TNCs to displace domestic firms, especially in the second half of the 1990s. Economic openness, especially in countries that used the exchange rate to control inflation, created even more severe problems for national enterprises producing tradable goods.

Transnational enterprises thus gained greater production and market share. In 1996, as public enterprises were declining in number, TNCs represented half of the 100 major enterprises. Although in 1990, TNCs had accounted for only 25 per cent of total sales of the 500 major enterprises, by 1999 when FDI reached its highest level, their share peaked at 43 per cent. In 1996, sales of the major 100 enterprises represented around 10 per cent of GDP, and those of the top 500 around one third of GDP.

TNCs have long had a strong presence in the manufacturing and services sectors. Many medium and high-technology industries (automotive, auto parts, electronics) are largely dominated by TNCs, which have concentrated their operations in assembly plants located in Mexico and, to a lesser extent, in Argentina and Brazil. Along with medium and high-technology industries, a wide range of low-technology manufacturing industries also operate assembly plants located in Mexico and the Caribbean.

The services sector also has a broad-based TNC presence, which has been growing steadily since economic reforms were implemented to privatize, deregulate and liberalize public utilities in most countries in the region. In the second half of the 1990s, this sector received the largest FDI inflows. The new regulatory context for the provision of public utilities allowed TNCs to gain ground by purchasing state-owned assets, mainly in energy, telecommunications, finance and infrastructure. This process explains the declining role of the largest firms in the primary and manufacturing sectors, although the latter still has the largest overall TNC presence (see ECLAC, 2004a). During the latter part of the 1990s (1996–2000), TNC sales in Brazil increased from 26.6 to 41.8 per cent of total sales, while employment in TNCs decreased from 17.0 to 10.9 per cent (Barros de Castro, 2003).

Transnational and large-scale national enterprises imposed new models of production with a high degree of standardization and interchange of inputs produced in different countries. Administrative reforms were also introduced. Employment and supply aspects of the rise of transnational enterprises caused net unemployment after introducing technical innovations with little more fixed capital. Types of products from the region also changed with the international pattern of consumption. Surviving large and medium-sized national enterprises adopted, to different degrees, new administrative patterns, conducive to higher productivity and net unemployment. This new pattern also contributed to inequality. In terms of inputs, products from other transnational factories replaced domestic suppliers, leading to pressure on the trade balance, thus increasing inequality.

The social strata associated with the top national and international enterprises benefited from the system, but many who lost their jobs had to find employment in low productivity enterprises. More importantly, perhaps, the youth and women trying to enter the labour market for the first time had increasing difficulty in finding jobs that could guarantee minimal welfare. After ten years, workers performing the same job functions received the same real income, despite having on average two more years of education (see ECLAC, 2004b).

In short, in the period under review, Latin America experienced significant economic change with reduced fixed capital investment. A majority of people failed to adjust to the new circumstances and became net losers in terms of both income and equity. While growth may be good for the poor, these reforms in Latin America resulted in slower growth and even stagnation, as well as greater inequality.

Labour Market

The uneven evolution of employment, productivity and income in the labour market played a central role in economic and social changes in Latin America. Large disparities in performance between large and small enterprises were a feature of the 1980s and 1990s. Large-scale enterprises recorded high rates of productivity growth with a shrinking labour force, while small enterprises and self-employment continued to grow and be associated with low productivity. In the 1990s, growth in production in the tradable sector was practically equal to that of the non-tradable sector, at an annual average growth rate of nearly 3 per cent. Non-tradables grew faster in most countries except Brazil, Costa Rica, Ecuador, Mexico, Nicaragua, Peru and Venezuela.

The low rate of job creation in the tradable sector was evident even in those countries where the sector's output increased relatively quickly. In Argentina, for example, the GDP of the tradable sector expanded at an annual rate of 3.6 per cent, while the change in total employment was-1.3 per cent. In Brazil, these figures were 2.4 per cent and 0.2 per cent respectively; in Chile, 5.6 per cent and -0.4 per cent; in Colombia, 1.7 per cent and-0.1 per cent; in Costa Rica, 5.5 per cent and 1.3 per cent; in Mexico, 3.4 per cent and 1.7 per cent; in Panama, 3.0 per cent and-0.6 per cent; in Uruguay, 1.1 per cent and-1.1 per cent; and in Venezuela, 2.7 per cent and 0.7 per cent. In some smaller and less developed countries, however, the tradable sector diverged from this trend. In

TABLE 10.1
Total and wage employment in 16 Latin American countries, 1990–1999

	Total employment			Waged employment [a]		
	Total	Tradable sector[b]	Non-tradable sector[c]	Total	Tradable sector[b]	Non-tradable sector[c]
Costa Rica	3.7	1.3	5.2	4.5	3.2	5.2
		[2.1]	[3.7]		[2.9]	[3.5]
El Salvador[d]	4.3	3.5	4.6	4.8	4.0	5.1
		[4.1]	[2.2]		[5.2]	[3.7]
Guatemala	3.6	2.2	5.6	2.7	2.9	2.6
		[6.0]	[2.3]		[4.4]	-[0.3]
Honduras	3.9	2.9	5.2	3.0	2.3	3.4
		[6.6]	[4.4]		[7.3]	[3.8]
Mexico	3.0	1.7	3.9	2.6	1.7	2.1
		[4.0]	[4.6]		[3.4]	[3.9]
Nicaragua	3.5	3.9	3.3	3.6	5.8	2.5
		[1.2]	[1.6]		[4.0]	[3.2]
Panama	3.5	-0.6	5.6	4.1	1.7	4.8
		[3.5]	[2.7]		[3.5]	[2.4]
Subtotal (weighted) average)	3.2	1.8	4.1	2.8	2.0	2.7
		[4.1]	[4.3]		[3.6]	[3.6]
Argentina[d]	1.2	-1.3	1.7	1.6	-1.4	2.5
		-[1.5]	[2.2]		-[1.6]	[2.4]
Bolivia[d]	5.0	7.6	4.4	3.8	3.6	3.9
		[8.1]	-[0.9]		[4.9]	[1.5]
Brazil	1.6	0.2	2.4	1.7	0.2	2.5
		[0.3]	[2.4]		[0.2]	[2.8]
Chile	2.3	-0.4	3.6	2.8	-0.1	4.3
		-[0.2]	[4.6]		[0.0]	[6.0]
Colombia	1.7	-0.1	2.8	1.2	0.2	1.9
		-[0.4]	[3.1]		-[0.4]	[2.1]
Ecuador[d]	3.6	2.2	4.1	3.5	1.6	4.1
		[1.4]	[4.2]		[0.6]	[3.1]
Paraguay[e]	4.1	3.9	4.1	4.7	4.7	4.7
		[4.5]	[3.3]		[5.6]	[3.5]
Uruguay[d]	1.2	-1.1	1.8	1.5	-0.3	2.0
		-[1.8]	[1.0]		-[2.0]	[1.1]

(contd)

TABLE 10.1 *(contd)*

	Total employment			Waged employment [a]		
	Total	Tradable sector[b]	Non-tradable sector[c]	Total	Tradable sector[b]	Non-tradable sector[c]
Venezuela	2.7	0.7	3.4	1.5	0.1	2.0
		[1.6]	[2.5]		-[0.3]	[1.3]
Subtotal (weighted average)	1.8	0.2	2.6	1.8	0.1	2.5
		[0.2]	[2.5]		-[0.1]	[2.6]
Total (weighted average)	2.2	0.8	3.0	2.1	0.7	2.6
		[1.5]	[2.9]		[0.9]	[2.9]

Source: ECLAC; estimates based on data tabulations from household surveys conducted in the respective countries.

Notes: [a] Figures are for wage earners between the ages of 25 and 59, working 20 hours or more per week. [b] The figures in brackets refer to manufacturing. [c] The figures in brackets refer to government, social, community and personal services. [d] Total for urban areas. [e] Asunción and the Central Department.

El Salvador, for example, employment in the tradable sector grew by 3.6 per cent, while total employment expanded by 3.5 per cent. In Honduras, employment in the tradable sector expanded by 3.2 per cent, and total employment by 2.9 per cent; in Nicaragua, these figures were 4.3 per cent and 3.9 per cent respectively.

In urban areas, creation of jobs differed between the tradable and non-tradable sectors, as it did between the formal and informal sectors. In most Latin American countries, employment expanded faster in sectors that produce non-tradable goods and services (see Table 10.1).[4] The two sectors' respective capacities to increase productivity and generate employment have evolved separately. In general, the tradable sector absorbed little labour, but achieved productivity gains. By contrast, the non-tradable sector showed a greater capacity to generate employment, but at the cost of low or negative rates of productivity growth.

The low rate of job creation in the tradable sector is evident even in countries where the sector's output has increased relatively quickly. This atypical trend can be observed in the development of the maquila industry. Although rising production of tradable goods helped to increase productivity, its effects on employment were weak except in countries with a growing maquila sector (Mexico and some of the Central American and Caribbean countries).

Although the maquila industry has generated employment, it has shown little capacity to increase productivity, and therefore cannot be expected to become the basis for a regional strategy for economic growth and employment in the medium or long term. Furthermore, in most recent years, this industry has lost ground to Chinese exports. In general, the responsibility for generating employment has fallen on the non-tradable sector, but this sector has not generated enough jobs.

The general asymmetry between the tradable and non-tradable sectors not only accentuated the heterogeneity of Latin American economies, but also had an impact on labour markets. The gap between the incomes of wage earners with different levels of schooling has widened, as the modernization of certain occupations has paralleled an increasing casualization of the workforce. Since there is little unemployment protection in Latin America, most workers prefer to avoid unemployment by turning to low-productivity, low-income jobs, as had been the trend in the 1980s and 1990s, although open unemployment also rose in the latter decade.

Much debate has surrounded the question of whether or not the tertiarization of employment is conducive to modernization. The answer depends on whether tertiarization is due to economic growth or the lack of momentum in the economy, which drives workers to seek employment in commerce and services. The two processes coexist in Latin America, although casualization prevails over modernization.

In effect, the 1990s saw intensive tertiarization, with 66 per cent of all new urban jobs generated in the informal sector[5] (see Table 10.2). Unskilled self-employed workers in commerce and services registered the largest increase (24.2 per cent), followed by workers (both employers and employees) in micro enterprises (18.2 per cent), domestic workers (9.4 per cent), unskilled self-employed workers in industry and construction (8.1 per cent), and in primary occupations (6 per cent). Most of these jobs were of low quality, reflecting the urban economy's poor capacity to raise labour productivity. This conclusion holds true for most of the 17 countries considered, particularly the most heavily populated ones, such as Brazil, Colombia and Mexico. In Argentina and Chile, by contrast, most new jobs were in the formal sector, although Argentina also recorded a substantial increase in open unemployment.

As a result of these patterns, informal employment expanded from 41.0 per cent of total employment in 1990 to 46.3 per cent in 1999. The contraction of the formal sector reflected a decline in the proportion of private sector employees other than professionals and technicians, from 35.9 to 29.1 per cent, and in the proportion of public sector employees, from 16.0 to 12.9 per cent. These relative decreases were not fully offset by increases in the share of professionals and technicians working in the private sector (from 4.7 to 7.8 per cent) and that of employers and independent professionals and technicians (from 3.8 to 4.3 per

TABLE 10.2
Distribution of urban employed in Latin America by labour market segment
and labour status, 1990–1999

Labour status	Share of urban employment		Share of each category during 1990–1999	
	1990	1999	%	Employed persons (000)
Total employed persons	100.0	100.0	100.0	26 216
Total formal sector	58.9	53.6	34.1	8 933
Public sector	16.0	12.9	2.1	551
Private sector	44.4	41.3	32.0	8 382
Employers, independent professionals and technicians	3.8	4.3	6.5	1 703
Employees	40.6	36.9	25.5	6 679
Professionals and technicians	4.7	7.8	20.1	5 260
Non-professional, non-technical workers	35.9	29.1	5.4	1 419
Total informal sector	41.0	46.3	65.9	17 284
Employment in microenterprises[a]	14.7	15.5	18.2	4 784
Domestic employment	5.4	6.3	9.4	2 466
Unskilled self-employed workers:	22.3	25.8	38.3	10 034
In agriculture, forestry, hunting and fishing	2.2	3.0	5.9	1 559
In industry and construction	4.3	5.2	8.1	2 131
In commerce and services	15.8	17.7	24.2	6 344

Source: ECLAC; from data tabulations of household surveys conducted in the various countries.
Notes: [a] Includes employers and employees in firms with up to five workers.

cent). Consequently, in 1990, value-added per employee was only 84 per cent of what it had been in 1980; in 2000, it was 93 per cent of the 1980 value, and in 2003, 90 per cent.

The wage gap between different segments of the workforce also widened. In general, occupational earnings were slow to increase, and grew at a lower rate than per capita income. Moreover, in most countries, these increases were too small to bring earnings back up to the levels recorded before the crisis of the 1980s. In almost every case, income increases reflected a combination of a large increase in the earnings of workers employed in the fastest-growing productivity activities of the modern sector and a slower (or even negative) growth of the earnings of all other urban workers. As a result, income gaps between the formal and informal sectors and between skilled and less skilled workers grew even wider (ECLAC, 2002).

Wage disparities between the formal and informal sectors increased in all countries for which data are available. The same was true for the average income of workers in these sectors in all countries in the study except Costa Rica, Honduras and Panama. Within each sector, income disparities between workers in higher and lower-skilled jobs also increased in every country except Argentina.[6] By contrast, and with few exceptions, income disparities between men and women tended to narrow. The main exception was Panama, where these disparities were smaller than in any other country in the region.

Poor and households with low per capita income generally experienced higher unemployment. During the 1990s, open unemployment in Latin America rose from 4.6 to 8.6 per cent, climbing steadily in Argentina, Brazil and Colombia, although only at half the rate in Brazil compared to the other two countries. Unemployment also increased in Bolivia, Chile, Ecuador, Paraguay, Uruguay and Venezuela. In Chile, it did not begin to rise until 1998, after having gone down since the beginning of the decade. By contrast, unemployment declined in Mexico and most Central American and Caribbean countries. After it recovered from the effects of the 1995 crisis, urban unemployment in Mexico declined to about 2.5 per cent. The figure also dropped in some Central American countries, such as El Salvador, Honduras and Nicaragua, while it stayed relatively moderate in Costa Rica.

Unemployment continued to affect the lower income groups the most. In 17 Latin American countries, and in the group of 8 countries that experienced a rapid increase in unemployment between the mid- and late 1990s,[7] the share of unemployed among the poorest 40 per cent of the population (quintiles I and II) continued to be considerably higher than the overall rate of unemployment, and, between 1994 and 1999, it increased significantly. Unemployment also rose in another 40 per cent of households (quintiles III and IV), particularly in the 8 countries worst affected by the crisis. Urban unemployment even increased among the highest-earning quintile. At the end of the decade, the three quintiles with the highest incomes recorded rates of unemployment twice as high—and in some countries, three times as high—as the rates that had prevailed in the middle of the decade.

From these changes in the labour market, primary income distribution became more unequal, as will be discussed in more detail below. Differences in unemployment and wages rose—both between professionals and non-professionals as well as between the formal and informal sectors. Public employment, which historically had provided comparatively higher incomes, lost importance vis-à-vis private employment. This also contributed to increasing inequality of income distribution.

SOCIAL POLICIES

Objectives

In the 1980s and 1990s, social policy proposals changed significantly. There was great confidence that countries would achieve higher rates of economic growth, with social policies playing a complementary role by ensuring more equity of opportunity.

In terms of equity objectives, governments generally preferred poverty alleviation measures to policies that sought to redress income inequality. This was in accordance with the dominant neoliberal argument, that capital would promote economic growth, which in turn was generally considered the best way to alleviate poverty. It was thought that emphasis on income redistribution, e.g., through higher taxes, would slow investment and growth, and therefore negatively affect the poor. Furthermore, if the public sector refrained from participating in the production of goods and commercial services, resources would be freed for public (social) expenditure, which would allow for increased education and health spending as well as direct transfers to the poor. It was also argued that there was a broad need for greater efficiency in public expenditure, both through the use of better technical solutions and by concentrating on the poor and reducing expenditure for strata which could manage without public assistance.

According to this view, the market would ensure economic growth, which in turn would reduce poverty, while the public sector could concentrate on social policy and equity through investment in human capital. In the 1990s, other objectives, such as safety nets, were added, in view of the repeated crises that rendered the labour market vulnerable, especially for the poor. Proposals relating to social capital and empowerment of the poor were also added to the policy agenda, with little success.

The influence of the United Nations was important in issues of equity. The UN's international conferences forced countries to incorporate human rights considerations, as well as democratic rights into their national constitution and legislation. The Copenhagen Summit set various social policy objectives, e.g., on equity, poverty and employment, and critics of neoliberal policies pointed out that reality was far from satisfactory in many respects.[8] The 2000 Millennium Declaration also raised issues relating to poverty, equity and international cooperation. Furthermore, a critical evaluation of social policies was gaining momentum.

The ageing of the population and the consequent reduction in the proportionate share of children and young people in the nation are new phenomena in Latin America. As the family is the main target and channel for social policy interventions, these will also have to change in recognition of the implications of recent population life-cycle changes. Gender also played an increasingly significant role in poverty alleviation policies in the 1990s, with some progress in women's education. Financial assistance is increasingly given directly to mothers in recognition of their role in nutrition, health, education, savings and consumption.

Outcomes

Social expenditure

Social expenditure in the form of transfers and human capital formation has been important for poverty alleviation both in the short and long term. Social spending rose considerably during the 1990s. In most countries, resources allocated to the social sector increased as a result of economic growth, increased budgetary pressure and the higher fiscal priority assigned to social expenditure.[9] In 17 countries in the region, per capita public spending rose by about 58 per cent on average between 1990–1991 and 2000–2001. From an average of $360 per capita at the start of the decade, social expenditure climbed to $540 per capita by the end of the decade.[10] The only countries that failed to significantly expand social expenditure were El Salvador, Honduras and Nicaragua (among the countries with low spending levels, or less than or close to $100 per capita) and Venezuela (among the countries with intermediate spending levels, or around $400). The increases were not uniform throughout the region, and tended to be greater in countries with moderate or low levels of per capita social expenditure. Social expenditure rose by over 100 per cent in Colombia, the Dominican Republic, Guatemala, Paraguay and Peru, whereas in countries with relatively high levels of spending (Argentina, Brazil, Costa Rica and Panama), the increases were somewhat smaller, amounting to between 20 and 40 per cent compared to the beginning of the decade.

Since the beginning of the 1990s, countries also made significant efforts to increase the share of GDP allocated to the social sector in order to compensate for the reduction in fiscal revenue due to a lower rate of economic growth. Accordingly, the ratio of social spending to GDP in the region increased from 12.1 per cent in 1996–1997 to 13.8 per cent in 2000–2001. This increase was only slightly smaller than the rise from 10.1 to 12.1 per cent between 1990/ 1991 and 1996/1997 (see Table 10.3). The increase was achieved despite a sharp downturn in growth of GDP per capita, which slowed from 2.1 to 0.2 per cent over the period. However, from 1998 onward, the economic slowdown and the contraction of GDP in a number of countries curbed the expansion of social spending. Although public spending in the social sector in the region as a whole continued to increase in per capita terms between 1998 and 2001 (from $501 to $552), its growth was slower than before. Per capita social spending expanded by 6.3 per cent a year between 1991 and 1997, but by only 4.2 per cent a year between 1998 and 2001 (see Figure 10.1 and Table 10.3).

The increase in social spending in the 1990s was partly associated with an effort on the part of these countries to raise spending levels by boosting government revenues and allocating a larger portion to the social sector. Social spending

TABLE 10.3
Latin America (18 countries): Public social expenditure as a percentage of GDP, 1990–2001 (percentages)

Country	Period					
	1990–1991	1992–1993	1994–1995	1996–1997	1998–1999	2000–2001
Argentina	19.3	20.1	21.1	20.0	20.8	21.6
Bolivia[a]	–	–	12.4	14.6	16.3	17.9
Brazil	18.1	17.7	19.3	17.3	19.3	18.8
Chile	11.7	12.4	12.3	13.0	14.7	16.0
Colombia	6.8	8.1	11.5	15.3	14.0	13.6
Costa Rica	15.6	15.2	15.8	16.8	16.4	18.2
Ecuador[b]	5.5	5.8	7.4	8.2	8.1	8.8
El Salvador[c]	–	3.1	3.4	3.8	4.1	4.2
Guatemala	3.4	4.1	4.1	˙ 4.3	6.0	6.2
Honduras	7.9	8.1	7.8	7.2	7.5	10.0
Mexico	6.5	8.1	8.8	8.5	9.2	9.8
Nicaragua	11.1	10.9	12.2	11.3	13.0	13.2
Panama[d]	18.6	19.5	19.8	20.9	21.6	25.5
Paraguay	3.1	6.2	7.0	8.0	8.5	8.5
Peru	4.0	5.3	6.7	7.1	7.7	8.0
Dominican Rep.	4.3	5.9	6.1	6.0	6.6	7.6
Uruguay	16.9	18.9	20.3	21.3	22.8	23.5
Venezuela	8.5	8.9	7.6	8.3	8.4	11.3
Latin America[e]	10.1	10.9	11.7	12.1	12.8	13.8

Source: ECLAC, social expenditure database.

Notes: [a] The figure in the 1994–1995 column refers to 1995.

[b] The figures in the 1990–1991 and 2000–2001 columns refer to 1991 and 2000, respectively.

[c] The figure in the 1992–1993 column refers to 1993.

[d] The figure in the 2000–2001column refers to 2000.

[e] Simple average for the countries shown, except Bolivia and El Salvador. If these countries are included, then the averages for Latin America are 11.3% for 1994–1995, 11.7% for 1996–97, 12.5% for 1998–1999 and 13.5% for 2000–2001.

FIGURE 10.1

Public social expenditure per capita in 18 Latin American countries, 1990–2001 (in 1997 US$)

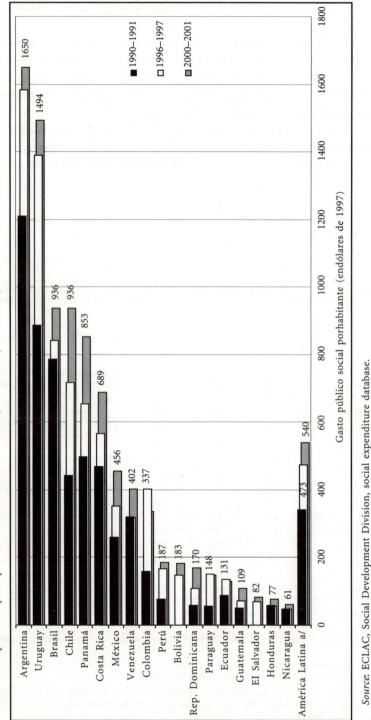

Gasto público social porhabitante (endólares de 1997)

Source: ECLAC, Social Development Division, social expenditure database.

[a] The first figure corresponds to the average for the two-year period, 1994–1995.

[b] The simple average of the countries, excluding Bolivia and El Salvador.

in the region thus climbed from nearly 42 to almost 48 per cent of total public expenditure. This trend was common throughout the region, except in Honduras and, to some extent, Panama.

The combined effect of increased budgetary pressure (public spending share of GDP) and greater fiscal priority for social expenditure (social sector share of total public expenditure) is reflected in a substantial increase in the share of GDP allocated to public social spending. In the region as a whole, this share rose from 10.4 to 13.1 per cent between 1990–1991 and 1998–1999. In any case, it is important to keep in mind that, as reflected in Figure 10.1, per capita social expenditure was near or below $100 in the poorest countries, which gives an idea of its potential effects and its limitations.

The increase in public social expenditure is especially important because its distribution is more equitable than the primary income distribution, mainly due to variations in employment and asset ownership. Not counting social security payments, the poorer quintile received 28 per cent of expenditure (compared to only 4.8 per cent of the primary income distribution), while the richest quintile received 12 per cent (compared to 50.7 per cent of the primary income distribution).

In considering the redistribution effects of increased public social expenditure in these countries, it is important to ascertain whether the substantial increase in per capita social expenditure during the 1990s went to its more progressive components. For the region as a whole, approximately 44 per cent of the growth in spending went to education and health (28 and 16 per cent respectively); 51 per cent to social security, mainly to retirement and other pensions; and the remaining 5 per cent to other expenditures, such as housing, drinking water and sanitation. This breakdown seems to indicate that in the region as a whole, the increase in spending went to both the most progressive and the least progressive social sectors. Furthermore, the equity effects were not uniform throughout the region. In countries with lower per capita income levels, spending increases were relatively greater in the more progressive components (education and health), accounting for 56 per cent of the total, while social security represented only 20 per cent. In contrast, social security accounted for around half the total increase in countries where expenditure was the highest.

The substantial increase in spending on education was for the implementation of reform programmes to improve the quality of and equity in education, especially at the primary and secondary levels. These reforms included teacher training and salary increases, the cost of which had a significant impact on the sector's budget. The rise in current and capital expenditure also contributed to this increase, especially in countries that sought to improve their physical and technological infrastructure, update teaching methods and materials, and establish systems for measuring educational output.

As for trends in health expenditure, the greatest progress was registered in Argentina, Chile and Colombia, where the increase was between $76 and $109 per capita, i.e., much higher than the regional average of $28. The biggest increases in spending on social security occurred in countries where that component already received a greater share of public resources (in Argentina, Brazil, Chile and Uruguay). In Argentina, Brazil and Chile, the increase ranged between $150 and $200 per capita, and in Uruguay, it was just over $500. These increases stemmed from adjustments in retirement benefits and other pensions, especially in Uruguay, where four-monthly adjustments were introduced in line with a constitutional amendment in 1989. Amortization of liabilities accumulated by the system and increases in coverage and benefits also contributed to the increases.

These trends indicate that the increased efforts of those governments that allocated lower shares of GDP to their social sectors had a more progressive effect on welfare distribution than did the efforts of countries with the highest per capita social expenditure levels where social security—which mostly benefits the middle and high-income strata—accounted for a much larger share of public spending.

Bearing in mind the distributive effects of social expenditure, there is a need to:

i)   Intensify efforts to increase social expenditure, as its level is quite low in most countries in the region;

ii) Stabilize the financing of social expenditure, to forestall the serious adverse effects of spending cuts during economic downturns; and

iii) Target public social expenditure more accurately, especially in programmes aimed at vulnerable or poor groups, by reallocating available funds so as to have the most impact.

In short, efforts should be made to maintain or increase resources, manage them more efficiently, and ensure that the programmes that are financed have the desired effect on the population segments they are intended to benefit.

Broad Social Outcomes

Although most governments in the region made poverty reduction an explicit priority, they were more cautious about taking steps to boost equity in income distribution. In most countries, progress was made with respect to legal equality, protection against discrimination, women's rights, labour rights and children's rights. Although there has been some delay in ratifying the UN Convention on

Indigenous People, many constitutions have recognized these rights. However, there has been little progress in other areas, such as the right to life, physical integrity and security.[11]

POVERTY ALLEVIATION

Global economic stagnation, volatility of growth and economic change not only limited efforts to fight poverty, but also had other negative effects due to the asymmetry between growth and poverty. Statistics show that increased poverty levels during the economic crisis only partially declined when the economies returned to pre-crisis per capita income levels. The percentage of the population in poverty in Latin America was higher in 2003 (44.0 per cent) than in 1980 (40.5 per cent).

The economic recession, expansion and stagnation that Latin American countries experienced in the 1980s and 1990s had a significant impact on

FIGURE 10.2
Annual growth rates of gross domestic product (GDP) and of the poor population in Latin America, 1980–1999 (in per cent)

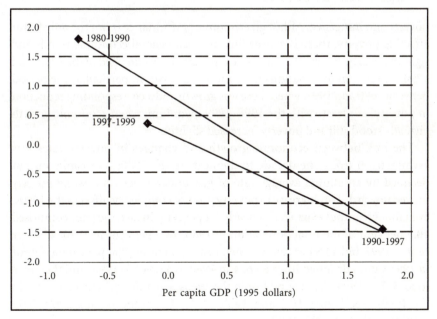

Source: ECLAC, on the basis of special data tabulations from household surveys conducted in the respective countries.

TABLE 10.4
Poor and indigent households and individuals in Latin America,[a] 1980–1999

	Poor[b]						Indigent[c]					
	Total		Urban		Rural		Total		Urban		Rural	
	Mil.	%	Mil.	%	Mil.	%	Mil.	%	Mil.	%	Mil.	%
					Households							
1980	24.2	34.7	11.8	25.3	12.4	53.9	10.4	15.0	4.1	8.8	6.3	27.5
1990	39.1	41.0	24.7	35.0	14.4	58.2	16.9	17.7	8.5	12.0	8.4	34.1
1994	38.5	37.5	25.0	31.8	13.5	56.1	16.4	15.9	8.3	10.5	8.1	33.5
1997	39.4	35.5	25.1	29.7	14.3	54.0	16.0	14.4	8.0	9.5	8.0	30.3
1999	41.3	35.3	27.1	29.8	14.2	54.3	16.3	13.9	8.3	9.1	8.0	30.7
					Individuals							
1980	135.9	40.5	62.9	29.8	73.0	59.9	62.4	18.6	22.5	10.6	39.9	32.7
1990	200.2	48.3	121.7	41.4	78.5	65.4	93.4	22.5	45.0	15.3	48.4	40.4
1994	201.5	45.7	125.9	38.7	75.6	65.1	91.6	20.8	44.3	13.6	47.4	40.8
1997	203.8	43.5	125.7	36.5	78.2	63.0	88.8	19.0	42.2	12.3	46.6	37.6
1999	211.4	43.8	134.2	37.1	77.2	63.7	89.4	18.5	43.0	11.9	46.4	38.3

Source: ECLAC, on the basis of special data tabulations from household surveys conducted in the respective countries.
Notes: [a] Estimates for 19 countries in the region.
[b] Households and population living in poverty. Includes indigent households (population).
[c] Indigent households and population.

poverty and indigence. Although economic performance is not the only factor affecting poverty, there is a clear link between general economic trends and signs of poverty. Figure 10.2 shows how poverty levels changed in the 1980s and 1990s in relation to variations in economic growth. In particular, the period between 1990 and 1997, when there was growth and a corresponding reduction in poverty, contrasts with the 1998–1999 biennium, when economic growth virtually stood still and poverty increased slightly.

The link between economic growth and changes in poverty rates was asymmetrical from one decade to the next. In the 1980s, per capita output declined by an annual average rate of just under 1 per cent, while poverty moved upward. This increase in poverty was not completely offset in the 1990s, even though output expanded at nearly 1.4 per cent. In fact, the poor comprised 40.5 per cent of the total population in 1980, 48.3 per cent in 1990, 43.5 per cent in 1997 and 43.8 per cent in 1999. Bearing in mind that per capita output in 1995 values dropped from $3,654 in 1980 to $3,342 in 1990, and then rose to $3,807 in 1999, the ground lost in the 1980s was only partially recovered in the 1990s (see Figure 10.2 and Table 10.4). The trend during 2000–2003 continued that of 1997–1999.

Changes in the spatial distribution of the population have resulted in poverty today being a largely urban phenomenon. In 1999, 134 of the region's 211 million poor people lived in urban areas and 77 million in rural areas. However, the incidence of poverty is still much higher in rural areas (64 per cent) than in cities (37 per cent). In addition, as shown in Table 10.4, poverty is more extreme in rural areas, with most of the rural poor being indigent (46 million), while most of the urban poor are non-indigent (91 million).

Migration of poor people from the countryside to cities increased the proportion of urban poor in the region's total poor population. As a result, the urban economy faced the challenge of absorbing a larger proportion of the nation's working-age population and of meeting an increased demand for social services. In spite of these challenges, the urban economy was able to absorb rural migrants into jobs at a higher level of productivity than what was available at their places of origin.

Of the 211 million Latin Americans living in poverty in 1999, about 22 million lived in households with a per capita income not less than 90 per cent of the minimum needed to meet basic needs. In other words, close to 10 per cent of the poor were relatively well placed to rise above the poverty line. On the other hand, 45 million of the non-poor population were categorized as most at risk of falling into poverty, as their income was not more than 25 per cent above the poverty-line. This population group is highly vulnerable to economic fluctuations, as the slightest negative impact on their income can lead to a significant decline in living standards.

Certain features that go hand in hand with poverty—such as an overcrowded dwelling, an unemployed head of household and a poor educational environment—exacerbate the vulnerability of poor households. These tend to occur in the context of a low-income environment and offer a more complete picture of the living standards of the region's poor.

Income Distribution

Historically, Latin America has shown the worst income distribution of the world's regions. This situation deteriorated further in the 1980s and the 1990s, even in countries that previously had relatively better distributions, such as Argentina, Chile and Venezuela. The fact that, in the late 1990s, the major portion of total income in Latin America was earned by the richest 10 per cent of households, who received more than 30 per cent, can serve as an illustration of the region's income distribution. In most countries (except El Salvador and Venezuela), that figure was over 35 per cent (45 per cent in Brazil). The average income of this decile was 19 times higher than the average for the 40 per cent of households with the lowest incomes, who received between 9 and 15 per cent

(Uruguay was an exception, with around 22 per cent). In the 1990s, the share of total national income accruing to the top 10 per cent of households continued to increase in most countries, raising inequality of income distribution in Latin America. During that decade, the share of income received by households in the top decile increased in eight countries, declined in five (significantly so in Honduras[12] and Uruguay) and remained steady in Mexico.

A comparison of the average income of various household groups also reflects a high degree of inequality in Latin America. In Bolivia, Brazil and Nicaragua, the average per capita income of the richest quintile (20 per cent of households) were more than 30 times greater than those of the poorest quintile. In the other countries, the average was also high, at around 23 times. The ratio of the average income of the wealthiest decile to that of the poorest four deciles also underscores the degree of concentration. The largest ratio was for Brazil, where the income of the most affluent was 32 times greater than the combined incomes of the bottom four deciles. The average difference region-wide was 19.3, which is extremely high compared to the ratios for Uruguay (8.8) and Costa Rica (12.6), the countries with the lowest income inequality in the region.[13]

The share of income received by the poorest 40 per cent of households differed in the region over the decade. The figure fell in five countries, rose in eight and held steady in Nicaragua. The steepest decreases were in Ecuador and Venezuela, countries that experienced major crises, and also in Costa Rica, El Salvador and Mexico. Where there were improvements, they were relatively minor, and surpassed two percentage points in only one case—Colombia from 1994 to 1997, but with a slight deterioration from 1997 to 1999. The improvements amounted to more than one percentage point in three others—Honduras, Guatemala and Uruguay—and were around 0.5 per cent in Argentina, Brazil, Chile and Panama.

Another indicator of income concentration is the percentage of people with a per capita income falling below the overall average. Between 67 to 77 per cent of the population in Latin America get less than the average per capita income. In most countries, this proportion was smaller at the beginning of the 1980s. At present, around 75 per cent of households have below-average incomes. Hence, a much larger share of the increased per capita GDP has gone to the top 25 per cent of households. Costa Rica and Uruguay have the lowest shares of persons receiving less than the average per capita income, while Brazil and Guatemala have the highest.

In summary, even though many countries did show a certain economic growth and considerably increased social expenditure in the 1990s, Latin America as a whole did not succeed in substantially improving primary income distribution. Although economic growth has made it possible to reduce absolute poverty, increased output has not altered the way in which the benefits of growth are distributed, nor are there any signs that this situation is likely to change significantly in the short or medium term.[14] Out of 17 countries analysed, only Honduras and Uruguay had reduced their rates of inequality by the end of the decade. Even in countries that achieved high and sustained growth rates, such as Chile, income distribution has not changed, and disparities persist. While social expenditure is presumably progressive, it is insufficient by itself to compensate for existing economic inequalities.

Sectoral Outcomes

Although the preceding review of broad social outcomes provides a useful framework to evaluate changes in equity, it is nonetheless necessary to complement the analysis by further examining certain areas which specifically influence equity. Increased social expenditure and progress on certain indicators do not, by themselves, ensure improved equity. Actual trends in key strategic areas of social policy—such as education, health, housing and social protection—must also be considered in this regard.

Education

As mentioned above, the region has increased its public expenditure on education. Policies in this area have taken into consideration international recommendations, such as the importance of educating women. Much emphasis has also been placed on the need to universalize education. Governments have made huge investments to try to ensure universal primary education and to significantly expand enrolment in preschool and secondary education. The gross enrolment rate for primary education is 100 per cent in most countries today; enrolment rates for secondary and tertiary education have also increased, although progress remains uneven across countries. Despite these efforts, only around half of those who start primary education actually complete it.

Although the region made significant progress in the 1990s, national and international tests suggest that there is considerable room for improvement in quality, which is also important for equity. In-depth analysis shows the magnitude of related problems in the region, such as the extremely low level of education of most parents, the need for children in poorer families to work, and the limited access to educational services in poor rural areas. The level of education received by children from poor households is generally too low to enable them to break out of the cycle of poverty.

The distribution of educational achievement remains extremely uneven, as inequalities persist and are carried over to the next generation, mostly through

FIGURE 10.3
Educational attainment of youths aged 20–24 compared with their parents
in Latin America, 2000 (in per cent)

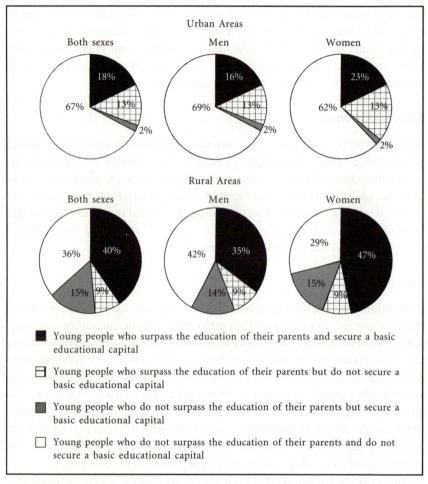

Source: ECLAC, on the basis of special tabulations of data from household surveys of the respective countries.

unequal opportunity and achievement in education. ECLAC studies show that, despite efforts to extend the coverage of formal education, socio-economic status and family origin continue to determine opportunities for education as well as for social and economic mobility. Educational opportunities—and consequently, access to more stable and better-paid employment—are inherited to a great degree, thus perpetuating socio-economic inequalities. Around 75 per cent of young people in urban areas are from households in which the parents have less than 10 years of schooling. On average, more than 45 per cent of them do not reach the educational threshold required for gaining a decent livelihood, which is currently around 12 years of schooling given some variation between countries (see Figure 10.3). In rural areas, opportunities for young people are even more limited: around 80 per cent do not attain the threshold level, even though this level is lower.[15]

Despite the significant extension of educational coverage that had taken place throughout the Latin American region over the previous 15 years, the proportion of young people who significantly exceed the educational level of their parents is low. This shows that inter-generational carry-over of educational achievement is still a dominant factor.[16] The average number of years of schooling of young people has risen from 7.1 to 10.4 years in urban areas and from 3.0 to 6.8 years in rural areas. Nevertheless, young people from the lower social strata have had few opportunities to achieve a level of education that would assure them a minimum livelihood level. At present, just over 30 per cent of young people, whose parents did not complete primary education, finish secondary school. In contrast, secondary schooling is completed by 75 per cent of the children of parents who had at least 10 years of schooling.

The link between access to education and social origin suggests that opportunities for young people today have already been shaped, to a large extent, by the inequalities of the previous generation. This implies a rigid social structure with little real social mobility, which again limits opportunities to improve income distribution in the medium term, since the number of years of schooling and quality of education are the main means for obtaining well-paid employment. For the majority of young people in the region, educational achievement and upward mobility continue to depend on parents' education and household means.

Unfortunately, the inequality of educational opportunities already manifests itself at the primary school level. Differences in years of schooling are not the only inequality in educational achievement. The quality of education that young people receive also varies with their social origin. Learning levels significantly differ between students in public schools and those in private schools. Delich (2002) notes that the average student in public schools barely learns 50 per cent of the official curriculum, but the average graduate of a private school has learned close to 100 per cent. Reading and writing tests show that two out of five pupils in the fourth or fifth grade, typically from families at a low socio-economic level, do not understand what they read. Those who complete more years of education have generally received better quality education.

Many governments in the region have carried out educational reforms focused on curricula, institutional change and allocation of financial resources. Such reforms may reduce disparities between private and public establishments in terms of student results and educational achievement, and thus reduce educational inequalities between different socio-economic strata. A substantial proportion of the educational inequalities transmitted from one generation to the next is related to the number of years of schooling completed, independent of the quality of education received. Attempts to improve education may have little effect if not accompanied by policies that lengthen the period that young people remain in the school system, since a high proportion do not stay in school for 12 years.

To ensure that young students from poor families remain in school, some countries have established programmes that motivate families to ensure their children's attendance. The Brazilian Bolsa Escola and the Mexican Progresa (now called Oportunidades) are examples of such programmes. The Bolsa Escola gives a monetary bonus to low-income families with children between 6 and 15 years who attend school. The Mexican system is more comprehensive in making transfers to poor rural families for children between the third year of primary and the third year of secondary school, with the transfers increasing with the number of years. To receive money for nutrition and educational materials, families must: enrol their children below 18 in school; guarantee their regular attendance; enrol in and regularly use the corresponding local health service; attend regular lectures on education and health; and use the monetary assistance for their children's nutrition. Specially trained state employees supervise compliance with these conditions. Since 2002, the programme has increased the coverage of benefits at the secondary and university levels and in poor urban areas.

Real income associated with years of schooling is lower now than in the 1980s. In fact, the increase in average years of study that occurred during the 1980s and 1990s did not increase per capita income per se. Most young people with between 9 and 11 years of schooling still only have access to occupations that provide insufficient well-being. This suggests that, as the coverage of secondary education has increased, the value of education in securing a livelihood has declined. The significant concentration of individuals with 13 or more years of schooling in occupations that provide adequate well-being underscores that this is an important educational threshold. Clearly, it is important to orient educational reforms to improving educational equity for children and adolescents from the lower-income social strata. However, reforms of the school system will not benefit those already aged 20 or more, who will constitute more than two-thirds of the labour force in the region within the next two decades.

Health and Housing

As discussed above, the poor in Latin America have not only the lowest income, and the worst opportunities for education, but the health sector also reveals a similar intergenerational persistence of poverty and inequality. The poor are especially susceptible to health problems, due to low incomes, poor sanitation, and low-quality housing and working conditions. Limited access to public health services exacerbates their health problems.

In the 1990s, governments in the region increased their expenditure on health, as did the private sector, and the financing increased for non-governmental organization activity. Increased public health expenditure is still insufficient to enable the public sector to cope with the increasing demand for health services. As in the case of education, some progress has been made, although these indicators do not reflect the variation in progress between social groups. The rate of infant mortality has fallen from 42 to 32 per thousand live births, while life expectancy has risen from 67 to 70 years, and sanitation facilities have improved.

In the 1990s, governments in the Latin American region made efforts to improve public services. Access to electricity, water and sanitation improved significantly in most countries. Although figures vary according to the standards used, access to safe water increased from 79 to 85 per cent, while access to sanitation increased from 74 to 82 per cent. In most of these cases, wider coverage benefited poor households and therefore contributed to increased equity.

The issues of overcrowding and poor quality in housing are more difficult to deal with. Poor neighbourhoods, due especially to their lack of schools and health services, tend to create conditions that entrench poverty from generation to generation. Furthermore, social discrimination makes it difficult for job-seekers from poor neighbourhoods to find good jobs.

Unregulated urbanization in many Latin American cities has created serious problems and left many neighbourhoods without basic infrastructure. Meanwhile, rising land prices have forced the poor to move further away from town centres. In the 1980s and 1990s, the shift from rural to urban poverty continued as the absolute number of the poor increased. The quality of life of the poor deteriorated, attended by problems such as growing insecurity, rising crime, drug trafficking and overcrowding. The cost of dealing with these problems has been high, undermining the commitment to poverty alleviation.

Increased Social Protection and Reduction of Risk

The debt crises of the 1980s, greater macroeconomic vulnerability in the 1990s as well as adjustment policies and reforms have all increased the vulnerability of the poor, often increasing drop-out rates and problems of nutrition and health. When critical situations arise, social protection may be pursued through public assistance to individuals, households and communities to ensure access to basic social services.

For the non-poor, insurance is a classic instrument against risk. For families and communities, social solidarity can be an effective tool against risk. However, for the poor, the possibilities for such solidarity are often limited. Although the public sector has supported the poor with emergency jobs, monetary subsidies, school assistance, food assistance, as well as childcare and health services, these traditional instruments were insufficient to deal with the crises in Latin America of the 1980s and 1990s.

Governments have introduced new programmes to reinforce these instruments. Unemployment insurance operates in few countries and offers very limited benefits. Presently, proposals to enhance this type of insurance include the need for employee savings, retrenchment of benefits, and free access to certain social services for the unemployed. Other alternatives—such as credit for the unemployed and funds financed by both employees and employers—are easier to finance.

Official figures show that, in 1999, 217 million persons in the region were not covered by social security. The nature of the labour market and the effects of unemployment due to crises are quite different across countries. Therefore, possible policies for social protection vary significantly. Recently, increased attention has been given to providing health services and covering social security contributions for the poor. Other policies include training and retraining for people who have lost their job.

Special funds to alleviate poverty, first introduced in reaction to the effects of the adjustment policies of the late 1980s, were reintroduced in the 1990s. Their focus on serving families in extreme situations and their relative autonomy distinguish these funds from other instruments. These funds operate through projects and require the beneficiaries to cooperate by contributing work or their own land as inputs. The main challenges are to identify those living in extreme poverty, to engage consultants to scrutinize and supervise projects, and to establish bureaucratic links with different public and non-public organizations.

Many of these funds have become permanent. The role of the funds is related to particular situations that require quick intervention and new institutional mechanisms that are more flexible and efficient. It has become clear that mechanisms for social protection must complement positive effects of economic and social policies, but cannot by themselves solve the perplexing problems of equity. Social protection should not be financed from a reduction in other social expenditure, which is, in essence, anti-cyclical in nature.

The Public Debate on Equity

The Latin American region experienced important political changes during the 1980s and 1990s. In the 1960s, 1970s and 1980s, many countries in the region were governed by authoritarian regimes. The 1990s was an unprecedented decade in which almost the entire region had democratic regimes. Equity is a basic component of democracy, and progress in political and citizenship participation constitutes an important aspect of equity. UNDP's 2004 report on democracy in Latin America in the previous twenty years points to the relative strength of democracy in Latin America.

The functioning of democracy has changed significantly since the first three post-war decades in terms of the relative power of economic and social actors. Economic change has been accompanied by a decline in the power of unions and those political parties associated with labour, a weakening of labour and a reduction of the public sector, while the power of large-scale private enterprises has been reinforced. There has been a significant loss of government autonomy. As mentioned above, government freedom to implement economic and social policy has been limited by explicit or implicit conditionalities imposed by creditors—such as international financial institutions, other foreign economic actors, as well as foreign governments—or by supposedly voluntary government commitments.

Control of communications has become more important for the consolidation of power, involving modern technology and closer association of powerful economic interests, as evidenced by the high cost of political campaigns and lobbying. The media have also contributed to the establishment of new consumption patterns favouring transnational enterprises and increasing their control of markets.

Public debate on equity has evolved in this context of concentrated power. In the past, political parties in many countries used to design programmes that proposed major social changes. In recent years, however, transnational media have promoted liberal values associated with individualism, to the detriment of the collective interest. Polls have gradually become more important in gauging and shaping public opinion. Governments have become increasingly involved in appearing to be responsive to the population, instead of debating alternative social, economic and political programmes with other political parties. There is a need to promote more substantive citizen participation in public affairs

(ECLAC, 2000b). Until recently, confidence prevailed that economic growth and public expenditure would solve the problems of poverty and inequality, but now, doubts have become widespread.

Neoliberals have pointed to certain positive outcomes of the recent economic changes and social policies as proof that their policies have benefited the majority of the population, especially the poor. The 2000 round of population and housing censuses have shown that the structure of consumption has changed considerably, especially in terms of access to durable goods, while public sector infrastructure expenditure has significantly increased access to safe water, sanitation and electricity. Progress has been made on these issues in all countries, despite variations in per capita income and growth.

However, critics claim that the poor quality of education, health, infrastructure and security as well as drug abuse and criminality in poor neighbourhoods are the results of those same neoliberal policies. Other problems that critics ascribe to neoliberal ideology include increased unemployment, lower wages and the vulnerability of small enterprises. The devaluation of education as a guarantee of income and security has also created dissatisfaction among young people and their families. The stagnation of per capita income during between 1999 and 2003 has strengthened critics of the prevailing system. In this context, the principle of equity has gained political momentum.

The Latinobarümetro is an annual survey that gathers opinions on topics associated with values, actors and equity covering 17 Latin American countries. The Latinobarümetro surveys of 2002 and 2003 showed the following results regarding values and the functioning of institutions.[17] Although democracy was preferred to authoritarian regimes (7 to 2), only 32 per cent in 2002 and 29 per cent in 2003 were satisfied with government performance. Confidence in government was below 50 per cent with very few exceptions, while confidence in legislatures and political parties was even weaker.

In relation to the respective roles of the State and the market, half the respondents believed that development was more important than democracy; 66 per cent believed that the market economy was a better option than State intervention; however, only 24 per cent in 2002 and 16 per cent in 2003 were satisfied with the actual performance of the market economy. In 2003, only 22 per cent believed that privatization had been good for the country, down from 46 per cent in 1998, and 28 per cent in 2002. In 2002, 70 per cent believed that the State should be in charge of providing electricity, water, health and other social services, while 21 per cent preferred these services to be in the hands of the private sector; 53 per cent believed that they would attain the level of welfare they desired in less than 10 years, while 67 per cent believed that their countries would need more than 10 years or would never develop; 56 per cent considered the economic situation of the country bad or very bad, and 48 per cent believed it was worse or much worse than in previous years; 57 per cent believed that their parents had been better off than they were themselves. Among problems felt to be the worst, unemployment, low wages and poverty accounted for more than 50 per cent, while 80 per cent of respondents judged the current income distribution to be unfair or very unfair. These opinions have been reflected in election results since 2000. Although democracy and a mixed market economy are desired as institutions, there is discontent with the way they have been functioning so far.

The economic stagnation during the five-year period, 1999–2003, is reflected in opinions that are increasingly critical of the system. Social unrest has increased and many political candidates strongly critical of prevalent economic and social policies have been elected. However, due to existing power structures, many newly elected officials have been unable to implement desired changes.

Most social and political actors strongly defend democracy. The significant change today as compared to earlier attitudes is a desire for stronger public policies for poverty alleviation and equality, at least in terms of opportunity. For the first time in many years, prevailing policies have been challenged in Argentina and Venezuela, and the principle of a new distribution of the costs of the economic crisis has been introduced.

The need for economic growth and economic transformation conducive to growth was also clearly stated during the Copenhagen Summit:

"To create a favourable economic environment that would help to bring about more equitable access to all income levels, resources and social services", to promote "dynamic, open and free markets, while recognizing at the same time the need to intervene in the market, as and when necessary, to prevent or stop markets from falling, to promote stability and long-term investments, to ensure fair competition and ethical conduct, and to harmonize economic and social development" (UN, 1996).

Patricio Aylwin, then President of Chile, stated in an address on 28 June 2000 on the occasion of the Copenhagen Plus 5 Conference in Geneva, "Moreover, civil society in most developing countries lacks the necessary organization and power to have effective influence on such matters, while the sorely needed and long hoped-for resources of the wealthy nations to be given in assistance to the poor countries are far from reaching the needed levels".

NOTES

[1] The author has heavily used ECLAC documents, especially ECLAC (2004b), of which he was coauthor. The author wishes to express his gratitude to Adolfo Gurrieri for his comments and suggestions.

[2] The disarticulation process is described in Sáinz and Calcagno (1992).

[3] For the influence of policies on globalization, see Ocampo (2001).

[4] In a number of countries, some non-tradable services, such as segments of the tourism sector, may be significant. However, since the national accounts estimates of most of the countries do not identify the amounts corresponding to these segments, growth rates in the tradable sector may, to some extent, be underestimated in cases where they are representative and have expanded rapidly.

[5] For detailed information, see ECLAC (2004b).

[6] Argentina's situation is not fully comparable to that of other Latin American countries, owing to the great increase in its open unemployment rate.

[7] Argentina, Brazil, Chile, Colombia, Ecuador, Paraguay, Uruguay and Venezuela.

[8] See, for example, the two ECLAC appraisals of the Copenhagen Summit Programme of Action (1997; 2000a).

[9] In the analysis of public expenditure, 'social sector' does not refer to social classes or groups, but rather to health, welfare, social security, housing, etc.

[10] These figures are simple averages for all countries in the study; per capita social expenditure is expressed in 1997 US dollars.

[11] For a complete and detailed description and analysis of national legislation improvement and shortcomings, see UNDP (2004).

[12] It should be noted, however, that the data for Honduras for the 1990s may not be fully comparable, owing to changes in the income-measurement methodology introduced with the 1994 household survey. These changes—which had to do with the breadth of the income definition used in the study—may have influenced the data on distribution of household income in 1990, compared to such data for subsequent years, and thus may have influenced analysis of the trend through the decade.

[13] Although no figures comparable with those for the rest of the region are available, Cuba has probably maintained a less regressive income distribution than the other countries, despite that country's economic deterioration in the 1990s.

[14] For details of structural factors underlying income distribution, see ECLAC (1998).

[15] For rural areas, the threshold for children is 9 years, while for their parents, less than 6 years of schooling was considered inadequate.

[16] Although there are other important factors, such as household demography, property and employment, for most people, education is the main factor determining their opportunities for future well-being.

[17] See press releases, Latinobarómetro 2002 and 2003. http://www.latinobarometro.org.

REFERENCES

Aylwin Azócar, Patricio (2000). Scant progress since the Summit. Translation of the Panel Address made on 28 June 2000 on the occasion of the Copenhagen Plus 5 Conference in Geneva by Patricio Aylwin, Former President of Chile. *South Letter* 36. South Centre, ISSN 1023–1366. Available from http://www.southcentre.org/southletter/sl36/sl36-02.htm (accessed 30 March 2006).

Barros de Castro, Antonio (2003). Brazil's Second Catch-up: Characteristics and Constraints. *CEPAL Review* 80, August: 71–80.

Delich, Francisco (2002). La Declinación Argentina. *Archivos del Presente* (Fundación Foro del Sur, Buenos Aires) 7 (27), October–December: 30, 33.

ECLAC (1984). The Latin American Crisis: Its Evaluation and Perspectives. E/CEPAL/SES.20/G.25, 08/02/1984. Economic Commission for Latin America and the Caribbean, Lima.

ECLAC (1997). The Equity Gap. LC/G.1954, March, Economic Commission for Latin America and the Caribbean, Santiago.

ECLAC (1998). *Social Panorama 1997.* Chapter 2. Economic Commission for Latin America and the Caribbean, LC/G.1982-P, February, Economic Commission for Latin America and the Caribbean, Santiago.

ECLAC (2000a). The Equity Gap: A Second Appraisal. LC/G.2096, May, Economic Commission for Latin America and the Caribbean, Santiago.

ECLAC (2000b). Equity, Development and Citizenship. LC/G.2071, March, Economic Commission for Latin America and the Caribbean, Santiago.

ECLAC (2002). *Social Panorama of Latin America, 2001–2002.* LC/G.2183-P/1, October, Economic Commission for Latin America and the Caribbean, Santiago.

ECLAC (2004a). Foreign Investment in Latin America and the Caribbean: 2003 Report. LC/G.2226-P/I, May, Economic Commission for Latin America and the Caribbean, Santiago.

ECLAC (2004b). *A Decade of Social Development in Latin America, 1990–1999.* LC/G.2212-P, April, Economic Commission for Latin America and the Caribbean, Santiago.

Latinobarómetro. http://www.latinobarometro.org. See press releases for 2002 and 2003.

Ocampo, José Antonio (2001). La Globalización y la Agenda del Desarrollo. Paper for the III Encuentro Internacional de Economistas, 'Globalización y Problemas del Desarrollo', Havana, 29 January–2 February.

Sáinz, Pedro, and Alfredo Calcagno (1992). In Search of Another Form of Development. *CEPAL Review* 48, December: 7–38.

UN (1996). Report of the World Summit for Social Development, Copenhagen Declaration on Social Development—Part C, Commitment 1, §b, e. A/CONF.166/9. United Nations, New York.

UNDP (2004). *Democracy in Latin America.* United Nations Development Programme, New York.

11
Income Distribution in the Middle East and North Africa, 1960–2000

MARIA CRISTINA PACIELLO

Over the last two decades, income concentration has risen in many nations of Latin America, Eastern Europe and the former Soviet Union, China, and a few African and Southeast Asian economies, accompanied by slower growth and stagnant poverty rates (Cornia and Kiiski, 2001). Elsewhere, there appears to be an association between rising within-country inequality and changes in policy regimes, particularly involving stabilization and structural adjustment policies. However, as far as the Middle East and North Africa (MENA) countries are concerned, this trend towards increasing inequality seems not to have occurred. Moreover, the relatively high inequality in some MENA countries seems to have changed little over fairly long periods of time. This chapter will attempt to explain the long-term trends in income distribution observed in MENA, and to highlight the distributive impact of stabilization and structural adjustment policies in the region. It will mainly cover six MENA countries: Algeria, Egypt, Jordan, Morocco, Tunisia and Turkey.

HAS INCOME INEQUALITY DECLINED IN THE MENA REGION?

Before proceeding, it is important to emphasize that analysis of poverty and income inequality is frustrated by the lack of comprehensive and comparable data, by the reluctance of some official sources to share primary survey data with researchers, and by irregular data collection and publication in individual countries (UNDP, 2002). Data on income distribution are available for 14 MENA countries (see Paciello, 2006). Gini coefficients for the MENA region are based on household consumption expenditures, with the exception of Turkey, Lebanon and Iraq for 2004. Household expenditure surveys are thus likely to miss the upper tails of the distribution because of the higher savings rates of upper income groups.

The MENA region is commonly said to compare favourably with the rest of the world in terms of income inequality and poverty (World Bank, 1995; Page and Van Gelder, 2002; UNDP, 2002). In comparing trends in income inequality in MENA with those of other regions of the developing world over the period 1970 to 1999, a recent study by two economists of the World Bank (Page and Van Gelder, 2002) underlines that the "MENA region recorded the largest improvement in income distribution of all regions of the developing world between 1970 and 1999" and, because of this, "it has now one of the most equal income distributions in the developing world, with an average Gini coefficient of 36.0" (Page and Van Gelder, 2002: 6).

This brief section will attempt to show that the above view is not entirely accurate, by providing a more nuanced picture of income inequality trends in the seven MENA countries for which long-term data exists. Firstly, it is important to note that regional averages may be misleading in so far as they cover a very limited sample of countries and mask different country trajectories in inequality. For example, income inequality ranges from a high Gini coefficient of 43 per cent in Iran to a medium 32 per cent in the West Bank and Gaza Strip. Secondly, by looking at the individual empirical case studies presented below for which data are available (see Table 11.1), contrary to the view that MENA recorded one of the largest improvements in income distribution over time, the relatively high inequality in seven MENA countries has changed little over fairly long periods of time and the trend in inequality has not been linear.

In Algeria, the Gini coefficient for inequality in Algiers only increased marginally between 1966 and 1980 (Belkacem, 2001). In the 1980s, the economic and social crises that followed the end of the oil boom, compounded by economic mismanagement, led to the adoption of a structural adjustment programme (SAP) and a significant deterioration in inequality, although poverty continued to decline. During the early phase of the SAP (1988–1995), Algeria recorded large improvements in inequality in the context of increasing poverty (see Tables 11.1 and 11.2). Moreover, while the top quintile lost in favour of all other income groups, the income shares of the first and second quintiles hardly changed (see World Bank, 1999b, 2000b). In other words, the gap between the income shares of the middle class and those of the poorest 40 per cent increased.

During the 1960s and 1970s in Egypt, income distribution improved (see Table 11.1), but slowed down in the latter part of the 1970s, with the oil boom (see Paciello, 2006). During the 1980s, with the collapse of oil prices and the economic crisis following it, Gini coefficients suggest a significant deterioration in inequality, both in urban and rural areas (see Amin, 1999; Korayem, 2002; El-Ghonemy, 1998; Page and Van Gelder, 2002).[1] Increasing inequality also coincided with fairly rapidly rising poverty. During the early phase of its SAP (1991–1995), according to the World Bank (1999b; 2000b), income

TABLE 11.1
Trends in income inequality, 1960–2000

	Gini coefficient			Gini coefficient
Algeria			Turkey	
1980	34.3		1963	55.0
1988	38.7		1973	51.0
1995	35.8		1987	44.0
			1994	49.0
Egypt				
1959	42.0		Iran	
1965	40.0		1969	41.9
1975	38.0		1970	45.5
1990–1991	32.0		1971	43.6
1995–1996	28.9/34.5		1972	42.3
1999–2000	37.8		1983	42.9
			1990	43.4
Jordan			1994	43.0
1986–1987	36.1		1998	43.7
1992	40.0			
1997	36.4			
Morocco				
1984–1985	39.7			
1990–1991	39.3			
1998–1999	39.5			
Tunisia				
1965	42.3			
1975	44.0			
1980	43.0			
1985	43.4			
1990	40.1			
1995	41.7			
2000	40.9			

Notes: Data from different sources are not comparable among them.

Sources: WIDER, *World Income Inequality Database*, http://www.wider.unu.edu/wiid/wiid.htm. For Algeria, Belkacem (2001). For Egypt, for 1990–1991 and 1995–1996, World Bank (1999b, 2000b); for 1995–96 and 1999–2000, El-Laithy, Lokshin and Banerji (2003). For Jordan, Page and Van Gelder (2002). For Morocco, Page and Van Gelder (2002). For Tunisia, UNDP (2004b). For Iran, from 1990 to 1998, Adams and Page (2003).

distribution began to improve, mainly due to the reduction in rural inequality. However, other estimates point to increasing inequality (Radwan, 1997; Kandeel and Nugent, 1998; El-Ghonemy, 1998) and poverty in urban areas increased (see Table 11.2). Finally, in the second half of the 1990s, inequality at the aggregate level unambiguously deteriorated, as poverty improved.

TABLE 11.2
Population below the poverty line in selected MENA countries, various years

	Headcount index		
	Overall	*Urban*	*Rural*
Algeria			
1988	12.2	7.3	16.6
1995	22.5	14.7	30.3
Egypt			
1990–1991	24.9	20.3	28.6
1995	22.9	22.5	23.3
1999–2000	16.7	9.2	22.1
Jordan			
1987	3.0	–	–
1992	14.4	12.4	21.1
1997	11.7	10.0	18.2
Morocco			
1990–1991	13.1	7.6	18.0
1998–1999	19.0	12.0	27.2
Tunisia			
1975	22.0	26.5	18.0
1980	12.9	11.8	14.1
1985	7.7	8.4	7.0
1990	6.7	7.3	5.8
1995	6.2	7.1	4.9
2000	4.2	4.9	2.9

Sources: For Algeria, World Bank (1999b); for Egypt, Adams and Page (2003); World Bank (2002b); for Jordan, World Bank (2004a); for Morocco, World Bank (2001); for Tunisia, UNDP (2004b); for Iran, Adams and Page (2003).

As for Jordan, there is evidence that income distribution improved during the period of positive economic growth from the 1960s to the 1980s (World Bank, 1994). However, the economic crisis following the end of the oil boom and the 1991 Gulf war completely offset such gains: between 1987 and 1992, inequality surged from 36.1 to 40.6, with evidence of fairly rapidly rising poverty (see Table 11.2). In the 1990s, under the SAP, income inequality almost returned to its pre-crisis level, decreasing to 36.4 per cent (see Table 11.1). However, the Jordan Living Conditions Survey carried out jointly by the Fafo Institute for Applied Social Science of Norway and Jordan's Department of Statistics in 1996 showed that income differences probably increased over the period

(Hanssen Bauer, Pedersen and Tiltnes, 1998). Moreover, poverty in 1997 was higher than in 1987.

While there is no Gini coefficient before the SAP in Morocco, over the 1980s and the 1990s, the Gini index remained almost unchanged, at around 39 per cent (Table 11.1). However, although income distribution was relatively stable during the 1990s, this appears to mask different patterns of inequality in urban and rural areas; the lowest decile gained in urban areas, whereas in rural areas the lowest decile lost (World Bank, 2001). Unlike during the first phase of adjustment, poverty increased, both in severity and incidence, from 13.1 per cent in 1990–1991 to 19.0 per cent in 1998–1999 (see Table 11.2).

In Tunisia, over the period 1965–2000, there was a slight reduction in inequality, although disparity was high in urban areas. Income inequality experienced the largest decline, by 3.3 percentage points in the early phase of the SAP (1987–1990), and remained almost unchanged at around 40 per cent in the 1990s, although it increased in urban areas (see UNDP, 2004b). Poverty has steadily decreased in both urban and rural areas since 1975. After adoption of the SAP, poverty reduction slowed down, especially in the first part of the 1990s (Table 11.2).

Gini coefficients in Turkey show that inequality declined in the 1960s and 1970s, and worsened after 1987, during the second phase of structural adjustment (Table 11.1; Yeldan, 2000). However, evidence other than the Gini coefficient points to increasing inequality in both rural and urban areas from the late 1970s (Hansen, 1991; Boratav, Türel and Yeldan, 1996; Arincali and Rodrik, 1990) and during the early phase of structural adjustment between 1980 and 1987 (Owen and Pamuk, 1998; Arincali and Rodrik, 1990; Boratav, Türel and Yeldan, 1996). Since 1987, the worsening of urban income distribution seems to account for almost all of the economy-wide concentration of income (Yeldan, 2000).

As for Iran, inequality increased slightly between 1969 and 1983, as indicated by Table 11.1. However, several studies reveal a large increase in disparity in consumption during the period preceding the Islamic revolution and covering the oil boom (1960–1978) (e.g. see Assadzadeh and Paul, 2001). For example, a higher Gini index of 53 per cent was noted in 1977 (Karshenas and Pesaran, 1995), reflecting a situation of profound inequality. During 1983–1988, Iran experienced an economic recession and increased poverty, mainly due to the war with Iraq and the drop in oil revenue (Assadzadeh and Paul, 2001). However, prolonged mobilization against Iraq and the safety nets for the poor probably contributed to avoiding increased inequality. In the 1990s, income inequality remained constant at around 43 per cent (Adams and Page, 2003).

For the six MENA countries that implemented SAPs under agreements with the International Monetary Fund (IMF) and World Bank, increasing inequality observed in several other developing countries following adoption of such policies seems not to have occurred, at least for the period under consideration.[2] Nonetheless, evidence on the pattern of inequality during the period does not reveal an indisputable and clear tendency towards declining income inequality in MENA. Moreover, in the second phase of economic reform, in the 1990s, inequality began to rise unambiguously in Turkey (from 1987) and in Egypt (from 1995).

EXPLAINING INCOME DISTRIBUTION TRENDS IN THE MENA REGION

Very little has been written on income distribution in the MENA region as a whole. It is argued that given the little evidence of growing integration of MENA in global markets, it is unlikely that trade has had much long-term impact on growth, income distribution, and poverty in the MENA region. Thus, the 'pro-poor' pattern of growth in MENA reflects another aspect of globalization—the substantial role played by remittances earned and sent home by workers labouring abroad and, to a lesser degree, the impact of aid flows, associated with oil rents and geopolitical concerns. In many Middle Eastern countries, these large resource flows helped to finance both a public investment boom and a comprehensive set of commodity-based consumer subsidies (Page and Van Gelder, 2002: 8–9).

Along with these factors, declining income inequality in MENA has also been attributed to government jobs and a strong social network in which families provide sustenance to one another during hard times, and income is redistributed through religious and charity arrangements (UNDP, 2002; Adams and Page, 2003).

In the 1960s, inequality in the region was high, with Turkey reporting the highest Gini coefficient at 55, while Egypt and Tunisia had similar levels of inequality, with Gini coefficients around 42. In the 1960s and 1970s, with rare exceptions, MENA countries pursued import-substituting industrialization (ISI) strategies, to varying degrees, with different ideological underpinnings, involving central planning and a large public sector. During the period, the MENA region as a whole experienced relatively high growth rates and poverty was reduced (Kossaifi, 1998).

The impact of the ISI strategy on income distribution is less clear, since no empirical study has attempted to establish a relationship between income distribution and industrial protection in MENA. From the experiences of the countries reviewed here, one may tentatively argue that ISI may initially have had a progressive distributional impact by generating significant economic growth and raising demand for labour. However, by the middle of the 1970s, the infant industries had difficulties growing up and becoming internationally competitive because of their high costs. They were highly capital intensive, and even in the best of circumstances, did not provide large numbers of jobs (Richards and Waterbury, 1998), thus failing to keep pace with the rapidly expanding workforces. Agriculture was generally penalized by exchange rate and pricing policies, despite the fact that the majority of the labour force was still in agriculture (Richards and Waterbury, 1998).

However, governments in MENA countries pursued generous employment policies in the public sector that helped to provide job opportunities to a growing part of the population in the region. This also meant that a large part of the labour force became eligible for formal modes of social protection. Nonetheless, while public employment is likely to have promoted a more equal income distribution (Adams and Page, 2003), upward mobility was confined to the middle class and most government jobs were for the educated (Amin, 1974; Hansen, 1991). Evidence also shows that the redistributive impact of social insurance systems has been limited and, in some cases, regressive, favouring certain groups like the military and technocrats (Nasr, 2001).

Moreover, the quadrupling of the international price of oil in 1973 led to a major economic boom in MENA, with both oil and non-oil countries sharing the massive rents that characterized the period. The benefits of the oil boom were partly redistributed to the population in the region through various channels: massive build-up of public investment, migration, remittances and high wages. However, the oil windfall also increased inequality in various ways. First, oil windfalls led to further concentration of power and wealth in the hands of a few elites, while corruption and family connections remained the main channel of social mobility (El-Ghonemy, 1998; Amin, 1974). Second, the impact of remittances on income distribution is less clear than their effect on poverty (Richards and Waterbury, 1998). In Egypt, for example, there is evidence from the 1980s that while emigrant remittances indirectly reduced rural poverty by raising the farm wages for those left behind, international remittances were mainly received by the higher income-earning villagers (see Richards and Waterbury, 1998). More data on the actual amounts of remittances received by the bottom decile are needed to fully evaluate the equity consequences of migration and remittances in MENA.

Third, with oil revenues, governments in both oil and mixed oil economies tended to ignore the need for structural reforms. As a result, to varying degrees, MENA countries failed to reduce their dependency on oil, keeping unchanged a distorted production structure characterized by a significant contribution of services to output and a limited role for manufacturing, including small and medium-sized enterprises (SMEs). This has, in turn, resulted not only in little change in the pattern of income distribution, but also in the inability of the economy to provide jobs to a growing population and improve economic performance.

From the 1950s through the 1970s, governments in the MENA region progressively redistributed income from the upper to the lower strata through land reforms, universal food subsidies and free access to education. However, while redistributive policies limited increases in the Gini coefficient, they were not sufficient to significantly reduce inequality. Land reform reduced inherited inequalities, but was not effective in either generating sustainable incomes for the lowest quintiles or providing land to the landless (see Paciello, 2006). While food subsidies helped mitigate income and asset inequality by protecting the purchasing power of the poor, it left untouched the structural causes of inequality. Finally, the distribution of education remained very uneven despite the emphasis of governments on expanding human capital, leaving a few highly educated people coexisting with relatively large numbers of people who were illiterate.

With the collapse of oil prices, oil revenues started declining after 1985. The 1991 Gulf war caused further damage to the region, and, although oil prices recovered modestly after the war, they later fell again, reaching a low in 1999, before rising again in recent years. Following the end of the oil boom, economic growth slowed down in all countries of the MENA region. The fall in oil prices dramatically affected the budgets of the oil exporting countries and international trade balances, while countries with significant out-migration to the Gulf, especially Egypt, Jordan and Yemen, experienced declining demand for their labour. Moreover, Arab workers in Gulf countries began to be replaced by emigrants from Asian countries, resulting in reduced demand for unskilled Arab workers in the Gulf. In addition, as demographic pressures in the Gulf states led to larger numbers of highly educated nationals seeking work, Gulf countries intensified efforts to nationalize their labour forces.

Thus, during the 1990s, the annual growth rates of foreign labour in the Gulf Cooperation Council (GCC) countries fell sharply. As labour migration decelerated and demand shifted away from unskilled Arab labour, the positive impact of remittances on income distribution diminished in the Arab countries, with large out-migration to the Gulf (see Paciello, 2006). Yet, although international migration and remittances continued to play a role in poverty alleviation, this was not large enough to prevent poverty from increasing. The prospects of Arab migration of skilled labour to Gulf countries are also likely to diminish since unemployment rates in the Gulf countries are on the increase and GCC nationals are entering the labour force with higher and higher levels of academic education (Girgis, 2002). Finally, although Algeria, Morocco and Tunisia have been less affected by the declining demand for labour in the Gulf countries since the majority of migrants seek work in Europe, restrictive European Union (EU) migration policy has increasingly hampered legal labour migration from the three countries. Probably because illegal migration has increased, and with it, disparities among migrants, benefits from remittances have decreased for those at the bottom rung of the income ladder (see Paciello, 2006).

Faced with rising economic difficulties associated with serious foreign debt problems and falling oil prices, many MENA countries implemented macroeconomic stabilization programmes in the 1980s. The implementation of orthodox policy reforms generated adverse distributive outcomes, except in MENA, which apparently did not experience a sharp increase in inequality. However, the evidence is often unclear and disputable; apart from Turkey, no serious empirical study exists that analyses the impact of either the overall SAP package or single policy components on inequality in the MENA region.

Overall, the pattern of income inequality observed in Algeria, Egypt, Jordan, Morocco and Tunisia can be explained by the following factors: (a) the lack of recent, good quality data; (b) the slow and gradual pace of structural reforms; and (c) varying social expenditure, despite fiscal adjustment. As structural reforms go ahead, income disparities are likely to widen, as indicated by the case of Egypt. In Turkey, where SAPs began earlier, in 1980, rising income inequality in the second phase of adjustment is associated with the deregulation of domestic financial markets and capital account liberalization (Yeldan, 2000).

THE IMPACT OF STABILIZATION AND STRUCTURAL ADJUSTMENT POLICIES ON INEQUALITY

This section seeks to highlight the distributional impact of structural adjustment policies in the MENA region. It shows that the slow and gradual pace of structural reforms in the region, with little impact on the economic structure and no major labour reallocation among sectors, has been responsible for the trends in income inequality observed in Algeria, Egypt, Jordan, Morocco and Tunisia.

The timetable for economic reform and liberalization in the MENA countries, with the exception of Turkey, has generally lagged behind other developing countries undergoing macroeconomic adjustment, perhaps owing to the protection offered by oil riches (Hakimian, 1998). A recent study by the World Bank concludes that while MENA countries have done very well in relation to economic stabilization, they have lagged behind in terms of structural reforms, with significant reform only happening from the mid-1990s (Dasgupta, Keller and Srinivasan, 2002). To avoid major social transformations and dislocations, and to maintain the political status quo, some governments in MENA opted for gradual economic reforms. This also means that, in MENA, control over the distribution of resources continued to be concentrated in the hands of the old ruling elites, while imposition of the SAPs was accompanied by significant repression and reduced political freedom (Dillman, 2001).

Macroeconomic Stabilization[3]

Under SAPs, all MENA countries in the sample, with the exception of Algeria, were successful in resuming growth.[4] All countries narrowed their budget deficits and improved their current account balance.[5] Moreover, while the consumer price index continued to rise in all the countries, its rate of increase slowed down in Egypt, Jordan, Morocco and Tunisia.[6] In addition, compared to the crisis periods before introduction of the SAPs, external debt as a percentage of gross domestic product (GDP) declined in all countries, with the exception of Algeria.[7] However, this reduction was mainly the result of debt relief obtained from official creditors. It is furthermore important to note that while resuming growth, such countries were not able to restore the sustained economic growth of the pre-crisis period. Also, economic growth remained unstable and susceptible to internal and external shocks over the 1990s. Moreover, as a result of budget deficit reduction, the rate of public investment fell in all the countries, while private investment did not recover as expected. Finally, in Turkey, inequality deteriorated in the context of an unstable macroeconomic environment during the second phase of SAPs (1989–1994), following the financial deregulation of 1989. The result was a financial crisis in 1994 (Yeldan, 2000).

Structural Reforms

Structural reforms here refer to sets of policies aimed at increasing an economy's market orientation. This subsection will assess the extent to which the main policy components of structural reforms have been implemented in the MENA region and are likely to have affected income distribution.

Globalization and trade liberalization
While standard theory predicts that trade liberalization will improve inequality between and within poor countries endowed with abundant labour, new evidence suggests that trade liberalization may play a significant role in raising inequality and limiting efforts at poverty reduction (Cornia and Kiiski, 2001; UNCTAD, 1997).

Under SAPs, MENA countries have reformed their economies pursuing trade liberalization gradually. Various studies have reached the conclusion that the region, excluding Turkey, lags behind, both in terms of speed of global integration and extent of trade liberalization (Srinivasan, 2002; Page and Van Gelder, 2002; World Bank, 1995). The MENA region's trade integration has generally remained unchanged over the last twenty years, in contrast to the increase observed for all other regions except Sub-Saharan Africa (Srinivasan, 2002). Growth of real trade ratios (exports plus imports as a share of GDP) in the MENA region—aside from oil-related volatility—has been weak and well below the world average, while foreign direct investment is among the lowest in the world (see Paciello, 2006). Moreover, with the exception of GCC countries, MENA continues to be sheltered by high protection levels (Srinivasan, 2002). This slow pace of dismantling trade barriers has made MENA trade protection the second highest among the world's developing country regions (Srinivasan, 2002).

The slow pace of trade liberalization is likely to have marginally affected the pattern of income distribution in MENA countries. Since the mid-1990s, all the countries reviewed in this chapter have committed to further liberalize their trade regimes, by joining the World Trade Organization (WTO) and the EU Mediterranean Partnership. The obligation to liberalize trade and reduce customs duties by joining the WTO or partnership agreements with the European Union is likely to speed up trade liberalization in the future. While little is known about the impact of such agreements on poverty and inequality, a few studies that have examined poverty and distributional outcomes of the trade policy reforms embodied in the Euro-Mediterranean agreements have underlined the regressive impact of those agreements (Diwan, 1997; Joffé, 1998; Henry and Springborg, 2001). The elimination of tariff barriers may increase imports and trade deficits, diminish state revenue from tariffs and adversely affect social welfare programmes administered by the state. MENA countries will need to fully benefit from trade liberalization and minimize the social costs of openness to ensure its costs are not larger than its benefits.

Financial liberalization
Domestic financial sector reform has been one of first structural changes introduced in many developing countries. It began in the 1970s in Latin America, spread to Africa and Asia in the 1980s, and to Eastern Europe in the 1990s. The distributive impact of such measures is difficult to capture, but the data are suggestive of a negative impact (Cornia and Kiiski, 2001).

With the exception of Turkey, the development of local capital markets and their integration into the international capital market appear to be less advanced in MENA than in Latin American and Asian economies, where financial reforms generally started earlier (Creane and others, 2003). While the speed and depth of the reforms have varied among countries, overall, the experiences of the MENA countries with financial sector reforms have been marked by gradualism and caution. MENA's record in attracting external equity capital has been even more dismal than in attracting foreign direct investment (FDI) (Hakimian, 1998). So, as capital accounts have not been fully liberalized, the immediate impact of the Asian upheaval on MENA countries, with the exception of Turkey, was limited.

While financial liberalization was a major feature of adjustment from very early on in Turkey, in the other MENA countries, important financial sector reform steps were only taken in the second half of the 1990s, with the gradual liberalization of interest rates. To avoid shocks that could undermine the stability of the financial system, greater interest rate liberalization was undertaken in Algeria, Jordan, Morocco and Tunisia, in parallel with strengthening the financial situation of banks (Jbili, Enders and Treichel, 1997; Creane and others, 2003). The reform of the domestic financial system was accompanied by gradual capital account liberalization. Full current account convertibility was generally established around 1993, but the process of foreign exchange market liberalization accelerated during the second half of the 1990s (see Paciello, 2006).

Labour market liberalization
Labour market reforms, which have taken place in several developing countries with structural adjustments in the 1980s and 1990s, include reducing minimum wages, workers' rights and employment protection. Under SAPs, MENA Governments have attempted to reform labour laws and regulations in areas such as job security and wage regulation. However, they have been cautious and, as noted in a World Bank (2004b: 150) report, "labour market reforms have been absent from the policy agenda in MENA for much of the past decade". Indeed, the MENA countries reviewed in this chapter, with the exception of Turkey, began to reform their labour laws for more labour market flexibility in the second half of the 1990s: in 1996, Algeria amended the labour law it passed in 1990; Jordan and Tunisia approved a new labour code in 1996, while Egypt and Morocco did so in 2003 (ILO, Natlex database). Nonetheless, despite slow labour institutional change, there is evidence of increasing labour market flexibility in MENA during the 1990s (see below).

Privatization
Many studies show that the MENA region lags substantially behind other regions with regards to privatization (ERF, 2002). However, MENA governments'

privatization efforts seem to have accelerated in the late 1990s. In Morocco, the privatization programme was announced in 1985, but only got under way in 1993 (Pfeifer, 1998; Richards and Waterbury, 1998). The monarchy favoured a gradual approach. One of the criteria for inclusion in the initial list of enterprises to be sold was lack of surplus labour, with all buyers required to retain the inherited workforce for at least five years. However, since 1999, privatization has been moving into more previously avoided strategic areas where there are more jobs at stake. Since then, the number of layoffs and company closures has increased (El-Mikawy and Pripstein Posusney, 2000). In Tunisia, privatization has been the weakest component of the reform (Richards and Waterbury, 1998; Dillman, 2001).

In Egypt in the early 1990s, mass lay-offs were avoided by an arrangement with the Government whereby workers were entitled to keep jobs in the privatized companies for at least three years (El-Mikawy and Pripstein Posusney, 2000). Early retirement schemes were widely used to reduce excess workers in the privatized companies (Korayem, 2002). In Jordan, moves toward privatization were sluggish over 1986–1995, and privatization of major firms, including telecommunications, did not occur before 1999 (World Bank, 2004a). In Algeria, despite a privatization law in August 1995 and a new telecommunications law in August 2000, no major state enterprise sale took place (ERF, 2002; Dillman, 2001; IMF, 2000). On the whole, privatization left unchanged the structure of power in MENA societies and actually reinforced the control of state elites and their allies over resources (Dillman, 2001).

Labour Market Performance

Wages

In the second half of the 1980s and through the 1990s, most countries of the region experienced significant declines in real wages, with Algeria and Egypt registering the largest declines (ERF, 2000; World Bank, 2004b). Between 1992 and 1996, Algeria experienced significant wage erosion, with real wages declining by more than 30 per cent in four years (World Bank, 2004b). In Egypt, real wages started declining across all sectors in 1982 and continued to fall under SAPs through the 1990s, albeit at a slower pace (ERF, n.a.). However, between 1998 and 2001, real wages appeared to improve, although at a faster rate in state-owned enterprises than in the formal private sector. In Morocco and Tunisia, in the first years of SAPs, while the expansion of labour demand for low-skill work was a key aspect of poverty reduction in both countries, an important element of cost reduction in export-oriented industries was substantial real wage compression and increasing labour flexibility (Berberoglu, 1998).

In the 1990s, average real wages in the manufacturing sector apparently stagnated in Morocco (World Bank, 2002a), while in Tunisia, compensation per salaried worker increased (Page and Van Gelder, 2002). However, there were differences among sectors. Average annual growth in real wages during 1989–1994 was negative in manufacturing, where most non-agricultural workers are employed, and in tradable services during 1989–1997. In construction, average annual growth of real wages turned negative in the second part of the 1990s. Such differences in the growth in real wages could be partly behind the increased income inequality in urban areas observed in Tunisia.

In Turkey, there was a sizeable regression in real wages during the 1980s, with the benefits mostly captured by rentiers through higher interest incomes (Boratav, Türel and Yeldan, 1996). Wage data in the 1989–1993 period strongly suggest that the substantial improvement in wages was almost totally due to what was happening in the formal sector (Boratav, Yeldan and Köse, 2000). Wage gaps between large/small and public/private enterprises widened significantly and exceeded the magnitude of the early 1980s.

Apart from Turkey, information on wage inequality in MENA is very scarce. Using a Theil wage inequality index based on data published by United Nations Industrial Development Organization (UNIDO), a World Bank (2004b) report concluded that, in the 1990s, MENA had some of the highest wage inequality levels for the manufacturing sector, compared to other regions. Non-oil exporting countries seem to have much lower levels of wage inequality compared to the oil-exporting countries. Moreover, wage inequality is said to have declined steadily between 1965 and 1985, and then risen until 1995, only to decline again thereafter. However, more research is needed in order to better understand how wage inequality has evolved in the MENA region under SAPs.

Unemployment

Despite shortcomings in employment and unemployment data in the world in general, unemployment has been on the increase in almost all MENA countries and is higher than anywhere else in the world, with Algeria, Iraq as well as the West Bank and Gaza Strip having the highest rates (UNDP, 2002; see Paciello, 2006). The estimates would be even higher if official estimates included underemployment and disguised employment (see Fergany, 2001). While this situation may be attributed to structural adjustments, there can be no doubt that implementation of current economic policies has led to the aggravation of unemployment in the absence of any job creation strategy. The result is that structural adjustment policies have been unable to create sufficient jobs to keep pace with the steady increase in the work force.

The way in which unemployment has affected inequality in the region has been little studied and remains unclear. For example, the period of adjustment in Algeria brought an improvement in income distribution, but unemployment increased dramatically, reaching the highest level in MENA, of 29.9 per cent in 2000. In Egypt, over the 1995–2000 period, for which more disaggregated data is available, unemployment improved at the national level, but rose in Metropolitan and urban Upper Egypt. In particular, these two regions also experienced worsening income distribution over the same period.

It is clear that the link between unemployment and inequality needs to be further investigated, especially in relation to the profile of the unemployed in the MENA region. It is commonly acknowledged that unemployment in the MENA region is characterized by the following main features: a) it tends to affect young people, with medium to high levels of education; b) it is essentially an urban phenomenon; c) it is higher for women than for men, with the exception of Algeria; and d) it is not correlated with poverty (World Bank, 2004b). Nonetheless, in Algeria, while the unemployed corresponded to the above-mentioned profile between 1987 and 1995, unemployment later spread to older adults and to those with lower levels of education, but declined for youth (World Bank, 1999a). In Morocco, in the late 1990s, unemployment in urban areas started increasing among household heads (primary breadwinners aged 35–44 years) (World Bank, 2002a). Finally, evidence from countries for which data are available, namely Algeria, Egypt, Jordan and Morocco, suggests that the poor are more and more likely to be unemployed (see Paciello, 2006).

Public employment
Under SAPs, the percentage of public sector workers in the labour force declined, largely in response to policies to reduce the size of budget deficits. Reduction in the role of government in employment creation has thus contributed to unemployment problems, especially among the youth. During the first phases of SAPs, albeit to different degrees, MENA countries reduced the size of their public sectors gradually. Thus, in the mid-1990s, in some countries, the state was still playing a major role as employer. However, efforts at reducing public sector employment, especially in state-owned enterprises, intensified after then. At the end of the 1990s, although most MENA countries still had a large share of public sector employment, the role of public sector employment as a tool to promote more equal distribution and ensure social mobility became questionable. Recent data on the distribution of wages in Egypt and Morocco suggest, for example, that between 40 to 60 per cent of public sector employees belong to the highest income quintile, whereas less than 5 per cent were in the poorest segment of the population (World Bank, 2004b).

Informal sector

During the 1990s, the informal market in MENA became the last resort for the unemployed and underemployed who could not be absorbed by the formal labour market. Despite the numerous problems with statistical data, there is evidence that, in most Arab countries, the 1990s witnessed steady growth in the number of those in the informal sector, where income is inadequate and social protection is lacking (ERF, 2000; El-Khawaga, 2000; World Bank, 2004b). In Turkey, even though informal employment is a perennial feature of Turkish labour markets, intensification of this process is observed, especially after 1989, the post-financial liberalization era (Boratav, Yeldan and Köse, 2000). In Egypt, the majority of jobs created in the private sector in the 1988–1998 decade were unprotected by legal contracts (Assad, 2000). For Morocco during the first half of the 1990s, the average annual growth rate of employment in the informal sector was about double that of the formal sector (El-Khawaga, 2000; World Bank, 2002a).

REDISTRIBUTIVE POLICIES

During the 1950s, 1960s and 1970s, Governments in the MENA region played a positive role in redistributing income from upper to lower strata. Land reforms, universal food subsidies and free access to education were the main redistributive policies implemented by Middle Eastern Governments at the initial stage of development. There were, of course, differences among countries in the emphases put on each redistributive policy component, but in general, quite high levels of public expenditure were allocated to social sectors, especially to education. Petroleum revenues in the 1970s permitted many Governments in the region to maintain very high levels of social expenditure and to finance generous welfare systems in the form of food subsidies and other social transfers to large portions of the population. The impact of social policy from the 1960s to the 1980s can be seen in the impressive progress in indices relating to health, education and welfare (Doraid, 2000). During the economic crisis that followed the end of the oil boom which preceded the adoption of SAPs, there was downward pressure on social spending in Algeria, Egypt and Jordan. In contrast, in Tunisia, the priority on social welfare remained: military spending was reduced and public expenditure on education, health and social security increased from 29.3 per cent in 1983 to 34.1 per cent in 1986 (El-Ghonemy, 1998). This may partly explain why inequality worsened in Algeria, Egypt and Jordan, but not in Tunisia, before the implementation of SAPs.

Even with SAPs, Governments in MENA, with the exception of Algeria, did not drastically cut social spending, at least over the period for which data are available (see Paciello, 2006). This was probably an important factor that helped to avoid a sudden increase in income polarization during the first phase of SAPs. However, MENA countries have differed in their efforts to adjust social spending, with Jordan and Tunisia allocating most to social expenditure. Thus, for Tunisia, during the early phase of SAPs, inequality improved, partly because the poor benefited from increased social transfers that helped to avoid falls in disposable household incomes and real wages (El-Ghonemy, 1998). Unlike the other MENA countries, social spending in Morocco, especially for education, fell in the first phase of restructuring (1986–1991), but then rose in the 1990s.

However, there is clear evidence that the redistributive role of the state has been eroding in MENA (see Paciello, 2006). Jordan increased social security and health expenditures, while public spending on education decreased with the expansion of the private university education system. Jordan continued to spend a larger share on defence, the highest in MENA. Also, in Morocco, the rise of social spending in the 1990s was driven by a major increase in social insurance expenditure, while public spending on health and social assistance programmes was almost unchanged. In Egypt, there was an evident increase in education expenditure and, while the health budget increased slightly in the second half of the 1990s, it remained under-funded at a low 1.3 per cent of GDP. Moreover, one should bear in mind that, while social spending was pro-tected, too much of it went for paying salaries of the large number of public employees.[8] Social spending has not been sufficient to prevent deterioration in the quality of health and educational services. Lastly, there is evidence from Egypt, Morocco and Tunisia that, although health care and education should be free, private expenditure on those services is on the increase, in particular for the poor.[9]

Two further considerations are needed with regard to tax policy and the system of social protection. Similar to other developing countries, tax policy in MENA has not been effective in redistributing income from the rich to the poor, as it has mainly relied on social security and indirect taxes (Islam,1998). Under SAPs, reforms calling for the institution of a value-added tax (VAT) have been adopted, and the general trend has been towards less tax progress-iveness.

The impact of formal social security schemes on income distribution is likely to have been regressive. Some schemes have generally covered only part of the formal sector by reflecting the ranking of the power structure, with correspondingly unequal benefits and unequal treatment of individuals (Nasr, 2001; El-Ghonemy, 1998). In Egypt, in 1998, nearly 47 per cent of all workers and 36 per cent of non-agricultural workers were without social insurance coverage (World Bank, 2004b; Loewe, 2000). In Morocco, in 1998, the social insurance system protected only about 23 per cent (2.3 million) of the total workforce of 10.1 million (World Bank, 2002a). In sum, because of significantly increased unemployment, lack of job creation and deterioration of real wages, social protection needs in MENA have increased, but the current social protection system is hardly sufficient to reach all in need (Nasr, 2001).

Food Subsidies

Food subsidy policies have been widespread in MENA countries, with the exception of Turkey and Lebanon, where food subsidies have been limited. Programmes of food subsidies were introduced in the 1970s, peaking in the 1980s. Prior to adjustment reforms, they were typically universal and were the largest social transfer programmes in the region, benefiting all consumers (World Bank, 1999c).

Although food subsidies have been widely criticized as being poorly targeted, fiscally unsustainable and a cause of macroeconomic problems (World Bank, 1999c), there is agreement that they have been a major tool of income distribution in the region and have made substantial contributions to the welfare and nutritional intake of the poor.[10] This helps to explain why food subsidies have been politically difficult to abolish in the MENA region, as illustrated by food riots in Algeria, Egypt, Jordan, Morocco, and Tunisia in the 1980s. Despite inadequate targeting of the poor when measured in terms of absolute incidence, subsidies have proved to be progressive in relative terms, constituting important transfers to the poor, particularly in Algeria, Egypt, Morocco and Tunisia, but less so in Jordan. In the 1980s and 1990s, food subsidy programmes became fiscally unsustainable, and many Governments in the region undertaking SAPs began to reduce the fiscal costs of such programmes. However, for political reasons, food subsidy reforms were implemented on a slow and gradual basis (see Paciello, 2006). This could partially explain why income distribution did not worsen during the earlier stage of SAPs. In 1995, food subsidies still represented large shares of GDP in all the countries, with the exception of Algeria (see World Bank, 1999c). By the end of the 1990s, Algeria and Jordan had completely abandoned their food subsidy schemes. Unfortunately, data on income distribution for these countries in the late 1990s are not available.

Education Policies

From the 1960s to the 1980s, Governments in MENA made considerable efforts to improve education. Education became accessible to almost all and typically received the largest share of social expenditure (see Paciello, 2006). Due to this strong emphasis on public provision of education, MENA countries made dramatic advances in educational indicators, starting from very low bases during this period (UNDP, 2002). Mass education systems set up in most Middle Eastern countries facilitated real social mobility, at least at the early stages (Richards and Waterbury, 1998). Despite SAPs, MENA countries have protected expenditures on education, albeit to different degrees, except in Algeria. Through the 1990s, enrolment rates at the primary, secondary and tertiary levels continued to improve, with the exception of Iran, Iraq and Oman (see Paciello, 2006).

Despite improvements in educational attainment since the 1970s, the distribution of education has been uneven in most MENA countries. A few highly educated people have coexisted with a relatively large number of illiterates (see Paciello, 2006). Since 1970, in all the countries reviewed in this chapter, primary school enrolment rates expanded slower than secondary school rates. Notwithstanding, secondary enrolment in most MENA countries lagged behind other countries at similar income levels (Shafik, 1994). There are, of course, differences among countries. In Jordan and Turkey, more than three quarters of adults could read and write in 2000, while the problem of illiteracy was particularly severe in Egypt and Morocco. In 2000, Morocco had the lowest ratios at the primary, secondary and tertiary levels. Secondary enrolment rates remain particularly low in Algeria, Morocco and Turkey. There are also significant disparities among regions and between rural and urban areas.[11]

Poverty is strongly associated with lack of education in all the countries reviewed in this chapter (see Paciello, 2006), further reducing the chances of good employment for the poor and for their children. In the context of structural adjustment, and as a result of further worsening of the quality of government education and increasing private expenditure on education, dropouts among the lowest deciles are high in the MENA countries.[12]

Education policies in MENA countries have been biased in favour of higher education, against rural areas and against females (Shafik, 1994), with adverse implications for inequality. Since the 1970s, despite high illiteracy rates and low primary school enrolments, MENA countries' public expenditures progressively have shifted towards higher education, at the expense of basic education for which public expenditure has been disproportionately low (see Paciello, 2006). Education expenditure seems less unbalanced in Tunisia and Turkey. Moreover, wages, salaries and benefits have constituted a very high share of current expenditure, especially at the primary level (Shafik, 1994; UNDP, 2002).

With the costly, but successful effort throughout the region to expand secondary and university education, straining budgets and raising enrolments, it was impossible to maintain education standards (Richards and Waterbury, 1998). The results were low-quality education services and a consequent bias against basic education and rural areas. In the 1980s, access to higher stages of education became critically dependent on financial means. Private tutoring in secondary and higher education, for example, became widespread as a supplement to public education. As students from low-income families could not afford private lessons, the constitutional guarantee of free education at all levels became skewed in favour of the well-to-do (UNDP, 2002).

As seen above, structural adjustment policies did not address the shortcomings of education systems in the region. Private tuition has become even more indispensable to obtain good grades in public examinations for access to higher education, especially in disciplines considered most likely to lead to better career prospects (UNDP, 2002). Yet, the expansion of expensive, privately-funded education in many countries is likely to further worsen the problem of distribution as long as only the better-off have access to it. In addition, the problems of low quality and relevance have persisted during the period of adjustment, leading to a significant mismatch between the labour market and development needs in MENA. Given the high rate of unemployment among the educated youth of the region and consequent low rates of return to education, education may be losing its ability to provide social mobility in MENA countries.

CONCLUSION

This chapter argues that the MENA region is characterized by two main income distribution trends. First, contrary to the idea that the region had one of the largest improvements in income distribution over time, the relatively high inequality in MENA countries seems to have changed little over fairly long periods of time. Second, the increasing inequality observed in several developing countries, following the adoption of stabilization and structural adjustment policies, seems not to have occurred in MENA, except in Turkey.

The oil-dominated economy has clearly affected income distribution in both oil and non-oil MENA countries. For countries with little or no oil, while the benefits of the oil boom were partly redistributed to the population in the region through various channels—migration, remittances, high wages and generous welfare policies—the powerful and rich gained more. Moreover, the economic policies of MENA countries failed to reverse dependency on oil, keeping intact distorted economic structures characterized by the significant contribution of services to output and a limited role for manufacturing. This has, in turn, not only resulted in little change to the pattern of income distribution, but also to the inability of the economy to provide and improve jobs for a growing population. In addition, while helping to limit increases in Gini coefficients, the redistributive policies pursued in MENA probably failed to address the causes of inequality at the source.

Under stabilization and adjustment policies, income inequality, as measured by the Gini coefficient, did not worsen in MENA countries, because the pace of structural reforms was slow and social expenditure was protected. However, people's living standards and labour market outcomes were negatively affected: poverty worsened, unemployment increased or remained unchanged, and real wages declined while the informal sectors experienced growth. Progress with stabilization remained fragile and structural reforms seemed to have accelerated towards the end of the 1990s. As the pace of structural reforms accelerates and the redistributive role of the state diminishes, MENA countries are more likely to experience further deterioration in their income distributions.

NOTES

[1] For Egypt during 1981–1991, evaluation of inequality trends is based on Gini indices for rural and urban areas.

[2] A full evaluation of the distributive effects of the SAPs is hampered by the lack of more recent data for Gini coefficients for Algeria, Jordan and Turkey.

[3] For data sources and discussion of macroeconomic stabilization in single MENA countries, see Paciello (2006).

[4] For Algeria, our considerations are based on the 1989–1994 period since data on income inequality only covers these years. Turkey is excluded from our evaluation of MENA adjustment experiences presented in this paragraph.

[5] No data on the current account balance is available for Algeria.

[6] Our consideration of trends in the consumer price index (CPI) is based on data until the mid-1990s.

[7] In Morocco, external debts increased until 1990, and then started declining.

[8] For Egypt, UNDP (1998); for Jordan, World Bank (2004a); for Morocco, World Bank (2002a).

[9] For Egypt, UNDP (1998) and Galal (2003); for Morocco, World Bank (2002a); for Tunisia, World Bank (2004c).

[10] For Egypt, Ali and Adams (1996); for Morocco, Morrisson (1991); for Tunisia, Ghazouani and Goaied (2001).

[11] For Algeria, World Bank (1999a); for Egypt, UNDP (1998); for Jordan, UNDP (2004a); for Morocco, World Bank (2001); for Tunisia, World Bank (2000c); and for Turkey, UNDP (1996).

[12] For Egypt, Abu Gazaleh and others (2004); for Jordan, Hanssen Bauer, Pedersen and Tiltnes (1998); for Tunisia, World Bank (2000c); for Turkey, World Bank (2000a). Unfortunately, information regarding trends in drop-out rates is lacking, with the exception of Tunisia.

REFERENCES

Abu Gazaleh, Kawther, Lamia Bulbul, Soheir Hewala and Suadad Najim (2004). *Gender, Education and Child Labour in Egypt.* Gender, Education and Child Labour Series, International Labour Office, Geneva.

Adams, Richard H. Jr, and John Page (2003). Poverty, Inequality and Growth in Selected Middle East and North Africa Countries, 1980–2000. *World Development* 31 (12): 2027–2048.

Ali, Sonia M., and Richard H. Adams Jr (1996). The Egyptian Food Subsidy System: Operation and Effects on Income Distribution. *World Development* 24 (11): 1777–1791.

Amin, Galal A. (1974). *The Modernization of Poverty: A Study in the Political Economy of Growth in Nine Arab Countries, 1945–1970.* Brill, Leiden.

Amin, Galal A. (1999). Globalization, Consumption Patterns and Human Development in Egypt. Working paper 9929, Economic Research Forum for the Arab Countries, Iran and Turkey (ERF), Cairo. www.erf.org/eg

Arincali, Tosun, and Dani Rodrik (1990). An Overview of Turkey's Experience with Economic Liberalization and Structural Adjustment. *World Development* 18 (10): 1343–1350.

Assad, Ragui (2000). The Transformation of the Egyptian Labor Market:1988–1998. Final Report, Economic Research Forum for the Arab Countries, Iran and Turkey (ERF), Cairo. http://www.iceg.org/NE/projects/labor/transformation.pdf

Assadzadeh, Ahmad, and Satya Paul (2001). Poverty, Growth and Redistribution. A Case Study of Iran. WIDER Discussion Paper No. 2001/124, UNU/WIDER, Helsinki.

Belkacem, Laabas (2001). Poverty Dynamics in Algeria. Paper presented to the Workshop on the Analysis of Poverty and its Determinants in the MENA Region, Sanaa, Yemen, 31 July–1 August. http://www.erf.org.eg/html/Laabbas.pdf

Berberoglu, Berch (1998). Unemployment, Low Wages, and Income Inequality: The Triangle of Poverty in the Middle East and North Africa. In Wassim Shahin and Ghassan Dibeh (eds). *Earnings Inequality, Unemployment, and Poverty in the Middle East and North Africa.* Greenwood Press, Westport: 185–204.

Boratav, Korkut, Erinc A. Yeldan and Ahmed H. Köse (2000). Globalization, Distribution and Social Policy: Turkey, 1980–1998. Working Paper No. 20, Series 1, Center for Economic Policy Analysis (CEPA), New York.

Boratav, Korkut, Oktar Türel and Erinc Yeldan (1996). Dilemmas of Structural Adjustment and Environmental Policies under Instability: Post-1980 Turkey. *World Development* 24 (2): 373–93.

Cornia, Giovanni A., and Sampasa Kiiski (2001). Trends in Income Distribution in the Post-World War II Period. Evidence and Interpretation. WIDER Discussion Paper No. 2001/89, UNU/WIDER, Helsinki.

Creane, Susan, Rishi Goyal, A. Mushfiq Mobarak and Randa Sab (2003). *Financial Development in the Middle East and North Africa.* International Monetary Fund, Washington, DC. http://www.imf.org/external/pubs/ft/med/2003/eng/creane/index.htm#fig2

Dasagupta, Dipak, Jennifer Keller and T.G. Srinivasan (2002). Reform and Elusive Growth in the Middle East. What Has Happened in the 1990s?. Working Paper No. 25, World Bank, Washington, DC.

Dillman, Bradford (2001). Facing the Market in North Africa. *The Middle East Journal* 55 (2): 198–215.

Diwan, Ishac (1997). Globalization, EU Partnership, and Income Distribution in Egypt. Working Paper No. 12, The Egyptian Centre for Economic Studies, Cairo.

Doraid, Moez (2000). Human Development and Poverty in the Arab States. Paper prepared for the Mediterranean Development Forum, Cairo, March 5–8.

ERF (2000). Economic Trends in the MENA Region. Economic Research Forum for the Arab Countries, Iran and Turkey, Cairo. http://www.erf.org.eg

ERF (2002). Economic Trends in the MENA Region. Economic Research Forum for the Arab Countries, Iran and Turkey, Cairo. http://www.erf.org.eg

ERF (n.a.). *Egypt Country Profile: The Road Ahead for Egypt.* Economic Research Forum for the Arab Countries, Iran and Turkey, Cairo. http://www.erf.org.eg/html/Country_Profile.asp

Fergany, Nader (2001). Aspects of Labour Migration and Unemployment in the Region. Almishkat Centre for Research, Cairo, February.

Galal, Ahmed (2003). Social Expenditure and the Poor in Egypt. Working Paper No. 89, Egyptian Centre for Economic Studies, Cairo.

Ghazouani, Samir and Mohamed Goaied (2001). The Determinants of Urban and Rural Poverty in Tunisia. Paper presented at the Workshop on the 'Analysis of Poverty and its Determinants in MENA Region', Sanaa, Yemen, 31 July–1 August. http://www.erf.org.eg/

El-Ghonemy, M. Riad (1998). *Affluence and Poverty in the Middle East.* Routledge, London.

Girgis, Maurice (2002). Would Nationals and Asians Replace Arab Workers in the GCC?. Paper submitted to the Fourth Mediterranean Development Forum, Amman, Jordan, 6–9 October.

Hakimian, Hassan (1998). From East to West Asia: Lessons of Globalization, Crisis and Economic Reform, SOAS Working Paper No. 82, School of Oriental and African Studies, London.

Hansen, Bent (1991). *The Political Economy of Poverty, Equity, and Growth: Egypt and Turkey.* Oxford University Press, New York.

Hanssen Bauer, Jon, Jon Pedersen and Åge A. Tiltnes (eds) (1998). *Jordanian Society—Living Conditions in the Hashemite Society of Jordan.* Fafo Institute for Applied Social Science, Oslo.

Henry, Clement M., and Robert Springborg (2001). *Globalization and the Politics of Development in the Middle East.* Cambridge University Press, Cambridge.

ILO. *Natlex database,* International Labour Organization. http://www.ilo.org/dyn/natlex/natlex_browse.home

IMF (2000). *Algeria: Recent Economic Development.* IMF Staff Country Report No. 00/105, August, International Monetary Fund, Washington, DC.

Islam, Muhammad Q. (1998). Fiscal Policy and Social Welfare in Selected MENA Countries. In Wassim Shahin and Ghassan Dibeh (eds). *Earnings Inequality, Unemployment, and Poverty in the Middle East and North Africa.* Greenwood Press, Westport: 95–110.

Jbili, Abdelali, Klaus Enders and Volker Treichel (1997). Financial Sector Reforms in Algeria, Morocco and Tunisia: A Preliminary Assessment. IMF Working Paper WP/97/81, International Monetary Fund, Washington, DC.

Joffé, George (ed.) (1998). *Perspective on Development: the Euro-Mediterranean Partnership.* Frank Cass, London.

Kandeel, Ayman, and Jeffrey B. Nugent (1998). Unravelling the Paradox in Egypt's Trend in Income Inequality and Poverty. In Wassim Shahin and Ghassan Dibeh (eds). *Earnings Inequality, Unemployment, and Poverty in the Middle East and North Africa.* Greenwood Press, Westport: 29–50.

Karshenas, Massoud, and Hashim Pesaran (1995). Economic Reform and the Reconstruction of the Iranian Economy. *Middle East Journal* 49 (1): 89–111.

El-Khawaga, Leila Ahmed (2000). Globalization, Social Policies and Labor Markets in Arab Countries: Concepts and Correlations. The Lebanese Center for Policy Studies, Beirut. http://www.lcps-lebanon.org/web04/english/activities/2000/ssprep/khawaja_word.pdf.

Korayem, Karima (2002). How Do the Poor Cope with the Increased Employment Inadequacy in Egypt?. Robert Schuman Centre Working Paper No. 39, European University Institute, Florence.

Kossaifi, George F. (1998). Poverty in the Arab World: Toward a Critical Approach. Paper submitted to the Second Mediterranean Development Forum, Amman, Marrakech, 3–6 September.

El-Laithy, Heba, Michael Lokshin and Arup Banerji (2003). Poverty and Economic Growth in Egypt, 1995–2000. Policy Research Working Paper 3068, World Bank, Washington, DC.

Loewe, Markus (2000). Social Security in Egypt: An Analysis and Agenda for Policy Reform. Working Paper No. 2024, Economic Research Forum for the Arab Countries, Iran and Turkey, Cairo.

El-Mikawy, Noha, and Marsha Pripstein Posusney (2000). Labor Representation in the Age of Globalization: Trends and Issues in Non-oil-based Arab Economies. Paper presented at the Third Mediterranean Development Forum, Cairo, March 5–8.

Morrisson, Christian (1991). Adjustment, Incomes and Poverty in Morocco. *World Development* 19 (11): 1633–51.

Nasr, Salim (2001). Issues of Social Protection in the Arab Region: A Four-Country Overview. Cooperation South 2: 31–48. http://tcdc.undp.org/coopsouth/2001_2/31-48.pdf.

Owen, Roger, and Sevket Pamuk (1998). *A History of Middle East Economies in the Twentieth Century.* I.B. Tauris, London.

Paciello, Maria Cristina (2006). Income Distribution in the Middle East and North Africa, 1960–2000. UN/DESA Working Paper, Department of Economic and Social Affairs, United Nations, New York.

Page, John, and Linda Van Gelder (2002). Globalization, Growth and Poverty Reduction in the Middle East and North Africa, 1970–1999. Paper presented at the Fourth Mediterranean Development Forum, Amman, Jordan, 7–10 April.

Pfeifer, Karen (1998). Does Structural Adjustment Spell Relief from Unemployment? A Comparison of Four IMF 'Success Stories' in the Middle East and North Africa. In Wassim Shahin and Ghassan Dibeh (eds). *Earnings Inequality, Unemployment, and Poverty in the Middle East and North Africa.* Greenwood Press, Westport: 111–52.

Radwan, Samir (1997). Towards Full Employment: Egypt into the 21st Century. Distinguished Lecture Series, The Egyptian Center for Economic Studies, Cairo. www.eces.org.eg

Richards, Alan, and John Waterbury (1998). *A Political Economy of the Middle East.* Westview Press, Boulder, Colorado.

Shafik, Nemat (1994). Big Spending, Small Returns: The Paradox of Human Resource Development in the Middle East. Paper presented at Economic Research Forum Workshop on the Labour Market, Cairo, December.

Srinivasan, T.G. (2002). Globalization in MENA—A Long Term Perspective. The Fourth Mediterranean Development Forum, Jordan, 6–9 October.

UNCTAD (1997). *Trade and Development Report.* United Nations Conference onTrade and Development, Geneva.

UNDP (1996). *Turkey Human Development Report.* United Nations Development Programme, New York.

UNDP (1998). *Egyptian Human Development Report.* United Nations Development Programme, New York.

UNDP (2002). *Arab Human Development Report 2002.* United Nations Development Programme, New York.

UNDP (2004a). *Jordan Human Development Report: Building Sustainable Livelihoods.* United Nations Development Programme, New York.

UNDP (2004b). *Stratègie de Rèduction de la Pauvretè, Etude du phènomène de la pauvretè en Tunisie.* Bureau du Coordonnateur Rèsident en Tunisie, Tunis.

World Bank (1994). *Hashemite Kingdom of Jordan Poverty Assessment.* Volume 1/2, Report No. 12675-JO, October, World Bank, Washington, DC.

World Bank (1995). *Changing the Future: Choosing Prosperity in the Middle East and North Africa.* World Bank, Washington, DC.

World Bank (1999a). *Algeria, Main Report.* World Bank, Washington, DC.

World Bank (1999b). *The World Development Report 1999/00.* World Bank, Washington, DC.

World Bank (1999c). *Consumer Food Subsidy Programs in the MENA Region.* Report 19561, November, World Bank, Washington, DC.

World Bank (2000a). *Turkey Economic Reforms, Living Standards and Social Welfare Study*. Report No. 20029-TU, January 27. World Bank, Washington, DC.

World Bank (2000b). *World Development Report, 2000/2001*. World Bank, Washington, DC.

World Bank (2000c). *Tunisia Social and Structural Review*. World Bank, Washington, DC.

World Bank (2001). *Kingdom of Morocco Poverty Update*. Volumes 1 & 2. World Bank, Washington, DC.

World Bank (2002a). *Kingdom of Morocco: Social Protection Note*. Report No. 22486-MOR, World Bank, Washington, DC.

World Bank (2002b). *Arab Republic of Egypt: Poverty Reduction in Egypt—Diagnosis and Strategy*. Report No. 24234-EGT, Volume 1/2, Main Report, June 29, World Bank, Washington, DC.

World Bank (2004a). *Jordan: Economic development in the 1990s and World Bank assistance, Operations Evaluation Study*. Report 29365, World Bank, Washington, DC.

World Bank (2004b). *Unlocking the Employment Potential in the Middle East and North Africa: Toward a New Social Contract*. MENA Development Reports, World Bank, Washington, DC.

World Bank (2004c). *Republic of Tunisia Development Policy Review: Making Deeper Trade Integration Work for Growth and Jobs*. Report No. 29847-TN, October, World Bank, Washington, DC.

Yeldan, Erinc A. (2000). The Impact of Financial Liberalization and the Rise of Financial Rents on Income Inequality: The Case of Turkey. WIDER Working Paper No. 206, UNU/WIDER, Helsinki.

12

Openness, Trade Liberalization, Inequality and Poverty in Africa

ALEMAYEHU GEDA and ABEBE SHIMELES[1]

For Africa, it is not yet clear if globalisation, defined by increased openness to trade and financial flows, will improve social development and equity or lead to rising inequality and poverty on the continent. In an effort to contribute to the discourse on this important question, this analysis provides a brief review of social development in Africa over the last few decades, while also exploring the patterns of trade and finance that have linked the continent to the rest of the world. The macroeconomic policy framework that guided African policymaking over the last three decades is the lens through which social development, poverty and inequality are further examined. This chapter highlights the major factors underpinning observable patterns of trade, poverty and inequality and concludes with policy recommendations.

SOCIAL PROGRESS IN AFRICA IN THE 1990s[2]

Improving health, education, employment and equality have been long-term, as well as recent Millennium Development Summit goals (MDGs) for Africa. Over the past few decades, the lessons learned, statistics, and data that have accrued now inform the debate on social development policy.

Comparative data from the 1990s show that human development is highly correlated with the status of and access to education and healthcare. A number of countries have reported tangible progress in these sectors as a result of increased spending. Illiteracy rates have declined by nearly half since 1990, though gender disparity has remained largely unchanged. Encouraging results were also recorded for gross enrolment ratios and infant mortality rates, in which North Africa, followed by Eastern and then Southern Africa, showed relatively improved performance (Alemayehu, 2006).

Except for Botswana, Mauritius and Seychelles, poverty appears pervasive in the Eastern and Southern African sub-regions (ESA), where an estimated 50 percent of the population live below the poverty line. In the Central and West

African (CWA) sub-regions, the dire economic situation severely affects the most disadvantaged segments of society, particularly in rural areas. Poverty incidence is lower in North Africa (NA), where approximately 22 per cent of the population live below the poverty line. Unemployment rates, especially in urban areas, remain disproportionately high.

Given the pervasiveness of poverty and the inadequacy of social progress, it is important to ask if there are special features specific to Africa that can help explain the massive privation and inequality overwhelming the continent. Some of the elements that may explicate Africa's severe under-development include; (1) weak initial conditions (such as ailing institutions, human capital and an extractive and lingering colonial history) at the time of independence; (2) the dependence of almost all African countries on primary commodity production and trade; (3) the lack of non-aid financial capital and the alarming level of aid-dependency; (4) the lack of ownership of policies that are invariably imposed on Africa by donors; and (5) the prevalence of conflict and poor governance. The rest of this study is devoted to an examination of these issues in the context of globalisation.

RECENT PATTERNS OF OPENNESS, INEQUALITY AND POVERTY IN AFRICA

The earlier literature written by Africans took extreme openness as one of the major obstacles hindering development[3]. ECA (1989) noted that weaknesses in Africa's productive base, the predominant subsistence and exchange nature of the economy, and its openness (to international trade and finance) have all perpetuated the external dependence of the continent. This report also pointed out that the dominance of the external sector is a striking feature of African economies that leaves them quite vulnerable to exogenous shocks (ECA, 1989). Some other analysts (see Collier and Gunning, 199), however, argue that "lack of openness explains why Africa has grown more slowly than other regions".

Although available data does not support the computation of a comprehensive measure of openness for Africa, the information provided in Table 12.1 and Figure 12.1 are instructive. Table 12.1 shows that exports and imports account for about 60 per cent of Africa's gross domestic product (GDP) (equally divided between exports and imports). In contrast, the share of tax revenue from international trade in total government revenue is only about 12 per cent. Figure 12.1 relates the share of exports and imports in GDP to real per capita growth for 46 countries during the period of 1990–2001. The figure shows a positive correlation between openness and growth (with a correlation coefficient of about 0.30).

TABLE 12.1
Africa: selected indicators of openness (averages for 1990–2001)

African Region	Ratio of exports (X) and imports (M) to GDP	Ratio of exports (X) to GDP	Ratio of foreign direct investment to GDP	Ratio of government subsidies to total public expenditure	Ratio of taxes on international trade to revenue
East & Southern Africa	52.9	25.8	0.6	1.3	9.3
North Africa	60.9	31.7	1.1	6.8	12.1
West Africa	69.8	34.8	1.9	2.5	19.7
Sub-Saharan Africa	57.8	28.5	1.0	1.6	12.2
All Africa	58.1	29.0	1.0	3.5	12.2

Source: Authors' computations based on World Bank (2003a)
Notes: Key: X: Exports of goods and non-factor services
M: Imports of goods and non-factor services
GDP: gross domestic product

FIGURE 12.1
African countries: relationship between openness and growth, 1990–2001

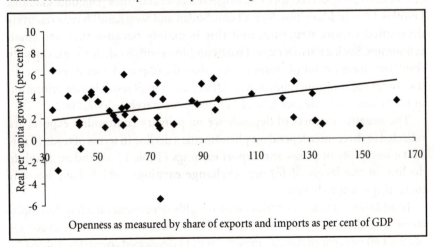

Source: Based on World Bank (2003a)

Openness: The Pattern of Trade in Africa

Table 12.2 shows a deceleration of growth in the volume of sub-Saharan African (SSA) exports from about 15 per cent per annum in the early days of independence to about 3 per cent today. The current level of growth is far below the average for other parts of the world. The share of sub-Saharan Africa in total world export values has also steadily declined by more than half during the period of 1980 to 2001 (see Table 12.3).

African exports are characterized by dependence on primary commodities, and consequently, vulnerability to global economic shocks. Such commodities are also typified by a low income elasticity of demand, volatility, and a secular decline in prices. They generally represent sectors where the scope for technical progress is limited. These characteristics have limited the growth potential of African countries (see, among others, Prebisch, 1950; Singer, 1950; Alemayehu, 2002).

For many African countries, more than 50 per cent of export earnings derive from only three principal primary commodities (see Alemayehu, 2006: Figure 3). For most small mineral exporting countries this figure increases to over 80 per cent. SSA as a whole depends on three major commodities for about 70 per cent of its total export receipts. Only eight out of 43 countries (Djibouti, Gambia, Lesotho, Liberia, Mauritius, Sierra Leon, Sudan and Swaziland) have a relatively diversified export structure, and this is mainly because they are small economies. Such a narrow export base combined with weak domestic capacity results in an export supply response less than the import demand response. In the context of trade liberalization in Africa, the overall result is a deterioration in the balance of trade (see UNCTAD, 2004; Alemayehu, 2002, 2003).

The negative impacts of dependence on primary commodity exports are reflected in three interdependent phenomena: a decline in terms of trade (Table 12.4); instability of prices and export earnings (Table 12.5); and an absolute decline in the levels of foreign exchange earnings, which have become increasingly unpredictable.

In addition, African countries are also highly dependent on a few developed countries as destinations for their exports. For the period of 1955–2000, an average of about 80 per cent of Africa's exports went to developed countries. Table 12.6 shows that this concentration was 84 per cent in 1955 and 71 per cent in 2000. The data also reveal a shift from the European Union to the United States of America, as a frequent recipient of African exports. Although the share of African trade in the world is limited, what happens globally, and in particular in the developed countries, has an enormous impact on Africa (see Alemayehu, 2002).

TABLE 12.2
Growth of export volumes for industrial countries, developing countries and
sub-Saharan Africa, 1965–2002

Region	1965–1973	1973–1980	1980–1986	1993–2002
Industrial countries	9.4	5.4	3.5	6.2
Developing countries	4.9	4.9	4.4	7.1
Sub-Saharan Africa*	15.0	0.1	-1.9	3.1

Sources: Based on World Bank (1987) for 1980–1986, and World Bank (2003c) for 1993–2002.
* Figures exclude South Africa except for 1993–2002.

TABLE 12.3
Trends in sub-Saharan African exports as a share of exports from the developing world,
and for the world as a whole, 1970–2001

Share of exports by region	Ratio of exports between world regions by year							
	1970	1975	1980	1985	1990	1995	2000	2001
Developing countries/world	22.9	27.5	30.1	25.1	19.7	19.9	23.0	23.5
SSA/World	2.0	2.1	2.2	1.6	1.0	0.8	0.8	0.8
SSA/Developing world	8.6	7.4	7.4	6.2	5.2	3.8	3.6	3.5

Source: World Bank (2003a).

TABLE 12.4
Africa: trends in terms of trade, 1990–2001

Year	Terms of Trade Index, 1995=100*				
	East and Southern Africa	North Africa	West Africa	Sub-Saharan Africa	All Africa
1990	101.1	104.4	122.1	108.3	106.9
1991	98.4	114.3	114.4	104.1	107.5
1992	96.1	108.9	106.2	99.6	102.7
1993	95.7	102.2	100.2	97.3	99.0
1994	98.4	98.1	98.6	98.5	98.4
1995	100.0	100.0	100.0	100.0	100.0
1996	100.2	103.6	120.8	106.9	105.7
1997	96.5	103.3	109.6	101.0	101.6
1998	92.4	93.5	91.4	92.2	92.4
1999	94.4	97.3	101.5	96.9	96.8
2000	102.5	115.5	133.5	112.4	113.3
2001	99.5	115.7	125.7	107.8	110.4
Average	98.0	104.7	110.3	102.1	102.9

Source: Computations based on World Bank (2003a)
Notes: * The terms of trade index is given by the ratio of export to import price

TABLE 12.5
Africa: price instability indices and growth in prices for selected primary commodities, 1962–2001

	Price instability index by period				
Commodity	1962–1980	1982–1990	1991–1994	1998–2001	1977–2001
All Non-Fuel Primary Commodities	15.2	8.8	5.0	4.1	11.6
Food	24.4	13.5	3.7	7.2	15.7
Tropical Beverages	25.5	14.1	20.6	5.1	20.8
Cocoa	27.7	15.1	10.2	15.8	18.6
Coffee	28.4	16.8	29.8	8.0	26.0
Agric. Raw Materials	16.6	5.7	4.6	4.4	11.7
Minerals, Ores, Metals	12.3	13.0	6.9	5.8	14.0

	Growth in prices of commodities*				
Commodity	1962–1980	1982–1990	1991–1994	1998–2001	1977–2001
All Non-Fuel Primary Commodities	1.1	-3.1	2.9	-2.1	-2.8
Food	1.0	-2.5	2.6	-0.1	-2.6
Tropical Beverages	2.9	-11.0	15.0	-17.5	-5.6
Cocoa	5.7	-11.7	5.9	-12.6	-6.9
Coffee	2.9	-10.3	17.1	-21.6	-5.1
Agric. Raw Materials	0.5	-1.9	2.3	-0.7	-2.0
Minerals, Ores, Metals	-0.5	0.3	-3.1	3.4	-1.9

Note: The measure of price instability used is:

$$\frac{1}{n}\sum_{t=1}^{n}\left[(|Y(t)-\hat{y}(t)|)/\hat{y}(t)\right]*100$$

Where Y(t) is the observed magnitude of the variable, $\hat{y}(t)$ is the magnitude estimated by fitting an exponential trend to the observed value, and n- is the number of observations. The index reflects the percentage deviation of prices from those predicted by an exponential trend for a given period.

*Data for 1962 to 1994 in constant 1980 dollars. Other years in 1985 constant dollar prices.
Sources: UNCTAD (2002a, 2002b).

TABLE 12.6

Share of African exports to specified destinations, 1955–2000

Year	Europe	USA	Japan	Destination of Exports				
				Other Developed Countries	All Developed Countries	Developing Countries	Former Socialist Countries
1955	70	10	1	3	84	12	4
1960	67	8	1	3	79	13	8
1970	70	7	4	1	82	10	8
1980	49	31	2	1	83	14	3
1990	57	19	1	2	79	17	4
1995	51	18	2	3	74	22	4
2000	43	23	2	3	71	25	4
Average	58.1	16.6	1.9	2.3	78.9	16.1	5

Sources: UNCTAD, *Handbook of International Trade and Development:* various issues.

Foreign Direct Investment (FDI) and Capital Fight

In addition to trade in goods and services, Africa's openness is also characterized by financial flows in and out of the continent. Financial flows include official flows (bilateral and multilateral), private flows, (such as FDI, bank flows, and bonds as well as portfolio flows) and capital flight.

The share of FDI in Africa's GDP, which was about 1 per cent in the 1990s, suggests that Africa's integration into the world financial economy is limited. For all of Africa, the share of FDI in GDP increased from 0.29 per cent (US$1.3 billion) in 1990 to 0.56 per cent (US$2.7 billion) in 1995 and to 1.2 per cent (US$6.3 billion) in 1998. The comparable figures for sub-Saharan Africa (excluding South Africa) during this same period were 0.41 per cent (US$0.76 billion), 1.61 per cent (US$2.7 billion) and 2.4 per cent (US$4.8 billion) respectively.

Relative market size, the existence of mining activity, and the historical pattern of investment together determine the flow of FDI to Africa (see Alemayehu, 2002, 2006). In another study, Bhattacharya, Montiel and Sharma (1997) grouped FDI recipients into three categories: (1) countries that are long-term recipients (Botswana, Mauritius, Seychelles, Swaziland, and Zambia); (2) countries that recorded large increases in the 1990s (Angola, Cameroon, Gabon, Ghana, Guinea, Lesotho, Madagascar, Mozambique, Namibia, Nigeria and Zimbabwe); and (3) countries that have low and/or declining levels of FDI, but with encouraging turnaround (Uganda). Despite overall low levels of FDI, the share of aid and hence debt creating flows, in the total budget of most African countries is significant.

Other private capital flows such as portfolio flows, bank flows and bonds also reflect the openness of African economies. During the late 1970s and early 1980s, private capital flows (described as FDI, private equity flows, and private loans, which included bank, bond and other flows) to SSA were about 9 per cent of total private flows to developing countries. This declined to 1.6 per cent during the period of 1990–1995. This sharp fall was mainly attributed to a rapid deceleration of private loans beginning in the mid-1980s (Bhattacharya, Montiel and Sharma, 1997).

Based on a case study of South Africa, Zambia, Tanzania, Uganda and Zimbabwe, Bhinda and others (1999) recently noted, however, that trends and perceptions are changing. South Africa has received higher flows than all four of the other countries combined (90 per cent of the total SSA since 1992) in absolute terms. However, relative to GDP, Tanzania, Uganda, Zambia and Zimbabwe have received levels ranging from 10 to 15 per cent of GDP. These percentages are as high as the fastest growing Southeast Asian and Latin American countries (see Bhinda and others, 1999; Taylor and Sarno, 1997; Calvo, Leiderman, and Reinhart, 1993, 1996; and Alemayehu, 2006).

Openness also means that Africans now have a choice, legal or illegal, to hold their assets in advanced countries—also known as capital flight. Notwithstanding the complications of measuring capital flight, a study using a rather large data set based on 22 countries from sub-Saharan Africa concluded that the continent has the highest incidence of capital flight, exceeding even the Middle East. Thirty-nine per cent of private portfolios were held outside the continent. Were Africa able to attract back this component of private wealth, the private capital stock would increase by approximately 64 per cent (Collier, Hoeffler, and Pattillo, 1999). Ajayi (1997) estimated capital flight from the severely indebted low-income countries of sub-Saharan Africa to be worth US$22 billion, which is nearly one half of the foreign aid needed in these countries in 1999–2000 (Amoako and Ali, 1998). A review of the empirical literature reveals that the high level of capital flight from Africa, despite the continent's capital scarce characteristics, attributes to overvalued exchange rates, its evaluation by international investors as the riskiest continent, and the level of indebtedness of African countries (Collier, Hoeffler, and Pattillo, 1999; Hermes and Lensink, 1992).[4]

Africa's External Debt Problem

For Africa, an examination of financial openness must also include a discussion of debt. The total external debt of Africa has increased nearly twenty-five fold from a relatively low level of US$14 billion in 1971, to more than US$300 billion in 2003. The major component is outstanding long-term debt, (bilateral followed by multilateral flows) which is generally obtained on concessional terms. Over time, International Monetary Fund (IMF) credits were also increasingly used, along with 'Structural Adjustment' and 'Enhanced Structural Adjustment' facilities until they also became a large component of debt. The accumulation of arrears from these flows is leading to an amassing of debt and its attendant problems. Indebtedness is aggravated by the capitalization of interest and principal arrears, which constitute nearly a quarter of the external debt burden of the continent (Alemayehu, 2003).

Although the share of African debt as a proportion of the total debt of developing countries is low, the relative debt burden born by Africa is extremely heavy compared to its capacity. Excluding grants and net FDI from total inflows, net transfers since 1990 have, in fact, been negative with net outflows actually rising from Africa to developed nations. These outflows from Africa increased from US$3.6 billion in 1985 to nearly US$12.5 billion in 1998. Further, in the 1990s, approximately 35 per cent of aid to Africa went to technical experts from donor countries, thereby increasing outflows from the continent.

The actual size of indebtedness does not typically represent an economic problem in itself, since such debt can usually be mitigated by rescheduling and similar short-term arrangements. However, three inter-related implications of the debt issue deserve mention. First, servicing external debt erodes foreign exchange reserves that might otherwise be available for the purchase of imports. In the past, this has led to an 'import compression problem', where a shortage of foreign exchange adversely affected levels of public and private sector investment and hence, growth and poverty reduction (see for instance, Ndulu, 1986, 1991; Ratso, 1994). Second, the accumulation of a debt stock results in a 'debt overhang' problem that tends to undermine the confidence of both foreign and domestic private investors (see for instance Elbadawi, Ndulu, and Ndung'u, 1997). Finally, debt servicing places enormous fiscal pressure on many African nations. This may explain to some extent, the high fiscal deficits and decline in the share of public investment in GDP since the late 1970s. Naturally, a reduction in public investment will tend to have adverse consequences for physical and social infrastructure, which are vital for social development. This outcome is significant given that public sector investments, in particular in the low income countries of Africa, crowd-in private investment (see Alemayehu, 2002, 2003).

The performance of African economies, coupled with a mounting debt burden, surely indicates that they are incapable of simultaneously servicing their debt and attaining a reasonable level of economic growth, let alone addressing the issues of poverty alleviation and social development. The options made available to highly indebted poor countries (HIPC) since 1996 are not only besieged by much conditionality, but also fail to offer a sustainable solution to Africa's financial and trade problems (see Alemayehu, 2003).

OPENNESS AND INEQUALITY IN AFRICA

Although global interdependence takes the form of both finance and trade, the focus here is on trade liberalization because of Africa's under-developed financial sector and its relative isolation (apart from aid) from global financial markets.[5] Africa's trade, though very small from the rest of the world's point view (SSA share in world exports is about 1 per cent), is dominant and vital, from the African perspective. Trade share in each country's GDP averages about 80 per cent.

The empirical literature identifies various channels through which trade liberalization has impacted Africa, including the levels and composition of investment, household welfare, the distribution of income, and the competitiveness of local firms. With respect to investment, Collier and Gunning (1996) noted that the literature does not unequivocally concur that trade liberalization positively affects aggregate investment. They examined this issue in African context much like Buffie (1991), who argued that if the protected imports substitutes sector is capital intensive then trade liberalization will reduce the returns on investment. In this view, liberalization is tantamount to a reduction of subsidies on capital goods. Based on the cases of Nigeria, Tanzania, and Uganda, Collier and Gunning (1996) argued that trade liberalization might result not only in a fall in aggregate investment but also in changes in its composition. Dividing investment into equipment (tradable capital) and structure (non-tradable capital), they found that in each country, equipment investment fell significantly both in absolute and relative (to GDP) terms.

Changes in investment might also be related to the terms of trade. Liberalization in Africa has led to specialization in primary commodities, which have been characterized by deteriorations in the terms of trade and market volatility (see Alemayehu, 2002). This, in turn, has brought about capital (and consequently investment) instability in most African countries (Fosu, 1991, 2000).

Another area of concern for African countries is the effect of liberalization on household welfare. UNCTAD (2004) shows that there is a general tendency for the incidence of extreme poverty to be more persistent in commodity dependent countries, such as those in Africa. In least developed, mineral exporting countries, extreme poverty (the proportion of the population living under US$1 per day) rose on average from 61 to 82 per cent between the periods of 1981–1983 and 1997–1999 (see also Haousas and Yagoubi, 2003; Chemingui and Thabet, 2001, for similar studies in Tunisia with different findings). Chemingui and Thabet (2001) and Litchfield, McCulloch, and Winters (2003) also found that trade liberalization hurt non-agricultural households while the combination of output and input market reforms dampened the effect on rural farmers.

In a similar vein, Blake, McKay, and Morrissy (2000) concluded that trade liberalization has modest positive welfare effects.[6] These authors noted that the welfare of agricultural producers has significantly improved, although the urban self-employed stood to gain more from freer trade. Ingco (1996), using data from a sample of developing countries, including those from Africa, noted that trade liberalization in agriculture has invariably led to a terms of trade deterioration. A number of the negative effects of trade liberalization on household welfare were also documented in Winters, McCulloch, and McKay (2002), as well as in Deininger and Olinto (2000), Head (1998), Henson and others (2000), and Elson and Evers (1997).

The loss in terms of welfare for Africa may also come, as noted by Dembele (2001), from the global unfairness of trade liberalization. Though most developing countries reduced import tariffs to less than 20 per cent and removed non-tariff barriers altogether, developed countries have not implemented their similar commitments. This unevenness in liberalization has caused cheap imports (including from newly industrializing Asian countries) to flood sub-Saharan African markets. This has resulted in the destabilization of many small scale private and public enterprises and the subsequent loss of a considerable volume of domestic jobs. Tekere (2001) similarly reported that liberalization in Zimbabwe put the country's economy in turmoil, and that growth was better in preceding years. Lall (1999) noted that the increased import competition in Africa has resulted in a substantial contraction in industrial employment. Rather than upgrading aggressively, firms in Kenya, Tanzania and Uganda contracted in response to the pressures of competition.

There are however, studies that point to gains in household welfare. Delgado, Hopkins and Kelly (1998) claim that an additional dollar of new farm income raises total household income by $2.88 in Burkina Faso, $1.96 in the Niger, $2.48 in the Central Groundnut Basin of Senegal, and $2.57 in Zambia. This increase in household incomes, Hazell and Hojjati (1995) argue, is due to the high marginal propensities to consume out of local non-tradable goods. Similarly, Anderson and Yao (2003) suggest that the welfare gains accruing to the SSA region from involvement in the World Trade Organization (WTO) rounds are twice as much than if the countries had forgone participation. On the other hand, using data for 14 countries, Hartel and others (2003) conclude that the impact of trade liberalization on different households can't be conclusively determined because the effects are fairly varied and not always positive.

Rodrik (1992) noted that the impetus for liberalization in Latin American and African countries primarily arose from the prolonged macro-economic quagmire in which developing countries were immersed during the 1980s. The liberalization hence pursued has generally led to five dollars of income being reshuffled within the economy for every dollar of efficiency gain. This huge distributional effect has enormous political implications, as the ratio of the net efficiency gain to the redistribution involved is very small.

While trade reform may improve equity, the prospect of too much redistribution may explain the central political difficulty in enacting trade reform. From the perspective of policymakers, Rodrik (1992) shows that the pure reshuffling of income must be counted as a political cost. The rents and revenues that accrue on a regular basis create entitlements, thereby increasing the political difficulty of instituting changes except, perhaps in times of crisis. It is thus instructive and important to consider the political context of such reform, particularly in Africa where the democratic tradition is generally nascent.

The existing empirical literature on Africa shows that the impact of trade liberalization on household welfare is mixed. In most cases rural households, relative to urban, seem to benefit during the initial stages of reform. On the other hand, liberalization changes the level and composition of investment and causes large redistributions in income that are politically costly and associated with de-industrialization. Which of these effects dominate in a particular country is largely an empirical question. In countries that are non-oil primary commodity exporters, trade liberalization has reinforced poverty. In general, as has been reported by UNCTAD (2004), the trade-poverty relationship improved between the first and the second half of the 1990s, with the greatest progress occurring in moderately open economies.

OPENNESS AND POVERTY IN AFRICA

Poverty is pervasive in Africa. As Table 12.7 demonstrates, North Africa has a relatively lower incidence of poverty when compared to Southern and Eastern Africa, which have the highest. In most countries, urban is lower than rural poverty by as much as 50 per cent, suggesting significant regional disparities in the standards of living. Overall, poverty and human development in sub-Saharan Africa did not change during the 1990s. As shown in Table 12.8, the number of poor people in sub-Saharan Africa in the 1990s increased by about 73 million and the incidence of poverty increased by one percentage point. ECA (2003)

TABLE 12.7
Selected African countries: incidence of poverty by urban/rural residence, 1990–2000

Region/Country	Survey year	Poverty incidence (Percentage)			Estimated poor population, 2003 (millions)			Total national population (millions)
		Rural	Urban	National	Rural	Urban	National	
West Africa								
Benin	2002	33.0	23.2	29.0	1.3	0.7	2.0	6.7
Burkina Faso	1998	51.0	16.5	45.3	5.6	0.3	5.9	13.0
Cote d'Ivoire	1998	42.0	23.0	33.6	4.0	1.6	5.6	16.6
Gambia	1999	73.0	28.0	69.0	0.7	0.1	1.0	1.4
Ghana	1999	36.0	17.3	27.0	4.8	1.3	5.7	20.9
Guinea	1996	52.0	24.0	40.0	3.3	0.5	3.4	8.5
Mali	1998	75.9	30.1	63.8	7.0	1.1	8.3	13.0
Niger	1993	66.0	52.0	63.0	6.5	1.1	7.5	12.0
Nigeria	1993	36.4	30.4	34.1	28.1	14.2	42.3	124.0
Senegal	2001	80.0	51.5	53.9	4.2	2.5	5.4	10.1
Weighted average		*44.4*	*29.5*	*38.1*	*65.5*	*23.5*	*87.0*	*226.3 (total}*
Central Africa								
Cameroon	2001	49.9	22.1	40.2	4.0	1.8	6.4	16.0
Chad	1996	67.0	63.0	64.0	4.5	1.2	5.5	8.6
Estimate		*56.9*	*29.1*	*47.6*	*8.5*	*3.0*	*11.9*	*24.6*
North Africa								
Algeria	1995	30.3	14.7	22.6	4.4	2.5	7.2	31.8
Egypt	2000	21.2	10.7	16.7	8.7	3.3	12.0	71.9
Mauritania	2000	61.2	25.4	46.3	0.8	0.4	1.3	2.9
Morocco	1999	27.2	12.0	19.0	3.8	2.0	5.8	30.6
Tunisia	1995	13.9	3.6	7.6	0.5	0.2	0.8	9.8
Weighted average		*24.4*	*11.7*	*18.4*	*18.2*	*8.5*	*27.1*	*147.0*
East Africa								
Burundi	2000	68.7	68.2	68.7	4.3	0.4	4.7	6.8
Djibouti	1996	86.5	–	45.1	0.1	–	0.3	0.7
Ethiopia	2000	45.0	37.0	44.2	26.9	4.1	31.2	70.7
Kenya	1997	53.0	49.0	52.0	11.8	4.8	16.6	32.0
Madagascar	2001	74.9	50.0	69.6	9.5	2.6	12.1	17.4
Rwanda	2000	67.9	22.6	64.1	5.9	0.1	5.4	8.4
Tanzania	1991	49.7	24.4	51.1	14.2	2.0	18.9	37.0
Weighted average		*52.8*	*40.3*	*51.7*	*72.7*	*14.0*	*89.3*	*173.0*

(contd)

TABLE 12.7 *(contd)*

Region/Country	Survey year	Poverty incidence (Percentage)			Estimated poor population, 2003 (millions)			Total national population (millions)
		Rural	Urban	National	Rural	Urban	National	
Southern Africa								
Lesotho	1993	53.9	27.8	49.2	0.8	0.1	0.9	1.8
Malawi	1991	66.5	54.9	54.0	7.1	0.8	6.5	12.1
Mozambique	1997	71.3	62.0	69.4	9.6	3.3	13.1	18.9
Swaziland	1995	70.6	45.4	65.5	0.6	0.1	0.7	1.1
Zambia	1998	83.1	56.0	72.9	5.4	2.4	7.9	10.8
Zimbabwe	1996	48.0	7.9	34.9	4.2	0.3	4.5	12.9
Weighted average		*66.3*	*43.9*	*58.4*	*27.7*	*7.1*	*33.6*	*57.6*

Source: World Bank (2004)

TABLE 12.8
Status of human development in sub-Saharan Africa

Indicator	1990	2000
People living on less than $1 (PPP)* a day (% of population)	45	46
Primary completion rate (% of relevant age group)	57	55
Country promotes gender equality and empowerment of women	79	82
Under five mortality rate (per 1,000 births)	187	174
Maternal Mortality Rate (per 100,000 live births)	920*	917
Access to an improved water source	54*	58
Access to improved sanitation facilities (% of population)	55*	54

Notes: *PPP (purchasing power parity)
Source: www.developmentgoals.org, *United Nations database.

noted that close to half of the African population lives on less than a dollar per day. However, a comparison of two surveys conducted for about 14 countries in the early and late 1990s shows that there may be a trend towards poverty reduction (see Tables 12.7 and 12.9).

ECA (2003) illustrated the spatial dimension of poverty when it reported that poor households tended to be in the most impoverished regions. These households were also likely to be larger in size, less literate, and suffering from insufficient nutrition. ECA (2003) approximated that a quarter of the people in many African countries are chronically poor, with up to 60 per cent of the population transitioning in and out of poverty. Their findings underscored the importance of reducing vulnerability as an anti-poverty strategy.

TABLE 12.9
Change in poverty during 1990s (based on $1/day and national poverty lines)

Country	P_0 ** (survey year)	P_0 ** (survey year)	Annual % change
Botswana	33.4 (1986)	23.5 (1993)	-4.23
Burkina Faso	61.0 (1994)	44.9 (1998)	-6.6
Cameroon	33.4 (1996)	17.1 (2001)	-9.76
Ethiopia	31.3 (1995)	26.3 (2000)	-3.19
Kenya	26.5 (1992)	23.0 (1997)	-2.64
Lesotho	43.1 (1993)	36.0 (1995)	-8.25
Madagascar	49.0 (1993)	49.0 (1999)	0
Mauritania	28.6 (1995)	25.9 (2000)	-1.89
South Africa	11.5 (1993)	7.1 (1995)	-19.13
Zambia	63.7 (1993)	63.7 (1998)	0
Cote d'Ivoire	12.3 (1995)	15.5 (1998)	6.88
Malawi*	54.0 (1991)	65.0 (1998)	2.40
Egypt*	22.9 (1996)	16.7 (2000)	-9.28
Zimbabwe*	25.8 (1991)	34.9 (1996)	5.20
Tunisia*	7.4 (1990)	7.6 (1995)	0.52
Tanzania*	41.6 (1993)	35.7 (2001)	-2.06
Uganda*	44.0 (1997)	35.0 (2000)	-6.82

Notes: * National poverty line is used instead of US$1/day. ** P_0= Head count ratio
Sources: World Bank (2001, 2003b)

Notwithstanding the complex relationship between growth and poverty, especially when income distribution is taken into account, the available data for Africa in the 1990s suggest that openness is negatively associated with the incidence of poverty. The relatively developed countries such as those in North Africa, South Africa, and Cote d'Ivoire had a high index of openness and a lower incidence of poverty (see Figure 12.2). Botswana, however, seemed to have more poverty even though it maintained a higher degree of openness. This case suggests the possibility of a non-linear relationship between the two variables. This outcome might be related to inequality, which often arises (or increases) in highly open countries characterized by dependence in a single commodity; such as diamonds in Botswana. Such data underscore the importance of addressing inequality.

Available data on the relationship between inequality and openness in Africa is presented in Figure 12.3, where openness (measured as exports and imports as the share of GDP) positively associates with income inequality. This data indicates that more open economies in Africa tend to have high levels of income

FIGURE 12.2
19 African countries: relationship between exports share in GDP and poverty in the 1990s

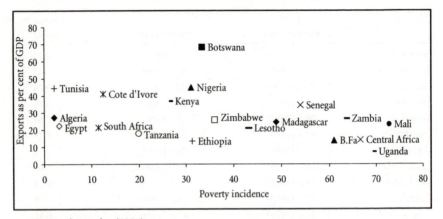

Source: Alemayehu (2006)

FIGURE 12.3
46 African countries: openness and inequality, 1990–2001

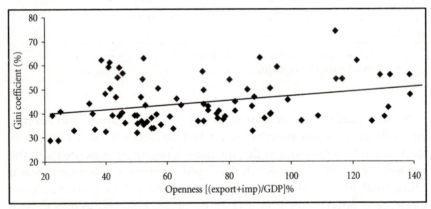

Source: Bigsten and Shimeles (2003)

inequality. Part of the reason for this outcome could be that SSA countries in the middle-income category derive a significant part of their GDP from trade in extractive industries. These sectors, due to political economy factors, are characterized by high initial inequality. The question arises; does this mean that more openness can lead to a worsening of income inequality and a higher incidence of poverty?

The answer depends on a number of factors. There are cases where increased trade liberalization might be beneficial to the poor. According to Winters,

McCulloch, and Mckay (2004), the net gain to household welfare could be positive in circumstances where the majority of the population works in tradable sectors, such as in the production of exportable crops or in the formal manufacturing sectors that trade internationally.

Inequality, in addition to income, shapes the relationship between openness and poverty. African inequality can be evaluated from two perspectives; (1) it can be appraised from a global viewpoint where Africa's position in the world distribution of wealth is considered (see Table 12.10); (2) the distribution of income and wealth can be examined from within the African continent, comparing countries or groups within countries (see Table 12.11).

Table 12.10 shows the striking divergence in the distribution of income across the world, despite fifty years of rapid globalisation. The table highlights the fact that the poor are growing more destitute while the rich are becoming even better off. Africa's per capita income as a percentage of high income OECD countries declined from 3.3 per cent in 1980 to 2.1 per cent during 1991–1995. This decline continued to 2.0 per cent in the second half of the 1990s and to 1.9 per cent in 2001.

Unlike the high income OECD countries, this worsening income gap was actually common for most developing countries, except for those in East Asia and the Pacific.[7] Moreover, Wade (2003) has shown that Africa's share of the bottom quintile of world income increased between 1990 and 1999. The continent of Africa is becoming worse off after opening its economy to international trade and finance. It is therefore important to examine whether openness in Africa, in particular international trade, is associated with persistent and rising inequality and poverty.

TABLE 12.10
Sub-Saharan African per capita income as share of high income OECD countries (1995 constant US$, percentage)

Region	1980	1981–1985	1986–1990	1991–1995	1996–2000	2001
Sub-Saharan Africa	3.3	3.1	2.5	2.1	2.0	1.9
South Asia	1.2	1.3	1.3	1.4	1.5	1.6
Middle East & North Africa	9.7	9.0	7.3	7.1	6.8	6.7
Latin America & Caribbean	18.0	16.0	14.2	13.5	13.3	12.8
East Asia & Pacific	1.5	1.7	1.9	2.5	3.1	3.3
High income non-OECD	45.3	45.3	48.2	56.1	60.2	59.2
High income	97.7	97.6	97.6	97.9	97.9	97.8
High income OECD	100.0	100.0	100.0	100.0	100.0	100.0

Source: Computations based on World Bank (2003b)

TABLE 12.11
Inequality measures for Africa and other world regions in the 1990s

Inequality Indicators	Africa				Other World Regions			
	Average	Standard Deviation	Max	Min	E. Asia & Pacific	South Asia	Latin America	Industrialized Countries
Gini Coefficient	44.4	8.9	58.4	32.0	38.1	31.9	49.3	33.8
Share of Top 20%	50.6	7.4	63.3	41.1	44.3	39.9	52.9	39.8
Share of Middle Class	34.4	4.3	38.8	38.8	37.5	38.4	33.8	41.8
Share of Bottom 20%	5.2	5.2	8.7	2.1	6.8	8.8	4.5	6.3

Source: ECA (1999)

The information contained in Table 12.11, which is based on the best available data, covers about 60 per cent of population of the continent (ECA, 1999). It shows that Africa is characterized by a high degree of inequality, with a Gini coefficient of 44 per cent. Latin America had a Gini coefficient of 49 per cent. The high standard deviation reflects the large variation in inequality among countries on the continent. Inequality was especially high in South Africa (58.5 per cent), Kenya (58.3 per cent), Zimbabwe (56.8 per cent), Guinea-Bissau (55.8 per cent) and Senegal (54.1 per cent) and lower in Egypt (32 per cent), Ghana (34.1 per cent) and Algeria (35.5 per cent). The top 20 per cent of the African population accounted for about half of total income; again the second highest among regions in the world, next to Latin America (see ECA, 1999).

Given these results, it is instructive to ask whether or not this pattern of inequality is associated with openness. Most cross-country regressions have found that openness, defined in different ways, is positively correlated with income inequality (e.g., see Fisher, 2001).[8] Again, as can be read from Figure 12.4, the correlation between a measure of openness and income inequality is positive and significant for selected African countries. Apart from the theoretical explanations for this evidence (such as the biased demand for skilled labour when developing countries liberalize their trade), political economy must also be taken into account. Easterly (2002) argues that resource rich countries that depend primarily on a few products for their exports tend to have institutions and political frameworks that favour the persistence of income inequality. In other words, more open economies in Africa tend to depend on one or two major export items (mineral, oil, or a primary commodity), and are characterized by high *initial* inequality. Trade liberalization could reinforce such initial inequality.

FIGURE 12.4
Africa: relationship between Gini coefficient and log per capita income

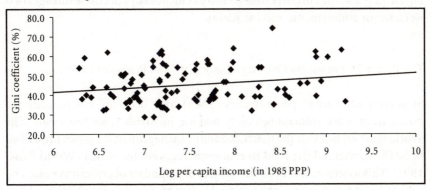

Source: Bigsten and Shimeles (2003)

FIGURE 12.5
Africa: land endowment and income inequality in the 1990s

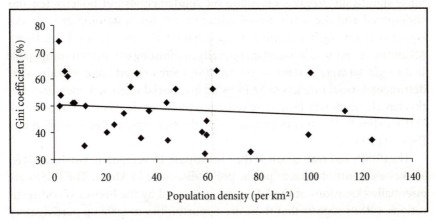

Source: ECA (2004)

The impact of the initial endowment differential on the distribution of income following liberalization is shown in Figure 12.5. Using population density as a crude indicator of endowment intensity, Figure 12.5 shows a negative association between population density (low density showing initial inequality of resource ownership) and the Gini coefficient for a number of African countries in the 1990s. This outcome suggests that countries abundant in natural resources, such as land, tend to experience a rise in income inequality following trade liberalization. The explanation follows that countries rich in natural resources or land are both capital and labour poor—factors represented by inequitable ownership in Africa (see Deininger and Olinto, 2000). Both Figure 12.5 and the current cross-country evidence support these linkages between factor endowments and inequality.

Structural adjustment programmes (SAPs) have been the macroeconomic policy framework informing policy making in Africa since the 1980s. The World Bank argued that the macroeconomic management strategies prescribed in SAPs represented the road to economic recovery for Africa (World Bank, 1994). This assertion has been the subject of a number of criticisms voiced by a diversity of actors in the international policy arena (see, among others, ECA, 1989; Adam, 1995; Mosley, Subasat, and Weeks, 1995; Lall, 1995; White, 1996; Alemayehu, 2002).

According to Mkandawire and Soludo (ECA, 1999), SAPs in Africa have made significant progress on economic fundamentals but poverty remains widespread and the institutional requirements for sustaining growth and equitably extending its benefits to the population remain onerous (ECA, 1999). Mkandawire and Soludo noted that poverty in adjusting countries is comparable to the regional average, if not worse. Initially, there were attempts to address the detrimental social impacts of SAPs by ad hoc 'social safety net' measures, but this has changed over time. The recent emphasis of the World Bank and the IMF is to link SAPs with poverty reduction through Poverty Reduction Strategy Papers (PRSPs).

The PRSPs and realization of the Millennium Development Goals (MDGs) are key elements of current public policy discourse in Africa. The PRSPs are essentially extensions of the SAPs and sponsored by the Breton Wood Institutions. PRSPs suggest that there are opportunities to scale up participatory learning strategies from grassroots to national levels, while also offering new possibilities to budget for these activities and increase public interest and participation in poverty monitoring (UNDP, 2002). The PRSP initiative created, at least in principle, an opportunity for building a national consensus on the critical causes of poverty and social development inequity, as well as how to design interventions. Thus, if appropriately implemented, the value of the PRSP initiative may go beyond the economics of poverty reduction all the way to improving democratic culture and developing social capital.

Currently, major donor countries are using PRSP and MDGs targets as their guide for development assistance, even though the resources required to attain the MDGs are so significant that they render achieving such targets unrealistic. This is further accentuated by the declining flow of official development assistance to Africa in recent years. The ECA's 1999 annual *Economic Report*, for instance, forecasted the required GDP growth to reduce poverty in Africa by half by 2015, to about 7.2 per cent (or 4.2 per cent in per capita terms). Given the problems of domestic resource mobilization, the required level of external financing is estimated at about 26 per cent of GDP, and well above the current official development assistance (ODA) to GDP ratio of about 12 per cent. This shows the difficulties of achieving the MDGs in Africa in general and of poverty reduction in particular (see ECA, 1999).

Since the MDGs basically comprise social development goals, the failure to achieve them is tantamount to a regression in social development, equity, and poverty reduction. The impacts of initial inequality on efficient growth and poverty reduction need serious consideration. Figure 12.6 illustrates how the responsiveness of poverty to growth (the growth elasticity of poverty) varies with initial income inequality in SSA. The figure shows that to halve poverty by 2015, countries with low levels of income inequality need a much lower rate of per capita income growth than those with high initial income inequality.

From the discussion in the preceding sections, it is noted that initial inequality in Africa strongly correlates with the degree of openness of the economy. That said, these countries need rapid and sustained growth in order to significantly reduce poverty. In fact, if these countries can contain income inequality to its existing level, modest growth would be sufficient to reduce poverty by half by 2015 (see Bigsten and Shimeles, 2005). Each country therefore

FIGURE 12.6
Initial inequality and overall growth required to halve poverty by 2015 in sub-Saharan Africa

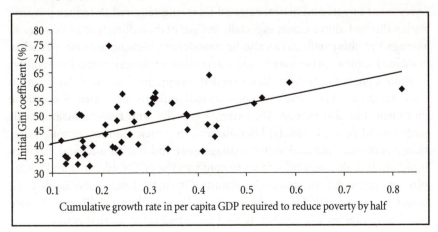

Source: Bigsten and Shimeles (2005)

needs to consider how the interaction of trade reform and income inequality affects poverty. The contributions of trade reform to growth however, should not be the only guide used to bring about poverty reduction.

CONCLUSIONS

There has been a recent revitalization of the economic fundamentals important to improving poverty and inequality in Africa. However, cautious optimism is required. Sustainable economic growth and development is precarious due to Africa's patterns of trade and finance, the prevalence of conflict, dependence on agriculture (the main stay of the majority of the rural population), the vagaries of nature, backward technology, and to a limited degree, dependence on the global commodity market.

International trade, finance, and aid link Africa to the world and in particular, to developed countries. These relationships are accentuated by the policy prescriptions of international financial institution (IFIs), which are in turn, complemented by global commitments like the MDGs and by African governments themselves. SAPs and the PRSPs were intended, in part, to speed up African engagement in global markets through a set of polices loosely termed 'liberalization'. Trade liberalization policies were critical instruments deployed in African countries during the SAP era, and trade remains the most significant channel through which global interdependence impacts the welfare level of ordinary African citizens.

Africa is effectively marginalized from global markets given its degree of trade and financial integration with the rest of the world. The high growth and investment targets and hence, external financing required to reduce poverty, makes this isolation a curse, especially in light of dwindling levels of domestic savings. Yet, this partition can also be considered a blessing because Africa has remained somewhat insulated from international financial market instability.

From a policy perspective, Africa's orderly integration into the global financial system requires the institution of policies that promote investment flows to the continent, but also manage the extreme volatility and risks associated with such capital flows. Financial liberalization in Africa requires, among other things, stronger financial sector management and institutions and capacity building. It is also very important to confront the policy dilemma and trade-offs between high flows and high volatility. Given, the huge cost of bailing out countries facing with financial crisis, Bhinda and others (1999) rightly note that "Africa has no 'big brother' to facilitate a bailout in the first place."

The global market remains extremely important to the African economy, especially given Africa's dependence on trade in a few commodities, the dominant effect of trade in the economy, and the secular deterioration and volatility of its terms of trade.[9] However national governments are required to adjust to 'economic reality' and 'market discipline' in order to stimulate exports and promote foreign investment. Certain dangers are ignored, such as the 'race to the bottom', as individual countries try to bend their labour standards, environmental safeguards and tax concessions to boost trade. Policymakers also ignore the 'fallacy of composition' inherent in the small-country assumption, causing over-expansion of commodity supplies and declining prices.

Economic *perception* is as vitally important as economic *reality*. External economic relations need to be examined as a variable, rather than as a given. Domestic economic events become endogenous to the operation of the global system rather than simply at the behest of policymakers. This shows, on one hand, how limited the options really are for domestic policymakers in Africa (especially if they act individually and only for short periods) and, on the other hand, the crucial importance of changing international arrangements, particularly trade and investment rules.

Africa's entrance into the global system has not been orderly, as can be read from its economic history, including the origins of its debt and external finance problems. As previously noted, debt issues stem from the structure of trade in general and from commodity trade in particular. Especially relevant are long-term declining terms of trade and high price volatility. The question then seems to be why Africa has not diversified its exports to manufactures, services or processed raw materials, all of which offer better growth prospects. One reason may be that such a switch requires capital (infrastructure) and skills (human capital) that Africa does not currently possess.

What lessons are relevant for shaping the future of economic growth and development in Africa? First, research amply confirms that the debt problem is essentially commodity based (see Alemayehu, 2002). Efforts such as the HIPC process, which at least indicates a political commitment to act, will have little lasting effect unless export capacity and prices are raised. Second, if international flows of capital to Africa (such as aid) are envisaged, then more aid should be channelled towards small export farmers to promote exports and reduce poverty. Aid should also be accompanied by expansionary policies in order to keep exchange rates competitive. Third, Africa is highly vulnerable to changes in world interest rates. This implies that the construction of a new 'global financial architecture' can only be undertaken at the international level. Fourth, fiscal deficits are mostly exogenously determined by aid flows. This has important implications in terms of the need for donors to coordinate their actions in order to ensure macroeconomic sustainability, rather than leaving this task to IFIs alone (Alemayehu, 2002).

These various policy implications imply that the trade relations of Africa with developed countries need to be strengthened. The question then, is how? Improved access to developed country markets for processed primary commodities, and, in particular, the replacement of the Lomé system with better access to the European and American markets (along Everything but Arms of EU and The African Growth and Opportunity Act of the US) would be a first and important step. Commodity price stabilization schemes are currently out of favour and would require the full cooperation of the major importing transnational corporations in order to work. However, this is a problem of price volatility around the trend, as well as the declining trend itself. Reducing this volatility would benefit both importers and exporters and thus should not be impossible to achieve through a properly administered buffer stock system. The market mechanism alone cannot produce this result since hedging ranges are so short. This would have to be a form of public intervention.

However, the long-term downward direction of the terms of trade is difficult. It would not matter so much if volume was increasing fast enough to raise the income terms of trade (as is happening with labour-intensive manufactures), but this is not, in fact, the case. The market for tropical commodities is oligopolistic and riddled with restrictive practices, for instance, sugar and cotton in the US and bananas and coffee in Europe. Therefore, a producers' cartel may be the only theoretically viable solution. However, in spite of the recent success of the organization of petroleum exporting countries (OPEC) in driving up oil prices, Africa is unlikely to be able to organize such a cartel given the worldwide competition in those commodities.

Africa needs to change the mix (or at the very least upgrade the quality) of its primary export products. This requires investment, which to date has been insufficient. More than savings, risk is the main problem, since there is plenty of capital held overseas and also plenty of liquidity within the banking system. These steps cannot be undertaken by each African country in isolation but rather, require an international agreement on investment rules and the stabilization of commodity prices; in other words, the *orderly* insertion of Africa into the global market.

The impact of trade liberalization on welfare depends to a certain degree on the state of income and poverty distribution in Africa. Existing income inequality is relatively high in most African countries, which makes the distributional consequences of trade policies a serious matter. Cross-country evidence shows the positive correlation between trade policies and income inequality through the channel of land abundance (e.g. Fischer, 2001), and through political economy factors for Africa (e.g. Easterly, 2002). In some cases, trade liberalization could also worsen income distribution by reducing the demand for unskilled labour.

Trade reform also affects intra-household inequalities and gender disparities. Even if the aggregate welfare of a household increases, it is possible for some measures of trade reform to increase intra-household inequality through changes in employment opportunities between male and female household members (Winters, 2000). Such reforms may also induce changes in the composition of the whole workforce (UNDP, 2003). For example, the garment industry, which mainly employed women, sharply contracted with the end of the Agreement on Textiles and Clothing (ATC) (Blackden, 2003). Lower wages for women in such labour-intensive sectors may also increase wage inequalities, even when more women are employed.

The positive effects of trade liberalization can be enhanced if policymakers act at the right time (Winters, 2000), and institute basic macroeconomic stability policies (e.g. Bhagwati and Srinivasan, 2001). For instance, inflationary trade policy measures can be controlled with appropriate macro-stabilization policies. These stabilization policies though, in most cases hurt the poor. Thus, it is important to decide the appropriate timing of trade reform in order to maximize gains and minimize the adverse effects on the least well-off. Poverty decomposition along sectoral lines can provide the analytical tools to evaluate who benefits from trade liberalization and help devise intervention strategies to mitigate welfare losses (Kanbur, 2000).

Finally, national ownership of development policies is crucial. Development strategies must be designed to ensure sustainable growth along with the equitable distribution of wealth. This can take the form of

1) Ensuring political stability and designing peaceful mechanisms of conflict resolution
2) Pursuing macroeconomic stability by emphasizing the savings–investment export nexus
3) Investing in human resource development through education and healthcare expenditures and institution building
4) Addressing each country's major structural problems, such as diversification.

Progress on each of these fronts can help mitigate the often inequitable consequences of rapid economic growth, and reduce poverty and inequality in Africa.

NOTES

[1] We would like to thank two graduate students of the Department of Economics, Addis Ababa University, Dawit Berhanu and Melesse Menale, for excellent research assistance. Any remaining errors are ours.

[2] This section is largely based on Alemayehu (2000).

[3] See Alemayehu (2002: Chapter 1) for a discussion of such studies.

[4] This finding about the impact of debt is, however, contested by Ajayi (1997) and Alemayehu (2002), who found no relationship between debt and capital flight.

[5] See UNCTAD (2004) for a detailed discussion about 'trade policy in general' and 'trade liberalisation' in particular and Alemayehu (2002) for both trade and financial linkage of Africa with the result of the world.

[6] The estimates are based on the assumption that the commitments of the Uruguay Round are implemented by 2002

[7] This result is even obtained using World Bank data, which Wade (2003) argues has a lot of problems and may give the wrong impression that poverty was declining in the recent past.

[8] Some disagree with the assertion that trade reform worsens income inequality on the grounds that the causation is weak (e.g., Srinivasan and Wallack, 2003). Dollar and Kraay (2001) also take the view that greater openness is neutral with respect to income distribution.

[9] See Alemayehu (2002) for details on this.

REFERENCES

Adam, Christopher (1995). Review article; Adjustment in Africa: Reforms, results and the road ahead. *World Economy* 18 (5): 729–35.

Ajayi, S. Ibi (1997). An analysis of external debt and capital flight in the heavily indebted poor countries of sub-Saharan Africa. In Zubair Iqbal and Ravi Kanbur (eds). *External Finance for Low-Income Countries*. International Monetary Fund, Washington, DC: 224–45.

Alemayehu Geda (2000). An assessment of the performance of African countries in implementing the Copenhagen Declaration and Programme of Action. Background paper prepared for Economic Commission for Africa, Addis Ababa.

Alemayehu Geda (2002). *Finance and Trade in Africa: Macroeconomic Response in the World Economy Context*. Palgrave Macmillan, London.

Alemayehu Geda (2003). The historical origin of African debt crisis. *Eastern Africa Social Science Research Review* 19 (1): 59–89.

Alemayehu Geda (2006). Openness, inequality and poverty in Africa. Working paper, United Nations Department of Economic and Social Affairs (DESA), New York, NY.

Amoako, K.Y., and Ali G. Ali (1998). Financing development in Africa: Some exploratory results. AERC Collaborative Project on Transition from Aid Dependency, African Economic Research Consortium, Nairobi.

Anderson, Kym, and S. Yao (2003). How can South Asia and sub-Saharan Africa gain from the next WTO Round? Processed, University of Adelaide, Adelaide.

Ben-David, Dan (1993). Equalizing exchange: Trade liberalization and income convergence. *Quarterly Journal of Economics* 108 (3): 653–79.

Bhattacharya, Amar, P.J. Montiel and Sunil Sharma (1997). Private capital flows to sub-Saharan Africa: An overview of trends and determinants. In Zubair Iqbal and Ravi Kanbur (eds). *External Finance for Low-Income Countries*. International Monetary Fund, Washington, DC: 244–65.

Bhinda, Nils, Stephany Griffith-Jones, Jonathan Leope and Matthew Martin (1999). *Private*

Capital Flows to Africa: Perception and Reality. Forum on Debt and Development (FONDAD), The Hague.

Bhagwati, J.D., and T.N. Srinivasan (2001). Trade and poverty in poor countries. Processed, Department of Economics, Yale University, New Haven.

Bigsten, A., and A. Shimeles (2003). Prospect for pro-poor growth strategies in Africa. Paper presented at the conference organized by World Institute for Development Economic Research (WIDER), May, Helsinki.

Bigsten, A., and A. Shimeles (2005). Can Africa reduce poverty by half by 2015: case for pro-poor growth strategy, Working paper in Economics No. 0177, Department of Economics, Goteborg University, Goteborg, Sweden.

Blake, Adam, Andrew McKay and Oliver Morrissey (2000). The impact on Uganda of agricultural trade liberalization. Processed, March, Centre for Economic Research and International Trade (CREDIT), University of Nottingham, Nottingham.

Blackden, M. (2003). Gender and growth in Africa: A review of evidence and issues. Processed, World Bank, Washington, DC.

Buffie, E. (1991). Commercial policy, growth and distribution of income in a dynamic trade model. *Journal of Development Economics* 37: 1–30.

Calvo, G.A. (1987). On the cost of temporary policy. *Journal of Development Economics* 27: 245–61.

Calvo, G.A. (1988). Costly trade liberalization: Durable goods and capital mobility. *IMF Staff Papers* 35: 461–73.

Calvo, Guillermo A., Leonardo Leiderman and Carmen M. Reinhart (1993). Capital inflows and the real exchange rate appreciation in Latin America: The role of external factors. *IMF Staff Papers* 40 (1): 108–51.

Calvo, Guillermo A., Leonardo Leiderman and Carmen M. Reinhart (1996). Inflows of capital to developing countries in the 1990s. *Journal of Economic Perspectives* 10 (2): 123–39.

Chemingui, Mohamed Abdelbasset, and Chokri Thabet (2001). Internal and external reforms in agricultural policy in Tunisia and poverty in rural area. Paper written for the Global Development Network (GDN) medal competition, December, Tunis.

Collier, Paul, and Jan W. Gunning (1996). Trade liberalization and the composition of investment: Theory and African application. Processed, Centre for African Economic Studies, University of Oxford, Oxford.

Collier, Paul, and Jan W. Gunning (1999). Explaining African economic performance. *Journal of Economic Literature* 37 (March): 64–111.

Collier, Paul, Anke Hoeffler and Catherine Pattillo (1999). Flight capital as a portfolio choice. Policy Research Working Paper Series No. 2066, World Bank, Washington, DC.

Cornia, Giovanni Andrea (1999). Liberalization, globalization and income distribution. UNU/WIDER Working paper No.157, March, United Nations University, World Institute for Development Economics Research, Helsinki.

Deininger, Klaus, and P. Olinto (2000). Asset distribution and growth. Policy Research Working Paper No. 2375, World Bank, Washington, DC.

Delgado, C., J. Hopkins and V. Kelly (1998). Agricultural growth linkages in sub-Saharan Africa. Research Paper No. 107, International Food Policy Research Institute, Washington, DC.

Dembele, Demda Moussa (2001). Trade liberalization accentuating poverty in sub-Saharan Africa. *South Bulletin* 16 (May): 11–15.

Dixit, A. (1989). Intersectoral capital reallocation under uncertainty. *Journal of International Economics* 26: 309–25.

Dollar, David (1992). Outward-oriented developing economies really do grow more rapidly: Evidence from 95 LDCs, 1976–1985. *Economic Development and Cultural Change* 40 (3): 523–44.

Dollar, David, and Aart Kraay (2001). Trade, growth, and poverty. Policy Research Department Working Paper No. 2615, World Bank, Washington, DC.

Easterly, William (2002). Inequality does cause underdevelopment: New evidence from commodity endowments, middle class share, and other determinants of per capita income. Working Paper No. 1, Centre for Global Development, Washington, DC.

ECA (1989). *African Alternative Framework to Structural Adjustment Programs for Socio-Economic Recovery and Transformation (AAF-SAP)*. United Nations Economic Commission for Africa, Addis Ababa.

ECA (1999). *Economic Report on Africa 1999: The Challenge of Poverty Reduction and Sustainability*. United Nations Economic Commission for Africa, Addis Ababa.

ECA (2003). *Economic Report on Africa, 2003: Accelerating the Pace of Development*. United Nations Economic Commission for Africa, Addis Ababa.

ECA (2004). *Economic Report on Africa, 2004: Unlocking Africa's Trade Potential*. United Nations Economic Commission for Africa, Addis Ababa.

Elbadawi, Ibrahim, B.J. Ndulu and N. Ndung'u (1997). Debt overhang and economic growth in sub-Saharan Africa. In Zubair Iqbal and Ravi Kanbur (eds). *External Finance for Low-Income Countries*. International Monetary Fund, Washington, DC: 234–55.

Elson, Diane, and B. Evers (1997). Gender aware country economic report: Uganda. Working Paper No. 2, Genecon Unit, Graduate School of Social Science, University of Manchester, Manchester.

Fisher, Ronald D. (2001). The evolution of inequality after trade liberalization. *Journal of Development Economics* 2: 555–79.

Fosu, Augustin (1991). Capital instability and economic growth in sub-Saharan Africa. *Journal of Development Studies* 28 (1): 74–85.

Fosu, Augustin (2000). The international dimension of African economic growth. Paper presented at the AERC/Harvard conference on Explaining African Economic Growth Performance, Harvard University, Cambridge, MA.

Frankel, Jeffrey, and David Romer (1999). Does trade cause growth? *American Economic Review* 89 (3): 379–99.

Haousas, Ilham, and Mahmoud Yagoubi (2003). Trade liberalization and labour demand elasticities: Evidence from Tunisia. Processed, University of Paris I, Paris.

Hartel, Thomas, Paul Preckel, John Cranfield and Maros Ivanic (2003). Poverty impacts of multilateral trade liberalization. Processed, Global Trade Analysis Project (GTAP), Purdue University, Purdue, March.

Hazel, P.B.R., and B. Hojjati (1995). Farm/Non-Farm Linkages in Zambia. *Journal of African Economies* 4 (3): 406–35.

Head, Judith (1998). Ik Het Niks'—I have nothing: The impact of European Union policies on women canning workers in South Africa. Processed, University of Cape Town, Cape Town.

Henson, S.J., R.J. Loader, A. Swinbank, N. Bredhal and N. Lux (2000). Impact of sanitary and phytosanitary measures on developing countries. Centre for Food Economics Research, University of Reading, Reading.

Hermes, Niels, and R. Lensink (1992). The magnitude and determinants of capital flight: The case for six sub-Saharan African countries. Development Economics Seminar Paper No. 92-1/3, Institute of Social Studies, The Hague.

Ingco, Merlinda D. (1996). Progress in agricultural trade liberalization and welfare of least-developed countries. International Trade Division, International Economics Department, World Bank, Washington, DC.

Kanbur, Ravi (2000). Income Distribution and Development. In A.B. Atkinson and F. Bourguignon (eds). *Handbook of Income Distribution*. North-Holland, Amsterdam.

Lall, Sanjaya (1995). Structural adjustment and African industry. *World Development* 23 (12): 2019–31.

Lall, Sanjaya (1999). *The Technological Response to Import Liberalization in sub-Saharan Africa.* Macmillan, London.

Litchfield, Julie, Neil McCulloch and Alan Winters (2003). Agricultural trade liberalization and poverty dynamics in three developing countries. *American Journal of Agricultural Economics* 85 (5): 1285–91.

Löfgren, H. (1999). Trade reform and the poor in Morocco: A rural-urban general equilibrium analysis of reduced protection. TMD Discussion Paper 38, Trade and Macroeconomics Division, International Food Policy Research Institute, Washington DC.

Mkandawire, Thandika, and Charles Soludo (1999). Special program of assistance—Phase five towards new aid relationships to reduce poverty. Processed, Economic Commission for Africa, Addis Ababa.

Mosley, Paul, Turan Subasat and John Weeks (1995). Assessing adjustment in Africa. *World Development* 23 (9): 1459–73.

Ndulu, Benno J. (1986). Investment, output growth and capacity utilization in an African economy: The case of manufacturing sector in Tanzania. *Eastern Africa Economic Review* 2 (1): 14–31.

Ndulu, Benno J. (1991). Growth and adjustment in sub-Saharan Africa. In Ajay Chhibber and Stanley Fischer (eds). *Economic Reform in sub-Saharan Africa.* World Bank, Washington, DC: 124–48.

Prebisch, Raul (1950). The economic development of Latin America and its principal problems. *Economic Bulletin for Latin America* 7 (1): 1–22.

Ratso, Jorn (1994). Medium-run adjustment under import compression: Macroeconomic analysis relevant for sub-Saharan Africa. *Journal of Development Economics* 45: 35–54.

Rodriguez, Francisco, and Dani Rodrik (2000). Trade policy and economic growth: A sceptic's guide to the cross-national evidence. Processed, Department of Economics, University of Maryland, and Kennedy School of Government, Harvard University, Cambridge, MA.

Rodrik, Dani (1992). The rush to free trade in the developing world: Why so late? Why now? Will it last? NBER Working Paper No. 3947, National Bureau of Economic Research, Cambridge, MA.

Rodrik, Dani (1998). Trade policy and economic performance in sub-Saharan Africa. NBER Working Paper No. 6562, National Bureau of Economic Research, Cambridge, MA.

Rodrik, Dani (1999). How far will international economic integration go? Processed, Kennedy School of Government, Harvard University, Cambridge, MA.

Rodrik, Dani (2001). The developing countries' hazardous obsession with global integration. Processed, Kennedy School of Government, Harvard University, Cambridge, MA.

Sachs, Jeffrey, and Andrew Warner (1995). Economic reform and the process of global integration. *Brookings Papers on Economic Activity* 1: 1–118.

Singer, H.W. (1950). US foreign investment in underdeveloped areas: The distribution of gains between investing and borrowing countries. *The American Economic Review: Papers and Proceedings* 40 (2): 473–85.

Srinivasan, T.N., and J.S. Wallack (2003). Globalization, growth and the poor. Processed, Department of Economics, Yale University, New Haven.

Taylor, Mark P., and Lucio Sarno (1997). Capital flows to developing countries: Long and short-term determinants. *The World Bank Economic Review* 11 (3): 451–70.

Tekere, Moses (2001). Trade liberalisation under structural economic adjustment: Impact on social welfare in Zimbabwe. The Poverty Reduction Forum (PRF), Structural Adjustment Program Review Initiative (SAPRI), April, Harare.

UNCTAD. *Handbook of International Trade and Development.* Various issues, United Nations Conference on Trade and Development, Geneva.

UNCTAD (2002a). *Commodity Yearbook, 2002.* United Nations Conference on Trade and Development, Geneva.

UNCTAD (2002b). *Handbook of Statistics, 2002*. United Nations Conference on Trade and Development, Geneva.

UNCTAD (2004). *The Least Developed Countries Report, 2004: Linking International Trade with Poverty Reduction*. United Nations Conference on Trade and Development, Geneva.

UNDP (2002). *UNDP support for poverty reduction strategies: The PRSP countries*. United Nations Development Programme, New York.

UNDP (2003). *Human Development Report 2003*. United Nations Development Programme, New York.

Wade, Robert (2003). Is globalisation reducing poverty and inequality? *World Development* 32 (4): 567–89.

Winters, Alan (2000). Trade, trade-policy and poverty: What are the links? Discussion Paper No. 2382, Centre for Economic Policy Research, London.

White, Howard (1996). Adjustment in Africa: A review article. *Development and Change* 27 (4): 786–815.

Winters, Alan, Neil McCulloch and Andrew McKay (2002). Trade liberalization and poverty: The empirical evidence. Discussion Paper in Economics No. 88, October, University of Sussex, Brighton.

Winters, Alan, Neil McCulloch and Andrew McKay (2004). Trade liberalization and poverty: The evidence so far. *Journal of Economic Literature* 42: 72–115.

World Bank (1987). *World Development Report, 1987*. World Bank, Washington, DC.

World Bank (1994). *World Development Report, 1994*. World Bank, Washington, DC,

World Bank (2001). *World Development Report, 2001*. World Bank, Washington, DC.

World Bank (2003a). *African Development Indicators, 2003*. World Bank, Washington, DC.

World Bank (2003b). *World Development Indicators, 2003*. CD-ROM. World Bank, Washington, DC.

World Bank (2003c). *Global Economic Prospects, 2003*. CD-ROM. World Bank, Washington, DC.

World Bank (2004). *World Development Indicators, 2004*. CD-ROM. World Bank, Washington, DC.

13

Inequality in India: A Survey of Recent Trends

PARTHAPRATIM PAL and JAYATI GHOSH

Officially, Indian policymakers have always been concerned with the reduction of poverty and inequality. However, between the first five year plan (1951–1956) and the turn of the century, economic policy making in India has gone through a sea of change. After independence and for a period of about forty years, India followed a development strategy based on central planning. As Chakravarty (1987) points out, one of the reasons for adopting an interventionist economic policy was the apprehension that total reliance on the market mechanism would result in excessive consumption by upper-income groups, along with relative under-investment in sectors essential to the development of the economy. According to Chakravarty (1987: 10), policymakers in India adopted a middle path, in which "there was a tolerance towards income inequality, provided it was not excessive and could be seen to result in a higher rate of growth than would be possible otherwise." In this context, however, the macro-economic sensitivity to inflation as a 'fallout' of growth reflected the concern of the government regarding the redistributive effects of inflation, which typically affected workers, peasants and unorganized sectors more.

From the mid-1980s, the Indian government gradually started to adopt market-oriented economic reform policies. In the early phase, these were associated with an expansionist fiscal strategy that involved additional budget allocations to the rural areas, and thus counterbalanced the redistributive effects of early liberalization. The pace of policy change accelerated during the early 1990s, when the explicit adoption of neo-liberal reform programs marked the beginning of a period of intensive economic liberalization and changed attitudes towards state intervention in the economy. The focus of economic policies during this period shifted away from state intervention for more equitable distribution towards liberalization, privatization and globalization. This study focuses on the period when these neo-liberal and market-oriented economic policies were being implemented in India. However, it should be noted that the Indian experience with such policies over this period was more limited, gradual and nuanced than in many other developing countries, with correspondingly different economic effects. This chapter gives an overview of the nature and causes of inequality trends since the mid-1990s and tries to explain the observed trends.

TRENDS IN INCOME AND CONSUMPTION INEQUALITY IN INDIA

The debate on economic policy and reform began in India in the 1980s, and still continues. Prior to the extensive introduction in 1991 of the new economic policy, as it came to be known, there was widespread apprehension that liberalization and excessive reliance on market forces would lead to increases in regional, rural-urban and vertical inequalities in India. Nearly fifteen years later, the issue is still debated since the various studies which have investigated this matter do not give an unequivocal verdict. There are substantial disagreements among economists about whether income and consumption inequality have increased in India during the reform period.

It is notable that during the reform period, urban inequality in India has been much higher than rural inequality for most states. According to the *National Human Development Report of India, 2001*, in 31 of the 32 states and union territories, urban inequality was higher than rural inequality. This is also reflected in the all-India figures, where it can be seen that urban inequality remained higher than rural inequality in all the reference years. Moreover, from 1983 to 1999–2000, the rural Gini declined consistently, but there was a

FIGURE 13.1
India: rural and urban Gini coefficients, 1983–2000

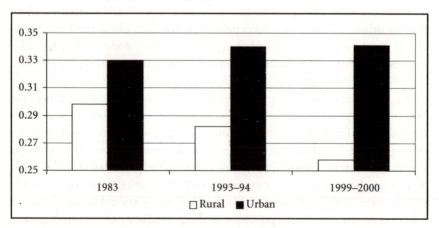

Source: National Human Development Report of India, 2001

gradual rise in urban inequality during the same period, as shown in Figure 13.1.

Most studies have used various rounds of National Sample Survey (NSS) consumption expenditure survey statistics for calculating per capita incomes and Gini coefficients. But there is a well known problem of lack of comparability of NSS statistics between earlier rounds and the latest (55th) round for 1999–2000. As Sen (2001) points out, the reference period for the Consumer Expenditure Survey of the 55th round of NSS was changed from the uniform 30 day recall period, used until then, to both 7 day and 30 day questions for food and intoxicants, and to 365 days for clothing, footwear, education, institutional medical expenses and durable goods. As Deaton and Dreze (2002) explain, the change from 30 to 365 day reporting periods for these low frequency items has possibly led to lower poverty and inequality estimates. According to them, the longer reporting period reduces the mean expenditures on these items, but because a much larger fraction of people report something over the longer reporting period, the bottom tail of the consumption distribution is pulled up, and as a result, both inequality and poverty are 'reduced'.

Thus, according to some estimates, the new methodology has lowered measured rural poverty in India by almost 50 million. As a consequence, rural inequality measures have also been affected. Revised estimates of rural in-equality, using adjusted data (Deaton and Dreze, 2002; Sundaram and Tendul-kar, 2003a, 2003b; Sen and Himanshu, 2005), indicate that rural inequality has, in fact, gone up in India between 1993–1994 and 1999–2000.[1]

Striking evidence of increased inequality in India in the post-reform period is provided by Sen and Himanshu (2005). Based on indices of real mean per capita expenditure (MPCE) by fractile groups, Sen and Himanshu show that whereas the consumption level of the upper tail of the population, including the top 20 per cent of the rural population, went up remarkably during the 1990s, the bottom 80 per cent of the rural population suffered during this period (Figure 13.2). This graph clearly shows that the consumption disparities between the rich and the poor and between urban and rural India increased during the 1990s. Similarly, Deaton and Dreze (2002) point out that over the 1990s, there was divergence in per capita consumption across states and a significant increase in rural-urban consumption inequalities within states and at the all-India level. Jha (2004) also concludes that in both rural and urban sectors, the all-India level of inequality was higher during the post-reform period than during the crisis of the early 1990s.

Banerjee and Piketty (2001) also highlight the disproportionately larger income/consumption gains by the upper tail of the population. Based on income tax reports, they find that the real incomes of the top 1 per cent of income

330 · Flat World, Big Gaps

FIGURE 13.2
India: indices of real per capita consumption by fractile groups, 1987–2002

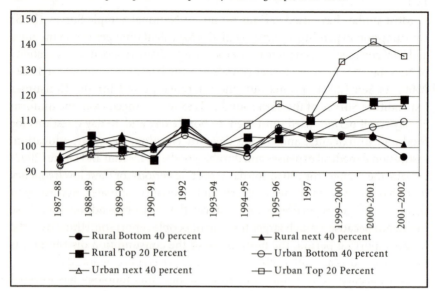

Source: Sen and Himanshu (2005)

FIGURE 13.3
India: real income of top 1 per cent of income earners as share of total income, 1956–1999

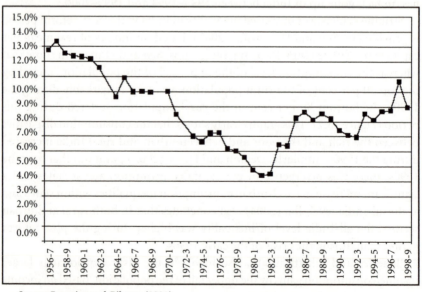

Source: Banerjee and Piketty (2001)

FIGURE 13.4

India: widening disparity between richest and poorest states, 1980–2002

Ratio of per capita net state domestic product of the richest (Punjab) and the poorest (Bihar) major state of India

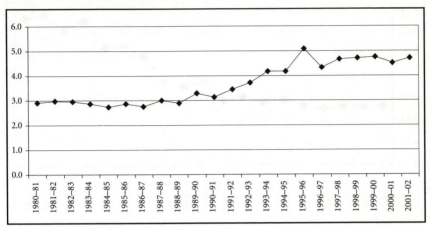

Ratio of per capita net state domestic product of richest states (Punjab, Haryana, Gujarat) and the two poorest states (Bihar and Orissa)

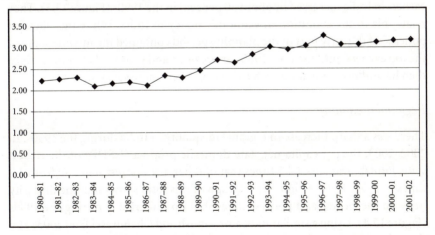

Source: Authors' calculations using data from the Reserve Bank of India, *Handbook of Statistics on Indian Economy*.

FIGURE 13.5

India: trend in inter-state inequality (Gini coefficient), 1980–1999

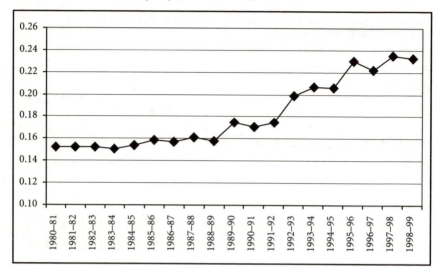

Source: Ahluwalia (2002)

earners in India increased by about 50 per cent in the 1990s (Figure 13.3). They relate this to the evolution of economic policy in India. While the 'socialist policies' of the early part of the planning period contained the income share of the top earners until the mid-1980s, more open and pro-market policies since then have allowed the ultra-rich to increase their share substantially.

Regional Inequality

There was a sharp increase in regional inequality in India during the 1990s. In 2002–2003, the per capita net state domestic product (NSDP) of the richest state, Punjab, was about 4.7 times that of Bihar, the poorest state, up from 4.2 times in 1993–1994. A time-series graph of this ratio shows that the disparity between the richest and poorest states shot up remarkably during the 1990s (Figure 13.4). Using a similar indicator, Ghosh and Chandrasekhar (2003) also show that inter-state inequality increased sharply in India during the reform period.

Trends in Poverty in the 1990s

Closely related to the discussion of inequality in India during the 1990s, there is a similar debate about the extent of poverty reduction in India during the same period. At one end of the spectrum is Bhalla (2003), who uses National

TABLE 13.1
India: trends in urban and rural poverty incidence, 1977–2000

	Urban			Rural		
	Planning Commission estimate	Method 1	Method 2	Planning Commission estimate	Method 1	Method 2
1977–1978	45.2	45.2		53.1	53.1	
1983	40.8	40.8		45.7	45.6	
1987–1988	38.2	38.2		39.1	39.1	
1993–1994	32.4	32.6	27.9	37.3	37	31.6
1999–2000	23.6		24.8	27.1		28.4

Sources: Government of India, *Economic Survey*; Sen and Himanshu (2005)
Note: Method 1 refers to the earlier pattern of questioning with 30 day and 365 day reference periods, while Method 2 refers to the new pattern, with 7 day questions also added, as well as different reference periods for particular commodities.

Accounts Statistics (NAS) for computation of poverty, and claims that there has been a very sharp decline of poverty in India. According to Bhalla, the official poverty figure of 27 per cent for 1999–2000 is a gross overestimate. His calculations indicate that for the year 1999, poverty in India was less than 12 per cent. However, Bhalla's optimism is not shared by others who use the NSS data. These researchers have generally found that the pace of poverty reduction slowed down in the 1990s.[2] Some indication of the varying results that can be obtained by using different methods is provided in Table 13.1.

Employment Growth and the Distribution of Income Generating Opportunities

The most significant link between growth and poverty reduction is employment generation, which is why patterns of employment growth are usually critical in determining both changes in income distribution and the incidence of poverty. During the 1990s, the employment growth rate in India plummeted. Table 13.2 shows significant deceleration of employment generation in both rural and urban areas, with the annual growth rate of rural employment falling to only 0.67 per cent over the period 1993–1994 to 1999–2000. This is not only less than one-third the rate of the previous period 1987–1988 to 1993–1994, it is also less than half the projected growth rate of the labour force in the same period. In fact, this is the lowest growth rate of rural employment in post-Independence history.

The decline in rural employment can be directly attributed to the stagnation of agricultural employment during the 1990s. NSS data indicate that total

TABLE 13.2
India: employment growth rate, 1983–2000

	Rural	Urban
1983 to 1987–1988	1.36	2.77
1987–1988 to 1993–1994	2.03	3.39
1993–1994 to 1999–2000	0.67	1.34

Source: Government of India, Economic Survey.

TABLE 13.3
India: employment in agriculture, 1983–2000

	1983	1987–88	1993–94	1999–2000
Employment (millions)	151.35	163.82	190.72	190.94
Annual growth rate (%)	1.77	2.57	2.23	0.02

Source: Government of India, Economic Survey.

employment in the agriculture sector increased from 190.72 million in 1993–1994 to 190.94 million in 1999–2000, registering an annual growth rate of only 0.02 per cent during this period. This is much lower than the population growth rate over the same period (1.67 per cent), and also lower than the corresponding figures for earlier periods. In fact, the agricultural employment growth rate has plunged to its lowest ever mark since the NSS began recording employment data in the 1950s.

There was also a sharp decline in the employment elasticity of output growth during this period. Among the sectors, employment elasticities fell in agriculture, mining and quarrying, manufacturing, electricity, gas and water, transport, storage and communication, finance and insurance and services sectors. In general, the employment elasticity of output growth was highest in the tertiary sector, followed by the secondary sector. In the reform period, the employment elasticity of agriculture was the lowest.

Along with low employment generation in the agricultural sector, real wage growth rate of agricultural labourers also stagnated during the 1990s. Real agricultural wages grew at about 2.5 per cent per year during the 1990s, whereas public sector salaries grew at about 5 per cent per year during the same period. This partly explains the increased rural-urban inequality of the 1990s in India.

Although real wage growth of agricultural labourers has been positive, its impact on rural per capita income has been less significant because the number of agricultural labourers grew faster than the available days for wage employment. While the rural population in agricultural labour households grew at an average rate of 3.7 per cent per year between 1993–1994 and 1999–2000, annual days of wage employment grew by less than 1.5 per cent per year (Sen and Himanshu, 2005). As a consequence, the increase in real wages has not resulted in an increase in the per capita income for rural agricultural workers, and agricultural unemployment is on the rise.

Another observable employment trend is a steady increase in the casualization of the labour force. In rural India, the proportion of casual workers has increased steadily. This has been matched by a decrease in the self-employment of workers. Currently, only about 7 per cent of rural workers find regular employment. However, for urban areas, the share of casual employment for female workers has come down over the years and regular employment has gone up. But for male workers, the shares of casual workers and self-employed workers have steadily increased, and there is a marginal decline in the share of regular employment.

The decline in self-employment in agriculture, which was especially sharp for women, may be related to changes in production conditions which have forced some peasants out of direct cultivation. There is strong evidence of the declining viability of cultivation in India during the 1990s. A recent study of farm business incomes (Sen and Bhatia, 2004) found that average farm business incomes at current prices deflated by the Consumer Price Index for Agricultural Labourers (CPIAL) grew at only 1.02 per cent per annum during the 1990s, compared to 3.21 per cent in the 1980s. Rising input costs and fluctuating output prices were found to be the dominant cause of this trend. These numbers are averages for farmers of all size holdings; clearly, the situation has been much worse for small and marginal farmers with inferior access to both input and product markets.

This, in turn, has led to a loss of assets, including land, by the small peasantry. It is now clear that this period witnessed a significant degree of concentration of operated holdings, reflecting changes in both ownership and tenancy patterns. Many small and very marginal peasants lost their land over this period, and therefore have been forced to search for work as landless labourers; meanwhile, micro-level surveys have reported increased leasing-in by large farmers from small landowners. According to NSS data, there has been a very large increase in landless households as a percentage of total rural households, from around 35 per cent in 1987–1988 to as much as 41 per cent in 1999–2000. This would definitely have affected the degree of labour intensity on farms.

The sector-wise distribution of the workforce shows some interesting patterns. Using a broad definition of agriculture that includes forestry and fishing, Sundaram (2001a, 2001b) shows that the labour force participation rate in agriculture declined between 1961 and 1999/2000, but there has been a reversal

TABLE 13.4

India: employment growth rate of India by sector, 1983–2000

	1983 to 1987–88	1987–88 to 1993–94	1983 to 1993–94	1993–94 to 1999–2000
Agriculture Industry	1.77	2.57	2.23	0.02
Mining and quarrying	7.35	1.00	3.68	-1.91
Manufacturing	3.64	1.23	2.26	2.58
Electricity, gas and water supply	2.87	7.19	5.31	-3.55
Construction	12.08	-1.38	4.18	5.21
Services				
Trade, hotels and restaurant	4.89	2.99	3.80	5.72
Transport, storage and communication	3.21	3.46	3.35	5.53
Financial, insurance, real estate and business services	4.72	4.50	4.60	5.40
Community, social and personal services	3.57	4.06	3.85	-2.08
All sectors	2.89	2.50	2.67	1.07

Source: Government of India, *Economic Survey*.

of this trend since. However, there has been hardly any change in the absolute number of workers in the agricultural sector. Agriculture still employs about 75 per cent of the total female workforce in India and 84 per cent of rural female workers are still dependant on agriculture. Meanwhile, there has been a decline in the proportion of male workers dependent upon the primary sector. Increasingly higher proportions of male workers (both rural and urban) are finding employment in secondary, tertiary and other non-farm activities. The percentage of male workers involved in these sectors has increased from 22 per cent in 1983 to 29 per cent in 1999–2000.

The lopsided nature of employment growth in India is evident from Table 13.4. The table shows that employment in all sub-sectors of the services sector (except community, social and personal services) increased much faster than in the rest of the economy. However, in spite of the high rate of employment generation in the services sector, poor performance in agriculture and in some industrial sectors has brought down the overall rate of employment generation.

In India, only about 8 to 10 per cent of the population is involved in the organized sector. But employment generation in this sector has suffered during the 1990s, mainly because of a decline in employment generated by the public sector. However, due to better performance of the private sector, total employment generated by the organized sector grew marginally in the period 1995–2001.

The deceleration in organized sector employment is one of the more disconcerting features of the 1990s, especially since industrial output has increased manifold and the service sector, in which much organized employment is based, has been the most dynamic element in national income growth. So, along with the deceleration of employment generation in the rural areas, urban employment generation has also suffered during the 1990s. However, there has been some increase in employment opportunities in certain service sub-sectors such as information technology, communications and entertainment related services. But the numbers involved remain very small (currently around 170,000 to 200,000) relative to the size of the labour force and these jobs remain concentrated in the larger cities.

There is also a strong gender dimension in the growth rate of organized sector employment. For male workers, employment in the organized sector has steadily declined since 1997. Both in private and public sector companies, employment of male workers has come down. Female workers, on the other hand, have done better, and there has been an increase in aggregate organized sector employment for them.

Employment generation data reveal higher levels of inequalities in 1999–2000 than in 1993–1994. The coefficient of variation across states increased from 53.7 in 1993–1994 to 63.7 in 1999–2000. Out of the fifteen major states and union territories, only three (Gujarat, Haryana and Karnataka) experienced a decline in the unemployment rate during this period.

Inequalities in Health, Nutrition and Education

India's performance in health is one area which has been extremely disappointing over the years. Though there have been improvements in some health related indicators like birth and death rates, India's performance in a number of health-related development indicators has been worse than Sub-Saharan Africa's. Also, the improvements have not been uniform throughout the country. Health services are much better in urban areas, and there are differences in the population's health across different regions.

Dreze and Sen (2003) point out that India has fared much worse than Sub-Saharan Africa in nutrition-related indicators such as the proportions of undernourished children, low birth weight babies and pregnant women with anaemia. The proportion of females to males in the population is also lower in India than in Sub-Saharan Africa. *World Development Indicators 2001* shows that about 53 per cent of children are undernourished, and the proportion of pregnant women with anaemia is as high as 88 per cent (World Bank, 2001). In fact, as far as these indicators are concerned, in all the countries for which data are available, none—except Bangladesh—has fared worse than India. Also, if one looks at basic gender inequality data, India is again right at the bottom of the world table, along with Pakistan.

On certain other indicators such as infant mortality and life expectancy, India's performance is relatively better, but these figures hide considerable inter-state variations as well as persistent vulnerabilities of some segments of the population.[3] For example, life expectancy at birth is about 55 in Madhya Pradesh, but in Kerala, it is more than 73 (1993–1997 data). Similarly, the number of women per 1000 males varied from 861 in Punjab to about 1058 in Kerala.

South Indian states have done much better on development-related indicators, including health indicators. Kerala's health indicators are in many ways comparable to those of mid-income and high income countries. On the other hand, the performance of Uttar Pradesh and Bihar, two of the most populous states of India, has been worse than many Sub-Saharan African countries on a large number of health indicators. The Human Development Index (HDI) of India also shows considerable variations across the states.[4]

Inter-state variations in health related indicators do not always correlate with poverty levels. Poverty, as measured by the head-count ratio, is higher in the eastern states of Bihar and Orissa, but child death rates are much higher in the central and northern states of Uttar Pradesh, Madhya Pradesh and Rajasthan. Despite poverty being lower in Uttar Pradesh, child mortality is more than twice as high in the state as compared to Tamil Nadu. Also, gender discrimination is most pronounced in the states of Punjab and Haryana, two of the most prosperous states of India. In fact, one of the most disturbing developments in the 1990s was the decline in the female-male ratios in the relatively prosperous states of India. The female-male ratio among children declined from 945 girls per 1,000 boys (in the 0–6 year age group) in 1991 to 927 girls per 1,000 boys in 2001.

This decline was mainly driven by a combination of social discrimination against girl children and the spread of prenatal sex-determination technology and sex-selective abortion. As the largest declines in the female-male ratios have occurred in the more prosperous states of Gujarat, Haryana, Himachal Pradesh, Punjab and Delhi, it appears that economic growth may have facilitated the spread of sex-selective abortion by making sex-determination technology and sex-selective abortion more affordable. Though prenatal sex determination has subsequently been banned by the government, given the social stigma, corruption and availability of technology, it is difficult to say how effective the ban will be.

One of the main reasons behind the poor state of health care facilities in India and the high health-related inequalities across the states is the very low level of public health expenditure, which happens to be among the lowest in the world at 5.1 per cent of gross domestic product (GDP). Further, nutrition conditions are acknowledged to have a close relationship with overall health, and here, the conditions may even have worsened in recent years. There have been disturbing changes in consumption patterns, as revealed by the National Sample Survey Organization (NSSO) and other sources. Thus, per capita food-grain consumption declined from 476 grams per day in 1990 to only 418 grams per day in 2001, and even aggregate calorific consumption per capita declined from just over 2200 calories per day in 1987–1988 to around 2150 in 1999–2000. This decline was marked, even among the bottom 40 per cent of the population, where it was unlikely to reflect Engels' curve type shifts in consumer choice, but rather relative prices and the inability to consume enough food due to income constraints.

In India, the literacy rate has been increasing at a slow pace over the last few decades. The Census of India has calculated the country's overall literacy rate at 65 per cent in 2001, up from about 43 per cent in 1981 and 52 per cent in 1991. The male-female gap in literacy has improved from 26.6 per cent in 1981 to 21.6 per cent in 2001, but remains large. There are significant inter-state inequa-lities in literacy rates. Even in 2001, Bihar, the state with lowest literacy rate (47.5), was about 18 percentage points below the national average (65.2). For female literacy, the gap was even wider at about 21 per cent. By contrast, Kerala, the state with the highest literacy, had an average literacy rate of 90.92 per cent, with more than 86 per cent female literacy. Though the difference in literacy rates between the top and the bottom states has narrowed in recent years, it remains significant. Along with inter-state differences, there are large disparities between the rural and urban sectors of the country, as Table 13.5 shows. In par-ticular, the literacy rate is still shockingly low among rural women, with less than half classified as literate, even with a restricted definition of literacy.

Primary school enrolment in India may have increased over the years, but is

TABLE 13.5
India: literacy rates by location and gender, 1991, 2001

	1991			2001		
	Male	Female	All	Male	Female	All
Rural Areas	57.90	30.60	44.70	71.40	46.70	59.40
Urban Areas	81.10	64.00	73.10	86.70	73.20	80.30
All Areas	64.13	39.29	52.21	75.85	54.16	65.38
Rural-urban differences	23.2	33.4	28.4	15.3	26.5	20.9

Source: Ministry of Education, Government of India website, based on census.

low even by South Asian standards. Countries such as Bangladesh and Sri Lanka have higher primary school enrolment rates than India. Estimates suggest that more than 70 million children in the 6 to 14 years age group are either school dropouts or have never been enrolled at all. Many more children may be formally registered, but barely attend. This is not surprising because the bulk of primary schools in the country lack the most basic resources: teachers, buildings, blackboards, toilets, textbooks, and so on. Dropout rates from schools are very high, with girls more prone to drop out. However, the dropout rate did decline marginally over the 1990s.

Another factor contributing to increased inequality in education in India has been the rapid growth of private schools. Over the years, the shares of private un-aided schools have gone up significantly at primary, mid-primary and secondary school levels. There has also been a commensurate decline in the share of government schools in these categories. The growth of private un-aided schools has been much higher at the secondary and higher secondary levels. These private un-aided schools are mostly located in urban areas, and charge much higher fees than the government or local school bodies. Since these private schools mainly cater to the richer sections of the population, their rapid growth is indicative of increasing education inequality in India.

FACTORS BEHIND GROWING INEQUALITY AND PERSISTENT POVERTY[5]

The earlier discussion shows a perceptible increase in inter and intra-regional inequality in India during the reform period, and this inequality is evident, not only in income terms, but also in terms of health and access to education. This section discusses some factors which might be responsible for the increase in inequality in India during the reform period.

Fiscal Policy

An important element of the economic reform process adopted in India was the belief that the high fiscal deficit level was responsible for the 1991 crisis, and the deficit should therefore be brought down to a certain pre-determined target. It was argued that a high fiscal deficit is bad for an economy because it can be inflationary, give rise to external deficits, lead to high interest rates and therefore crowd-out private investment, and put an unsustainable interest rate burden on an economy through accumulation of public debt.[6] The International Monetary Fund (IMF) structural adjustment and stabilization programme required the government to bring down the fiscal deficit to a level of 5–6 per cent of GDP from an average of 7 per cent of GDP for the period 1985–1990.

However, it was also part of the new macro policy paradigm that taxes should be rationalized and direct tax rates should be cut so as to improve 'efficiency' and provide incentives to private investors. In addition, indirect tax rates were cut because of import liberalization and associated domestic duty reductions. This meant that fiscal balance could not be achieved through increased tax revenues, but would have to depend upon expenditure cuts. Therefore, to achieve this targeted fiscal deficit, the government undertook major expenditure cuts during the 1990s (Figure 13.6). As the government found it difficult to cut current expenditure, massive reductions were made in capital expenditure.

As a result, central government capital expenditure, as a share of GDP, declined steadily from 7.02 per cent in the late 1980s to 2.74 per cent for the period 1999–2000 to 2002–2003. Public investments in crucial areas like agriculture, rural development, infrastructure development and industry were scaled down. This adversely affected the already fragile state of infrastructure in the economy and led to a virtual collapse of public services in areas like education, public health and sanitation. As discussed by Chandrasekhar and Ghosh (2004), not only were the plan targets for expenditure scaled down, but there were also huge shortfalls in public investment, even relative to these reduced targets, during most years of the decade.

In addition, there was a decline in the central government's current expenditure on rural development accompanied by an overall decline in per capita government expenditure in rural areas. The decline of government investment in the rural areas marked a sharp turnaround from the trend observed during the early 1980s, when there was a large increase in expenditure on the rural

FIGURE 13.6
India: capital and current expenditure as shares of GDP, 1986–2003

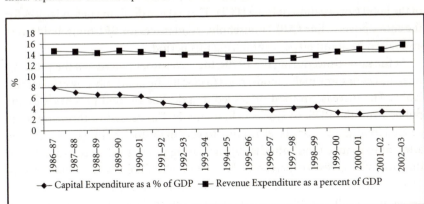

Source: Reserve Bank of India, *Handbook of Statistics on Indian Economy*

sector. Political developments of the 1980s induced various governments to increase the flow of resources to this sector. This led to higher demand generation in the rural sector, and consequently resulted in lower poverty, economic diversification and increased rural employment generation. However, over the 1990s, many policies which had contributed to the development of the rural areas were reversed. Central government expenditure on rural development schemes like agricultural programs, rural employment programs and anti-poverty schemes were cut. This had a negative effect on rural poverty and employment generation during the 1990s.

Along with the cutback of central government expenditure on the rural sector, there was a gradual reorganization of the tax system which led to reduced financial transfers to state governments. The central government reduced the Central Sales Tax (CST), introduced non-shareable levies in direct taxes, and adopted a value-added tax, all of which reduced the ability of states to generate resources. As state governments are the dominant provider of basic services and rural infrastructure, the reduced ability of the state to finance these activities resulted in even lower levels of investment in rural sectors. This again adversely affected demand and employment generation in the rural sector.

As part of the cost cutting exercise, subsidies given for food, fertilizer and exports were also reduced significantly. The reduction of the food subsidy crippled the public distribution system (PDS) for food, which provided fair-priced food items to a very large number of low-income households. To reduce the food subsidy, the government introduced the targeted public distribution system (TPDS). In this system, only the households that belong to the Below Poverty Line (BPL) category were eligible for subsidized food through the public distribution system. To reduce the budgetary expenditure on food, in 1999–2000, the government tried to increase food prices to equal the economic cost of the Food Corporation of India (FCI). This led to a doubling of food prices for the above poverty line (APL) household. Food prices for BPL households were also raised by about 80 per cent during this period.

At the same time, during the 1990s, the government increased the procurement prices of some major food-grains to placate the politically powerful farmer lobby. The increase in food prices led to a decline in food purchases by the public from the PDS, so stocks held by the FCI increased to three times the desired food-grain stock level, leading to very high stock holding costs. So, the attempt to reduce food subsidies by increasing prices paid by consumers had the paradoxical effect of increasing the public costs of holding food-grain stocks, and thus increased the food subsidy! Over this period, per capita food-grain availability in the country actually declined from 510 grams in 1991 to 458 grams in 2000.

Downsizing of employment in a number of key public sector industries was also undertaken in line with the expenditure-cutting exercise. This severely affected employment generation in the public sector but, as most studies point out, generated only notional fiscal benefits. Widespread disinvestment and sale of the equity of profitable public sector units were also undertaken during the 1990s. It was argued by the policymakers that disinvestment of public sector units (PSUs) would ensure fiscal discipline and lead to higher levels of efficiency.

However, as many economists suspect, the real motivation behind the sale of PSUs was the accumulation of resources to meet the IMF fiscal deficit target. The disinvestment process pursued throughout the 1990s turned out to be a disaster, as the controversial disinvestment of PSUs involved a number of profit-making PSUs being sold at low and discounted prices to their global and domestic competitors. Not only did this result in a loss to the government exchequer, putting a recurring burden on the treasury, but it also distorted the markets for several commodities and services. There were also persistent allegations about corruption and malpractice in the sale of PSUs.

As part of fiscal consolidation, a number of loss-making PSUs were closed down. Since some of these actually provided important services to farmers, small enterprises and people in general, their closure also had unfortunate productive and distributive implications. Many of these PSUs were not established solely as profit making companies, but were supposed to achieve various socio-economic targets. So, as a result of this process of disinvestment, the fiscal situation of the government did not improve while many were deprived of the socio-economic benefits provided by these PSUs. This is one reason why the new government of the United Progressive Alliance, led by the Congress Party, declared that it would halt this process of mindless privatization, especially of profit-making public companies. Privatization of basic services like electricity and transport has also raised the prices of these services in many places across India. This has definitely contributed to the increased inequality observed during the 1990s. The worst hit have been the relatively less developed regions where private participation in industry is low.

The attempt by the government to undergo fiscal adjustment was essentially a one-track approach. In line with the expenditure cutting exercise, very little emphasis was put on improving revenue generation in the economy. As noted above, the dictates of market-friendly neo-liberal economic policies did not allow for increases in direct tax rates or import tariffs. As a result, the central government's tax to GDP ratio declined from about 11.8 per cent for the period 1987–1988 to 1989–90 to about 9.6 per cent from 1999–2000 to 2002–03.

A number of factors contributed to this decline. First, India initiated trade liberalization from the early 1990s, and levels of customs duties were reduced on a large number of goods. During the mid-1990s, tariff rates were reduced further, sometimes even going far beyond the level required by World Trade Organization (WTO) obligations. As a result, customs duties declined steadily from about 3.6 per cent of GDP in 1990–1991 to about 1.8 per cent in 2001–2002. Secondly, a range of excise duty concessions were introduced to boost private sector demand and to encourage the growth of private industry. Also, to attract foreign direct investment and foreign portfolio investment, a number of fiscal concessions were given to foreign investors. Huge amounts of tax revenue were foregone on these accounts. Consequently, excise taxes declined from 4.3 per cent of GDP in 1990–1991 to 3.2 per cent in 2001–2002. During the mid-1990s, a number of direct tax concessions were also given as incentives to boost domestic savings and investment.

It was argued that lowering direct tax rates would lead to higher tax revenue following the Laffer curve argument and would increase the buoyancy of tax receipts. However, between 1991–96 and 1997–2001, the buoyancy of central government taxes deteriorated from 0.9 to 0.8. Though this decline happened mainly on account of indirect taxes, the buoyancy in direct tax collection stagnated at 1.3, and did not compensate adequately for the fall in buoyancy of indirect taxes. The restructuring of both direct and indirect taxes effected since the early 1990s, coupled with the structural shift in the composition of GDP towards the less-taxed services sector, appears to have affected the growth in tax revenue.

It can be concluded that the fiscal policy measures initiated in the reform period did not allow the government to build up productive capacity in the economy. Lack of public investment dampened aggregate demand, negatively affected private investments, created infrastructure bottlenecks to future growth, and adversely affected the provision of important public services. Moreover, in a developing country, where capital expenditure on infrastructure and social services tends to crowd in private investment, reduced expenditure on these sectors led to the crowding out of private investment. As a result of reduced public and private investment, there was inadequate productive employment generation, both in rural and urban areas. This worked as a key factor behind the increased inequality and slowing down of poverty reduction in the country.

Financial Sector Reform

The crisis of 1991 hastened the process of financial liberalization pursued by the Indian government since the mid-1980s. Financial liberalization was designed to accomplish the following objectives: a) make the central bank more independent; b) relieve financial repression by freeing interest rates, and introduce various new financial instruments and innovations in the Indian financial system; c) reduce directed and subsidized credit; and d) allow greater openness and freedom for various forms of external capital flows. It should be noted that these objectives were not realized in full, and indeed, the lack of completeness of such financial liberalization has been one important reason for the relative financial stability of the country, unlike several other 'emerging markets'.

The most adverse effect of financial liberalization on inequality has come from policies which eased 'priority sector'[7] lending norms for nationalized banks. Until the 1980s, nationalized banks had obligations to fulfil priority sector lending targets. But post-liberalization, the priority sector definition was widened to include many more activities, and the emphasis in banking shifted instead towards maintaining the capital-adequacy level prescribed by the Basle accord. As a result, most banks now avoid lending to small farmers and small scale industries as they are perceived to be less creditworthy customers. This has had dramatic effects on the viability of cultivation and of small enterprises, which are the largest employers in the country. Consequently, the adverse effects of these policies were felt on income distribution and poverty reduction.

Decline in priority sector lending has led to a significant decline in rural credit from formal channels, which has had major effects in terms of the costs and feasibility of cultivation. The irony is that the rural sector continues to contribute savings in the form of deposits into the banking system, leading to low and falling ratios of credits to deposits in rural banks. The reduced access to and higher cost of agricultural credit obviously means not just increased costs of cultivation, which has not been given adequate policy attention, but also adversely affects private investment in agriculture.

Another consequence of financial liberalization has been the high inflow of foreign private capital into India. Since the late 1990s, there has been a sharp increase in the Net Foreign Assets of the Reserve Bank of India (RBI). This affects monetary management for obvious reasons, but it also constrains fiscal behaviour by creating pressures for reducing central bank credit to the government. This substantially increases the fiscal vulnerability of the state, reducing its ability to stimulate growth, sustain welfare measures like subsidies, and increase outlays on the social sectors.

Liberalization of Foreign and Domestic Investment

One factor contributing to increased inter-regional disparities has been the extremely skewed inter-state distribution of domestic and foreign direct investment (FDI) in India. Only a handful of states have managed to attract a very high share of FDI. There is also a strong regional disparity in the pattern of FDI flows: the southern and western states have fared much better than the other parts of the country. Three southern states (Andhra Pradesh, Karnataka and Tamil Nadu) have received more than 20 per cent of total FDI, while Maharashtra and Gujarat (both in Western India) have received 17.35 per cent and 7.7 per cent of FDI respectively. In contrast, the seven north-eastern states together have received only 0.03 per cent of total FDI during the same period. This unequal distribution of FDI across states in India is not unexpected as FDI inflows tend to go to states where the infrastructure and level of development are better. Concentration of FDI in a few pockets in India has therefore not helped to reduce inequality during the reform period.[8]

Apart from its skewed regional distribution, FDI flows in India also exhibit a strong sectoral bias. A very high proportion of FDI has gone into high-end consumer goods and financial services like banks, insurance companies and consultancy services. It has also gone into information technology related areas where India's human resources and research and development base have pockets of international competitiveness. A large part of the inflow has also gone into the non-tradable infrastructural sector, attracted by special concessions, including guaranteed returns, offered by the government for such investments.

However, benefits accruing from FDI in terms of fixed investments, exports and technological upgrading have been less than expected. This has happened because, since the 1990s, a significant part of FDI has come in the form of mergers and acquisitions. As opposed to green-field FDI investment, mergers and acquisitions do not create new productive capacity and hence do not benefit the host country as much. In fact, there are some negative consequences if they lead to the formation of monopoly powers in an industry. Also, typically with such mergers, employment stagnates or falls. This often counterbalances or even negates the increase in employment of multinational corporation (MNC) affiliates, so that employment increases tend to be the least buoyant of all the major variables associated with MNC production.

Secondly, though FDI worth around $30 billion has come into India since 1991, it has not contributed to an increase in exports. Most analysts suggest that a high proportion of FDI came into India in the early 1990s to jump the 'tariff wall' and service the Indian market, rather than to use the country as an export hub. There are also apprehensions that the initial inflow of direct investment would be followed by large and persistent outflows on account of imports, royalties, technical fees and dividends, with adverse balance of payments consequences. There have also been a few cases of anticompetitive practices by some large foreign companies in India. The most famous cases include the tussle between the government of Maharashtra and the energy giant Enron, and the buyout of a rival Indian cold drink company Parle Exports by Coca Cola.

However, despite the liberalization of rules regarding FDI, India's perform-ance in attracting foreign direct investment has not been particularly impressive in the post-liberalization period. Whereas China has managed to increase its FDI stock from around $24 billion in 1990 to around $448 billion in 2002, India's FDI stock has increased from $1.6 billion in 1990 to $25.7 billion in 2002. FDI also financed only about 2–3 per cent of India's gross domestic capi-tal formation, whereas the corresponding figure for China was around 10–11 per cent (UNCTAD, 2003).

The concentration of FDI in relatively small areas has created some illusion of prosperity, but has hardly done anything to reduce overall levels of poverty or inequality in India. On the other hand, in a bid to attract FDI to their states, many state governments have completely overlooked the rural sector and con-centrated their development expenditures in the urban areas. This has resulted in increased rural-urban inequality, and has given rise to political tension in these states.

Along with FDI, domestic private investment has also been regionally skewed. In the reform period, decontrol of investment licensing eliminated the central government's ability to direct investment to particular areas, especially to less developed or undeveloped regions. As a result, private corporate investment has increasingly tended to locate in areas which can provide them with better support at lower cost. Ahluwalia (2000: 1643) argues "Private corporate invest-ment is potentially highly mobile across states and is therefore likely to flow to states which have a skilled labour force with a good 'work culture', good infra-structure especially power, transport and communications, and good gover-nance generally."

As a result of the increased mobility of private capital and the reduced power of the state to direct investment to certain areas, the poorer performing states, which suffer from infrastructure deficiencies, are at a serious disadvantage in attracting private investment. This has led to the concentration of domestic investment in a few enclaves, and resulted in higher levels of inter-state inequal-ity in India. To address this disparity, it is essential that public investment be used to build economic and social infrastructure in these states to help them attract a larger flow of private investment.

Trade Liberalization

Trade liberalization is essentially inequitable in nature as it distributes income in favour of the export sector and against the import-competing sector. Unless the gains from trade are redistributed, trade liberalization will always change income distribution, which may imply higher inequality. In India, a similar phenomenon can be observed, but not necessarily along lines predicted by traditional trade theories. The more employment-intensive sectors have been adversely affected, rather than encouraged, by trade liberalization. Opening up trade has helped certain sub-sectors, both in manufacturing and services, where India is internationally competitive, but mainly in activities using relatively skilled labour in the Indian context.

By expanding the markets for these sectors, trade liberalization has definitely created some pockets of prosperity in India, but on the other hand, it has negatively affected most other manufacturing sectors and agriculture. The situation in agriculture is most disturbing because about 70 per cent of the population is dependent upon this sector. Continued subsidization of agriculture by developed countries and the resultant distortion of global agricultural trade is one of the factors behind the poor performance of agriculture. But other domestic macroeconomic policies, such as patterns of public spending and financial policies, have also played a role. Small and medium enterprises (SMEs) in the manufacturing sector have also been hit by trade liberalization. Typically, employment intensive domestic production has been displaced by imports of similar goods using more capital intensive production methods abroad.

There is also a possibility that increased globalization and reforms may increase the cost of labour and that this would encourage capital intensive industrialization (Goldar, 2002). This can happen because: a) an increase in relative food prices would increase the cost of labour in the form of higher wages; b) a reduction of tariffs in the capital goods sector may lead to cost advantages in favour of capital; and c) foreign competition and a greater export drive may also encourage more capital intensity. Therefore, a freer trade regime may not necessarily lead to higher employment generation in a country; this is supported by India's experience thus far.

In this context, it is notable that in a liberalized trade regime, it is important that most workers possess some ability to shift jobs between sectors because trade liberalization is likely to induce relocation of workers. Opening up trade leads to job losses in import-competing industries and increases employment opportunities in export sectors. If socio-economic conditions prevent workers from making this transition smoothly, or if the rate of new job creation is not fast enough, then it may result in even higher levels of inequality than those already prevailing in the economy. It is the duty of the government to equip and train workers to build up the requisite skills to make such inter-sectoral shifts. However, the increased withdrawal of the state in India from most welfare-related issues suggests that the adjustment to trade liberalization is going to be a painful process, and the gap between the beneficiaries of trade liberalization and those who have not managed to benefit from it will increase in the immediate future unless alternative policies are introduced.

CONCLUSION

In India, although there are claims that inequality has decreased in the post-liberalization period, careful analysis of data shows that these views are mostly misplaced. Inequality has increased both in rural and urban India. While the richer sections of the population have benefited, there has been stagnation of incomes for the majority, and the bottom rung of the population has been severely affected by this process. There is also evidence that, both at the national and the state levels, income disparities across states and between urban and rural populations have increased during this period. Similarly, the pace of poverty reduction has slowed down and there have been alarming increases of poverty in some pockets, including in the north-eastern states.

One important factor behind these trends is the stagnation of employment generation in both rural and urban areas across the states. Open unemployment has increased in most parts of the country. The rate of growth of rural employment has hit an all time low. Falling employment generation in the agriculture sector has been associated with a steady, but significant increase in casualization of the labour force in India. Downsizing and privatization of public sector units have affected organized sector employment. While the employment growth rate in services has been higher than in other sectors, this reflects contrary trends. The more dynamic sub-sectors like information technology, communication and entertainment employ a very small section of the labour force, and their positive impact on the overall employment scenario has been minimal. Other service sector employment expansion reflects the move to refuge employment, given the lack of dynamism in other sectors.

One countervailing force to the lower employment generation has been increased economic migration, typically to other countries in Asia and the Middle East, which has been especially important in certain regions and provided an important alternative source of transfer income to local residents through remittances. However, these flows have had little to do with domestic policies and more to do with international economic processes.

Progress in terms of health and education indicators has been unsatisfactory, even when compared to other developing countries. There exist huge inter-state disparities in health and education related indicators across India. State involvement and investment in these sectors has historically remained low and come down even further during the 1990s. Gradual withdrawal of the state from these sectors and increased reliance on the private sector are likely to further exacerbate the already inequitable distribution of health and education services in India.

A number of policies adopted during the reform period have essentially increased the level of inequality in India. Liberalization of trade has helped some sectors where India is internationally competitive, but has also negatively affected the other sectors. The agriculture sector as well as SMEs, which account for the bulk of employment, has been the worst hit by the trade liberalization undertaken by policymakers since the mid-1990s. The inflow of FDI into India has only marginally improved gross domestic capital formation, but its incidence has been confined to very small pockets, both geographically and sectorally. This has increased inter-state and inter-sectoral inequalities in the country.

Emphasis on reduction of the fiscal deficit, in a context of falling tax-GDP ratios, is another factor which has increased inequality in India in the reform period. The government's failure to reduce current expenditure has implied that most of the adjustment to reduce the fiscal deficit has been carried out by reducing capital expenditure and rural expenditure generally, as well as by selling PSUs to generate one-time revenue. Reduction of capital expenditure has reduced public investment in key infrastructural areas and social welfare schemes. Attempts to reduce government expenditure on food subsidies and social welfare schemes have also had serious negative effects on inequality in the country.

Other market-oriented reform measures, like closure of non-profit making PSUs, have seriously undermined the social objectives of the PSUs and negatively affected employment and economic development in some parts of the country, especially in less developed regions. Opening up the economy and financial sector liberalization have also had major negative consequences for weaker sections of the population. Credit flows to agriculture and to SMEs have gone down drastically in recent years. This has reinforced the problems faced by these sectors due to trade liberalization and the complete removal of quantitative restrictions on imports.

All these point to some conclusions, which have implications for government policy. The first is the crucial importance of continued and increased public expenditure for productive investments in infrastructure as well as for social expenditures and ensuring food access. Both aggregate expenditure and the pattern of public expenditure are important. In addition, fiscal federalism is very significant in large countries like India. Policy must also incorporate clear perceptions of the relationship between growth patterns and the extent and type of employment generated.

NOTES

[1] Sen and Himanshu (2005) argue that their adjusted figures indicate an almost three Gini point increase, rather than a two Gini point decline in rural inequality between the 50th and 55th rounds.

[2] Deaton (2005), using adjusted and comparable estimates of poverty for 1993–94 and 1999–2000, finds that poverty declined from 37.3 per cent in 1993–1994 to 30.2 per cent in 1999–2000. Sundaram and Tendulkar (2003b, 2003c) estimate that poverty declined from 32.15 per cent in 1993–1994 to 27.32 per cent in 1999–2000, which indicates an even smaller decline in poverty. According to Sen and Himanshu (2005), the head-count poverty ratio in India declined over this period by three percentage points at most, but the number of poor in the country actually increased.

[3] These variations increase with the level of disaggregation. For example, according to Census 2001, district-level female literacy rates range between 9 and 84 per cent in India.

[4] However, the dispersion of HDI was lower in 2001 (coefficient of variation 18.4 per cent, range 0.283) than in 1991 (coefficient of variation 15.7 per cent, range 0.271).

[5] Unless otherwise specified, data for this section are from Government of India, *Economic Survey* and Reserve Bank of India, *Handbook of Statistics on Indian Economy*.

[6] These arguments against high fiscal deficits are often not supported by economic theory. Chandrasekhar and Ghosh (2002) and Patnaik (2000, 2001a, 2001b) discuss problems of the neo-liberal arguments against high fiscal deficits.

[7] Priority sector includes agriculture and small and medium scale enterprises (SMEs).

[8] Data for this section are from India Investment Centre, Government of India.

REFERENCES

Ahluwalia, Montek S. (2000). Economic performance of states in post-reforms period. *Economic and Political Weekly*, May 6–11: 1637–48.

Ahluwalia, Montek S. (2002). State level performance under economic reforms in India. In Anne Krueger (ed.). *Economic Policy Reforms and the Indian Economy*. University of Chicago Press, Chicago: 91–128.

Banerjee, A., and T. Piketty (2001). Are the rich growing richer: Evidence from Indian tax data. Processed, MIT, Cambridge, MA, and CEPREMAP, Paris. http://www.worldbank.org/indiapovertyworkshop.

Bhalla, Surjit S. (2003). Recounting the poor: Poverty in India, 1983–1999. *Economic and Political Weekly*, January 25–31: 338–49.

Chakravarty, Sukhamoy (1987). *Development Planning: The Indian Experience*. Oxford University Press, New Delhi.

Chandrasekhar, C.P., and Jayati Ghosh (2002). *The Market that Failed: A Decade of Neoliberal Economic Reforms in India*. Leftword Books, New Delhi.

Chandrasekhar, C.P., and Jayati Ghosh (2004). *The Market that Failed: A Decade of Neoliberal Economic Reforms in India*. Second Edition. Leftword Books, New Delhi.

Deaton, Angus (2005). Adjusted Indian Poverty Estimates in 1999/2000. In Angus Deaton and Valerie Kozel (eds). *Data and Dogma: The Great Indian Poverty Debate*. Macmillan, New Delhi.

Deaton, Angus, and Jean Dreze (2002). Poverty and inequality in India: A re-examination. *Economic and Political Weekly*, September 7: 3729–48.

Deaton, Angus, and Valerie Kozel (eds) (2005). *Data and Dogma: The Great Indian Poverty Debate*. Macmillan, New Delhi.

Dreze, Jean, and Amartya Sen (2003). *India: Development and Participation*. Oxford University Press, New Delhi.

Ghosh, Jayati, and C.P. Chandrasekhar (2003). Per capita income growth in the states of India. http://www.macroscan.com/fet/aug03/fet100803SDP_1.htm.

Goldar, Bishwanath (2002). Trade liberalization and manufacturing employment: The case of India. Employment Paper No. 2002/34, International Labour Office, Geneva.

Government of India (2001). Census 2001. http://www.censusindia.net/.

Government of India. *Economic Survey*. Various issues. Government Printing Office, New Delhi.

Government of India. India Investment Centre. http://iic.nic.in/default.htm.

Government of India, Ministry of Education. http://www.education.nic.in/.

Government of India, National Planning Commission (2002). *National Human Development Report of India, 2001*. Government Printing Office, New Delhi.

Jha, Raghbendra (2004). Reducing poverty and inequality in India: Has the liberalization helped? In G.A. Cornia (ed.). *Inequality, Growth and Poverty in an Era of Liberalization and Globalization*. UNU-WIDER Studies in Development Economics, Oxford University Press, New York: 297–327.

Patnaik, Prabhat (2000). On some common macroeconomic fallacies. *Economic and Political Weekly*, April 8: 1220–22.

Patnaik, Prabhat (2001a). On fiscal deficit and real interest rate. *Economic and Political Weekly*, April 14: 1160.

Patnaik, Prabhat (2001b). On fiscal deficit and real interest rate: A reply. *Economic and Political Weekly*, July 28: 2898–99.

Reserve Bank of India. *Handbook of Statistics on Indian Economy*. Various issues. Reserve Bank of India, Mumbai.

Sen, Abhijit (2001). Estimates of consumer expenditure and implications for comparable poverty estimates after the NSS 55th Round. Paper presented at NSSO International Seminar on 'Understanding Socio-economic Changes through National Surveys', 12–13 May, New Delhi. Reprinted in Angus Deaton and Valerie Kozel (eds). *Data and Dogma: The Great Indian Poverty Debate*. Macmillan, New Delhi (2005): 203–38.

Sen, Abhijit, and M.S. Bhatia (2004). *Cost of cultivation and farm income—A study of the comprehensive scheme for studying the cost of cultivation of principal crops in India and results from it*. Ministry of Agriculture, New Delhi. http://www.academicfoundation.com/n_detail/farmer.asp.

Sen, Abhijit, and Himanshu (2005). Poverty and inequality in India: Getting closer to the truth. In Angus Deaton and Valerie Kozel (eds). *Data and Dogma: The Great Indian Poverty Debate*. Macmillan, New Delhi: 306–70.

Sundaram, K. (2001a). Employment-unemployment situation in nineties: Some results from the NSS 55th Round Survey. *Economic and Political Weekly*, March 17: 931–40.

Sundaram, K. (2001b). Employment and poverty in the 1990s: Further results from NSS 55th Round Employment-Unemployment Survey 1999–2000. *Economic and Political Weekly*, August 11–17: 3039–49.

Sundaram, K., and Suresh D. Tendulkar (2003a). Poverty has declined in the 1990s: A resolution of comparability problems in NSS consumer expenditure data. *Economic and Political Weekly*, January 25–31: 327–37.

Sundaram, K., and Suresh D. Tendulkar (2003b). Poverty in India in the 1990s: An analysis of changes in 15 major states. *Economic and Political Weekly*, April 5–11: 1385–93.

Sundaram, K., and Suresh D. Tendulkar (2003c). Poverty in India in the 1990s: Revised results for all-India and 15 major states for 1993–94. *Economic and Political Weekly*, November 15–22: 4865–72.

UNCTAD (2003). *World Investment Report, 2003: FDI Policies for Development: National and International Perspectives*. United Nations Conference on Trade and Development, Geneva.

World Bank (2001). *World Development Indicators, 2001*. World Bank, Washington, DC.

14
Growth with Equity in East Asia?[1]

JOMO K.S.

The 'growth with equity' said to characterize East Asia has been explained by various factors. These include regime initiatives to secure greater political support and legitimacy (such as land reforms and rural development efforts), human resource development (HRD) efforts (especially meritocratic publicly-funded education to the tertiary level), as well as significant household savings ('forced' or otherwise) and the greater role of government more generally. Rapid economic growth in much of the region has undoubtedly raised living standards by various means. For example, 'trickle down' inducements to increase labour productivity as well as tight labour markets have pushed up real incomes despite repressive labour policies—particularly in the Republic of Korea (South Korea) and more recently in Southeast Asia—and the declining terms of trade of manufactured exports from the South generally. Hence, any consideration of the distributive implications of growth as well as economic liberalization must take into account both their inherent consequences as well as redistributive policy mechanisms. This chapter focuses on the social record of East Asia, especially in the decade since the 1995 World Summit for Social Development held in Copenhagen.

While government interventions have been crucial to rapid growth and structural change in the region, there has been considerable liberalization in the last two decades, largely due to international pressures, especially from the West. The consequences of this liberalization of trade regimes and foreign direct investment rules as well as financial regulation—especially in the Republic of Korea (South Korea), Taiwan Province of China, Malaysia, Thailand and Indonesia (i.e., in both first and second-generation newly industrializing economies [NIEs])—will be considered here. Besides such liberalization and globalization, there has also been subsidization of efforts in human resource development (especially education and training), redistribution and poverty targeting, more effective social safety nets, social corporatist and communitarian initiatives, quality-of-life improvement efforts, technology promotion, more gradual agricultural trade liberalization, as well as more effective and efficient, but indirect, governance of foreign direct investment and international finance, which have been differently affected by developments of the last decade, perhaps most significantly by the East Asian currency and financial crises of 1997–1998.

Many East Asian economies have achieved remarkable economic growth over the three decades or more preceding Copenhagen, which helped improve living standards generally. Besides the eight high-performing Asian economies (HPAEs)—Japan, South Korea, Taiwan, Hong Kong SAR, Singapore, Malaysia, Thailand and Indonesia—identified by the World Bank (1993), the People's Republic of China too has grown very rapidly in the last two and a half decades. According to the Bank, rapid growth of manufacturing and exports in these economies has been accompanied by falling poverty levels and better income distribution. While extensive interventions in the market have been important for late industrialization, most governments implemented substantial liberalization from the mid-1980s. Such liberalization can be attributed largely to pressure from the major Western powers and, often, recognition of the desirability of deregulation following unpopular, regressive, burdensome and counter-productive government interventions. The World Trade Organization (WTO) has joined the international financial institutions and powerful governments in further promoting liberalization. It is thus important to examine the distributive implications of such liberalization and globalization.

This brief review of the distributional effects of liberalization in the region will compare the major East Asian economies except Japan, namely South Korea and Taiwan from Northeast Asia, Indonesia, Malaysia and Thailand in Southeast Asia, as well as China. Urban economies such as Hong Kong and Singapore have long been far more unequal with inequality rising, while the Philippines has experienced modest growth during recent decades. All these economies have experienced unprecedented growth and structural transformation in the last few decades (see Table 14.1). Average annual gross domestic product (GDP) growth rates exceeded 7 per cent and 6 per cent in the periods 1970–1980 and 1980–1996, respectively, with the manufacturing sectors growing fastest to become the most important contributors to growth in most of these economies until de-industrialization began in some economies, beginning with Hong Kong, but also affecting Singapore, Taiwan and arguably, South Korea. Exports grew at double-digit levels annually over the period 1980–1992, and average per capita incomes increased greatly as a consequence. As a proportion of total growth, primary exports fell sharply, while machinery and transport equipment production grew significantly in the manufacturing sectors.

The success of East Asian economies in reducing poverty has been spectacular, largely attributable to growth and structural change. Income inequality

TABLE 14.1
Six HPAEs: economic indicators, 1970–2002

Economy	Per capita income (US$)		Average annual GDP growth (%)			Manufacturing/GDP share (%)						Agriculture/GDP share (%)					Services/GDP share (%)				
	1995	2002	1970–80	1985–95	1995–02	1970	1980	1990	1995	1999	2002	1980	1990	1995	1999	2002	1980	1990	1995	1999	2002
Korea	9700	9930	10.1	7.71		21.0	29	28.8	27.0	31.8	29.2	15.0	8.5	7.0	5	4	45	48.4	50	51.5	55.1
Taiwan	8788[a]	n.a	10.0[b]	7.5[c]		35.0[d]	na	na	42.0[a]	na	n.a	na	na	na	na	n.a	na	na	na	na	n.a
Malaysia	3890	3540	7.9	5.7		12.0	21	24.2	33.0	31.6	30.7	22.0	15.2	13.0	10.8	9.1	40	44.2	44	43.1	46.4
Indonesia	980	710	7.2	6.0		10.0	13	20.7	24.0	25.8	25.0	24.0	19.4	17.0	19.4	17.5	34	41.5	41	37.7	38.1
Thailand	2740	1980	7.1	8.4		16.0	22	27.2	29.0	32.4	33.8	23.0	12.5	11.0	10.4	9	48	50.3	49	49.6	48.5
China		940				na	42.2	37.0	na	43.1	44.9	30.1	27.0	na	17.3	14.5	21.4	31.3	na	32.9	33.7

Notes: [a] for 1991; [b] for period 1963–80; [c] for period 1981–93; [d] for industry.
Sources: World Bank (1997: Tables 12, 13, 15); Taiwan figures from Yu (1994) and Lee (1994); 2002: ADB (2003).

has been low in South Korea and Taiwan, but has risen in recent years with economic liberalization, including international integration or globalization. Trends in Indonesia, Malaysia and Thailand in Southeast Asia have been less clear, with poverty going down, but inequality apparently increasing in recent years with economic liberalization. With rapid growth and strengthened (private) property rights, China has experienced rapidly increasing inequality and unemployment despite high growth and considerable poverty reduction. The evidence suggests that the World Bank's (1993) claim of egalitarian growth in East Asia may be exaggerated. 'Initial conditions' seem to be primarily responsible for the more egalitarian experience of Northeast Asia compared to Southeast Asia, but has not been enough to prevent the rapid growth in inequalities in China. Growth has been critical in raising overall real incomes and thus alleviating poverty, but there is less clear evidence of the growth process directly contributing to more equitable income distribution, except perhaps in Northeast Asia, where low unemployment and skill enhancement strengthened the bargaining power and remuneration of labour generally. South Korea has probably been unique in East Asia in experiencing some significant institutionalization of redistributive and welfare measures with recent democratization.

Available evidence does not allow much robust and comparable commentary on recent trends in distribution of assets, work and employment, social services and benefits (especially health and education) as well as power in terms of access to information and political participation. Hence, the following discussion focuses on poverty and income distribution trends; but even here, most available evidence ends in the early part of this decade. Hence, it is very difficult to assess the impact of the heads of governments' declarations at the 1995 Copenhagen Social Summit on equity in the region. For most economies in the region, the 1997–1998 regional financial crises had a far greater impact on equity. The considerable rhetoric on social safety nets during the period obscured the consequences of economic liberalization, especially since the 1990s, which undermined earlier redistributive and welfare rights, provisions and institutions. However, there has been some retreat from the more extreme policies of the Washington Consensus in recent years, reflected in the involvement of the World Bank and the International Monetary Fund (IMF) in poverty reduction and the World Trade Organization's stated commitment to the Doha 'Development Round'. Nevertheless, the depth of these reforms is yet to be made wholly apparent.

POVERTY ALLEVIATION AND REDISTRIBUTION

The incidence of poverty declined sharply in all six East Asian economies, as shown in Table 14.2. With the exception of Thailand, which has not had a significant commitment to and mechanisms for more egalitarian redistribution, income inequality declined or did not worsen in Indonesia, South Korea, Malaysia and Taiwan over the 1976–1985 period. All five economies have had explicit poverty alleviation and redistribution policies, though their actual significance has varied among individual countries. With strong commitments to achieving growth and redistribution, the regimes in these economies were able to direct developmental efforts independently of outside pressures.

The first important initiative for poverty alleviation and more equitable distribution came from land reforms in South Korea and Taiwan in the late 1940s (see Hamilton, 1983; Hsiao, 1996). In 1947, during the Korean War, the United States of America military forces distributed land confiscated from the Japanese colonial government to the tillers, charging low rents. Later, after the Korean War, the South Korean government acquired land from landlords, reselling it at subsidized prices to 90,000 tenants (Amsden, 1989). In Taiwan, the Kuomintang government seized land from landlords in return for shares in public companies, and sold them at favourable prices to the tillers of the land. Reforms in Taiwan led to a reduction of land rents to 37.5 per cent of the yield for major crops, sale of public land to cultivators and tenants, and limited ownership by landowners (Yu, 1994: footnote 1).

The Southeast Asian experiences have been somewhat different. Unlike

TABLE 14.2
Five HPAEs: poverty incidence, 1970–2002

Economy	Poverty Incidence (%)							
	1970	1976	1980	1985	1993	1998	2000	2002
S. Korea	23.4	14.8	9.8	n.a.	n.a.	4.5 [c]	3.6	n.a.
Taiwan	n.a.	5.0	n.a.	n.a.	n.a.	n.a.	n.a.	n.a.
Malaysia	52.4	42.4	29	20.7 [a]	13.4 [b]	7.5 [c]	5.5 [d]	5.1
Thailand	39.0	30.0	23.0	29.5	n.a.	12.9	13.1	n.a.
Indonesia	57.1	50.1	39.8	21.6 [a]	n.a.	23.4	n.a.	18.2

Notes: [a] 1984; [b] 1989; [c] 1999; [d] 2002; n.a.—not available.
While inter-country comparison of changes is possible, cross-comparisons of rates in particular years is not possible due to classification differences.
Sources: Medhi (1995: 58–73); Malaysia (1996); Habibullah (1988); Yu (1994: 6); Chowdhury and Islam (1993); data for 1998 and 2000 from ADB, Key Indicators (various years) Asian Development Bank; data for Malaysia from Malaysia (1999, 2003).

natural resource-poor South Korea and Taiwan, land reforms have been less significant in the resource-rich Southeast Asian economies. Political circumstances have also been less favourable to inducing pro-active redistribution measures as in Northeast Asia. Resource wealth may also have weakened the imperative to industrialize, especially to promote export-oriented manufacturing. Political considerations as well as ethnic diversity may have also prevented the regimes from promoting domestic industrialists through more activist industrial policy initiatives. After seceding from Malaysia in 1965, the Singapore leadership sought to quickly develop a large foreign stake in the Singapore economy to secure protection against potentially belligerent neighbours. With the introduction of pro-Malay affirmative action policies from the early 1970s, it is widely believed that foreign investment was encouraged to 'balance' the ubiquitous ethnic Chinese presence in the Malaysian economy.

As a consequence, the region, especially Singapore and Malaysia, has relied far more on foreign direct investment (FDI) to industrialize, and especially for export-oriented manufacturing capacity. Labour, especially wage repression, has been an important incentive to such FDI to relocate in the region. From the mid-1980s until the mid-1990s, currency undervaluation was an important incentive to attract FDI. Compared to Northeast Asia, Southeast Asia has done less well in terms of educational and training efforts, which in turn has limited development of industrial and technological capabilities, and hence, prospects for greater productivity growth as well as labour remuneration. However, the Southeast Asian experiences have also been diverse in other respects.

Although there has not been any major land reform in Malaysia, new agricultural land has been distributed to the land-hungry through land development schemes managed by government agencies. Although the land schemes have had some effect on poverty alleviation, the impact has been limited (see Halim, 1991; Jomo, 1986). Malaysia deepened its rural development efforts following the 1971 introduction of the New Economic Policy (NEP), which was committed to poverty reduction and redistribution to achieve greater inter-ethnic parity. Besides extensive investments to develop infrastructure in rural areas, where Bumiputera[2] are heavily concentrated, special ministries and government agencies have also been set up to enhance the socio-economic standing of the Bumiputera. With rapid economic growth, led by export-oriented manufacturing in the 1970s and since the late 1980s, poverty rapidly declined. In addition, the Green Revolution in rice cultivation—involving double cropping, green revolution strains, fertilizers, pesticides, ploughing and harvesting machinery—helped raise yields and incomes. Income inequality trends are unclear, but seem to suggest that inequality grew in the 1960s, declined in the 1970s and 1980s, and increased since then (Jomo and Ishak, 1986; Hashim, 1997).

Not unlike Malaysia, the Thai authorities emphasized agricultural diversification and the opening up of new land in the 1960s (Onchan, 1995: 7–8), with little emphasis on land or income redistribution to help disadvantaged groups. Land reforms were formally introduced in Thailand in 1975 with the Agricultural Land Reform Act. However, little real progress was made; a significant amount of land was transferred to wealthy, politically influential businessmen instead (Onchan, 1995). Hence, despite important initiatives, land reforms have generally been unsuccessful. However, growth helped lower the overall incidence of poverty (except in the mid-1980s), although income inequality worsened (see Tables 14.3, 14.4a and 14.4b). The government has also fairly successfully raised rural household incomes by promoting off-farm rural work, as in Japan, South Korea and Taiwan. As a consequence, the proportion of rural household incomes from off-farm activities rose from 46 per cent in 1971–1972 to 63 per cent in 1986–1987 (Onchan, 1995: 32). Off-farm activities helped further reduce rural poverty in the period 1985–1990, when urban poverty rose as well (see Rasiah, Ishak and Jomo, 1996: Table 4).

Investments in human resources have also helped reduce poverty and inequality. Through government efforts, South Korea and Taiwan have developed highly educated labour forces. While primary education has been universal in these economies, at least since the 1960s, there have also been high rates of transition to the secondary and tertiary levels, and strong emphasis on technical and engineering disciplines. Clearly, these economies' investments in human capital went well beyond the primary schooling limit recommended by the World Bank, with labour market interventions based on long-term considerations beyond current prices (Rodrik, 1994). The expansion of education not only helped generate technical and professional human resources for industrial upgrading, but also enhanced opportunities for upward socioeconomic

TABLE 14.3
Six HPAEs: household income distribution Gini coefficients, 1970–2002

	1970	1976	1980	1985	1999	2000	2002
S. Korea	0.332	0.391	0.389	0.357[d]	0.3204	0.32	n.a.
Taiwan	0.294	0.28	0.277	0.29	0.325	n.a.	0.345
Malaysia	0.506	0.529	0.493[e]	0.474[a]	0.4432[b]		0.4607
Thailand	n.a.	0.451	0.473[c]	0.500[b]	0.444	0.43	0.428
Indonesia	0.35	0.34	0.34[d]	0.33	0.31	0.30	n.a.
China					0.32[g]		

Notes: a 1984; b 1989; c 1981; d 1982; e 1979; f 1998; n.a.—not available.

Sources: Medhi (1995: 58–73); Malaysia (1996); Habibullah (1988); Taiwan Gini coefficients are from Yu (1994: 6); Chowdhury and Islam (1993); 1999, 2002: ADB website; Sunantha (2002)

TABLE 14.4a
Household income Gini ratios for eight East Asian economies, 1961–1993

Year	Asian NIEs				ASEAN 4			
	Hong Kong	South Korea	Singapore[a]	Taiwan	Indonesia[b]	Malaysia	Philippines	Thailand
1961							0.49	
1962							(0.486)	0.414
1964				0.36				
1965		0.344					0.49 (0.491)	
1966	0.487 (0.407)		0.498	0.358				
1967						0.498		
1968				0.362 0.321				0.429
1970	(0.430)	0.332		(0.295)		0.506 (0.502)		
1971	0.439 (0.430) (0.409)						0.480 (0.478)	
1972				0.318				
1973			(0.46)					
1974			(0.45)	0.319 (.0288)				
1975	[0.429]		0.448 (0.45)					0.451 (0.426)
1976	(0.435) (0.409)	0.391	(0.44)	0.307 (0.280)	0.34 (0.492)	(0.529)		
1977			(0.46)	(0.284)				
1978			(0.42)	0.306 (0.287)				
1979			0.424 (0.42)	(0.285)		0.493 (0.493)		
1980	(0.373)	0.389	(0.41)	0.303 (0.278)	0.34			
1981	0.481 (0.453) (0.451)		0.443 (0.44)	(0.281)	0.33	0.443		0.473 (0.453)
1982		0.357	0.465 (0.46)	0.308 (0.283)		0.465		(0.453)
1983			(0.48)	(0.288)				

(contd)

TABLE 14.4a *(contd)*

Year	Asian NIEs				ASEAN 4			
	Hong Kong	South Korea	Singapore^a	Taiwan	Indonesia^b	Malaysia	Philippines	Thailand
1984			0.474 (0.47)	0.312 (0.288)	0.33	0.474 (0.480)		
1985	(0.453)		(0.46)	0.317 (0.290)			0.452 (0.446)	
1986	(0.420)		(0.46)	(0.297)				(0.500)
1987			(0.47)	(0.299)	0.32	(0.458)		
1988		(0.400)	(0.48)	(0.303)			(0.445)	(0.479)
1989			(0.49)	(0.303)				
1990	[0.476]			(0.311)	0.32			(0.504)
1991	(0.451)							
1993					0.34			

TABLE 14.4b
Household income Gini ratios for eight East Asian economies, 1985–2001

Year	Asian NIEs				ASEAN 4			
	Hong Kong	South Korea	Singapore^a	Taiwan	Indonesia^b	Malaysia	Philippines	Thailand
1985							0.4446	
1987					0.32			
1988				0.303			0.4466	0.485
1989		0.304		0.303				
1990		0.295		0.312	0.32	0.446		0.524
1991	0.476	0.287	0.471	0.308		0.4680		
1992		0.284	0.475	0.312				0.536
1993		0.281	0.474	0.316	0.34	0.459		
1994		0.285	0.474	0.318			0.4507	0.527
1995		0.284		0.317		0.464		
1996	0.518	0.291	0.473	0.317	0.356			0.515
1997		0.283	0.472	0.320		0.470	0.470	
1998		0.316	0.470	0.324	0.319		0.494	0.511
1999		0.320	0.476	0.325	0.334	0.443		0.533
2000		0.317					0.496	
2001	0.525	0.319						

Notes: ^a For employed population, not households; ^b Based on expenditure.
Sources: Hong Kong, Census and Statistics Department (2001); Korea National Statistical Office (2002); Singapore, Mukhopadhaya (2000); Taiwan, Taiwan (undated); Indonesia, 1987–1993: Asra (2000); 1996–1999: Ali Said and Widyanti (2002); Malaysia: Ragayah (2002); Philippines, 1985–1994: Yap (1997), 1997–98: Tabunda and Albert (2002); 2000: Albert and others (2002); Thailand: Sunantha (2002), as cited by Ragayah (2005: Table 1).

mobility, including skills enhancement and higher remuneration (Deyo, 1989).

Achievements in secondary and especially in tertiary education in Indonesia, Malaysia and Thailand have not been comparable to South Korea and Taiwan. Interestingly, the Philippines has performed better than Indonesia, Malaysia and Thailand on many such indicators of educational achievement, raising serious doubts about the actual role and contribution of human resource development to growth and equality. While basic education has offered access to low-skilled jobs, schooling has offered limited upward social mobility. In addition, while South Korea and Taiwan have generated ample supplies of technical labour, Malaysia, Thailand and Indonesia continue to face serious shortages of such labour. In 1990, Malaysia, Thailand and Indonesia had around 400 technologists and scientists per million people, compared to 2,200 for South Korea; 2,100 for Taiwan; and 6,700 for Japan (UNDP, 1994: 17). While Malaysia and Indonesia managed to reduce inequality over long periods, unlike in Thailand, these limited successes were not due to market forces, as both governments spent a great amount on redistribution and did much to generate employment.

Rapid growth, rising education levels and declining unemployment have pushed up real wages in these economies (see Table 14.5), despite the weakness of organized labour. Real wages grew at average annual rates of 10.0 per cent and 8.2 per cent over the periods 1970–1980 and 1980–1992, respectively, in South Korea (World Bank, 1995: 175). In Taiwan, real wages grew by 6.0 per cent (computed from Deyo, 1989: 93) and 7.5 per cent (Lee, 1994: 16) over the periods 1970–1980 and 1976–1986 respectively. Hence, although labour was

TABLE 14.5
Five HPAEs and China: wage employment, growth and unemployment rate, 1970–2002

Economy	Average annual growth of wage employment (1970–1990) (%)	Unemployment rate (%)				
		1970	1983	1992	2000	2002
S. Korea	6.6	n.a.	4.1	2.4	4.5	3.1
Taiwan	n.a.	1.7	2.7	1.51	2.99	5.17
Malaysia	8.2	8.0	6.0	4.1	3.1	3.5
Thailand	6.6	n.a.	2.9	3.0	3.6	2.2
Indonesia	n.a.	n.a.	2.0	8.0	6.2	n.a.
China					3.1	4.0

Note: n.a.—not available.
Sources: World Bank (1995); Taiwan figures from Yu (1994: 6); Ragayah (2005).

harshly repressed in South Korea and Taiwan until democratization from the late 1980s, efforts to enhance labour productivity, product quality and the competitiveness of private firms helped raise wages. Some of these trends also reduced occupational hierarchies and income differentials within enterprises. Hence, by the time unions grew in strength, real wages had already risen substantially.

The growth of wage labour in Indonesia, Malaysia and Thailand intensified, following rapid export-oriented manufacturing expansion from the 1970s or 1980s, which also reduced disguised unemployment and raised household incomes. Wage labour grew by annual average rates of 8.2 per cent and 6.6 per cent in Malaysia and Indonesia, respectively, in the 1970–1990 period (see Table 14.5), with female participation growing especially strongly (see Kamal and Young, 1985; McGee, 1986; Onchan, 1995; World Bank, 1993). The out-migration of rural labour to urban industrial areas was pronounced enough to put upward pressure on wages.

In Malaysia, the growing presence of foreign labour from the early 1980s, commodity price depression and union problems undermined real wage increases in plantation agriculture (Jomo and Todd, 1994). However, inter-ethnic and other redistribution efforts as well as the expansion of more remunerative employment—especially the absorption of Bumiputera in the public sector, manufacturing and modern service wage employment—caused the Gini coefficient to decline to 0.474 in 1984, 0.445 in 1990 and 0.4607 in 2002 (see Table 14.3). However, overall growth in wage employment and consequent increases in household income reduced poverty and inequality.

There has also been less corporatism at the firm level in Malaysia, Thailand and Indonesia compared to Taiwan, and especially South Korea. In export-oriented high-technology firms (semi-conductor firms, in particular), enter-prise-level corporatism has involved mutually beneficial cooperation between management and labour, but such enterprises tend to be much more exceptional in Southeast Asia. Meanwhile, rising demand for skilled labour in Malaysia and Thailand pushed up wages of skilled workers substantially (World Bank, 1995; Rasiah and Osman-Rani, 1995), increasing wage differentials between skilled and unskilled labour, with the latter's welfare also undermined by labour imports.

While unions and labour militancy have been treated unsympathetically, if not brutally, in all five economies, the second-tier newly industrializing countries (NICs) of Malaysia, Thailand and Indonesia have experienced much poorer wage and working conditions than in South Korea and Taiwan, with labour protests routinely suppressed. In Thailand and Indonesia, militant lead-ers have been beaten and murdered (Narayanasamy, 1996), unions weakened, and sometimes even destroyed. Collective bargaining rights for labour continue to be minimal in practice. Wages have risen, but mainly due to the exhaustion of labour reserves and technological deepening in a few export-oriented industries, rather than due to union strength.

Unlike in South Korea and Taiwan, industrial policy in Malaysia, Thailand and Indonesia has sought to attract investments by emphasizing low production, including labour costs, thus militating against rapid wage growth in these countries. Real wages in Malaysia and Indonesia grew by 2.0 per cent and 5.2 per cent, respectively, on average over the 1970–1980 period, and by 2.3 per cent and 4.3 per cent, respectively, over the 1980–1992 period (World Bank, 1995: 1974–1975). Real wages in Thailand grew by 2.0 per cent and 2.8 per cent, respectively, over the 1973–1981 and 1981–1989 periods (Rasiah, 1994: 210).

Besides poverty alleviation and redistribution mechanisms, the five governments have, to varying extents, also introduced some social safety nets to reduce the dislocation caused by rapid structural changes and cyclical influences. The effects of such instruments have, however, been mixed. In Malaysia, the cost-of-living-allowance (COLA) for workers is one such provision, but the unemployed do not qualify for it. However, there has been a pronounced tendency to minimize such provisions on the presumption that full employment could be indefinitely assured, and would ensure 'work-fare' and thus eliminate the need for 'welfare' provisions. It was often also claimed that the unemployed could always count on 'traditional' social safety nets provided by families, communities and informal sector participation. The social dislocations during the recessions following the 1997–1998 East Asian financial crises have underscored the inadequacy of such provisions and the need for broad social protection measures.

It is generally agreed that South Korea and Taiwan were far more interventionist in the 1950s and 1960s than Malaysia and Thailand have been in recent decades. Yet, income distribution fared well in Northeast Asia during high growth, although less so in Southeast Asia. Contrary to the Kuznets' (1955) hypothesis, the cases of South Korea and Taiwan suggest that lower inequality can be complementary to rapid growth in its early stages. The Northeast Asian experiences suggest a strong case for intervention to improve asset distribution and to enhance human resources in order to generate rapid growth. However, the South Korean and Taiwanese experiences were portrayed by the World Bank (1993) as special cases unsuitable for emulation by other developing countries.

The experiences of Malaysia and Thailand offer different lessons. The Malaysian economy remained largely laissez-faire until around 1970 (World Bank, 1995), with income distribution worsening in the 1960s. After interventionist redistribution policies were adopted, growth, industrialization and income distribution improved in the next two decades, before deteriorating again in the 1990s with economic liberalization. While Thailand did not pursue redistribution policies, and also did not have much of an explicit industrial policy, its income Gini coefficient continued to rise. With increasing liberalization since the 1980s, income inequality in South Korea and Taiwan began to worsen.

These experiences suggest that poverty alleviation and reduction of income inequality can not only accompany, but may even be conducive to rapid growth and industrialization, while income inequalities tend to worsen with economic liberalization, especially in the absence of effective provisions for redistribution. Also, the fact that income inequality in Taiwan and South Korea declined in the initial stages of growth, and worsened as the two economies liberalized, turns the Kuznets (1955) hypothesis on its head. However, the unique circumstances of post-war asset redistribution (including land reforms) suggest that their initial conditions—rather than subsequent growth itself—may better explain these Northeast Asian exceptions.

EAST ASIAN CONTRASTS

The World Bank's *East Asian Miracle* volume claimed that "The positive association between growth and low inequality in the HPAEs, and the contrast with other economies, is illustrated…. Forty economies are ranked by the ratio of the income share of the richest fifth of the population to the income share of the poorest fifth and per capita real GDP growth during 1965–89…. There are seven high growth, low inequality economies. All of them are in East Asia; only Malaysia, which has an index of inequality above 15, is excluded" (World Bank, 1993: 29–30). However, as Rao (1998) notes, "All that the data… can convey is that there are 22 (out of 40) economies with low relative inequality and varying economic growth rates. Thus, the evidence is not strong enough to establish a firm relationship between growth and relative inequality, notwithstanding the fact that seven high growth and low relative inequality economies are located in East Asia."

Hence, the available evidence suggests that Taiwan is almost unique in East Asia in having established and sustained an egalitarian income distribution—as indicated by the Gini coefficient remaining close to the 0.3 level, although there was no significant decline in the Gini coefficient after the late 1960s. In the case of South Korea, too, there was no continuous decline of the Gini coefficient after 1965. In Indonesia, there was some decline in the Gini coefficient for household expenditure, but no evidence to show that income inequality had declined. Reduction of inter-ethnic income differences has been the main factor behind the reduction of the Gini coefficient for Malaysia from 0.5 to around 0.45 in the 1970s and 1980s, before rising again in the 1990s. Meanwhile, the Thai Gini coefficient for income distribution rose from 0.41 in 1962 to a little over 0.5 in 1992.

Regardless of trends, income inequality in Southeast Asia seems to be significantly higher than in South Korea and Taiwan, where significant asset redistribution took place with land reforms in the late forties and early fifties. Malaysia, Thailand and possibly Indonesia have income Gini coefficients of 0.45 or more. None of them had low Gini coefficients at the beginning of their rapid growth phases or have had sustained reductions in income inequality since then. Only in South Korea and Taiwan did land reforms contribute to low initial levels of income inequality. The subsequent evidence suggests maintenance of these relatively low levels of inequality at best.

The evidence on income inequality in these five HPAEs does not support *The East Asian Miracle*'s claim of declining income inequality during the rapid growth phase after 1965. Corroborating Rao, You (1998) also found that, among the World Bank's eight HPAEs, only Japan, South Korea and Taiwan have had unusually low inequality. He argues that they were able to combine low inequality with rapid growth because:

1) they started rapid growth with an exceptionally egalitarian distribution of real and financial assets as a result of post-war, mainly agrarian, reforms;
2) rapid income growth was based on capital accumulation as well as employment expansion;
3) high profit shares were crucial for accumulation, by generating high savings rates and inducing high investment rates (though high profits are not sufficient for rapid growth, the three achieved rapid accumulation because effective institutions and policies translated large profits into high savings and investment rates);
4) wealth distribution was relatively even due to the highly egalitarian post-war redistribution and the unusual savings behaviour of low-income households, especially in Japan and Taiwan; and
5) although wage distribution has not been particularly egalitarian, rapid employment expansion and near full employment has probably meant wider and more even distribution of wage-earning opportunities among households.

For You, the future prospects for income distribution in the relatively egalitarian Northeast Asian three (Japan, South Korea and Taiwan) are not good. The favourable influence of the initially egalitarian wealth distribution will only continue to diminish over time, and little more can be achieved from further employment expansion. In fact, there is evidence of growing wealth concentration in all three relatively egalitarian HPAEs, especially with the recent asset-price bubbles from the late 1980s. It appears that income inequality rose in Japan, South Korea and Taiwan during the 1980s.

Only South Korea and Taiwan have had relatively low Gini coefficients from the 1960s, while there were significant reductions in the Gini coefficients of the five economies by the 1980s, compared to the 1960s. Thus, the World Bank's generalization about income inequality reduction is erroneous. Gini coefficients in South Korea and Taiwan have been low, but relatively unchanging, while declines have only been observed for Indonesia, Malaysia and perhaps Thailand.

The relatively low Gini coefficients for South Korea—0.34 in 1965 and 0.33 in 1970—have been attributed to a number of factors. The most important of these include the land reforms of 1947 and 1949 (which reduced income inequality among farm households), asset destruction during the Korean War, and confiscation of illegally accumulated wealth (Choo, 1975). Rao (1998) found no evidence of a continuing decline in income inequality, as suggested by the World Bank (1993).

The available evidence suggests that the Gini coefficient for Taiwan declined from the 1950s until the early 1970s, then stayed in the range of 0.28-0.30 during most of the 1970s and in the early 1980s, and has risen slightly since the mid-1980s. Land reform, labour-intensive industrialization, full employment, off-farm work, educational expansion and industrial organization (with large state-owned enterprises coexisting with small and medium-sized private firms) are believed to have contributed to the relatively egalitarian income distribution of Taiwan.

The World Bank and others have argued that, owing to the exceptional nature of Japan and the first generation newly industrialized economies (NIEs) of East Asia, the rest of the developing world should emulate the second-tier Southeast Asian newly industrializing countries (NICs) instead. While the more recent experiences of the second-tier Southeast Asian NICs may be more relevant to the rest of the South in some respects (e.g., resource wealth), the superior industrial policy as well as the more egalitarian initial conditions and development outcomes of Japan, South Korea and Taiwan should not be lost to others.

IMPLICATIONS OF ECONOMIC LIBERALIZATION FOR EQUITY IN EAST ASIA

Policies of economic liberalization and globalization have been advocated or even imposed on many developing countries, ostensibly to spur economic growth. However, economic growth slowed dramatically during 1980–2000, compared with the previous two decades (1960–1980) in most developing countries (Weisbrot, Naiman and Kim (2000). The only regional exception to this trend was East Asia, which grew faster from 1980 to 1998 than in the previous period. However, this was largely due to the quadrupling over the last two decades of GDP in China, which has 83 per cent of the population of East Asia. In Southeast Asia, high growth rates were achieved, especially during 1987–1997.

East Asian countries that did not follow the economic programmes and prescriptions of the Bretton Woods Institutions (BWIs) have seen more of their people lifted out of poverty due to more rapid economic growth than economies that have pursued such policies. This has happened despite increased inequality and consequently slower poverty reduction in recent decades in some of these economies. While economic welfare has often been adversely affected, some waste and undesirable regulation have also been eliminated in the process. However, available information does not allow a carefully considered assessment of the welfare consequences of recent liberalization and globalization for different socioeconomic groups, including those in poverty.

The consequences of globalization and liberalization for growth, poverty and income inequality in East Asia are quite complicated and also quite contingent. South Korea and Taiwan have lacked natural resources, but have transformed their economies through interventionist industrial policies. Indonesia, Malaysia and Thailand have relied more on resource rents to alleviate poverty, though growth has also been important. Export-oriented industrialization, driven primarily by foreign capital in Southeast Asia, has helped reduce unemployment, and thus raised household incomes in these economies.

The fiscal and foreign debt crises of the early and mid-1980s took a heavy toll on many governments in the region. Most governments emerged leaner by the late 1980s, though not necessarily meaner, i.e. more effective, partly due to economic liberalization. Government expenditure as a percentage of total economic activity has been reduced, public sectors checked, state-owned enterprises constrained and privatization policies pursued. Government regulations have been reduced, mainly to induce greater private, especially foreign, investments. Emergency loan policy conditionalities exacerbated the 1997–98 financial crises in the region by requiring pro-cyclical macroeconomic responses.

Nonetheless, the East Asian economies reviewed here seem to be examples of economies that have managed to grow rapidly without seriously worsening income distribution. Fuelled by rapid growth, poverty, both urban and rural, has generally continued to decline. Most of these economies introduced policy instruments to alleviate poverty and, to a lesser extent, to improve income distribution.

Income distribution in Indonesia, South Korea, Malaysia and Taiwan has intermittently experienced some improvements. Only Thailand, the least committed to redistribution, has experienced worsening income distribution over the long term. Thailand, which has historically been the most liberal of the six main economies under consideration, has experienced the most sustained long-term tendency toward greater income inequality. In fact, it was the only economy among the six that recorded increased poverty in the mid-1980s, and greater urban poverty in 1990.

Before the currency and financial crises of 1997–1998 induced a regional recession in 1998, liberalization had not significantly increased poverty in the region (except perhaps in Thailand), but seems to have worsened inequality in Malaysia, South Korea and Taiwan—a trend more consistently pronounced in Thailand from earlier on. In other words, although poverty in these economies continued to fall with rapid growth, productivity gains and declining unemployment, income inequality worsened in Malaysia, South Korea and Taiwan from the 1980s.

Liberalization since the 1980s seems to have adversely affected income distribution in the region. Rising income inequality under essentially laissez-faire conditions in the past have re-emerged as the economies of the region liberalized once again. Deregulation, reduced government intervention, declining commitment to earlier redistributive mechanisms, and greater government efforts to meet investor expectations probably all contributed to increased inequality in the region. Recent and current trends suggest the likelihood of worsening inequality in the future (see Ishak, 1996; Onchan, 1995). Redistributive policies have been discouraged by liberalization as well as renewed commitments to protecting property rights, aggravating social inequality in these countries. More liberalization is likely to further exacerbate such regressive trends.

Hence, the East Asian economies do not demonstrate any clear relationship between export-oriented industrialization and better income distribution (also see Alarcon-Gonzalez, 1996). While export orientation may have sustained long-term growth, equity may not improve without effective mechanisms for redistribution, usually implemented through government intervention. The World Bank recommends that other developing countries try to emulate the second-tier Southeast Asian NICs, especially since the mid-1980s, when they liberalized. However, the evidence suggests that South Korea and Taiwan have had much more egalitarian growth compared to Indonesia, Malaysia and

Thailand, and that inequality has increased all round since liberalization from the mid-1980s, especially in Southeast Asia.

The simplistic generalization of East Asian 'growth with redistribution' or 'egalitarian growth' does not stand up well to careful empirical scrutiny. Northeast Asia has been distinctly more egalitarian than Southeast Asia, and recent economic liberalization has exacerbated inequality in the region. Interestingly, those economies with more elaborate, effective and successful industrial policies have also been more egalitarian, although available data do not allow meaningful testing for correlation, let alone causality.

In light of these developments, it is important to consider possible measures to try to sustain poverty decline and reduce inequality in the face of continued pressures for trade, financial and investment liberalization, and especially with the unprecedented regional recession in the aftermath of the 1997–1998 currency and financial crises. Poverty alleviation and redistribution policies are still needed, particularly in Thailand, where such policies have been absent and income distribution has been worsening over a few decades. Evidence from the region suggests that efforts targeting poor groups—e.g. land reform, subsidized housing, and subsidized access to education—have been successful and should be emulated elsewhere.

Liberalization of agricultural—especially food—trade should be gradual to facilitate adjustment. With real wage increases in South Korea and Taiwan from the late 1980s, such agricultural trade liberalization led to cheap food imports from abroad, destroying the livelihoods of many farmers in South Korea, though the problem has been less in Taiwan, due to greater agricultural productivity and the importance of off-farm work. Similarly, Indonesia, Malaysia and, to a lesser extent, Thailand, will face similar challenges as cheap rice imports from China and Viet Nam enter their economies. The livelihoods of farmers would have been negatively affected, though the collapse of many Southeast Asian currencies since mid-1997 has changed the terms of trade for agriculture once again, at least for the near future. Alternative employment sources also need to be developed by the governments concerned, e.g., the promotion of industrial dispersal to raise off-farm incomes, as in Japan and Taiwan. The regional recession in 1998 temporarily revived interest in questions such as food security, which had been largely forgotten with the enthusiasm for liberalization and globalization in the preceding decade.

While direct subsidies may be difficult to sustain, new forms of indirect subsidization may well compensate. For example, increased government education and training efforts can become an important means of advancing industrial and technological capabilities. South Korea and Taiwan have successfully pursued such efforts for some time. While the demand for skilled labour has risen substantially in Malaysia and Thailand, earlier government efforts have been inadequate to meet these requirements. The improvement of the labour force should help raise the competitiveness of firms and economies, and narrow wage differentials and income inequality more generally.

The East Asian experience with labour market liberalization has therefore been quite complicated. Labour market liberalization has undoubtedly undermined labour market segmentation in significant ways, but such labour market rigidities still prevail. Some rigidities are becoming even more pronounced with more educational and skill specialization as well as greater use of foreign labour—with reduced 'citizenship rights'—at both ends of the labour force. In most East Asian economies, except for the 'new democracies' of South Korea and Taiwan, labour regulations have not improved significantly in the last decade, resulting in greater casualization of labour relations, thus enhancing labour flexibility without a concomitant improvement in labour security. The significance of corporate savings in explaining the high savings rate associated with the East Asian region suggests that this may have been at the expense of labour incomes.

While changing production relations at the international level—variously described as international or global 'production networks' or 'value chains'—have brought about some of this greater flexibility, much of this has been promoted by governments trying to attract investments and thus enhance growth. However, there has been relatively little resistance to such casualization, as its negative consequences were partly offset by the post-1985 boom (after the appreciation of the yen and the currencies of the first-tier East Asian NIEs), which has been accompanied by declining unemployment as well as improved labour remuneration to retain employees. However, such casualization negates the likelihood of corporatism, and hence of greater commitment by workers as 'stakeholders', as in Japan, South Korea and Singapore. Weak institutional development governing labour relations exacerbated the welfare of workers in the region. Liberalization also weakened the bargaining power of workers in Indonesia, Malaysia and Thailand, and may thus have worsened income distribution.

Unions could instead be encouraged to collaborate with management and the government to enhance social corporatism so that enhanced trust, commitment and efficiency from such collaboration could help raise competitiveness and workers' remuneration. This would probably involve more multi-skilling, cross-skilling and institutionalization of the work process, including union participation in worker training to strengthen effective tripartism. Such flexible work practices could also reduce occupational hierarchies, status differentials and income inequalities.

Technological development is essential for the success of such efforts. Growth should become a shared responsibility, with all parties partaking of its fruits. Commitment to technology development—e.g., through subsidization of catching-up activities—will become increasingly crucial to sustaining industrialization, growth and improved living standards. However, technology development efforts should not merely focus on firms alone. The broader institutional set-up for promoting a better national system of innovation, including upgrading labour force skills, will be critical for such efforts.

As traditional industrial policy measures are increasingly negated, there is likely to be greater interest in and attention to human resource development (HRD) efforts, offering a rare window of opportunity for social development proponents to advance their agenda. However, there is also a danger that only social development measures considered supportive of economic growth and industrialization, especially in the short and medium term, will be adopted, as others are neglected and eventually quietly forgotten.

In the long term, continued progress in health, education and labour productivity will be necessary to sustain economic growth and improve standards of living. Economic growth and social development should increase in tandem. Ramirez, Ranis and Stewart (1997) postulate a cumulative cycle of economic growth and human development, based on two chains: one linking economic growth to human development, the other linking human development to economic growth. They found that higher social expenditure improves human development, and that high investment rates and more equitable income distribution bolstered economic growth. Some East Asian economies seem to have such 'virtuous circles' category, with relatively high literacy rates and life expectancies, among other positive social indicators. These countries are well poised for further social development and economic growth in the future, but as the South Korean experience suggests, the institutional reforms to ensure this will only come about due to public pressure for such reforms to ensure that governments are committed to social development measures, especially through social reforms and expenditures.

NOTES

[1] Assistance from Mohd Aslam, Foo Ah Hiang, Lee Hwok Aun and Ragayah Mat Zin is gratefully acknowledged. The usual caveats apply.

[2] *Bumiputera* translated literally means "'sons of the soil'", but is generally used to refer to ethnic Malays and other indigenous people of Malaysia.

REFERENCES

ADB. *Key Indicators* (various years). Asian Development Bank, Manila.
Alarcon-Gonzalez, Diana (1996). Trade liberalization and income distribution: Lessons for Mexico from East Asia. In John Borrego, A.B. Alvarez and K.S. Jomo (eds). *Capital, the State and Late Industrialization: Comparative Perspectives from the Pacific Rim*. Westview, Boulder: 69–80.
Albert, José Ramon, Ana Maria L. Tabunda, Ofelia Templo and Ragayah Haji Mat Zin (2002). Poverty profile of the Philippines for 2000. Paper presented at the 'Poverty Analysis and Data Initiative (PADI) for East Asia' workshop, Bangkok, 28 February.
Ali Said, and Wenefrida D. Widyanti (2002). The impact of economic crisis on poverty and inequality in Indonesia. In Shahid Khandker (ed.). *Impact of the East Asian Financial Crisis Revisited*. World Bank Institute, Washington, DC, and Philippine Institute for Development Studies, Manila: 117–92.
Amsden, Alice O. (1989). *Asia's Next Giant*. Oxford University Press, New York.
Asra, Abuzar (2000). Poverty and inequality in Indonesia: Estimates, decomposition and key issues. *Journal of the Asia Pacific Economy* 5 (1&2): 91–111.
Choo, Hakchung (1975). Some sources of relative equity in Korean income distribution: A historical perspective. In Harry Oshima and Toshiyuki Mizoguchi (eds). *Income Distribution, Employment and Economic Development in Southeast Asia*. Japan Centre for Economic Research, Tokyo, and Council for Asian Manpower Studies, Manila: 48–72.
Chowdhury, Anis, and Inayatullah Islam (1993). *The Newly Industrializing Economies of East Asia*. Routledge, London.
Deyo, Fred (1989). *Beneath the Miracle: Labor Subordination in East Asia*. Cornell University Press, Ithaca, NY.
Habibullah, K. (1988). Development planning in ASEAN: Lessons of experience. *Economic Bulletin for Asia and the Pacific* 39 (2): 1–20.
Halim Salleh (1991). State capitalism in Malaysian agriculture. *Journal of Contemporary Asia* 21 (3): 327–243.
Hamilton, Clive (1983). Capitalist industrialization in East Asia's four little tigers. *Journal of Contemporary Asia* 13 (1): 35–73.
Hashim, Shireen M. (1997). *Income Inequality and Poverty in Malaysia*. Rowman, Boulder.
Hong Kong Census and Statistics Department (2001). Household income and Gini coefficient information note. Government of Hong Kong. www.legco.gov.hk/yr01-02/English/panels/fa/papers/fa1108cb1-346-ole.pdf.
Hsiao, Michael H.H. (1996). Agricultural reforms in Taiwan and South Korea. In John Borrego, A.B. Alvarez, and K.S. Jomo (eds). *Capital, the State and Late Industrialization: Comparative Perspectives from the Pacific Rim*. Westview, Boulder: 97–112.
Ishak Shari (1996). Liberalisasi ekonomi dan implikasinya terhadap usaha pembasmian kemiskinan di Malaysia (Liberalization of the Malaysian economy and its implications for the eradication of poverty). Paper presented at a seminar on 'Rancangan Malaysia Ketujuh: Penerusan Usaha Pembasmian Kemiskinan' (Seventh Malaysia Plan: Continuing Efforts for the Eradication of Poverty), 7–8 May, Kota Kinabalu, Sabah.
Jomo, K.S. (1986). *A Question of Class: Capital, the State and Uneven Development in Malaya*. Oxford University Press, Singapore.
Jomo, K.S., and Ishak Shari (1986). *Development Policies and Income Inequality in Peninsular Malaysia*. Institute for Advanced Studies, University of Malaya, Kuala Lumpur.
Jomo, K.S., and Patricia Todd (1994). *Trade Unions in Peninsular Malaysia*. Oxford University Press, Kuala Lumpur.
Kamal Salih, and M.L. Young (1985). Penang's industrialization: Where do we go from here? Paper presented at the 'Future of Penang' conference, 6–8 May, Penang.

Korea National Statistical Office (2002). http:www.nso.go.kr/eng/qna/view.html?num=2826

Kuznets, Simon (1955). Economic growth and income inequality. *American Economic Review* 45 (1): 1–28.

Lee, J.S. (1994). The role of the state in economic restructuring and development: The case of Taiwan. Occasional Paper Series No. 9403, Chung-Hua Institute for Economic Research, Taipei.

Malaysia, Government of (1996). *Seventh Malaysia Plan, 1996–2000.* Government Printers, Kuala Lumpur.

Malaysia, Government of (1999). *Mid-term Review of the Seventh Malaysia Plan, 1996–2000.* Government Printers, Kuala Lumpur.

Malaysia, Government of (2003). *Mid-term Review of the Eighth Malaysia Plan, 2001–2005.* Government Printers, Kuala Lumpur.

McGee, T.G. (ed.) (1986). *Industrialization and Labour Force Processes: A Case Study of Peninsular Malaysia.* Australian National University, Canberra.

Medhi Krongkaew (1995). *Thailand's Industrialization and Its Consequences.* Macmillan, London.

Mukhopadhaya, Pundarik (2000). Education policies as a means to tackle income disparity: The Singapore case. *International Journal of Sociology and Social Policy* 20 (11/12): 59–73.

Narayanasamy, N. (1996). Social standards in the marketplace. In Rajah Rasiah and V.N. Hofmann (eds). *Social and Environmental Clauses and Free Trade.* Friedrich Ebert Stiftung, Bonn.

Onchan, T. (1995). Economic growth, income distribution and poverty in Thailand. Paper presented at the Fifth Tun Abdul Razak Conference, 12–13 April, Athens, OH.

Ragayah Haji Mat Zin (2002). Income distribution in East Asian developing countries: The aftermath of the crisis. Paper presented at the 8th Convention of the East Asian Economic Association, Kuala Lumpur, Malaysia, 4–5 November.

Ragayah Haji Mat Zin (2005). Income distribution in East Asian developing countries: Recent trends. *Asian-Pacific Economic Literature* 19 (2), November: 36–54.

Ramirez, Alejandro, Gustav Ranis and Frances Stewart (1997). Economic growth and human development. Discussion Paper No. 787, Economic Growth Center, Yale University, New Haven.

Rao, J. Mohan (1998). Openness, poverty and inequality. Paper prepared for the Human Development Report Office, United Nations Development Programme, New York.

Rasiah, Rajah (1994). Capitalist industrialization in ASEAN. *Journal of Contemporary Asia* 24 (2): 197–216.

Rasiah, Rajah, and H. Osman-Rani (1995). Enterprise training and productivity in Malaysian manufacturing. Paper presented at the World Bank Conference on Enterprise Training and Productivity, 12–13 June, Washington, DC.

Rasiah, Rajah, Ishak Shari, and K.S. Jomo (1996). Globalization and liberalization in East and South East Asia: Implications for growth, inequality and poverty. In UNCTAD (ed.). *Globalization and Liberalization: Effects of International Economic Relations on Poverty.* United Nations Conference on Trade and Development, Geneva: 181–200.

Rodrik, Dani (1994). Getting interventions right: How South Korea and Taiwan grew rich. NBER Working Paper No. 4964, National Bureau of Economic Research, Washington, DC.

Sunantha Natenuj (2002). Poverty and inequality during the crisis period in Thailand. In Shahid Khandker (ed.). *Impact of the East Asian Financial Crisis Revisited.* World Bank Institute, Washington, DC, and Philippine Institute for Development Studies, Manila: 63–100.

Tabunda, Ana Maria L., and Jose Ramon G. Albert (2002). Philippine poverty in the wake of the Asian financial crisis. In Shahid Khandker (ed.). *Impact of the East Asian Financial Crisis Revisited.* World Bank Institute, Washington DC, and Philippine Institute for Development Studies, Manila: 223–92.

Taiwan, undated. The Story of Taiwan's Economy. http://www.gio.gov.tw/info/taiwan-story/economy/edown/table/table-10-1.htm.

UNDP (1994). *Human Development Report 1994*. Oxford University Press, New York, for United Nations Development Programme.

Weisbrot, Mark, Robert Naiman and Joyce Kim (2000). The emperor has no growth: Declining economic growth rates in the era of globalization. Processed, Center for Economic and Policy Research, Washington, DC.

World Bank (1993). *The East Asian Miracle*. Oxford University Press, New York.

World Bank (1995). *World Development Report, 1995*. Oxford University Press, New York.

Yap, Josef (1997). Structural adjustment, stabilization policies and income distribution in the Philippines: 1896–1996. Paper presented during the workshop on 'Impacts of macroeconomic adjustment policies on growth and equity in the Philippines', Makati City, 30 September.

You, Jong-Il (1998). Income distribution and growth in East Asia. *Journal of Development Studies* 34 (6), August.

Yu, T.S. (1994). Does Taiwan's industrialization have its own paradigm? Occasional Paper Series No. 9404, Chung-Hua Institute for Economic Research, Taipei.

15
Understanding the Extent and Evolution of Inequalities in China

RANJA SENGUPTA and JAYATI GHOSH

Along with spectacular economic growth, China has displayed high and increasing economic inequality in recent times, leading to some speculation on the relationship between growth and inequality. This has generated much international interest because China and India account for around one-third of the world's population, so inequalities within these countries are major determinants of world inequalities in general. Both rural-urban as well as regional disparities, partly overlapping concepts in China, have played major roles in determining the magnitude and growth of China's inequalities. Vertical inequalities within rural and urban areas also increased in the 1990s, although there is some evidence that these have declined slightly in the most recent period.

The rising inequalities have been attributed to many causes, ranging from the impact of opening up and other economic reforms, to the effects of China's geography and history. The impact of the Chinese government's economic policy regime, especially in the reform era, has emerged as a major contributory factor. Rising inequalities have also affected poverty reduction, despite a high rate of output growth and a significant poverty reduction programme. This chapter attempts to show that poverty and inequality have moved in synchronicity, both being crucially determined by the same set of macro-economic policies and contributing to each other.

The literature on economic inequality in China has mainly focused on income and consumption variables. However, the more basic and underlying factors—such as inequality in access to employment, wage differentials across sectors as well as the extent of social inequalities in terms of access to education and public health—must also form major areas of concern. This chapter attempts to document the inequalities that exist in China today: firstly, by surveying the inequality estimates in income and consumption; secondly, by discussing more basic inequalities in terms of employment and wages and social factors such as access to education and health facilities. In addition, trends in poverty reduction are examined. The chapter then goes on to analyse the causes of the current pattern of inequalities. It shows how, apart from China's historical policy regime and geographical endowments, the pattern of external trade, the nature and pattern of foreign direct investment (FDI) and the choices of government policy have helped to exacerbate inequalities. The need for a multi-dimensional approach to the problem is highlighted.

TRENDS IN ECONOMIC INEQUALITY IN CHINA

Rural-Urban Disparities in Per Capita Income and Consumption

Most studies have found relatively high levels of inequality in China and an increase in overall inequality in China over the 1990s. Most measures of inequality based on consumption or income data suggest some decrease from the mid-1970s to the mid-1980s, but major increases thereafter (Table 15.1). Intra-rural and intra-urban inequalities also increased over the 1990s, with a brief reversal in the middle of the decade. Meanwhile, inequality between urban and rural areas rose over the 1990s. The ratio of urban disposable income to rural net income increased from 1.86 in 1985 to 2.20 in 1990 (*China Statistical Yearbook, 2003*). While there was a short period of decline between 1995 and 1997 (Yang and Fang, 2003; Zhao Renwei, 2001; UNDP, 1999; Anderson, Huang and Ianchovichina, 2003), the post-1997 period saw a dramatic and continuous increase in this ratio between 1997 and 2002, from 2.47 to 3.11. The same pattern can be adduced from the consumption figures from National Bureau of Statistics (NBS) data, which show even higher disparities (Figure 15.1). Moreover,

FIGURE 15.1
China: urban/rural incomes and consumption ratios, 1978–2002

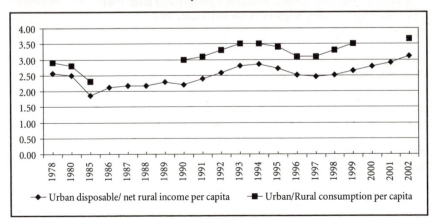

Source: Data from National Bureau of Statistics

TABLE 15.1
China: inequality trends, 1984–2002

| | Kanbur and Zhang | | | | Chen & Wang | | | Khan and Riskin | | |
| | Gini (%) | GE (%) | GE (Theil) | | (Gini, %) | | | (Gini, %) | | |
			Rural-Urban	Inland-Coast	Rural	Urban	National*	Rural	Urban	National
1984	25.6	10.9	6.3	0.4						
1985	25.8	11.1	6.6	0.5						
1986	26.8	11.9	6.9	0.5						
1987	27.0	12.0	6.8	0.6						
1988	28.2	13.1	7.7	0.8						
1989	29.7	14.4	9.3	1.0						
1990	30.1	14.9	9.5	1.0	29.87	23.42	33.34			
1991	30.3	14.9	9.9	1.2						
1992	31.4	16.0	10.2	1.5	32.03	24.18	37.23			
1993	32.2	16.8	10.9	1.7	33.70	27.18	40.18			
1994	32.6	17.2	10.8	2.0	34.00	29.22	41.46			
1995	33.0	17.7	11.5	2.3	33.98	28.27	39.84	41.6	33.2	45.2
1996	33.4	18.2	11.7	2.6	32.98	28.52	38.16			
1997	33.9	18.9	11.7	2.7	33.12	29.35	38.21			
1998	34.4	19.6	12.2	2.9	33.07	29.94	38.70			
1999	36.3	23.4	12.8	3.2	33.91	29.71	39.97			
2000	37.2	24.8	13.9	3.8						
2001@							44.7			
2002								37.5	31.8	45
2002#									33.8	44.8

Sources: Kanbur and Zhang, 2005a; Chen and Wang, 2001.
* Assumes 10 per cent price difference between urban and rural
@ Estimates from consumption inequality figures, (World Bank, 2004)
# Calculations including migrants (Khan and Riskin, 2005)

TABLE 15.2
China: Gini coefficients, 1978–2002

	Rural	Urban	National
1978	22	16	30
1988	30	23	37
1997	33	28	
2002	37	34	45

Source: UNDP (2005a). Calculation of the National Bureau of Statistics, based on household consumption surveys conducted by Chinese Academy of Social Sciences.

there was a lot of variation within both rural and urban consumption per capita, with the disparities being much higher in rural than urban consumption.

Khan and Riskin (2005) suggest that the urban-rural income gap increased from 2.47 in 1995 to 3.01 in 2002. Their study includes migrants, who were previously excluded from inequality calculations. This makes urban inequality higher than previously estimated, but reduces the divide between rural and urban China because average rural incomes rose while average urban incomes fell. It is likely, however, that actual rural-urban income gaps are still underestimated. As the *China Human Development Report, 2005* (CHDR) points out,

> if public housing subsidies, private housing imputed rent, pension, free medical care, and educational subsidies were included, the actual per capita income of urban residents in 2002 would increase by 3,600 to 3,900 yuan, bringing the urban-rural income ratio to about four-fold instead of the 3.2-fold acknowledged by official figures (UNDP 2005a: 27).

This would make rural-urban inequality in China among the highest in the world.

The CHDR also points to widening inequality within rural and urban areas as well, based on data from a household survey conducted in 2002 (Table 15.2). These increases in inequality are ascribed to the economic growth process, which has meant that rural non-farm income opportunities are concentrated in a few areas, while some urban areas have grown more rapidly than others. This relates directly to regional inequalities, which are considered below.

Regional Inequality

Regional inequality in China declined from 1979 through 1990, but then reversed to a rising trend. The increase between inland and coastal China grew particularly wide, especially in the late 1990s. The increase between 1990 and 2000 is startling—the Theil general entropy (GE) index increased from 1.0 in 1990 to 3.8 in 2000 (Table 15.1).

According to UNDP (2005a), the ratio of the per capita incomes of the eastern to the central regions increased from 1.42 in 1997 to 1.52 in 2003. However, Khan and Riskin (2005) suggest that inequality among provinces actually declined between 1995 and 2002. Most of the regional inequality in China is to be found between three large regions and within provinces (i.e. between districts within provinces). Coastal-inland inequality has always been much lower compared to rural-urban inequality, even though it has been rising sharply in recent years.

As is well known, the gross domestic product (GDP) of China has grown ·

TABLE 15.3
China: GDP growth rates, 1970–2000

	Pre-Reform	Reform Period		
	1970–78	1979–84	1985–95	1996–2000
GDP	4.9	8.8	9.7	7.9
Agriculture	2.7	7.1	4.0	3.4
Industry	6.8	8.2	12.8	9.6
Services	n.a.	11.6	9.7	8.3

Source: Anderson, Huang, Ianchovichina, 2003.

TABLE 15.4
China: per capita GDP by region at constant 1980 prices, 1980–2000

Year	1980	1990	1995	2000
Yuan per year				
East	598	2240	7247	11334
Centre	391	1338	3708	5982
West	308	1156	3035	4687
As % of East:				
Centre	65	60	51	53
West	53	52	42	41
Growth rates (% per annum)	1981–1999			
Eastern Region	10.90			
Central Region	8.40			
Western Region	8.10			

Source: Weiss (2002).

rapidly for a prolonged period, at an average rate of 9.8 per cent since 1980, although this has involved some degree of volatility around the high trend rate. While agriculture was responsible for the spurt in growth in the early phase of reforms during 1979–1984, subsequently, industrial growth has dominated, followed by services (Table 15.3). Such high growth notwithstanding, GDP per capita and its growth have shown wide variation across regions. The eastern coastal region has the highest GDP per capita as well as the highest rates of growth, the central region has been in the middle, while the western interior region has lagged behind (Table 15.4). The ratio of GDP per capita of the top five provinces to the bottom five provinces increased from 3.28 to 3.59 between 1985 and 1998. The inequality estimates are therefore corroborated by trends in GDP per capita.

The three largest cities of Beijing, Tianjin and Shanghai account for a large part of the variation in regional incomes.[1] Wu (1999) argues that if these three cities are excluded, regional inequality has not risen, especially post-1993. These large metropoles, which enjoy a high level of industrialization and have over 71 per cent of their population living within 100 kilometres of the coast or navigable waters, were able to reap the full benefits of public infrastructure expansion and export promotion, and therefore, attracted substantial FDI inflows. All this contributed to aggregate GDP growth of nearly 12 per cent per annum during the 1990s.

The central region, the agricultural heartland, reaped benefits from deregulation in the early phase of the reform period (with a growth rate of 7.7 per cent, higher than the national average between 1979 and 1984). However, the subsequent period saw growth rates fall as agricultural expansion reached its limit. With the lack of access to the coast or major waterways, both the north and the south in western China have lagged behind average growth rates in the post-planning period, especially in the 1990s. Dogged by difficult terrain and a lack of mineral resources, the south-west has always lagged behind the north-west, except in the 1990s. Growing disparity has also marked consumption per capita trends across regions in China and corroborates the income patterns.

Employment and Wages

Employment in China has increased steadily over the last two decades, much of it fuelled by the industrial and service sectors, and has registered an average annual growth rate of 2.55 per cent between 1980 and 2002. However, growth has been much slower in the period after 1990, at 1.09 per cent per annum, compared to 4.33 per cent in the earlier decade. Some of this deceleration has come from the agriculture sector, but much more has been contributed by the deceleration in industrial and service sector employment, which had recorded very high growth rates over the 1980s.

The share of agriculture in aggregate employment has declined steadily from 68.7 per cent in 1980 to 50 per cent in 2000–2002. However, rural employment is still dominated by agriculture, which accounts for two-thirds of rural workers, and therefore, slow rates of expansion of agricultural employment have reinforced widening rural-urban inequality. Total rural employment has been almost stagnant between 1995 and 2002. Employment has grown at a low 0.22 per cent per annum over 1990–2002, much lower than the 4.13 per cent of the previous decade of structural reform in agriculture. Urban employment, on the other hand, has grown much faster.

The stagnation in rural employment partly reflects an economy in the process of industrialization and development. The urban areas have absorbed part of the workforce from the rural areas, reflected in large scale migration, and this has compensated, at least partially, for stagnating rural employment. However, migration has also been part of the reason for increasing urban unemployment post-1985. Unemployment (in terms of absolute numbers of people) has risen steadily since 1985, reaching a high of 7.7 million in 2002. This rise has been particularly sharp since 1990, recording an annual growth rate of 6 per cent, compared to −3.4 per cent between 1980 and 1990. Most other indicators of urban unemployment also show a rise over this period.[2]

The problem is deeper than revealed by official statistics, which do not capture a significant proportion of jobless rural migrants and do not include the number of laid off workers from state-owned enterprises (SOEs) and urban collectives. When laid off workers from SOEs are included in the official unemployment figures, the actual rate thrown up is much higher, at around 12.5 per cent of the working population in 2000 (Riskin and others, 2004). Since the rate of urbanization in the east has been much higher than in other regions, higher growth rates in urban China have also compounded the problem of regional disparities in employment. In general, the unemployment rate in larger cities and provinces is lower than that in smaller cities and provinces (Riskin and others, 2004), and poverty rates are also comparatively lower. Regional disparity is also evident in the distribution of laid-off workers, who have been more concentrated in the north-west.

There is a marked gender dimension to employment patterns. In rural areas, the share of women in agriculture has been high, but their share in non-farm work has been much lower. This bias was especially pronounced in the poorer central and western regions, where women accounted for only 24.9 per cent and 22.5 per cent respectively of the total labour force in non-agricultural township and village enterprises (TVEs), against 42.6 per cent in the eastern region (National Bureau of Statistics, 1997). In urban China, the share of employment in every sector of activity has been much lower for women compared to men, and in most sectors that experienced an absolute decrease in employment between 1994 and 2000, the decrease has been more pronounced for women (Riskin and others, 2004). In manufacturing, this disparity has been very sharp. In overall employment, agriculture, mining, as well as manufacturing, construction, transport, and trade, the absolute number of women has been decreasing. The CHDR 2005 points out that fewer women work in white collar jobs than men, and also that layoffs in urban enterprises have affected women disproportionately.

Wage Differentials

According to the Khan, Griffin, and Riskin (1999) estimation from survey data, wage inequality accounted for about half of overall income inequality in China between 1988 and 1995. Knight and Song (2003) found that while all urban wages increased between 1988 and 1995, all measures of wage inequality also increased quite sharply.[3] Wages have been a large and growing contributor of urban inequality, but a declining contributor to its rural counterpart.

However, disparity between rural and urban areas has been significantly accounted for by the growing gap between wages in agriculture, which is dominant in rural areas, and wages in industry and services, which predominate in urban areas. The ratio of industrial wages to agricultural wages, which has been high since 1980, has generally experienced a rising trend (Figure 15.2). This rising pattern is even sharper in the ratio between most service sector wages and agricultural wages, with declines only between 1993 and 1996. The remarkable rise in service sector wages and, to a certain extent, in industrial wages over the period of liberalization, has therefore not benefited the rural population much.[4]

Wage rates have also varied widely within the dominant sectors and between various sub-sectors within urban China, adding to urban inequality. Wages in new sectors—such as telecommunications, banking and insurance, and real

FIGURE 15.2
China: wage ratios across sectors, 1978–2000

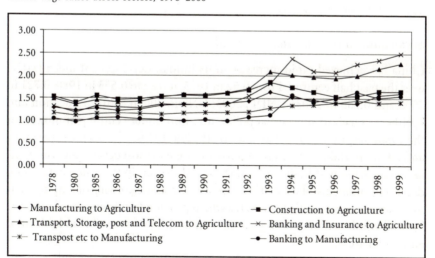

Source: Calculated from *China Statistical Yearbook* estimates.

estate—have increased significantly in recent years. Meanwhile, the government's recent attempts to stimulate domestic consumption have raised average wage levels in state-owned industries—such as health care, sports, education, culture, and scientific research—and in government, whereas wage levels in more traditional manufacturing industries, with older SOEs, have stagnated throughout the decade because of the cuts in government subsidies.

Urban wage disparities have also emerged across different types of enterprises. The difference between SOEs in urban areas and urban collectives has been increasing, with average wages offered by the latter lagging far behind. While the gap between the various levels of average wages in state-owned units and collectively-owned units has remained large, the difference in average wages between SOEs and enterprises having other forms of ownership (joint ownership, stock ownership, limited-liability corporations, foreign investment, etc.) has been reduced (Social and Economic Policy Institute, 2002). However, the positive impact of this phenomenon is limited since the share of SOEs in total urban employment has been coming down sharply.

While gender wage differences have been smaller in China than in some other countries, they are increasing. Between 1988 and 1995, the aggregate ratio of female-to-male earnings dropped from 0.84 to 0.82, and the urban gender wage gap increased from 1.6 per cent to 16 per cent (UNDP, 2005a). Since gender differences tend to be much lower in the state sector than in the non-state sector, the relative decline in public employment has been particularly adverse for women workers.

Social Indicators: Education and Health

China has achieved rapid increases in its human development index (HDI) over the past half century. From 0.52 in 1975, it rose to 0.553 in 1980, 0.721 in 2000 and 0.755 in 2003 (UNDP, 2003; UNDP, 2005b: 220).[5] Education and healthcare received substantial policy attention under central planning from the 1950s despite a clear urban bias. By the late 1970s, China's life expectancy and infant mortality rates were much better than in most developing countries, and even many middle-income countries. However, in the following period, decentralization, dissolution of the communes and the growing unemployment in urban areas, especially from SOEs which provided extensive social services, have all combined to make education and health less accessible in both rural and urban areas.

Despite major strides in the reduction of illiteracy and other indicators of education,[6] this sector showed a definite regression in infrastructural support and efficiency, as evident in the student-teacher ratios which increased over the

1990s until 1998. The distribution of education also became more unequal between rural and urban areas, and within rural areas. After falling for two decades, the gap between rural and urban illiteracy rates actually increased between 1990 and 1995, with rural rates 78 per cent higher than urban ones in 1995 (Kanbur and Zhang, 2005b). Gender has been another basis for the growing inequalities in education: within the adult population, the illiteracy rate for women is 2.6 times the rate for men, and female enrolment rates are lower than male rates at all levels.

The percentage of the population above 15 that is illiterate or semi-literate varies widely across regions. In 2002, Tibet had the highest rate of 54 per cent, while Beijing had the lowest rate of 5 per cent. Furthermore, disparities in educational attainment across regions have been increasing.[7] The poorer regions have fared worse in terms of higher education as well. Dropout rates have been much higher at all levels, especially for females. These regions also suffer from the problem of outflow of educated people.

There were significant improvements in health care along with better nutrition as public health infrastructure improved during the central planning era. Of course, there were significant rural-urban disparities. However, from 1985, both rural and urban infrastructure worsened, and so did the disparity between rural and urban areas. While the national infant mortality rate (IMR) is low (at 31 per 1,000 live births in 2003), disparities have grown.[8] In 2002, under-five mortality was 16 per cent in urban areas, but 40 per cent in rural ones. Urban infant mortality was 14 per cent, while rural infant mortality was 34 per cent. The maternal mortality rate in rural China (at 0.62 per cent) was nearly double the urban rate. These indicators also vary widely across provinces, with health standards generally much lower in western China. However, regional variation has declined over the 1990s, largely because of growing unemployment and the withdrawal of state health services in the more advanced industrial provinces.

Poverty in China

Given China's history, it is not surprising that poverty in rural China has been widespread. During the central planning period, urban poverty was hardly present as urban residents were assured jobs and provided with a widespread network of social security. Rural areas were discriminated against as the government concentrated on industrial development. The ancient *hukou* system, which tied citizens to their original place of residence, discouraged migration between the rural and urban areas, and helped to extract the surplus from agriculture to aid industrial development in the urban and outer regions.

From the onset of the reforms, this picture has changed considerably. As a result of agricultural reforms, consequent output growth, and favourable terms of trade, rural incomes went up and China's huge poverty numbers came down significantly. Meanwhile, urban areas began to experience poverty for the first time in Chinese history due to the easing of migration laws and illegal migration from rural areas. Effectively, part of rural poverty was transferred to the urban areas.

It can be argued that China's overall macroeconomic regime has been more influential in determining poverty reduction than official poverty reduction programmes (Riskin and others, 2004). Active poverty reduction programmes have not coincided with significant reductions in poverty. As evident from Figure 15.3, much of the decline in rural poverty occurred between 1978 and 1984, and during 1993–1996. From the mid-1980s to the mid-1990s and during 1997–1999, rural poverty increased. This happened in spite of the establishment of a coordinated institutional framework for a development-oriented poverty reduction programme by the Chinese government in 1986.

In this period, macroeconomic trends and development policies were not pro-poor. There was a shift in focus and a transfer of resources from the interior agricultural rural areas to the urban coastal areas. The terms of trade also moved against agriculture. All concessions, in terms of taxes and otherwise, went to trade and FDI-related sectors. Similarly, in the period after 1996, poverty reduction efforts were stepped up, but poverty estimates stayed more or less rigid, or actually increased for the next three years. The poverty reduction programme did not effectively reach the needy, largely rural, interior western

FIGURE 15.3
China: rural poverty incidence, 1980–2001

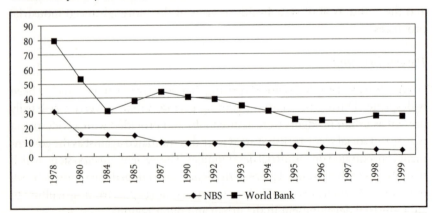

Source: Based on National Bureau of Statistics and World Bank estimates

regions with a concentration of minorities. Again, this period was marked by a reversal in the terms of trade against agriculture.[9] The movement in the agricultural terms of trade seems to be a common determinant in the different phases of rural poverty in China.

The first period of significant poverty reduction, corresponding to the beginning of the era of reform and transition, was when reform focused on the countryside. Over these years, the rural communes were dismantled, land was parcelled out to households on an essentially egalitarian basis, farmers were encouraged to abandon the previous 'grain first' policy and to diversify production, and farm prices were raised 30 per cent. In addition, chemical fertilizer supplies increased rapidly.

The second period of sharp decline in rural poverty occurred in the middle years of the 1990s. In the first third of the decade, the rural poverty rate was running at over 40 per cent of the population; it dropped to about 24 per cent by 1996. This was mainly because of a very steep rise in farm purchase prices, especially of food grain, which doubled in the middle of the decade. This increase in income benefited middle-income families reliant on agricultural returns. The real per capita incomes of rural Chinese increased by 21 per cent in the three years from 1993 to 1996 (*China Statistical Abstract, 1998*). Thus, rural poverty reduction proved to be highly income-elastic: a 21 per cent increase in rural income was accompanied by a 40 per cent decrease in rural poverty.

Both periods of decline in rural poverty were also periods of significant drops in national and rural inequality. The period of declining poverty between 1978 and 1984 coincided with a decline in the national Gini coefficient (from 30.8 to 25.6 per cent), after which it started rising. Regional inequality in favour of the coastal areas had a direct and crucial link with both national inequality and rising rural poverty during this period. In the 1990s as well, the period of falling rural poverty, 1993–1996, was also roughly the period that experienced declining rural and national inequality. Subsequently, both rural poverty and inequality increased until the end of the decade.

After the turn of the century, official rates of rural poverty showed major declines, to as little as 3 per cent in 2002. However, it has been argued (Hu, Hu and Chang, 2003) that despite China's substantial improvement in poverty reduction since 1978, the pace of poverty reduction has slowed down and new forms of poverty have arisen. The annual decrease in the poor population was reduced by half, with the number of poor decreasing only by 8 million annually; the average growth rate of farmers' consumption per year was only 2.5 per cent; the average growth rate of farmers' per capita net income was just 3 per cent. This is explained by the authors in terms of two factors: the deteriorating quality of growth and increased inequality.

In contrast to at least two significant periods of major declines in rural poverty, urban poverty has been steadily rising in China (Figure 15.4). As of mid-2002, the urban poverty headcount rate was officially put at 19.3 million, using an income poverty threshold of 152 yuan per month. This comes to about 4 per cent of the full status urban population (i.e. excluding the 'floating population' of migrants living in towns and cities), which is an increase from a rate of around 2 per cent in the early 1980s. Another study (ADB, 2002), led by Athar Hussain based on a higher poverty line of 192.5 yuan per month, found the proportion of urban poor to be about 11 per cent in 1998 based on expenditure, or 4.7 per cent based on income. This study also included a survey of migrant residents of 31 cities, and found that the poverty rate among migrants, averaging 15.2 per cent, was 50 per cent higher than among full-status residents in the same sample cities.

Trends in poverty have also been closely linked with trends in employment and the social sectors, and associated inequalities. In the rural areas, slow growth in the agricultural sector resulted in almost stagnant rural employment after the mid-1990s. Rising unemployment was a major driver of urban poverty in the post-1985 phase, especially after 1990, a period synonymous with sharply rising urban poverty. As the demand for skills grew and the SOEs downsized considerably, the job market became more narrow and skewed in favour of educated workers. This had a severe negative impact on the uneducated migrant

FIGURE 15.4
China: urban poverty incidence, 1981–1999

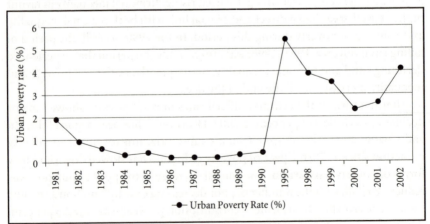

Source: Based on official estimates of urban poverty, Government of China

community, among whom the poverty incidence is very high, as well as on the growing population of registered unemployed. Inequalities in access to education accentuated this tendency. Despite high output growth in industry and services, the urban poor suffered the adverse effects of growing inadequacies in state-sponsored health and educational facilities, which were not at all available for the rural migrant population, among whom poverty was highest.

All this has also had much to do with macroeconomic policies. Obviously, the relevant policy regimes—including policy shifts favouring FDI, urban and coastal areas, trade openness, financial deregulation, fiscal discipline, migration as well as agricultural and industrial policies and terms of trade movements—have all affected poverty, as well as social, employment and income-consumption inequalities in similar ways that have reinforced poverty trends. These issues are explored in greater detail below.

CAUSES OF INEQUALITY IN CHINA

Structural Factors

Overall inequality was relatively low until 1956, but increased during the period of the 'great leap forward' culminating in the 'great famine', and again between 1966 and 1976 during the Cultural Revolution. However, in general, the extent of inequality, especially regional inequality, was much lower compared to the more recent reform period. The central planning period was marked by relatively low levels of regional disparity. However, policies adopted after 1972—that saw a shift towards the development of the coast at the expense of the interior regions—saw the beginning of a long period of rising regional inequalities in Chinese history as coastal regions were expanded to develop export capacity. This bias has been continued and carried forward with greater vigour during the reform period.

Meanwhile, rural-urban disparities have been present in China for a long time. The disparity between agriculture and industry, and therefore, between rural and urban areas, had grown continuously over the planning period as a result of the industry bias of the development policy. The Government used three strategies—including the household registration system that restricted migration from rural areas (in order to ensure enough labour for food production), unified procurement and sale of agricultural commodities sing price control mechanisms, and the people's communes—to extract the agricultural surplus for industrial growth.

The Effect of Geography

It has been suggested that geography has played a major role in determining regional disparity in China, because of the presence of large areas with particularly difficult terrain. This has specifically been linked to poorer infrastructure and weaker access to markets (for inputs as well as sale of output), and therefore, lower stimuli for growth in the interior regions. Of course, though geography may play a role in determining growth differences, policy could reverse or strengthen these conditions. So the important question is, if a region starts off with a locational disadvantage, can it be overcome by subsequent policies, or does policy continue to generate or perhaps increase differences?

It has been argued that over the 1990s, lack of access to the coast, and therefore, to international markets and FDI, has been a critical factor in China. Flatness of the ground, a topographical feature, probably also influenced provincial incomes. However, the relative impact of policy and geography has varied somewhat between provinces, being particularly significant for areas with access to the coast, i.e., the metropoles and the coastal provinces.

Policies of Economic Openness and FDI Flows

It is widely accepted that opening up to FDI flows and trade has helped boost China's growth performance considerably. FDI flows did not initiate China's growth story, which really began in the 1980s, but have helped sustain growth by increasing capital formation, total factor productivity and export performance. FDI inflows into China began in 1984 and the increase has been dramatic since the early 1990s.

However, the open door policy initiated in China in 1979—to attract FDI and encourage foreign trade in specific areas—very much involved preferential policies for the coastal regions, including the three metropoles. This involved tax and duty exemptions as well as labour laws favouring investors in Special Economic Zones or Open Economic Zones. At first, this preference was given to coastal areas in the south, and then, gradually extended to other coastal areas. Restrictions on FDI and foreign trade in the inland provinces continued until the early 1990s, and a national treatment policy for foreign investment only came after 1992. Even then, differences between levels of deregulation or preferential policy vis-à-vis FDI were still quite large in the late 1990s, most evidently in the sizeable tax concessions to foreign invested enterprises (FIEs). This preferential policy treatment also created a dualism between the domestic private economy and foreign funded industries.

While this may have facilitated more rapid growth, China's open door policy has been a major factor behind increasing inequalities. Part of this is due to the basic nature of FDI flows, which choose safe destinations that are already somewhat developed. Capital tends to favour the more developed, accessible 'safe' regions, and often tends to flow from low-growth to high-growth areas. This tendency was significantly compounded by government policy. It is therefore unsurprising that foreign investment in the coastal regions exceeded that in the interior regions by far. Thus, the gaps between investment rates across the major regions increased between 1980 and 2000, driven to some extent by FDI flows. In 2000, foreign investments in the eastern region were more than 85 per cent of total FDI.

Further, FDI has shown a strong sectoral bias in favour of manufacturing. In total FDI between 1999 and 2001, the share of agriculture was only 1.8 per cent, while the share of manufacturing was as high as 62 per cent. Much of this, at least initially, went into export oriented manufacturing, with weak linkages to the domestic economy. Services received relatively more, but infrastructure sectors—such as transport and storage—have received only 2.7 per cent, while electric power, gas, etc. received 6.4 per cent.

Despite an increase in the employment share from 0.1 per cent in 1986 to 3 per cent in 2001, the employment impact of FDI has also been a factor in exacerbating inequalities in China. Since the mid-1990s, and more actively since World Trade Organization (WTO) accession, FDI policies have shifted from attracting export-oriented and labour-intensive industries to capital- and technology-intensive industries. Recent patterns indeed suggest that FDI inflows are becoming more employment-averse and skill-biased (Riskin and others, 2004), which reduces aggregate employment growth and discriminates against poorer and rural regions. According to OECD calculations, the share of labour intensive industries in total FIEs' assets declined from 50 per cent in 1995 to 41.44 per cent in 1999. FDI share in value added by labour intensive industries also decreased to 40.75 per cent from 46.8 per cent in 1995. Meanwhile, most urban employment generated by FIEs has been concentrated in the eastern region.

International Trade and WTO Accession

The coastal region—with its already developed industrial base and access to transport and communication with the outside world—clearly gained from opening up to international trade. Accession to the WTO in 2002 brought further benefits to these regions while implying losses for agricultural areas in the interior. The disparity could be strengthened by weak linkages between the domestic economy and foreign trade, a large part of which revolves around the processing and re-export of imported materials and components.

Agriculture in interior areas of China is dominated by small farms which find it difficult to compete with the subsidized industrial agriculture of the North. Although expansion of the textile, apparel and service industries should open up a large number of positions for rural migrants, the necessary transition to non-farm employment will be difficult and painful in the short term. In its WTO Accession Agreement, China has also made many more concessions for the agriculture sector than for manufacturing industries, in terms of reducing import tariffs and Aggregate Measure of Support (AMS), a factor that could substantially increase inequalities over the next few years.

Domestic Economic Reforms: Decentralization and Resource Mobilization

The history of resource mobilization in China has shown an increasing inequality-exacerbating tendency and a bias towards richer, coastal areas. Before economic reform, there was a centralized budget and a more equitable distribution of resources, which were generated from the profits of and taxes on the SOEs. Also the rich provinces were required to turn over large surpluses to the government while the poorer provinces received large subsidies. However, as the profitability of the SOEs declined in the reform era, the system was marked by chaos, with local governments imposing other revenue raising measures. There was a proliferation of ad hoc, extra-budgetary projects monitored through the banking system, which continues even today. The share of central revenues, and consequently, its ability to spend on infrastructure, declined considerably.

The 1994 tax reforms, in which the value added tax (VAT) was introduced, exacerbated the inequality-exacerbating tendencies of the revenue system. The centre started a system of providing rebates to each province for any reduction in its tax base under the new formula, plus 30 per cent of any increase in revenues raised in the province after 1993. This formula favoured rich provinces and militated against a process of redistribution across regions. Leaving aside the special case of Tibet, the biggest beneficiary of this provision was Shanghai, China's wealthiest province. Inequality-exacerbating tendencies were compounded by the fact that richer provinces were no longer required to turn over their surpluses under the new system, and each region's ability to raise revenues was determined by the economic capacities in the area. Agricultural interior regions, dependent on levies and compulsory apportionments, suffered relative to advanced regions with more diverse economic structures and larger revenue bases. Furthermore, advanced regions had a larger degree of freedom to finance their economic development.

However, the crucial factor was the disparity in expenditure across regions.

First, the redistributive nature of the state fiscal system disappeared under a system where most local expenditures were supposed to be undertaken by local governments. Not surprisingly, the poorest provinces collected very little revenue, and their local governments had sharply lower per capita expenditures between 1990 and 2000, increasing the gap over this period. Second, the fall and then stagnation of total revenues as a share of GDP meant an absolute constraint on the spending of both central and local governments, and this specifically affected social security, health, education and infrastructure spending, all of which declined in per capita terms.

Lack of Diversification of Financial Structures

The banking and financial sectors in China remain highly centralized. While this has been an important source of macroeconomic stability (as elaborated in Chandrasekhar and Ghosh, 2006), the network has not diversified into providing channels of credit at a more decentralized level, and therefore has not served the cause of equality through local credit disbursement systems. However, some efforts have been made by the government in the recent past by integrating micro-finance into the formal financial sector.

The impact of the limited financial reforms only compounded the problem over the 1990s, given the overwhelming emphasis on financial risk reduction and control along private sector guidelines. This has been a reason why the financial sector has not really attempted to meet the financial needs of the non-state sector, especially those of the loan-dependent SMEs or TVEs, a phenomenon more pronounced in the case of privately owned enterprises. This is despite the fact that over the recent period, this segment of the economy has had a large impact on growth performance, employment and poverty outcomes, especially in the poorer regions.

The disbursement bias has had a distinct regional dimension. Most funds have gone to SOEs in the traditionally rich areas of the coast and the northeast. On the other hand, new businesses and small businesses, especially in the interior regions, have suffered. The new guidelines on strengthening credit support to SMEs, issued by the government in 2002, did not address this disparity either, since they singled out for support those enterprises with greatest 'development potential' and higher technology. Further, in spite of the positive role of the formal rural institutions—the Agricultural Bank of China, the Agricultural Development Bank of China and the rural credit cooperatives (RCCs)—financial reforms have also displayed an anti-rural bias, manifested in a significant reduction in the number of rural finance outlets and adverse shifts in the geographical distribution of rural finance, thus affecting access to formal and informal credit of both enterprises and households in rural areas.

Patterns of Industrial Development

Industrial growth in the reform era has been very high, but even then, patterns of development have encouraged the forces of inequality. First, there has been a complete change in the nature of this sector, marked by acute capital-deepening in new enterprises, which have replaced traditional ones. Employment elasticity in manufacturing has been very low. Between 1990 and 2002, industrial employment growth has been only 1.9 per cent, and the output elasticity of employment has been 0.01. The service sector has done better, with a higher growth rate of 4.83 per cent annually and employment elasticity of 0.2 per cent between 1990 and 2002. But this is inadequate to meet the needs of the labour force, and typically, service sector employment has required a higher level of skill, which much of China's population, especially in rural interior areas, has not possessed.

The second major feature of China's industrial development has been the role of SOEs. Reduced subsidies and greater external competition have reduced their profitability and employment generation potential. The share of SOEs in total urban employment has come down from 76 per cent in 1980 to 29 per cent in 2002. Simultaneously, pressure on urban employment has increased following the easing of migration restrictions. This has also had a severe negative impact on the social services provided by SOEs.

The role of the TVEs has strengthened the forces of inequality. While the TVEs have shown innate dynamism and have recorded high rates of growth,[10] the ability to adjust well to market conditions had an adverse impact on employment. In absolute terms, employment in urban collectives fell by 27.06 million persons between 1990 and 2001. In addition, since TVEs have had to raise their own resources and maintain their own profitability, they have shown both an urban and a regional bias, flourishing in urban and coast-biased sectors such as industry, commerce and restaurants, transport, services and construction (Riskin and others, 2004). The percentage of TVE jobs in total employment ranges from only 6 per cent in Guizhou (southwest) to 32 per cent in Zheijiang (coast). TVEs depend crucially on local government support, which has obviously been greater in the more advanced regions where governments have more fiscal strength as well as greater control over markets.

Agriculture and the Dissolution of the Communes

As discussed earlier, the planning period was marked by a clear exploitation of the agricultural sector for the development of industry. The early period of reform, between 1979 and 1984, saw the dissolution of the communes and organization of production following the household responsibility system. A spurt in agricultural growth followed, and consequently, rural poverty and inequalities declined, as did the gap between rural and urban incomes. But since 1984, when the benefits of the agrarian reform were exhausted, agricultural growth has decelerated and lagged behind industrial and service sector growth rates. During the early 1990s, more attention was paid to rural industries, which provided the new impetus for growth. However, over 65 per cent of the rural population still continues to be employed in the agriculture sector. Unlike the industrial sector, this sector has not received much state patronage in terms of investment, nor has it seen proliferation of small enterprises on the scale of the industrial and service sectors.

An additional threat is posed by new agricultural policies now trying to regularize land rights. This is likely to have severe adverse impacts on most of the rural population. In fact, China's egalitarian distribution of land has had a strong equalizing effect on the distribution of farm income (Khan and Riskin, 2005). However, recently, there have been sharp increases in wealth inequality, driven by land ownership in particular (UNDP, 2005a). Since universal land access is now the main form of social security available to the poorer Chinese farmers, any market collapses, natural disasters, or change in demographic conditions, could result in catastrophic outcomes. In addition, laws governing access to land typically tend to discriminate against women, exacerbating gender inequalities.

Price Deregulation

The deregulation of prices that followed in the wake of the reform period saw prices being gradually released from controls. A dual track price system was used until 1991 to ensure industrial inputs at lower prices while output prices of industrial goods were deregulated. This system was, in effect, transferring incomes from interior central and western regions, which were the main suppliers of industrial raw materials, to the coastal regions. While the abolition of the dual track pricing system helped to counter a tendency towards regional disparities, free price movements have tended to strengthen rural-urban disparities in the recent period. The terms of trade between industry and agriculture had moved in favour of agriculture during the early post-planning period, largely driven by agricultural growth after 1979. However, after a brief resumption of this trend between 1993 and 1995, there was a clear deterioration in the terms of trade against agriculture in the second half of the 1990s (Figure 15.5).

Given the lack of control over the declining terms of trade for agriculture,

FIGURE 15.5

China: industry–agriculture terms of trade, 1990–2000

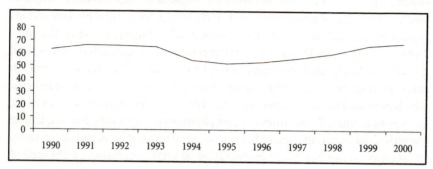

Source: Data from National Bureau of Statistics (2003)

increases in wages and in the costs of other factors of production over the 1990s resulted in increases in the price of industrial outputs. Higher input prices of industrial raw materials after the abolition of dual track pricing have also caused industrial prices to rise. On the other hand, agricultural prices have been declining from the late 1990s, reflecting growing openness to world markets. The joint impact of these price movements has resulted in increasing deterioration in the terms of trade against agriculture. This phenomenon has been clearly correlated with increases in rural poverty in China (Riskin and others, 2004).

Patterns of Internal Labour Migration

Restrictions on the movement of labour have been one important factor behind rural-urban inequalities in China. The origin of this lies in the hukou, or household registration system, started during the central planning era. Individuals were tied to their birthplace and given a household-based residence status at birth. Only approved urban registered residents were allowed to live and work in urban areas, and in consequence, rural residents were forced to stay and work within rural areas. More importantly, only urban-hukou holders were entitled to receive the social service benefits—such as education, housing and healthcare—in the urban areas. This system was aimed to ensure adequate labour supply in rural areas, which could then guarantee a supply of food and other agricultural goods for the industrial sector.

In the reform period, this system imposed enormous restrictions on labour movements from the poorer rural areas of interior China to the prosperous urban areas of the coast. Some modifications in the hukou system have made the system less stringent. From the 1980s onwards, some rural migrants have been granted temporary residence permits that allow them to remain in cities and enable them to access some social services, though at excessively high fees, especially when compared to urban residents.

However, the larger part of the migrant population did not qualify for temporary residence permits, and had to remain in the informal sector without access to the public utilities and other benefits available to urban residents. It is estimated that about half the total flow of migrants have been denied any kind of legal status in the form of temporary permits or urban hukous. In addition, rural migrant workers in cities often face discrimination as a result of local regulations, and are consequently charged various 'administration fees' (UNDP, 2005a). They also face harsher, more unhealthy and dangerous working conditions. This has added to inequalities in access to income and public services among migrant communities and led to severe poverty among migrants.[11]

Increasing unemployment has compounded the problem of labour management and inequalities in China. There is tremendous political pressure, especially within the most advanced industrialized regions, to restrict labour inflows. Currently, the basic responsibility of managing labour and migration issues lies with local governments, who, in response to their constituents, discourage in-migration so as to minimize unemployment in their own areas.

Social Security and Health Spending

Chinese citizens living in rural areas have always had much lower levels of social security compared to their urban counterparts. Even in the pre-reform era, while urban residents received unemployment relief, pension benefits and guaranteed access to health and education, rural residents enjoyed no such guarantees. However, at that time, the commune system provided relatively extensive education and health services in the rural areas. While the infrastructural provisions were much lower compared to urban areas, there was widespread access to such facilities. The existence of the cooperative medical insurance system also helped ensure basic access to public healthcare.

That situation changed in the wake of market-oriented reforms. Access to health and educational facilities for rural residents started declining with the dissolution of the commune systems. Simultaneously, the cooperative medical insurance scheme collapsed. In urban China, the change came in the early 1990s when competition in the industrial and service sectors led to a revamping of SOEs, with increased unemployment and withdrawal of their education and health coverage. The intention has been to transfer welfare provisions, including healthcare and housing, to social insurance agencies and individuals. Despite a nascent pension and social security system, an adequate and comprehensive social security net is not in sight. In rural areas, common and universal access to land has been the only social security available, a system now increasingly threatened under the regime of market-driven economic forces.

Its implications—in terms of a deteriorating public infrastructure and widening rural-urban gaps in education and health indicators—have already been discussed. Part of the deterioration stemmed from decentralization of the fiscal structure and the lower capacity of both central and state governments to raise revenues, which led to declines in the ability to provide public health and education facilities as well as to spend on social welfare. Government spending on health, education, social welfare and poverty alleviation programmes (as shares of GNP) fell over the 1990s, and though it has recovered somewhat in recent years, it was still lower than the 1988 level at the turn of the century. The resource constraint has also been the reason for cuts in subsidies to the SOEs.

The higher share of local governments in total government expenditure on social services has introduced severe inequality in the provision of these services. The current decentralization of the fiscal system has meant lower revenues for the largely rural, less developed regions mainly located in central and western China. Under pressure on the revenue front, local governments in general, and those of largely rural interior regions in particular, have tended to cut social expenditure.

Private healthcare and education, against the payment of full user-fees, have increasingly replaced government provision of such services. In healthcare, the percentage share of personal expenditure has increased from 16 per cent in 1980 to 61 per cent in 2001. This has obviously had a rural-urban dimension. In 1998, public paid healthcare coverage was 16 yuan per capita for cities, compared to 1.2 yuan for the countryside, while self-paid coverage was 44.1 yuan per capita for cities and 87.4 yuan for the countryside (Kanbur and Zhang, 2005b). Education expenditure has followed a similar trend, though the pattern has been less dramatic.

In addition, low educational attainments of the rural poor restrict them from moving to better-paying, off-farm jobs. This has a clear regional angle. Most of the rural labour force in the western region does not have education levels beyond middle school. The percentage of the 'just literate' is the highest here, and the percentage of college graduates the lowest. Unfortunately, the type of jobs that have grown and have better earnings potential, namely service sector jobs, have also been the ones requiring higher skill and education levels. Therefore, these have been out of reach for the largest part of the Chinese population.

Meanwhile, conditions faced by urban workers have also deteriorated. The growing unemployment—generated by retrenchment in the SOEs and an increase in the employment share of private enterprises—means that new jobs, especially for unregistered rural migrants, often come with little or no social security benefits. The problem has been compounded by the fact that migrants, who are officially registered in rural areas under the hukou system, are not entitled to social security benefits received by registered urban residents, such as unemployment benefits.

INEQUALITY AND CORRECTIVE POLICIES: A CONCLUDING NOTE

A case can be made that increasing inequality during this phase of the economic transition in China is inevitable. Thus, a government official has recently argued that:

> Looking at income inequality as a whole, it may be the case that rational, and thus inevitable, disparities are more significant than irrational disparities. The widening of income disparities occurred, on the one hand, during a process when overall incomes increased steadily and, on the other, where economic efficiency has also been continuously improved. In this regard, the process has helped overall economic growth and social development (Han, 2005: 11).

However, it is also accepted that widening income disparities can impose a number of negative effects in economic and social development.

The government of China seems to have recognized the growing problems of inequality and poverty. Recent official 'White Papers' on employment, poverty and women have acknowledged the need to correct regional imbalances as well as rural-urban and gender disparities. There have been specific attempts to develop the infrastructure and natural minerals of the interior regions to generate incomes. The recent strategies of developing the west and revitalising the northeast have involved funding new infrastructure projects and increasing fiscal transfers to these areas. Other recent efforts include expanding program-mes started in the 1980s to widen the social security net and provide pension and unemployment insurance. Migration norms were also relaxed and poverty relief programmes (including the aid-the-poor fund) were launched on a much wider scale than before. Further, the banking sector was decentralized to make credit more accessible to interior and rural areas. However, much of the 'Development of the West' strategy (such as the Three Gorges dam project) has had adverse environmental and livelihood implications. These strategies have generally involved undue exploitation of natural resources.

Addressing the problems of poverty and inequality requires wide ranging and multi-pronged policies. While the natural tendency of capital to concentrate in safe areas and safe sectors cannot be changed, its inequality-exacerbating tendencies need to be strictly countered and not aggravated by domestic policies. While maintaining broad state control over the banking and financial system is crucial, this should enable the diversification of banking institutions and widening the credit network, so important for the development of less developed areas and sectors. The tax system must be adjusted to take into account new income disparities and enable more resource mobilization from the higher income groups. This will also enable greater use of fiscal transfers to develop less developed regions and sectors.

Though China's agriculture is more competitive than in most developing countries, this sector needs greater protection from externally generated volatility as well as some concessions. Very recently, the government has recognised the need for policy measures to redress the imbalance between agriculture and industry. Starting in early 2004, the agriculture tax was reduced or eliminated in most provinces, and will be ended nationwide by 2006. The government has also extended direct subsidies to grain farmers, set price support for major grain crops, and in some areas, subsidized the purchase of improved seed varieties and machinery.

In terms of generating employment, there is an overwhelming emphasis on general economic growth and developing the tertiary sector. But obviously, that is not enough for addressing employment inequalities. The tertiary sector specifically shows a pro-education and pro-skill bias, which goes against the rural areas. Therefore, unless rural access to public education is improved rapidly, the rural population is not likely to reap benefits from the new development regime. Simultaneously, the hukou system has to be amended significantly, if not abolished. This is already occurring in some regions, where the system is being reformed to integrate rural and urban components, and the problem of wage arrears for migrant workers is being given some attention. Under a central government directive, local authorities in urban areas are taking steps to ensure that the children of migrant workers are enrolled in school.

Social security benefits must be extended to all citizens. The government's official position on women has been to grant equal legal rights in politics, marriage, work and property ownership, and to provide certain guarantees of the rights and interests of women. However, widely adopting these rights in practice has been a major problem. There is a need to redress the growing gender imbalances in employment patterns with special attention to provide rural women with more education and skills training. Fortunately, the government still retains enough control over crucial economic levers to ensure redirection of growth in more progressive ways.

NOTES

[1] The high regional variation of 65.9 falls to 38.7 once they are excluded (Demurger and others, 2002).

[2] Registered unemployment rates increased from 1.8 per cent of the labour force in 1985 to 4 per cent in 2002. The average number of employed persons per household as well as the percentage of employment per household in urban areas has gone down steadily over this period. The output elasticity of employment in industry has been close to zero in the 1990s, even decreasing from 0.08 in the first half of the 1990s to 0.01 for the period 1996–2001.

[3] The ratio of 90th percentile wages to the 10th percentile wages increased from 2.58 to 4.27. The ratio of median wages to the 10th percentile increased from 1.62 to 2.26. The Gini coefficient increased from 22.9 to 30.7, while the coefficient of variation increased from 57.2 per cent to 62.2 per cent.

[4] These conclusions are confirmed by the study of wage inequalities in China by Galbraith, Krytynskaia and Wang (2003).

[5] However, the income index is also responsible for this high value—in fact, the difference in ranking by GDP per capita and by HDI is very low in the case of China.

[6] Primary school enrolment rates increased continuously over several decades and reached 98.6 per cent in 2002. The percentage of primary school graduates entering secondary school also increased to reach 97 in 2002. The illiteracy rate has also shown a steady decline over a long time, from 33.9 in 1981 to 15.1 in 1999 (Kanbur and Zhang, 2005b; Woo and Bao, 2003).

[7] The coefficients of variation increased from 44.5 per cent in 1981 to 49.2 per cent in 1990 and to 67 per cent in 1999 (Woo and Bao, 2003).

[8] According to Kanbur and Zhang (2005b), there was a dramatic increase in the rural IMR between 1990 and 1995 from 32.2 to 44.8, a trend in clear contradiction to trends in most other Asian countries and a sharp reversal of the decline between 1981 and 1990. Even in urban China, the IMR rose between 1990 and 1995, from 19.3 to 21.1, in contrast to the decline between 1981 and 1990.

[9] During these years, the general index of farm prices fell by 23 per cent. Wheat and corn prices dropped by between 20 to 30 per cent in 1999 alone (Riskin and others, 2004).

[10] The TVEs contributed more than half of industrial valued added in the recent period, and accounted for over 30 per cent of GDP and nearly half of China's exports.

[11] According to a survey covering 31 cities, poverty incidence among migrant workers in urban areas is 50 per cent higher than among 'regular' urban residents (ADB, 2002).

REFERENCES

Anderson, K., J. Huang and E. Ianchovichina (2003). Long-run impacts of China's WTO accession on farm-non farm income inequality and rural poverty. Poverty Reduction and Economic Management Network, Economic Policy Division, World Bank, Washington, DC.

ADB (2002). Urban poverty in PRC. Final Report, TAE: PRC 33448, Asian Development Bank, Manila.

Chandrasekhar, C.P., and Jayati Ghosh (2006). Macroeconomic policy, inequality and poverty reduction in India and China. In G.A. Cornia (ed.). *Macroeconomic Policy and Poverty Reduction*. Palgrave, London.

Chen, Shaohua, and Yan Wang (2001). China's growth and poverty reduction: Trends between 1990 and 1999. Development Research Group, Poverty Reduction Division, July, World Bank, Washington, DC.

Demurger, Sylvie, Jeffrey Sachs, Wing Thye Woo, Shuming Bao, Gene Chang and Andrew

Mellinger (2002). Geography, economic policy and regional development in China. Discussion paper no. 1950, Harvard Institute of Economic Research, Cambridge, MA.

Galbraith, James K., Ludmila Krytynskaia and Qifei Wang (2003). The experience of rising inequality in Russia and China during the transition. University of Texas Inequality Project Working Paper No. 23, University of Texas, Austin. http://utip.gov.utexas.edu/papers/utip_23.pdf.

Government of China (1994). Government White Paper on the situation of Chinese women. June, Beijing.

Government of China (2004a). Government White Paper on China's employment situation and policies. April, Beijing.

Government of China (2004b). Government White Paper on China's social security and its policy. September, Beijing.

Han Wenxiu (2005). The evolution of income distribution disparities in China since the reform and opening-up. In *Income Disparities in China: An OECD perspective, China in the Global Economy*. Organisation for Economic Cooperation and Development, Paris: 9–26.

Hu Angang, Linlin Hu and Zhixiao Chang (2003). China's economic growth and poverty reduction (1978 to 2002). Paper presented at the conference on 'Tale of Two Giants: India's and China's Experience with Reform and Growth', organized by the International Monetary Fund and National Council for Applied Economic Research, New Delhi, 14–16 November.

Kanbur, Ravi, and Xiaobo Zhang (2005a). Fifty years of regional inequality in China: A journey through central planning, reform and openness. *Review of Development Economics* 9: 87–106.

Kanbur, Ravi, and Xiaobo Zhang (2005b). Spatial inequality in education and healthcare in China. *China Economic Review* 16 (2): 189–204.

Khan, Azizur Rahman, Keith Griffin and Carl Riskin (1999). Income distribution in urban China during the period of economic reform and globalization. *American Economic Review* 89 (2): 296–300. Reprinted in Carl Riskin, Zhao Renwei and Li Shi (eds). *China's Retreat from Equality*, M.E. Sharpe, Armonk, NY, 2000.

Khan, Azizur Rahman, and Carl Riskin (2005). China's household income and its distribution, 1995 and 2002. *The China Quarterly* (182), June: 356–84.

Knight, John, and Lina Song (2003). Increasing urban wage inequality in China. *The Economics of Transition* 11 (4): 597–619.

National Bureau of Statistics (1997). *China Agricultural Census*. China Statistical Press, Beijing.

National Bureau of Statistics (1998). *China Statistical Abstract*. China Statistical Press, Beijing.

National Bureau of Statistics (2003). *China Statistical Yearbook 2003*. China Statistical Press, Beijing.

Riskin, Carl, Nathalie Bouché, Li Shantong, Ashwani Saith, Wu Guobao (2004). Pro-poor macro policies for China. Paper originally prepared for the Regional Workshop on Macroeconomics of Poverty Reduction, UNDP, Kathmandu, 4–6 January 2003.

Social and Economic Policy Institute, Hong Kong (2002). Overview of current labour market conditions in China. Submitted to the Global Policy Network, by the Social and Economic Policy Institute, Hong Kong.

UNDP (1999). *China Human Development Report: Transition and the State*. China Financial and Economic Publishing House, Beijing, for United Nations Development Programme, New York.

UNDP (2003). *Human Development Report, 2003*. United Nations Development Programme, New York.

UNDP (2005a). *China Human Development Report, 2005*. United Nations Development Programme, Beijing and New York.

UNDP (2005b). *Human Development Report, 2005*. United Nations Development Programme, New York.

World Bank (2004). *World Development Indicators, 2004*. World Bank, Washington D.C.

Weiss, John (2002). Explaining trends in regional poverty in China. Processed, December, Asian Development Bank Institute, Tokyo.

Woo, Wing Thye, and Shuming Bao (2003). China: Case study on human development progress towards the Millennium Development Goals at the sub-national level. Background paper for *Human Development Report 2003*, United Nations Development Programme, New York.

Wu, Y. (1999). Income disparity and convergence in China's regional economies. Working paper, Department of Economics, University of Western Australia, Nedlands.

Yang, Dennis Tao, and Cai Fang (2003). The political economy of China's rural-urban divide. In Nick Hope, Dennis Tao Yang and Mu Yang (eds). *How Far Across the River? Chinese Policy Reform at the Millennium*. Stanford University Press, Stanford: 389–416.

Zhao, Renwei (2001). Increasing income inequality and its causes in China. In Carl Riskin, Zhao Renwei and Li Shi (eds). *China's Retreat from Equality: Income Distribution and Economic Transition*. M.E. Sharpe, New York: 25–43.

Contributors

ABEBE SHIMELES is a Research Fellow in the Department of Economics, University of Goteborg, Sweden.

ALEMAYEHU GEDA is Associate Professor and Head, Department of Economics, Addis Ababa University. He can be reached at: AG@ethionet.et and www. Alemayehu.com.

DEAN BAKER is Co-Director of the Center for Economic and Policy Research (CEPR), Washington, DC.

JACQUES BAUDOT is a retired international civil servant of the United Nations Secretariat. He was Coordinator of the World Summit for Social Development and Director of the Division for Social Policy and Development, among others. After his retirement, he coordinated the International Forum for Social Development. He can be reached at jbaudot@charter.net.

ALBERT BERRY is Professor Emeritus of Economics at the University of Toronto and Research Director of the Programme on Latin America and the Caribbean at the Munk Centre for International Studies, University of Toronto.

HEATHER BOUSHEY is Senior Economist at the Center for Economic and Policy Research, Washington, DC.

JAYATI GHOSH is Professor at the Centre for Economic Studies and Planning, Jawaharlal Nehru University, and Executive Secretary of International Development Economics Associates (IDEAs). She has published widely on issues pertaining to development, international economics, employment, gender and macroeconomic policies. She can be contacted at jayatig@vsnl.com.

JOMO KWAME SUNDARAM (Jomo K.S.) has been Assistant Secretary-General for Economic Development, Department of Economic and Social Affairs (DESA), United Nations, since 2005. Until 2004, he was Professor in the Applied Economics Department, University of Malaya, Kuala Lumpur.

BRANKO MILANOVIC is an economist in the World Bank Research Development Department, fellow at Carnegie Endowment, and visiting professor at Johns Hopkins University. His work is focused on the social consequences of transition from planned to market economy, and issues of global inequality. He is the author of the first detailed study of inequality among world citizens based entirely on household surveys. His most recent book, *Worlds Apart: Measuring International and Global Inequality*, studies inequality between the countries and peoples of the world over the last two centuries.

MARIA CRISTINA PACIELLO is a Ph.D. candidate in the Politics and Economics of Developing Countries at the University of Florence, Italy. Her research interests include gender inequality, child welfare, inequality and poverty, with a focus on the Middle East and North Africa.

PARTHAPRATIM PAL is a Fellow at the Indian Council for Research in International Economic Relations, New Delhi. He has a Ph.D. from Jawaharlal Nehru University and has worked in the areas of macroeconomics, development, financial markets and international economy.

JOSÉ GABRIEL PALMA is Senior Lecturer at the Faculty of Economics, Cambridge University. He is also Joint Editor of the *Cambridge Journal of Economics* and member of Joseph Stiglitz's Initiative for Policy Dialogue, based at Columbia University. His main research interests are in the economic, historical, institutional and political development of Latin America and East Asia, and in the history of ideas on development economics and politics.

DAVID ROSNICK is a Senior Research Associate at the Center for Economic and Policy Research (CEPR), Washington, DC.

PEDRO SÁINZ is now a consultant for the Inter-American Development Bank, UNDP, INE Chile and IBGE on public information systems as well as poverty analysis and policies. He was Director of the Economic Projections Center and of the Statistical Division of the Economic Commission of Latin America and the Caribbean, Santiago (ECLAC). Since his retirement in 2000, he has written articles on Latin American social development and given advice to Latin American institutions on public information systems.

RANJA SENGUPTA is a senior economist at the Economic Research Foundation, New Delhi, and has worked extensively on behalf of International Development Economics Associates (IDEAs). Her research interests include agricultural economics, international trade, poverty and inequality.

JOHN SERIEUX is an Assistant Professor in economics at the University of Manitoba, and a Research Associate at the Munk Centre for International Studies, University of Toronto. Besides his work on the global distribution of income with Albert Berry, he has published extensively and continues to work on developing country debt issues.

MIHALY SIMAI is a member of the Hungarian Academy of Sciences, former Chairman of the Council of the United Nations University (UNU), and former Director of the World Institute for Development Economics Research (UNU/WIDER). He currently works in the Institute for World Economics of the Hungarian Academy of Sciences as a Research Professor. He is the Honorary President of the World Federation of UN Associations.

BOB SUTCLIFFE is a writer on development and international economics. He has taught these subjects in universities in the UK, the USA, Nicaragua and Spain. He is the author of *100 Ways of Seeing an Unequal World* and *Nacido en otra parte: un ensayo sobre la migración internacional, el desarrollo y la equidad.* He lives in the Basque Country.

JOHN WEEKS is Director of the Centre for Development Policy and Research at the School of Oriental and African Studies (SOAS), University of London. He has published books and many articles on economic analysis and developing countries, and, most recently, has worked on pro-poor growth.

MARK WEISBROT is Co-Director of the Center for Economic and Policy Research (CEPR), Washington, DC.

CHRISTIAN WELLER is a senior economist at the Center for American Progress, Washington, DC.

Index